Ruling Performance

To four people without whom the Institute of
Contemporary British History would never
have been realized . . . Sir Frank Cooper, David
Butler, Lady (Olive) Wood and David Severn

Ruling Performance

British Governments from
Attlee to Thatcher

Edited by
Peter Hennessy &
Anthony Seldon

Basil Blackwell

Copyright © Institute of Contemporary British History 1987

First published 1987

Basil Blackwell Ltd
108 Cowley Road, Oxford, OX4 1JF, UK

Basil Blackwell Inc.
432 Park Avenue South, Suite 1503
New York, NY10016, USA

British Library Cataloguing in Publication Data
Ruling performance: British governments
   from Attlee to Thatcher.
   1. Great Britain—Politics and government
   —1945-
   I. Hennessy, Peter   II. Seldon, Anthony
   320.941   JN231
   ISBN 0–631–15645–3

Typeset in 11 on 12½ pt Caslon
by Joshua Associates Limited, Oxford
Printed in Great Britain by T. J. Press Ltd, Padstow

Contents

Acknowledgements

Many people helped in the publication of this book, but we should like to thank in particular the following: Kathleen Townsend and Andrew Thomas for preparing the index; David Baker, an undergraduate at Durham University, for work in the Public Record Office; David Lawrence for help with the chronologies and proof-reading; Graham Eyre for copy-editing the typescript; and Claire Andrews and the indefatigable Sean Magee of Basil Blackwell. Thanks also to Michael Brock, Warden of Nuffield College, for permission to hold the inaugural conference of the Institute of Contemporary British History, at which the papers in this book were given their first airing, in embryonic form. This book is also dedicated to the first benefactors of the Institute: The Nuffield Foundation, The Wolfson Foundation, Rio Tinto-Zinc and Marks and Spencer.

PH
AS

Introduction

Peter Hennessy and Anthony Seldon

General elections provide convenient dividing lines in history, much as the reigns of monarchs did in the past. In this volume is surveyed the 'ruling performance' of all the administrations from the general election of May 1945 to that of June 1987. This collection is the first publication of the Institute of Contemporary British History. It is based on papers originally presented to the Institute's inaugural conference at Nuffield College, Oxford, on 31 October 1986. The authors have prepared their papers as donations in kind to the Institute, for which we, the editors, are immensely grateful. Our contributors are authorities in their own right, and possess strong personalities both in their patterns of thought and in their styles of writing. We have therefore kept editorial interference to a minimum to ensure that the individual flavours reach the reader's taste buds unsullied.

There are, however, common ingredients. This book is not intended, to use Churchill's famous jibe at a Shadow Cabinet lunch at the Savoy Hotel in the late 1940s, to be a 'pudding lacking a theme'. For each post war administration, consideration is given to Cabinet style, relations between ministerial colleagues, priorities, the degree to which manifesto pledges were redeemed and the treatment of public expenditure. Almost every chapter inevitably is the story of a struggle to match aspirations with resources as the British economy failed to live up to hopes and expectations.

The postwar years are a period of paradox. At the time of the general election which swept Attlee to power in 1945, unemployment stood at 112,000.[1] The figures for May 1987 were 2,986,453.[2] Yet the standard of living – real income per head – more than doubled in that time. In 1945 work was plentiful and goods to buy in short supply. Forty years later the position was reversed. Attlee's settlement, as Professor John

Vincent pointed out at the inaugural conference, was designed to benefit poor manual workers (more than three-quarters of the adult male population were engaged in manual work in 1945). As Mrs Thatcher sought to undo key elements of that settlement, the figure had dropped to around a half, and the labour force had been reshaped by the shift from manufacturing to service industries and by the increase in female and part-time employment. But whether these changes amounted to 'the rise of the suburban hegemony', as John Vincent put it, is debatable.

Britain's external position, too, was changed dramatically over the four decades. From being one of the three great powers in 1945 with its vast empire still intact, the country has been reduced to the status of a medium power of the second rank, albeit still a pivotal member of NATO, in whose creation the Attlee government played a crucial role. The postwar consensus on defence and foreign policy has crumbled, with Labour, creator of the original British atom bomb, pressing for Britain to be the first nation to relinquish its nuclear status.

The great shifts in postwar British history and the perpetual problems – the weakness of sterling, uncompetitive industrial costs, the waxing and waning of trade union power – all are chronicled in the studies of successive administrations. The early chapters have the benefit of access to official archives at the Public Record Office. This does not solve every problem or answer each puzzle, as Lord Radcliffe realized when he inquired into the subject of Cabinet secrecy and ministerial memoirs: 'Government is not to be conducted in the interests of history', he wrote; 'the historian cannot have as of right a smooth highway conducted for him through the intricate plans of public administration and statecraft.'[3] Nevertheless, a smooth path into the PRO is a great help. Our contributors writing on administrations whose records remain closed to access under the thirty-year rule have had a much tougher time in acquiring the inside story. Provisional though their work must be, we nevertheless feel that it is valuable as an attempt to say what can already be said about the recent past.

Ruling Performance is as much about explanation as it is about judgement. As one of our contributors, Professor David Marquand, wrote in his authoritative biography of Ramsay MacDonald, 'The historian is not a kind of celestial chief justice, sentencing the guilty and setting free the innocent. He is part of the process he describes, and his judgements can never be more than provisional.'[4] Nor is there anything final or complete about our terminal date, despite the conventional wisdom that Mrs Thatcher has ruptured for ever the postwar consensus. It is not the job of any historian, least of all the contemporary historian, to set the past in concrete.

But there is such a thing as a usable past. We may not be able to stop history from repeating itself, but we can use the past to explain how our society and economy and politics came to be as they are, and to work towards an understanding of how things might be. This, in fact, is the *raison d'être* of the Institute of Contemporary British History and why we hope such studies as this will appeal as much to the general reader as to the professional historian or the political scientist.

On a point of nomenclature, the singular form 'government' is strictly speaking correct where only a general election has punctuated a term of office by a Prime Minister. However, as it is more common to use the plural form 'governments' where a general election occurs, we, as editors, have decided to term the relevant chapters the Attlee, Wilson and Thatcher 'governments'.

Notes

1   *Keesing's Contemporary Archives*, 1945.
2   Figure supplied by the Department of Employment Information Office, 27 June 1987.
3   *Report of the Committee of Privy Councillors on Ministerial Memoirs*, Cmnd 6386 (Her Majesty's Stationery Office, 1976), p. 31.
4   David Marquand, *Ramsay MacDonald* (Cape, 1977), p. 791.

1

The Road from 1945

Paul Addison

Discussions of British government since 1945 are overshadowed by two main assumptions. The first is that for a period of about thirty years after the war the leaders of the Conservative and Labour parties were agreed on the fundamentals of a 'postwar consensus', or 'postwar settlement'. The second is that governments were mainly responsible, as the managers of a mixed economy, for the relative decline of the British economy. Much of our political thought since the 1970s has consisted of attempts to find causal connections between political consensus and economic decline. There are socialist, devolutionary, Keynesian and free-market theories of the failure of the postwar state. But there are also sceptics: some who doubt whether there ever was a consensus, and others who doubt whether the policies of governments have had much effect on the long-term fortunes of the economy. In my opinion there did exist an elite consensus which succeeded in narrowing the range of political debate and marginalizing dissent; but I very much doubt whether it was a major cause of Britain's economic decline.

These issues enter into the analysis of every government since the war, but we must begin at the beginning. The aim of this preliminary chapter is to discuss the wartime origins of the consensus, to reflect on its peacetime consequences, and to query its relationship to economic decline. But I must admit that the term 'consensus' is open to question. However valuable as shorthand for the ascendancy of a ruling oligarchy which included Labour, Liberal and Conservative politicians, it can be very misleading if taken to imply a society free of conflict, or a natural harmony of opinion between the rank and file of the two main parties. To avoid ambiguity I shall therefore refer to the 'postwar settlement' rather than the 'postwar consensus'.

Of what did the postwar settlement consist? A comprehensive

definition would have to include external economic policy as well as foreign policy and defence: the International Monetary Fund, the Anglo-American special relationship, the North Atlantic Treaty Organization, the Commonwealth, and the British atom bomb. But, as this chapter will deal mainly with internal affairs, it would be hard to improve on the definition put forward by Alan Bullock in the wartime volume of his life of Ernest Bevin. Writing in 1967 he described the kind of society that had developed in Britain during the twenty years since the war, and classified it under six main headings:

First, a mixed economy, partly in public, partly in private ownership, with both sectors subject to constant intervention by Government, a managed as well as a mixed economy.
   Second, a commitment by all parties to the maintenance of full employment.
   Third, the welfare state.
   Fourth, extension of the State's provision of education in order to provide greater equality of opportunity.
   Fifth, great improvements in the position of the industrial worker and increased recognition of the role of unions in industry, even if this still falls far short (on both sides) of Bevin's conception of a partnership between management and men.
   Sixth, a great increase in Government consultation of interest groups (chief among them, the TUC and the employers' associations) and the attempt to build up a tripartite pattern of co-operation (Government–unions–employers) in carrying out economic policy.[1]

The coalition government of Winston Churchill, which took office on 10 May 1940, was formed for the sake of national unity and an all-out effort in the struggle against Nazi Germany. To this end it pressed ahead with the task of mobilizing resources for total war. By the end of 1941 a command economy had been established on the basis of state control of industry without state ownership: socialism without tears. In his determination to mobilize every resource and fling it into the battle, Churchill reflected the general will. But he could not have anticipated that wartime collectivism would metamorphose, at a later stage of the conflict, into peacetime collectivism. Between 1942 and 1945 the coalition government committed its successors, in a series of White Papers, to major initiatives in the fields of education, health, housing, employment, social security, industry and environmental planning. But this is to say nothing of the preparations made for the liberalization of world trade, the reform of the colonial empire, the setting up of the

United Nations, the manufacture of the atom bomb, the occupation of Germany, the settlement with the Soviet Union and, most importantly of all, the maintenance of the 'special relationship' with the United States. The Churchill coalition was truly seminal.

Much has been written about the making of social and economic policy in wartime and the policies were, of course, important. But more important still was the new structure of power, and the new apparatus of administration: the context within which policies were conceived. The Second World War gave rise to a revolution in government: not a social or an intellectual revolution, but an expansion in the role of government in society. By the end of the war a new administrative order was rapidly coming into existence. New peacetime departments were in place, new administrative procedures were at an advanced stage of preparation, and new mentalities were ingrained in officials. As J. M. Lee explains, the Cabinet Secretary, Sir Edward Bridges, 'felt confident that the policy outlined in the 1944 White Paper on employment policy would be followed by whichever party won the election, and he prepared for the new government's requirements on that assumption'.[2]

The Labour manifesto of 1945, *Let us Face the Future*, was super-imposed on an adminstrative revolution that was already taking place. In effect, the party was proposing to carry it through and extend it in a socialist direction. This helps to explain the speed with which the Attlee government was able to implement its remarkable legislative pro-gramme of 1945–8. By the late 1940s the collectivist hour was over, but the new collectivist state was set in concrete. In all its fundamentals, the Conservatives accepted it. The Churchill government of 1951 had no intention of dismantling the Beveridge system of social security, or challenging the power of the trade unions. Party antagonisms were real and deeply felt, but a hegemony of enlightened opinion succeeded in preserving the postwar settlement from its enemies until the mid-1970s.

How and why did the wartime revolution in government occur? The problem could be explored on many levels: in its widest sense it is a problem of social history. But in this chapter the discussion will be confined to three aspects of change at the top: high politics, the trans-formation of the Civil Service, and the trend towards corporatism.

First, then, high politics. When Churchill formed his coalition in May 1940, he turned Labour into an effective governing party for the first time. That was his intention. Passionately convinced that nothing should stand in the way of the prosecution of the war, he expected Labour ministers to shoulder the responsibility of mobilizing the working classes. As he was later to discover, however, it was impossible to devolve power to Labour for the purpose of winning the war, while denying the party the right to share in the creation of postwar Britain.

One of Churchill's first acts as Prime Minister was to offer the Ministry of Labour to Ernest Bevin, the general secretary of the Transport and General Workers Union. Churchill's aim was to enlist the co-operation of the trade unions in the drive for war production, and he appointed Bevin as a representative of the trade unions rather than as a Labour politician. At the very beginning, a bargain was struck. When Churchill offered Bevin the post, Bevin replied listing four conditions of acceptance. First, the Ministry must be involved in the organization of production as well as the supply of labour. Secondly, Bevin would not have to accept the *status quo* in the matter of the social services for which the department was responsible. Thirdly, the Trade Disputes Act of 1927 would have to be revised. And, fourthly, there must be a new attitude towards international labour policy. Churchill accepted the conditions – though he was later to refuse to agree to the amendment of the Trade Disputes Act.[3] In truth, Churchill valued the physical force of the trade unions more highly than the intellectual force of socialist politicians. Consequently he allowed Bevin greater latitude than other Labour ministers, and treated him with a respect bordering on deference. He proposed that, in the event of a German invasion, Britain would be governed by a Committee of Public Safety consisting of himself, Lord Beaverbrook and Bevin.

The Churchill–Bevin axis may be read both as the highest expression of a patriotic *détente* between capital and labour, and as a measure of the power of over-mighty personalities to change the course of history. It symbolized and at the same time facilitated the incorporation of trade union leaders in the war effort. Bevin was resolved not only to improve wages and conditions during the war, but also to employ the power of the trade unions to mould postwar planning. According to his biographer, Bevin had four main ideas for positive action by the state, with full employment at the top of the list.[4] Though sometimes out of step with the Labour Party, Bevin was the most powerful of the Labour ministers, and the most influential in the discussions leading up to the publication of the White Paper on employment policy in May 1944.

The other leading Labour ministers were Clement Attlee, Arthur Greenwood, Hugh Dalton and Herbert Morrison. Sir Stafford Cripps, who joined the Government in February 1942, cannot be included: he had been expelled from the Labour Party in 1939, and did not rejoin until 1945. Perhaps the name of Tom Johnston should be added. This former red Clydesider, appointed by Churchill as Secretary of State for Scotland in January 1941, ran his own form of coalition with the aid of a Council of State comprising all the surviving ex-Secretaries of State for Scotland. Under his guidance, Scotland enjoyed the best of both worlds: devolution and the Union manipulated for the benefit of industry and the social services. But Johnston gravitated away from Labour into an administrative type of Scottish nationalism.

Attlee, the leader of the Labour Party, was ineffectual in his first two posts as Lord Privy Seal and Secretary for the Dominions. In 1941 the Secretary of the War Cabinet, Edward Bridges, reported to Churchill that Attlee was incapable of dominating powerful departments.[5] But as leader of the party he was indispensable, with time to play himself in. He began to make a mark after his elevation to the Lord Presidency, the most powerful post on the home front, in September 1943. Greenwood failed as a minister and was sacrificed by Attlee in February 1942. Morrison, after a brief and unhappy period as Minister of Supply, found his métier as Home Secretary and Minister of Home Security from October 1940. Entering the War Cabinet in November 1942, he was just in time to play a decisive part in swinging the government behind the principles of the Beveridge Report.

Hugh Dalton, a rebarbative character in many ways, has been restored to his true stature as a major politician in Ben Pimlott's masterly biography.[6] In 1940 Churchill gave Dalton the Ministry of Economic Warfare, with secret responsibility for black propaganda and subversive operations in Europe. After fierce departmental battles with Anthony Eden and Brendan Bracken, he was transferred by Churchill to the Board of Trade in February 1942. In his new capacity, Dalton was responsible for the postwar planning of industry and so entered the field of postwar reconstruction. Like Morrison, he was of great significance as a bridge between the coalition and the National Executive of the Labour Party, revising the party's programme to accommodate the latest thinking in Whitehall. With his disciples, Hugh Gaitskell and Douglas Jay, he was the principal author of Labour's major declaration of economic policy *Full Employment and Financial Policy*, adopted by the party conference in 1944. As Pimlott observes, Dalton was busy redefining 'socialism' to mirror the postwar thinking of Whitehall.[7] Though Labour ministers were often riven by personal animosities, they succeeded in making their collective presence felt. When the Ministry of Reconstruction was set up under Lord Woolton in November 1943, the four Labour members of the Reconstruction Committee formed a powerful bloc.

While the Labour Party was gaining in authority, the Conservative Party was losing its sense of direction. Churchill, who assumed the leadership of the party in October 1940, took very little interest in its affairs. Absorbed in the problems of grand strategy and the conduct of relations with Roosevelt and Stalin, he ruled with the aid of a personal entourage of favourites and professional advisers, supplemented by a trio of Tory mavericks: Bracken, Beaverbrook and Frederick Lindemann (who became Lord Cherwell in 1941). With the partial exceptions of Eden and Oliver Lyttelton, no major Conservative politician was a member of the inner circle. Churchill had precious little time for the party, which had excluded him from office for nine long years before the war. He therefore tended to treat Conservative politicians as administrative ballast. Since they represented the majority party in the House, they commanded the majority of posts in the government. But it never occurred to Churchill to establish a Conservative high command to define the party's view of the war economy, or co-ordinate its approach to postwar problems. Key offices that might have been given to Conservatives were often awarded to outsiders or independents. When Neville Chamberlain resigned as Lord President in October 1940, Churchill replaced him with Sir John Anderson, a lofty independent and former civil servant. When he removed the former Chief Whip, David Margesson, from the War Office in February 1942, he replaced him with the permanent secretary of the department, P. J. Grigg, once Churchill's private secretary at the Treasury. Since Anderson and Grigg were conservatives with a small 'c', they were politically safe appointments from Churchill's point of view. But they were no substitute for an active party presence and strategy.

The nearest that Churchill came to recognizing this was in the sporadic encouragement he gave to the activities of R. A. Butler. Butler was the one Conservative minister who argued from 1940 onwards that the party should examine the impact of the war on the home front and begin to prepare itself for the postwar world. Churchill allowed Butler to explore the possibilities. In 1941 he appointed him President of the Board of Education and chairman of the party's committee on reconstruction problems. In November 1943 he put him on the Reconstruction Committee. But, for all that, Butler alone could not fill the void created by Churchill's abdication of leadership. Woolton, who was wholly in sympathy with the Conservative Party and might have done much to revive it at this juncture, preferred to maintain the persona of a non-party businessman.

Much more could be said about the political dimension of wartime change, but it is time to switch the focus from Westminster to Whitehall, and the impact of war on the Civil Service. This is not to imply that postwar planning was an exercise conceived and directed by civil servants: that would exaggerate their autonomy. The point is rather that the Civil Service was transformed by the war, and that, as a consequence, postwar planning acquired an institutional momentum that was practically irreversible by 1945.

In the eyes of administrators, a tolerably clear distinction could be drawn between the emergency collectivism of the war effort, and the collectivism of postwar planning. A government in time of war could exercise powers of compulsion that would inevitably lapse in peacetime. Though it was generally accepted that some emergency regulations would have to be retained for a transitional period after the war, no informed observer imagined that rationing would last for ever, or peacetime governments retain indefinitely the power to monopolize the purchase of imports, control the allocation of raw materials, forbid the manufacture of some products, command the manufacture of others, fix prices and ban strikes.

But the command economy had an indirect influence. In a general sense, it was taken to prove the efficacy of state action. But the wartime economy prescribed the ends, rather than the means, of postwar reconstruction. Wartime Britain served as an example of full employment and maximum industrial output. It served as an example of social welfare. The problem of reconstruction planning was to discover methods by which a peacetime state could achieve the same objectives. Hence the fact that, when it came to specific proposals, postwar planning owed more to the political thought of the 1930s, which was concerned with the problems of a peacetime society, than to the 'lessons of the war economy'.

The 1944 Education Act is an extreme case in point. There was nothing in it that had not been proposed by educational reformers between the wars. If there were specific lessons to be learnt from the experience of education in wartime, or the requirements of the war economy, they were ignored. The one change that did animate the Board of Education was change in Whitehall: the impact of Labour and the general trend towards collectivism. The permanent officials of the Board decided that, unless they took the lead and formulated their own ideas, they might have proposals thrust upon them from outside. They also recognized the change in the balance of party politics. As the deputy secretary, R. S. Wood, noted on 17 January 1941, 'While policies will have to command the support of the main elements in all parties, it is clear that the war is moving us more and more in the direction of Labour's ideas and ideals, and the planning for a national "New Order" will be more towards the Left than may generally be imagined now.'[8] In the shape of a 'Green Book', the outline of an Education Bill awaited R. A. Butler on his arrival at the Board in July 1941.

In the main, the 1944 Education Act was the work of permanent officials. But wartime Whitehall also witnessed an influx of 'temporaries': outsiders recruited for the duration only. As the command economy was established, there was a massive increase in the volume of administration. New ministries rose like mushrooms – Supply, Information, Food, Aircraft Production, Economic Warfare, Fuel and Power – while old departments had fresh responsibilities thrust upon them. Between 1939 and 1945 the number of full-time, non-industrial civil servants increased from 374,300 to 667,100, a leap of 79 per cent. The great majority of the extra staff recruited consisted of executive and technical officers, or cleaners and secretaries. But, at the apex of government, the number of civil servants in the administrative grade more than doubled, from 2100 in 1939 to 4900 in 1945.[9]

No satisfactory analysis has ever been made of the impact on wartime government of the influx of temporary civil servants. Perhaps the problem is too diffuse. Some were in external and some in internal affairs. On the home front the temporaries were extremely diverse: scientists at the service ministries, nutritionists at the Ministry of Food, captains of industry at Supply and Aircraft Production; literati at the Ministry of Information. For present purposes the most important category of temporaries were the reforming liberal academics recruited from the universities. Two of them stood out as pre-eminent and proto-typical: William Beveridge and John Maynard Keynes.

There were many parallels between the careers of these two very different personalities. Both were late-Victorian progressives from the upper middle class. Both had served twice before as civil servants: once during the Edwardian period, and once during the First World War. Both had led an active life between the wars as academics and publicists. Both were convinced by the late 1930s that a further instalment of liberal collectivism was inevitable and desirable. Both entered the service of the coalition government in 1940: Keynes as an unpaid adviser with a room at the Treasury, and Beveridge as a full-time official of the Ministry of Labour.

The history and significance of the Beveridge Report have been so exhaustively discussed that a few brief generalizations must dispose of the subject here. It was, of course, an accident. In 1941 Bevin, who found Beveridge insufferable, decided to remove him from the Ministry of Labour and persuaded Greenwood to appoint him chairman of a committee to inquire into social insurance. As originally conceived, the committee was a modest affair intended to rationalize and co-ordinate existing schemes of social insurance. Beveridge followed his brief to the extent that he did indeed prepare a detailed report on social insurance. But he exceeded the spirit, if not the letter, of his terms of reference. Social insurance was enlarged into a comprehensive scheme for the abolition of poverty, and Beveridge maintained that his social insurance plan would only be viable if three other assumptions were accepted: family allowances, a national health service, and policies to maintain a high level of employment – by which he meant a level of unemployment of up to 8.5 per cent. To heighten the significance of his proposals still further, Beveridge declared that poverty was one problem only among the 'five Giants' that government must tackle on the road to reconstruction: Ignorance, Want, Squalor, Idleness and Disease.

The Beveridge Report, though largely derivative as a synthesis of expert opinion, was in effect a political manifesto published over the signature of one man. It was also the most spectacular example of the consequences of introducing ambitious academics into Whitehall. No permanent official could have exceeded his terms of reference as Beveridge did, and got away with it. Unlike Beveridge, no career civil servant could have waged an open campaign to publicize himself and his proposals.

In Whitehall the Report had two main effects. It obliged the War Cabinet to give sustained attention for the first time to postwar planning and therefore to set up, in January 1943, a Reconstruction Priorities Committee. The second effect is well summed up by J. M. Lee: 'it posed in an acute form the basic question of what the country would be able to afford in providing public services after the war. Everything seemed to depend on the buoyancy of the nation's postwar economy.'[10] The Report started a debate in Whitehall over the future of public expenditure and the order of priorities among conflicting claims to resources.

In retrospect we see the Report, correctly enough, as the source of postwar consensus on social policy and full employment. But in January

1943 that consensus did not exist: it had to be hammered out through bargaining and compromise within the coalition. In principle, all three parties to the coalition accepted the proposals contained in the White Papers of 1943–5. But all the proposals would have to depend, for their implementation, upon the decisions taken by postwar governments about public spending. The coalition could make estimates of postwar revenue and expenditure, but it could not predetermine the judgement of postwar Chancellors of the Exchequer. With the exception of family allowances, none of Beveridge's proposals reached the statute book in wartime. Nevertheless the government issued its own proposals for social insurance and a national health service, and a Ministry of Social Insurance was created in October 1944. It is as certain as anything can be that a postwar Conservative government would have carried out its pledge to implement the social insurance plan and establish, in some form, a national health service.

By 1940 Keynes was already famous as the prophet of full employment. His *General Theory*, published in 1936, was rapidly gaining ground among the academic economists. But his influence in domestic reconstruction was largely indirect. Once installed at the Treasury, he devoted most of his energies to the problems of external finance, and the reconstruction of the international economy through the creation of the World Bank and the International Monetary Fund. On internal policy there was never a prospect that the Treasury would take the lead in pressing for a Keynesian policy to maintain full employment after the war. The leading Treasury officials were inclined to be pessimistic about the postwar economy, and dubious about the efficacy of Keynesian policies.

There is much debate over the extent to which the Keynesians succeeded in penetrating the thinking of the coalition government. But no one would doubt that the war marked an important stage in the reception of Keynesian ideas of demand management, which were officially acknowledged in the 1944 White Paper on employment policy. The Keynesian advance was the work of three groups of academic economists with a power base in Whitehall. Evan Durbin, Douglas Jay and Hugh Gaitskell were Keynesians with a socialist slant, working under the patronage of Hugh Dalton. A second group of economists were members of the Prime Minister's Statistical Section, a band of irregulars introduced into Whitehall by Lord Cherwell, who advised Churchill on economic as well as scientific affairs. The head of the section, Donald MacDougall, was a convinced supporter of Keynesian policies and converted Cherwell to the gospel of full employment. Cherwell, in turn, advised Churchill strongly in favour of public spending in a slump. 'It is, I think, generally agreed', wrote Cherwell in January 1944, 'that if money could be put into circulation when a depression began, and if the very natural reaction of government and people to cut down expenditure because times were bad could be overcome, we should have gone a long way to solving the problem.'[11]

The third and most important group of Keynesians belonged to the Economic Section of the War Cabinet, set up at the end of 1940 and attached to the office of the Lord President, Sir John Anderson. The director, from 1941 to 1945, was Lionel Robbins. Broadly speaking, the Economic Section was Keynesian: though the term itself is controversial. Some authorities maintain that Keynes was less prepared to accept inflationary risks in the pursuit of full employment than his followers. Others, with the evidence of the archives on their side, deny this by demonstrating that there was very little to separate Keynes from the economists of the Economic Section.[12]

The consideration of postwar employment policy began with a paper prepared by James Meade of the Economic Section in the spring of 1941. After the Beveridge Report, the issue was taken up by the Reconstruction Priorities Committee. The decision to produce a White Paper on the subject, itself a defeat for the Treasury, resulted in a prolonged debate between the Treasury and the Economic Section. The Section wanted to define full employment as an unemployment rate of 2.5 per cent or below; for the Treasury the permanent secretary, Sir Richard Hopkins, preferred to stick to Beveridge's yardstick of 8.5 per cent.

It is interesting in reviewing the debate to see how each side appeared to the other. Durbin, who was Attlee's personal assistant in economic affairs, was scornful of Treasury obscurantism. According to Dalton's diary,

He said that none of the Treasury officials knew any economics and this might have disastrous consequences. They knew only about a few strictly limited topics – Public Finance in the narrower sense, Foreign Exchange and the technique of Public Borrowing. If left to themselves, half a dozen high officials at the Treasury would land us with two million unemployed at the end of the war.[13]

From the other side of the fence the Treasury view is succinctly described by the economic historian Rory McLeod:

They did not deny that the fundamental cure of the trade cycle was to stabilise demand, but they felt that the remedies suggested by the economists would be difficult to implement and would have undesirable side effects. Politicians would be tempted to unbalance the budget and raise public spending by borrowing money, citing Keynesian doctrine to provide intellectual justification for a populist move. The public would become used to high employment financed by permanent deficits and would object to any attempt to cut the deficit by raising taxes. Inflation would quickly result, and there would be a collapse in business confidence.[14]

The final document, *Employment Policy*, represented a compromise. No quantitative definition of 'full employment' was attempted and the phrase itself was avoided. In the opening sentence the government pledged itself more cautiously to maintain 'a high and stable level of employment'. The White Paper stressed that certain preconditions, such as mobility of labour and the stability of prices and wages, were essential to the success of the policy. Deficit budgeting was ruled out as a deliberate policy in time of recession, but the principle of demand management, including state investment in public works, endorsed. To sum up, the White Paper was a qualified victory for the Keynesians, but as yet a fragile one, papering over divisions in Whitehall and disguising elements of resistance in both the main parties.

The White Paper on employment policy was the outcome of a series of negotiations within the government, and the Distribution of Industry Act, which Dalton managed to place on the statute book in spring 1945, was proof that the policies of the White Paper were already taking administrative form. But the consideration of industrial policy leads us to a third strand in the pattern of change: the corporate trend towards a tripartite structure of relations between Whitehall, the employers and the trade unions. This development has been placed in a long-term context by Keith Middlemas in his book *The Politics of Industrial Society*.[15] Middlemas argues that from about 1911 onwards there was a long-run tendency towards 'corporate bias' in the government's handling of industrial problems. When intervening in industry, governments attempted to do so by enlisting the co-operation of trade unions and employers' associations, thus turning them, in part, into 'governing institutions'. But Lloyd George's attempt to achieve this in the First World War collapsed. A modest revival of corporatism occurred during the 1930s, but the Second World War marked its restoration as an alternative system of government rivalling the party system.

The Ministry of Labour, which controlled manpower, and the three supply departments – Supply, Admiralty and Aircraft Production – had the task of implementing the manpower and production programmes of the War Cabinet. In March 1942 Churchill superimposed a Ministry of Production responsible for co-ordination with the US War Production Board. All these departments depended upon the active co-operation of employers and trade unions in the industries concerned. To this end, central and regional boards were established consisting of departmental officials, and representatives of the unions and employers. At the centre, representation was dominated by the Trades Union Congress and the two main employers' organizations: the British Employers' Confederation and the Federation of British Industries. Middlemas therefore argues that, as the government turned its attention towards problems of social reconstruction, so the pattern of 'corporate bias' was built into the workings of postwar government. Just as the political parties were drawing apart, in the latter stages of the coalition, so the 'two sides of industry' came to occupy a middle ground based on a common rejection of a competitive, free-market economy. The parties wanted to revive the politics of class: but the big battalions on both sides of industry favoured accommodation. In *Power, Competition and the State*, Middlemas argues that the 1944 White Paper on employment was the most important expression of the new industrial equilibrium.[16]

There are some problems in treating unions and employers' associations as governing institutions in a positive sense. They were agents of policy, or bodies to be consulted, rather than makers of policy. According to J. M. Lee, in his anatomy of the coalition, the central tripartite bodies were relatively ineffective: the really constructive work took place in the regions.[17] The postwar Labour government took over the system and extolled the advantages of consultation with unions and employers. But, in his unpublished doctoral thesis on economic planning under the Labour government, Martin Chick comments,

While much of the secondary literature and the publications of the Federation of British Industry and the Trades Union Congress themselves indicate that there were numerous meetings and exchanges of opinion and information between government, industry and the trade unions, the archives of all three sides indicate that this high level of activity cannot be equated with a high level of achievement. The actual influence of the unions and industry on government economic policy was much less than has been claimed both by the representative organisations themselves and by some analysts of the political development of corporatist industrial society.[18]

It may be more realistic to regard the employers and unions associations as veto groups, with the power to prevent governments from acting when their vested interests were threatened, rather than as architects of policy. If so, the effect of the war must still be reckoned as far-reaching. The veto groups were now entrenched at the centre of power.

It would be misleading to give the impression that by the time of the break-up of the coalition, the role of postwar government had been fully determined. No agreement was possible under the coalition over the nationalization of industry. The Conservatives had no plans for national-ization, while Labour had a long shopping list, including the iron and steel industry. But even here differences can be exaggerated. The formula for the reconstruction of basic industry accepted by many leading industrialists during the war was greater state regulation without state ownership. In social, economic and industrial policy change was deeply embedded in administrative practice by spring 1945. Middlemas goes so far as to say, 'The state apparatus bequeathed to the Labour government of 1945–1951 was not only not susceptible of amendment; it contained within itself a blueprint for economic management intrinsi-cally hostile to the decisions of the 1944 Labour party conference and to the spirit if not the letter of *Let us Face The Future*.'[19]

The new collectivism was a very British transformation: an acceleration of previous trends towards state intervention rather than an outright break with the past; a drive to build a range of new institutions alongside the old, rather than to overthrow them. In places, the laws of inertia con-tinued to operate. Proposals for the reform of local government were shelved. Though housing was a vast and urgent problem, the Ministry of Health still bore the dual responsibility for housing and the reform of the health services. Yet the extent of the change in Whitehall, and its compression within a short period, justify the term 'revolution'. Historians today are less likely to disagree over its extent than over its merits.

Generally speaking, British historians still hold the Churchill coalition and the war effort in high esteem. The official histories of the war, divided into a military and a civil series, were scholarly and critical, but in a deeper vein celebratory. Attempts to debunk Churchill have for the most part failed, and academic accounts of government and people in wartime are still highly charged with social or patriotic idealism. The Beveridge Report, and the Labour victory of 1945, may no longer be regarded in the old-fashioned way as milestones on the road to a peace-ful social revolution. But there is still an immense fund of respect among historians for the high-minded intelligentsia of the war years, and the principles of social reconstruction.

No doubt this says as much about historians, and the many ties that bind them to the period and its rulers, as it does about the British war effort. But there it is: a massive historical orthodoxy whose authority ranges far beyond the war years to validate the reputation of postwar governments and their leaders. It was inevitable that sooner or later the wartime orthodoxy would be challenged. Angus Calder, in *The People's War*, challenged it from the socialist point of view. Maurice Cowling, in *The Impact of Hitler*, introduced into his epilogue a note of dissenting Tory scepticism. But the most thorough and sustained assault so far is Correlli Barnett's *The Audit of War*.[20]

To appreciate Barnett's analysis it is essential to understand the point of view from which he writes. Barnett is a withering critic of nineteenth-century *laissez-faire* capitalism and its legacy for twentieth-century Britain. To this extent he shares some common ground with Marxist historians and quotes E. P. Thompson with approval. But his ideal model of the relationship between state and society is Bismarckian. The development of modern Germany, through the creation of a state dedicated to the pursuit of national efficiency in a ruthlessly Darwinian world, is held up as the example Britain ought to have followed. The British tradition of collectivism he interprets as a decadent, romanticizing humanism, anti-industrial, riddled with illusions, and perpetuated by the public-school system. Bishops and headmasters are treated as figures of fun.

As for the 'audit of war', Barnett's argument may be summarized as follows. The Second World War demonstrated that British industry was retarded and inefficient. The defects were obvious: backward technology, a shortage of skilled workers, an amateurish management, an obstructive trade union movement, a lack of investment in research and development. This was 'the audit of war', fully documented at the time by confidential inquiries and reports and well known to the inner circle of ministers and civil servants. The insiders also realized, as Barnett points out, that Britain would face an economic emergency after the war that could only be overcome by effective competition in world markets. The Board of Trade was already worried about the competition Britain would face in the long run from Germany and Japan.

According to Barnett, the Churchill coalition ought therefore to have adopted as the first priority in reconstruction the re-equipment, re-training, and reorganization of British industry. But, instead of planning for an economic miracle, the government planned for a New Jerusalem. The New Jerusalem movement, as Barnett calls it, was inspired by soggy liberal idealism and a lofty disdain for industry and the means by which wealth was created. But this movement, spearheaded by Beveridge, overrode opposition within the government and imposed a costly programme of social reform on a decaying industrial base. One of its most notable follies, according to Barnett, was the adoption of regional policy to direct industry to the depressed areas. In Darwinian terms, these regions were 'a species at the end of its evolutionary line', and the correct solution would have been to encourage migration to green-field sites of new technology in the South of England.[21] In the long run, the consequences of the coalition programme were inevitable: the New Jerusalem crumbled as British industry declined, and the illusion of full employment, as Barnett calls it, was destroyed. The Churchill coalition can therefore be held responsible for the postwar economic decline of Britain.

Barnett's book has many virtues. It is enterprisingly researched, spirited in style and irreverent in its judgements. There are kernels of truth in the analysis. His demonstration of the inefficiency of major industries in wartime would be hard to refute. His criticisms of the 1944 Education Act are damning. But it is facile to condemn some past administration for failing to behave like a philosopher king with prophetic powers and a magical authority over an obedient people. If Barnett had concluded that, owing to the force of historical circumstances, the coalition failed to attach a sufficiently high priority to the reconstruction of industry, the conclusion would be hard to dispute. But, following in the tradition of the 'guilty men' thesis, Barnett seeks to convict the reformers within the coalition of wilful stupidity and irresponsibility. They are alleged to have missed a historic opportunity for the modernization of the economy, and the prosecution grows into an assault on the postwar welfare state, which is represented as the root cause of Britain's industrial decline since 1945.

Barnett's thesis rests on a number of simplifications. First, he divorces the history of Britain from its European context and thereby distorts the perspective. Secondly, he fails to acknowledge the political imperatives behind the reconstruction programme. Thirdly, he neglects the politics of industrial conservatism. Fourthly, his analysis is remarkably selective, singling out one factor – the welfare state – and one government, as uniquely responsible for difficulties that no other government, before or since, has surmounted.

In writing of the wartime movement for social reform, Barnett treats it as a peculiarly British phenomenon, a reflection of the role in British life of a decadent, romanticizing intelligentsia. The welfare state and the mixed economy are thereby made to appear a uniquely British creation, responsible for Britain's postwar malaise. But how can this be, when similar conceptions inspired the resistance movements of occupied Europe, and were adopted by so many other countries after the war? As Walter Laqueur observes in *Europe since Hitler*, social reforms were carried out all over Europe. The pattern varied, of course. Some countries, such as Britain and West Germany, provided free medical care to all insured persons, while others, including France and the Scandinavian countries, demanded a contribution from the sick. Family allowances were universal, but much higher in Italy and France than in Britain. Everywhere the trend was towards higher social expenditure: 'Western European expenditure on social services quadrupled between 1930 and 1957; in Sweden it was six times higher in the latter year, in France seven, in Italy fourteen times.'[22] If, however, other countries succeeded in combining industrial advance with a welfare state, welfare programmes cannot be the root cause of Britain's poor industrial performance.

Barnett interprets the wartime movement for social reform in Britain as the creation of an intelligentsia who manipulated popular opinion in their favour and thereby created unrealistic expectations of the Promised Land. As everybody knows, the intelligentsia were ambitious and active during the war, and very effective in putting their message across. But their role in the pattern of wartime change was secondary. The primary factor was a shift in the balance of power between capital and labour that enhanced the bargaining power of the trade unions, established the Labour Party as an equal partner in the coalition, and rendered the state dependent upon popular morale. In other words, the dynamic for social reconstruction lay in the politics of class: the price of working-class participation was working-class welfare. The role of the intelligentsia was a consequence, rather than a cause, of the new dispensation, and their function was to define the terms of a new social contract between the classes. From Barnett's language, one might suppose that wartime social reformers were millenarians who promised the people heaven on earth. This may have been true of idealists on the fringes of politics, such as Sir Richard Acland and the Common Wealth movement. But it was not true of the Whitehall reformers who determined the course of events. Beveridge himself disliked the phrase 'welfare state', with its overtones of philanthropy and dependence, and would not use it. His plan rested on the insurance principle of benefits in return for contributions. The benefits were intended to ensure the bare minimum necessary to sustain a healthy existence. Beveridge made no allowance in his calculations for the purchase of such luxuries as beer and tobacco, and assumed that the insured would purchase stale rather than fresh bread as it was cheaper. The postwar welfare state, it has always to be remembered, was conceived in a period of austerity.[23] Similarly the policy of encouraging new industries in the prewar depressed areas, which Barnett treats as an act of romantic folly, was a modest and sensible project. There were plenty of green-field sites in the industrial regions, and there was no geographical reason why a business in the North of England should find itself at a dis-advantage, compared with a business in Surrey, in competing for markets at home or abroad.

A major omission from the book is the subject of industrial politics. But the industrial politics of the period ruled out, *a priori*, the strategy of modernization that Barnett believes ought to have been adopted. This renders still more implausible the idea that there was a great missed opportunity.

Barnett would appear to assume that, since the relevant government departments and their ministers were aware of the deficiencies of British industry, they ought to have drafted a radical blueprint for industrial modernization. But the wartime production drive rested on the co-operation of employers' associations and trade unions. The coalition was dependent upon these institutions, and, although it could bring pressure to bear on them, it was in no position to impose solutions on them. The government was aware of the need to improve productivity and efficiency in general, as the 1944 White Paper on Employment made perfectly clear. Indeed the White Paper never promised that any govern-ment could deliver full employment unconditionally: full employment was expressly stated to be conditional on the improvement of industry's performance. There was, in other words, an implied contract.

The government's own strategy was to work for this improvement through the system of voluntary co-operation between government, employers and unions. But one major obstacle was the fact that both the trade unions and the employers' associations had a vested interest in maintaining restrictive practices. To complicate the picture still further, many politicians were also strongly influenced by the prewar trend in political thought against the 'anarchy of competition' and in favour of a corporate structure. Industrial politics, therefore, tended to bind the coalition to the *status quo*.

Barnett's vision of the causes of industrial decline is highly selective. In a powerful critique of the coalition's housing policy he shows that the government was divided over the issue of the competing claims of the housing and factory-building programmes. For two years, from January 1943 to January 1945, a spluttering debate prevented a decision. At last the Reconstruction Committee decided that homes should be given priority over factories and infrastructure. The effects, as Barnett argues, were long-lasting: a bias over the next two decades in favour of capital investment in housing at the expense of industry.[24]

Where comparisons are possible, it seems that Britain did divert much greater resources into housing in the late 1940s: 31.6 per cent of fixed capital investment in 1947, as compared with 2.9 per cent in Italy, 11.8 per cent in Belgium, and 12.3 per cent in Norway.[25] But one query must be raised: if Barnett is right to attribute the low level of postwar investment in industry to the long-term burden of the housing programme, why should the long-term burden of defence expenditure, which diverted resources from the export trades, be left out of the reckoning? Barnett acknowledges the problem in a single paragraph on the last page of his book, where he notes the impact of war in fostering the illusion that Britain was still a great power:

The pursuit of this hallucination in the next quarter of a century was to cost Britain in defence expenditure up to double the proportion of GNP spent by European industrial competitors. . . . It was to impose a heavy dead weight on Britain's sluggish economy and on her fragile balance of payments, suck away from exports scarce manufacturing resources in advanced technology, and continue the wartime concentration of much of Britain's scarce R and D resources on defence projects.[26]

A telling judgement: but one that calls into question Barnett's verdict on the housing programme. For, as Martin Chick writes, 'Neither the British housing programme nor the British defence programme were unique. West Germany had a large housing programme. The French ran a considerable defence programme. What was unique was that only Britain tried to run both a large housing programme and a large defence programme at the same time.'[27]

Why should the coalition government in particular be saddled with the responsibility for Britain's postwar economic decline? Economic historians have long accepted that Britain's relatively poor economic performance dates from the 1870s. Indeed, the argument is often pushed back to the start of the Industrial Revolution, and Barnett himself, in a retrospective chapter of his book, argues that industrialization in Britain was a shambles from whose consequences the nation has suffered ever since. There are many possible explanations, some of which stress the responsibility of government, while others emphasize the inability of governments to change deeply ingrained patterns of behaviour in industry. If industry had practised what governments preached from 1945 to 1974, an economic miracle would have been assured.

The postwar settlement was of its time: an attempt to solve the problems of the interwar years. For twenty years it appeared to be working well but from the 1960s the rot set in. The social insurance principle failed to prevent poverty. The housing programme accelerated the disintegration of working-class communities. The managed economy failed to prevent the raging inflation and rising unemployment of the 1970s. The machinery devised in the 1940s was rusting away, and so was the social order it was invented to serve.

Social democracy depends upon social controls. In the war years reformers erred on the side of optimism in supposing that people would control themselves – co-operating with one another in peacetime as readily as they did in the Home Guard or the air-raid warden's post. But there was also an authoritarian side to wartime collectivism. A prominent feature of wartime political thought was elitism: the belief that society was divided into leaders and followers. Churchill possessed the aristocrat's version of this. He issued instructions to his subordinates with all the assurance of the infant Winston ringing for his nanny; and he addressed the British public with the natural authority of a born leader. Bevin exemplified a working-class form of authoritarianism. He expected the rank and file of the movement to comply with the terms of the bargains that he and other trade union leaders struck with the employers and the government. Under Bevin's regime, strikes were illegal, a situation that prevailed until 1951. When the postwar Labour government was discussing the introduction of peacetime National Service, Bevin argued that the rights conferred by the welfare state on its citizens imposed reciprocal duties.

Last but not least, there was the Beveridge version of elitism: the belief in an intellectual aristocracy actuated by service to the community, released from the trivial round and the common task by a high income, and rewarded by the deference of the uneducated. In Beveridge's vision, the role of the expert was first to research a problem and then, having reached his conclusions, to persuade the politicians and the public, by reasoned argument, to accept them. The rising young Oxford revisionists in the Labour Party shared this outlook.

These three elites – the old governing class, the trade union oligarchy and the intellectual mandarins – interlocked during the Second World War to create a new establishment and a new political settlement. The decline of that settlement can therefore be read, in part, as the story of the gradual erosion of their authority from the 1960s. The makers of the postwar state did not foresee the consumer society with its anarchic scramble for private gains at the expense of the public interest. They did not anticipate the collapse of intellectual authority as populism swept aside the conclusions of the experts, and rational debate was replaced by gut conviction. They did not imagine that Tory grandees, trade union oligarchs, and public-school socialists, would be overthrown by their followers. Nor could they see far enough ahead to envisage a society in which the Second World War was regarded as old hat. The class of '45, the generation of young adults for whom the war was the decisive experience of their lives, rose to power as the leaders of the war effort disappeared from the scene. Harold Wilson, who was twenty-three at the outbreak of war in 1939, and a temporary civil servant during the war years, was in the first year of his premiership when Churchill died. But within a few years there will be no one left in public life who made a name in wartime Whitehall, or served in the armed forces, or stood for Parliament in 1945.

The postwar settlement is crumbling away, but some things do not change. In a society of great inequalities, social justice is a selfish as well as an altruistic cause. It will remain high on the agenda, with the lower income groups appealing to the state to rectify the injustices produced by the working of market forces. It is modish in the 1980s to write off 1945 and all that as ancient history, and it is of course possible that Britain is finished as a self-governing nation with a distinctive political culture. But the British live in an old country where radical innovations have often been inspired by a revival of traditional values. When Enoch Powell and Tony Benn challenged the consensus in the 1970s, they appealed with good reason to aspects of British history the modernizers had forgotten about. The likelihood is that sooner or later another great reconstruction will occur, quite different in method from that of Keynes, Beveridge and Attlee, and attuned to the requirements of a different society, but inspired by the same tradition of progress and reform.

Notes

1 Alan Bullock, *The Life and Times of Ernest Bevin*, vol. II: *Minister of Labour 1940–1945* (Heinemann, 1967), p. 192.
2 J. M. Lee, *The Churchill Coalition 1940–1945* (Batsford, 1980), p. 138.
3 Martin Gilbert, *Finest Hour: Winston S. Churchill 1939–1941* (Heinemann, 1983), p. 331.
4 Bullock, *Bevin*, vol. II, pp. 190–1.
5 Paul Addison, *The Road to 1945: British politics and the Second World War* (Cape, 1975), p. 280.
6 Ben Pimlott, *Hugh Dalton* (Cape, 1985).
7 Ibid., pp. 396–7.
8 Addison, *The Road to 1945*, p. 172.
9 Political and Economic Planning, *Government and Industry* (PEP, 1952), p. 96.
10 Lee, *The Churchill Coalition*, p. 113.
11 Cherwell Papers, F256, War Cabinet memorandum by the Postmaster General dated 13 January 1944, Nuffield College, Oxford.
12 Alan Booth, 'The Keynesian revolution in economic policy-making', *Economic History Review*, 36 (1983), pp. 103–23.
13 Ben Pimlott (ed.), *The Second World War Diary of Hugh Dalton 1940–1945* (Cape 1986), p. 626.
14 Rory McLeod, 'The promise of full employment', in Harold L. Smith (ed.), *War and Social Change: British society in the Second World War* (Manchester University Press, 1986), p. 87.
15 Keith Middlemas, *Politics in Industrial Society: the experience of the British system since 1911* (André Deutsch, 1979).
16 Keith Middlemas, *Power, Competition and the State*, vol. I: *Britain in Search of Balance, 1940–1961* (Macmillan, 1986).
17 Lee, *The Churchill Coalition*, p. 103.
18 Martin Chick, 'Economic Planning, Managerial Decision-Making and the Role of Fixed Capital Investment in the Economic Recovery of the United Kingdom 1945–1955' (Ph.D. thesis, London School of Economics, 1986), p. 256.
19 Middlemas, *Power, Competition and the State*, vol. I, p. 111.
20 Correlli Barnett, *The Audit of War: the illusion and reality of Britain as a great nation* (Macmillan, 1986).
21 Ibid., p. 247.
22 Walter Laqueur, *Europe since Hitler*, 2nd edn (Penguin, 1982), p. 248.
23 Sir Norman Chester, 'The Austere Crusader', '*The Times*, 1 December 1982.

24 Barnett, *The Audit of War*, pp. 243–6.
25 Alan S. Milward, *The Reconstruction of Western Europe 1945–1951* (Methuen, 1984), p. 38.
26 Barnett, *The Audit of War*, p. 304.
27 Chick, 'Economic Planning . . . 1945–1955', p. 43.

2
The Attlee Governments, 1945–1951

Peter Hennessy

The scene is the Treasury some time in 1947. An under secretary has been summoned out of the blue to brief a Cabinet committee in session at No. 10 with the Prime Minister in the chair. It is an unusual event. The Treasury official has not seen Clement Attlee in action before. He returns to Treasury Chambers and delivers his verdict to the curious members of his policy division. 'Britain', he says, 'is being run by a senior executive officer.'[1] Slotting a minister hypothetically into the Civil Service hierarchy is a pretty pointless exercise. After all Roy Jenkins, that fastidious connoisseur of Westminster and Whitehall, said of Ernest Bevin, titan of the Attlee Cabinet, that he started as Foreign Secretary 'with the qualification that there was no other position in the Foreign Office, unless it was that of a rather truculent liftman on the verge of retirement, which it would have been possible to imagine his filling'.[2]

Our senior Treasury man can be forgiven for underestimating Attlee. He did possess the air of a middle-ranking civil servant of advancing years working out his time in an obscure corner of Whitehall. In an earlier study I described him as 'a deeply underwhelming figure even at the zenith of his titular power – he had no physical presence and on the equivalent of the Richter scale for oratory, the needle scarcely flickered'.[3] Yet his reputation and that of the administration to which he gave his name has steadily increased with the passage of time, a process which the release of official papers at the Public Record Office since 1976 (under the thirty-year rule) has accelerated rather than halted.

In 1986, with the deluge of Whitehall documentation virtually complete[4] and two major biographies published inside three years,[5] Attlee, as the twentieth anniversary of his death approached,[6] was paid the compliment of a revisionist history-in-the-making. Professor George Jones, Herbert Morrison's biographer[7] and a scholar deeply familiar with the Attlee years, criticized Trevor Burridge's biography on the grounds that it 'never confronts major criticisms of Attlee's leadership, in particular that at really important moments he dithered and never gave a lead, even perhaps succumbing to psychosomatic illness, as at the start of the Second World War, during the convertibility crisis, over devaluation and the 1951 Budget. He misjudged the timing of the elections in 1950 and 1951, and stayed on as Prime Minister when he had lost the zest to govern' – an interpretation vigorously rebutted by Professor Burridge, who gave clinical chapter and verse on Attlee's ailments to show they were not psychosomatic.[8] For good measure, in a flurry of correspondence about the Burridge book, Paul Addison revived the 'little man' thesis, comparing Attlee to Mr Pooter, and, shortly after, Eric Hobsbawm described the period 1945–51 as having acquired 'a mythical halo in retrospect'.[9] The time is clearly ripe for a reappraisal of the man and his governments.

The election of the first majority Labour government in July 1945 is the fourth of the five great benchmark dates of twentieth-century British political history. (The other four are 1906, formation of the first of the reforming Edwardian Liberal administrations; 1914, the outbreak of the First World War; 1939, the start of the Second; and 1979, the election of the first Thatcher government, which set its face against the fundamentals of post-1945 political economy.) But the key date for the politicians who wrought the Attleean revolution is May 1940, when Labour entered the wartime coalition government under Winston Churchill, its immediate price being the removal of Neville Chamberlain from 10 Downing Street.[10] Once inside Whitehall for the first time since the traumatic economic crisis of 1931, labour ministers began to exact a steady and longer-lasting price for their co-operation which by the end of the war had changed the language and the battleground of British politics, a process described by Paul Addison in his *The Road to 1945* (1975), a study of British politics in the Second World War which genuinely merits its description as a seminal work.[11] In 1940 Labour's impact was swift. The key figure was not Attlee but Ernest Bevin, creator and leader of the Transport and General Workers Union. Bevin was not even an MP when the coalition was formed. Almost to his dying day he denied that he was a politician.[12] But he embodied the might of the Labour movement and was the symbol and the talisman of the trade unions' indispensable collaboration in the war effort.[13] Bevin's status was quickly recognized by Churchill. If the Germans had invaded in 1940, three ministers – Churchill, Lord Beaverbrook[14] and Bevin – would have repaired to the War Cabinet's last redoubt as a 'Committee of Public Safety' to organize resistance.[15] Bevin demanded and won genuine concessions for 'my people', as he invariably referred to them. The status and condition of the British labour force underwent one of its most significant and dramatic advances.[16]

While Churchill concentrated on running the war with the Chiefs of Staff, Labour ministers such as Bevin, Attlee, Herbert Morrison and Arthur Greenwood tended to make the running on home policy and, crucially, from early 1943, on postwar reconstruction. Indeed, the influence of Labour ministers in the coalition, and the tide of reformist opinion on which they capitalized after Dunkirk, has gained a peculiarly diabolical place in the demonology of the free-market Right, who see in the collectivism of the home front in the forties several causes of the travails of the British economy in the seventies and eighties. For Correlli Barnett, whose *The Audit of War* acquired an instant vogue when published in 1986,[17] it was a straight choice between a New Jerusalem and an economic miracle.[18] For Barnett the verdict of the British electorate in 1945 was catastrophic in its long-term consequences:

by the time they took the bunting down from the streets after VE-Day and turned from the war to the future, the British in their dreams and illusions and in their flinching from reality had already written the broad scenario for Britain's postwar descent to the place of fifth in the free world as an industrial power, with manufacturing output only two-fifths of West Germany's, and the place of fourteenth in the whole non-Communist world in terms of annual GNP per head.

As that descent took its course the illusions and the dreams of 1945 would fade one by one – the imperial and Commonwealth role, the world-power role, British industrial genius, and, at the last, New Jerusalem itself, a dream turned to a dank reality of a segregated, subliterate, unskilled, unhealthy and institutionalised proletariat hanging on the nipple of state maternalism.[19]

But for other scholars of the Fighting Forties writing in the 1980s, the legacy of 1945 was very different. To Kenneth Morgan, whose masterly study *Labour in Power* appeared in 1984 (as Labour painfully emerged from the ashes of its worst electoral performance since 1918 in terms of proportion of votes cast),

The Attlee government was . . . unique in its structural cohesiveness and in its legislative vitality. Its legacy lived on in a broad influence over the Labour and progressive left, over political and economic thought and, indeed, over much of cultural life for a full quarter of a century after 1951. It was without doubt the most effective of all Labour governments, perhaps amongst the most effective of any British government since the passage of the 1832 Reform Act.[20]

The legacy of 1945 was more than a dry dispute among scholars in the 1980s. The performance of the Attlee government in its six and a quarter years of power was a live issue among the political practitioners themselves. Michael Foot as Labour leader made frequent and favourable reference to it. Shortly before the 1983 election was called, he said in an interview on Granada Television's *World in Action*, 'the Labour Party doesn't believe in authoritarian methods. It's one of the reasons why the Labour Party is better qualified to govern this country; why at some of the most critical moments in this century, 1945 for example, when we came out of a terrible war and hideous problems, couldn't have been dealt with by a Conservative government at those times'.[21] In June 1983 Mrs Margaret Thatcher was returned to power with a majority of 144, only two seats short of Attlee's postwar record thirty-eight years earlier. Significantly, the Conservatives' first party political broadcast after the 1983 general election took on the one Labour leader Conservatives had tended to exempt from their strictures. The broadcast began with a 'voice-over' which claimed that

To understand why today we are fighting a war against rising prices we need to go back to the end of the Second World War, to 1945. The people of Britain had a new vision of how they wanted life to be. An end to proverty and squalor, decent homes for families and plenty of jobs for everyone. To pursue this vision, the Attlee Government committed itself to spending virtually half of what this country earned. The intentions were good but such massive spending soon made the people feel poorer, not richer, and it created even more problems than it seemed to be tackling.[22]

Indeed, as the *Economist* noted when Kenneth Harris's biography was published in autumn 1982, 'Mrs Margaret Thatcher sees her task as replacing the Attleean consensus which left Britain with low industrial productivity, resource-hungry State concerns and a welfare system that discourages thrift and breeds bureaucracy. She says that it will take two parliaments to break that mould and is privately uncertain whether even she can pull it off.'[23]

It is a glowing tribute to the Attlee administrations that after forty years their light should shine sufficiently brightly to illuminate contemporary debate. 26 July 1945 was a day of political drama. (The election had taken place on 5 July, but the results were delayed for three weeks to allow the overseas forces' vote to be counted.) At the Savoy Hotel in the Strand a now immortal lady diner said, 'But this is terrible – *they've* elected a Labour Government, and *the country* will never stand for that.'[24] Attlee was his customary prosaic self. Mrs Attlee drove him to Buckingham Palace at 7.30 p.m. in the family car. To George VI he was 'looking very surprised indeed'.[25] (Gallup had forecast a Labour win. It had been suggesting 'for years that an election would produce a Labour majority'.[26] Nobody took any notice of opinion polls in those days, though Aneurin Bevan and Emanuel Shinwell were later credited with having foreseen the outcome.[27]) According to an unverified story, the two shy, retiring men began their official relationship with Attlee saying, 'I've won the election', and the King replying, 'I know. I heard it on the Six O'Clock News.'[28] According to legend George VI urged the new Premier to appoint Bevin to the Foreign Office rather than Dalton. Bevin *was* a surprise choice as Foreign Secretary, but Attlee, as he later explained, wanted to separate Bevin from Morrison, with whom he frequently quarrelled and 'if you'd put both on the home front there might have been trouble'.[29]

It was Bevin who flew with Attlee from Northolt to Berlin to represent Britain at Potsdam. But Bevin, despite impressions to the contrary, did not go green into the conference chamber. As the third volume of Lord Bullock's biography makes plain, Attlee and Bevin had been intimately involved in the coalition's postwar foreign policy preparations, and Professor Harold Laski, chairman of Labour's National Executive Committee, and others like him were quite wrong to expect a personal Churchillian foreign policy to be replaced by a distinctly socialist one.[30] In fact, no postwar British Cabinet has been better prepared for power than Attlee's. In any audit of the pluses and minuses of their inheritance in the last week of July 1945, experience gained from participation in the wartime coalition is high on the list. Of the Cabinet of twenty, only Bevan at the Ministry of Health and Shinwell at Fuel and Power were unseasoned by office in 1940–5.

Another huge advantage was the highly disciplined condition of the British people. No social engineer could have wished for more promising material with which to experiment. Almost six years of total war had left no citizen untouched by its rigours, whether in the form of the siege economy on the home front or by military service abroad. The population was used to receiving orders and to strict regulation in the face of shared dangers. This new condition of the people had left a deep impression on the Civil Service and helped create an atmosphere in which carefully conceived and centrally directed schemes of national improvement became a norm and not a pipedream. As Sir Richard Hopkins, Permanent Secretary to the Treasury and Head of the Civil Service from 1942 to 1945, wrote shortly after the war, 'However ingeniously and wisely the civil and industrial controls and rationing schemes may have been devised, they would not have achieved that full success but for the goodwill with which amid the strain and stress of war they were accepted by industry and the community as a whole.' This goodwill, he added, 'went beyond – in my judgement much beyond – any forecast which could reasonably have been made before hostilities began.'[31]

But the debit side of the Attlee Cabinet's inheritance was enormous, daunting. Expectations were high. Labour's manifesto *Let us Face the Future*[32] reflected them. The wherewithal to pay for the social transformation was seemingly non-existent. The manifesto was built round the Beveridge proposals for comprehensive social insurance and a national health service as the weapons for slaying 'the five Giants on the road to recovery', identified by Beveridge in 1942 as Ignorance, Want, Squalor, Idleness and Disease.[33] The manifesto's wholesale adoption of the Beveridge Report (whose author sat in the Commons as a Liberal in 1944–5) distinguished Labour's platform from the Conservatives' and caught the political mood and tide. It is misleading to suggest that Labour's social programme after 1945 was merely a continuation of coalition policies with a red tinge. Apart from R. A. Butler's Education Act of 1944, the Labour government created a legislative reform machine which went further and faster than anything a Churchill Cabinet would have undertaken after 1945. And, even in the education field, it is unlikely that the raising of the school-leaving age would have enjoyed under a Conservative Minister of Education the priority it had under Ellen Wilkinson, who fought it through Cabinet in early 1947, the last act of her political life.[34]

The scope and ambition of Labour's social pledges in *Let us Face the Future* cannot be seen as a disadvantage to the new Cabinet; after all, they helped win the 1945 election. The proposals on nationalization possibly were. The Labour leadership was not keen on the programme of public ownership foisted upon it at the party's annual conference at Blackpool in 1944 by Ian Mikardo, then a fledgling but already formidable political operator on the Labour Left.[35] The social legacy of

1945–51 has brought a warm glow to all sections of the party ever since. The debate about the scope and shape of public ownership has continued from 1948, when Herbert Morrison, the high-priest of 'socialization' as it was then called, began to preach 'consolidation', through to the present day, when Labour's mid-eighties Shadow Cabinet emphasizes the concept of 'social ownership' rather than public ownership.

Overshadowing every comma in *Let us Face the Future* was Britain's economic position. Within days of the war ending in the Far East, the Truman administration abruptly and surprisingly ended Lend–Lease and turned off what had been the financial life-support machine of the British economy since 1941. During the war Britain, in Keynes' homely if dramatic phrase, 'threw good housekeeping to the winds. But we saved ourselves, and helped save the world'.[36] The cost of profligate housekeeping was appreciated well enough in the corridors of the Treasury and the backrooms of the Cabinet Office occupied by its Economic Section, but the arcana of economics in which it was expressed – disinvestment, balance-of-payments forecasts, share of world trade and sterling balances accumulated by creditors in the Empire – were lost on most ministers, let alone Labour MPs, Labour supporters and the general public. More than £1000 million worth of British investments were sold during the Second World War. Sterling and dollar liabilities climbed to £3500 million by the end of 1945. The war finished with Britain carrying the largest external debt in its history.[37] The magnitude of the problem can be gauged by the haemorrhage of national wealth since the last reforming administration to occupy the Cabinet Room, H. H. Asquith's Liberal government. As Sir Alec Cairncross, author of the authoritative *Years of Economic Recovery*, puts it,

There had been a time, before the First World War, when the United Kingdom was by far the world's largest creditor. In 1913 her net overseas assets were comparable in magnitude with the net value of her domestic stock of fixed assets other than dwellings. By 1945 net overseas assets were a minus quantity. In the First World War 15 per cent of the country's wealth had been wiped out by disinvestment in foreign assets and increased foreign indebtedness; in the Second World War the loss was 28 per cent – nearly twice as great proportionately. . . . No other major country suffered such a setback.[38]

In stark terms, Britain in 1945 no longer had the economic sinews to sustain a world and imperial role abroad while constructing a welfare state at home. This was not a prospect either of the main political parties addressed in 1945. Few in politics or in Whitehall did and when they tried they were shunned. One who did try, albeit privately, was Sir Henry Tizard, Chief Scientific Adviser to the Ministry of Defence. In 1949 he minuted, 'We persist in regarding ourselves as a Great Power, capable of everything and only temporarily handicapped by economic difficulties. We are not a Great Power and never will be again. We are a great nation, but if we continue to behave like a Great Power we shall soon cease to be a great nation.'[39] Tizard's warning was received in Whitehall 'with the kind of horror one would expect if one made a disrespectful remark about the King'.[40]

The Attlee government in its domestic and foreign policy behaved throughout its six and a quarter years as if it was, in Tizard's words, 'only temporarily handicapped by economic difficulties'. A priority was to restore some kind of economic lifeline from across the Atlantic. A protracted and difficult negotiation began in Washington, led by Maynard Keynes. Brightness took on mightiness. A yellowing scrap of paper survives in the British files on which an unknown wag scrawled, 'In Washington Lord Halifax[41] once whispered to Lord Keynes: "It's true *they* have the money bags, but *we* have all the brains." '[42] Keynes in a famous passage had warned the new Labour government of its predicament, saying, 'the financial problems of the war have been surmounted so easily and silently that the average man sees no reason to suppose that the financial problems of the peace will be any more difficult'. In reality, Britain was facing 'a financial Dunkirk'.[43] Keynes secured a loan of $3750 million from the United States and $1250 million from Canada meant to tide Britain over a three-year transition from war to peace[44] and came home to die in Sussex at Easter 1946.[45] Without it the welfare state could not have been built.[46] Its construction was the showpiece of the first phase of the Attlee administration.

At some risk of simplification, the history of the Attlee governments can be divided into three phases.

Phase 1　July 1945–August 1947. From general election to convertibility crisis.

Phase 2　August 1947–February 1950. Convertibility crisis to general election.

Phase 3　February 1950–October 1951. The second Attlee government.

The first phase was what Hugh Dalton later called Labour's 'high tide'.[47] In terms of social and health policy and the nationalization of what used to be called the 'commanding heights' of industry (with the exception of iron and steel, which was delayed until 1949–50), it was a period of unprecedented legislative activity. The Bills rolled in and the Acts rolled out as if on a parliamentary production line. Dalton was probably unique among postwar Chancellors of the Exchequer in being as zealous as his social-spending ministerial colleagues in his appetite for funds. He budgeted for the new commitments 'with a song in my heart'.[48] The welfare state was brought into being by a pair of Welsh ministers: Griffiths at National Insurance, solid and competent; and Bevan at Health, brilliant and mercurial, possessing a fierce command of language and considerable administrative flair – a combination rare in political life. Like his fellow countryman, Lloyd George, himself a master-builder of the early welfare state, Bevan was, in Kenneth O. Morgan's phrase, an 'artist in the use of power'.[49]

As Griffiths recalled, Labour's plan for welfare legislation was as simple as it was comprehensive:

The 1945 Labour Government boldly aimed to implement the Beveridge Plan in full within three years, and bring it into operation on the third anniversary of the great electoral victory – 5 July 1948. This was a formidable task. It would necessitate five Acts of Parliament, scores of regulations and the creation of a nationwide [social security] organisation.[50]

The plan was achieved with what 1980s Whitehall would call 'efficiency and effectiveness'. The statutes rolled off the line – or, to be precise, four of them did. The Family Allowances Act 1945 had been pushed ahead by the coalition and was already law. It was followed in 1946 by the Industrial Injuries Act, the National Insurance Act, the National Assistance Act and the National Health Service Act. As if on cue, the jewel in Labour's crown, the National Health Service, came into being on 5 July 1948. A historian of postwar Britain, Peter Calvocoressi, has with justification written of the NHS,

For its customers it was a godsend, perhaps the most beneficial reform ever enacted in England, given that it relieved so many not merely of pain but also of the awful plight of having to watch the suffering and death of a spouse or a child for lack of enough money to do anything about it. A country in which such a service exists is utterly different from a country without it.[51]

The social security legislation aroused little controversy, not merely because the Conservatives in 1945–6 were shell-shocked by the magnitude of their electoral defeat but also because there was a high degree of consensus for the policies the bills embodied. Bevan's NHS bill was a different matter. He faced fierce opposition from the British Medical Association, which fought him to the last ditch, such was its horror of doctors as salaried servants of the state (a compromise was eventually found).[52] But from within the Cabinet Room Bevan found himself confronted by a formidable adversary in Herbert Morrison, apostle and protector of local government. The clash stemmed from Bevan's determination to go much further than plans developed by the coalition. As Kenneth Morgan noted,

the National Health Service is a prime exhibit illustrating the danger of making too much of the continuity between the social consensus of the war years and the post-war Labour welfare state. . . . The ideas of Henry Willink, Churchill's Minister of Health in 1944, especially in their final watered-down form, fell short of Bevan's later proposals in vital respects, notably on hospitals and health centres.[53]

In a Cabinet paper discussed on 18 October 1945 Bevan proposed the nationalization of the hospitals. Morrison wanted to preserve municipal and voluntary hospitals. The issue was settled at Cabinet on 20 December, when the bulk of its members, including Attlee, firmly swung behind Bevan.[54]

On the industrial front, nationalization advanced apace in 1945–6 with Morrison the key figure as chairman of the Cabinet's Socialization of Industry Committee and, as Leader of the House of Commons, the minister responsible for piloting the hefty tranche of legislation through Parliament. In the protracted parliamentary session of 1945–6 no fewer than seventy-five measures passed through the legislative process.[55] By autumn 1946 four nationalization statutes were in place – covering the Bank of England, civil aviation, cable and wireless, and, most emotive of all for the Labour movement, coal. The nationalization of railways, electricity and long-distance transport followed in 1947. None of the measures caused any real controversy. The model, much derided in later years from left and right,[56] was Morrison's beloved London Passenger Transport Board of 1934, created in his London County Council days[57] along lines adumbrated earlier in his first book, *Socialisation and Transport*.[58] Whitehall departments would sponsor public corporations. Ministers would appoint efficient expert people to boards which would run the industries at arm's length from Whitehall, Westminster and, it should be added, the workforce. There was no question of industrial democracy. Sir Stafford Cripps, President of the Board of Trade, in what Kenneth Morgan described as 'a moment of appalling frankness',[59] said in October 1946 that workers' control or co-partnership could not be considered, as the workers as a whole were not competent in management skills.[60] At the time nobody took offence.

Advances on the social and industrial front in 1945–6 and the huge demobilization operation returning men and women from the forces to civilian life were matched by an impressive economic recovery and an energetic performance in regional policy from Cripps at the Board of Trade.[61] But in foreign and defence policy the picture was grim. Bevin is remembered, rightly, as a titanic figure at the Foreign Office. But during the early phase of the Cold War problems crowded in as the wartime Grand Alliance broke up at a series of acrimonious foreign ministers' conferences. The Soviet Union became increasingly hostile. The United States was a very uncertain ally. With James Byrnes as US Secretary of State, Bevin was subjected to regular harangues about the evils of the British Empire and on British policy in Palestine (a perhaps inevitable disaster), while consistent efforts were made in Washington to dismantle the trading system based on imperial preference. The United States broke the Quebec and Hyde Park agreements on atomic energy reached in wartime. Britain once again seemed to stand alone. It was in this international climate that another much criticized decision was taken – to go it alone and build a British atom bomb. At the momentous Cabinet committee meeting on 8 January 1947 it was the United States, not Russia, which fuelled the Foreign Secretary's insistence that Britain have its own nuclear weapon. 'We could not afford to acquiesce', said Bevin, 'in an American monopoly of this new development'.[62] At a meeting the previous October which had authorized the building of a gaseous diffusion plant, Bevin had mounted a furious assault on the criticisms of Dalton and Cripps that the atomic programme was proving too costly:

That won't do at all. . . . We've got to have this. . . . I don't mind for myself, but I don't want any other Foreign Secretary of this country to be talked to or at by a Secretary of State in the United States as I have just had in my discussions with Mr Byrnes. We have got to have this thing over here whatever it costs. . . . We've got to have the bloody Union Jack on top of it'.[63]

Bevin was dead and Attlee was out of office when the bomb was tested in October 1952. But there was 'a bloody Union Jack on top of it'. There still is. The one early success of the early phase of Labour's overseas policy was Indian independence, a decision which Attlee made his own (Bevin was dismayed at the prospect of a scuttle 'without dignity or plan'[64]). It was bought at a heavy price in Indian blood, Sikh, Hindu and Muslim. Some half a million died in communal rioting.[65] But it was one of the most historic decisions taken by any British administration.

It would be wrong to see the Attlee government as anti-imperialist. A new settlement for the Indian sub-continent and the withdrawal from Greece in 1947 as an economy measure[66] were but one side of the imperial coin. A new emphasis on colonial development in tropical Africa was to be, as Jack Gallagher put it, 'a surrogate for India, more docile, more malleable, more pious'.[67] Attlee, Bevin and A. V. Alexander at the Ministry of Defence were convinced Empire men south of the Sahara. Bevin saw Africa as provider of food and raw materials for a resource-starved mother country. Its scarcely scratched mineral wealth could solve the dollar problem and might make even 'the United States dependent on us'.[68] There were dissenters from this view in the Cabinet Room. Dalton, in language highly offensive to post-imperialist ears, refused to see the tropical colonies as a source of 'geological jackpots',[69] speaking instead of 'pullulating, poverty-stricken, diseased nigger communities, for whom one can do nothing in the short-run and who, the more one tries to help them, are querulous and ungrateful'.[70]

He was in a minority. Bevin wanted the Empire to become a single defence and economic unit with its own customs union. Cripps as Chancellor after 1947 tried to integrate domestic and colonial investment programmes. A pair of corporations designed on Morrisonian lines were created as, in effect, nationalized industries for the Empire. The Overseas Food Corporation achieved notoriety as the patron of the ill-fated ground-nuts scheme, which, in Conservative propaganda terms, became the colonial equivalent of the whelk stall that socialists proverbially could not run.[71] For its part, the Colonial Development Corporation had a less controversial life as a sponsor of economic advance in the colonies.

Bevin, who thought instinctively in geopolitical terms, made huge efforts to prop up Britain's system of informal empire in the Middle East. Keeping the lifeline of Middle East oil in good repair was a prime concern. It coloured all his local policies in the area, such as his near-successful attempt to reach accommodation with the Egyptians over the British base in the Suez Canal Zone;[72] his truculence with advocates of the Jewish cause in Palestine sprang not from anti-semitism but from his overwhelming desire to preserve Britain's position in the Arab world.

It is easy to see why the politics of raw materials played such a part in the calculations of the Attlee government. It was still presiding over a siege economy created during the war. It operated five main types of control: price control, particularly of food; production controls such as the 'utility' clothing scheme; food rationing; control of trade through export and import licences and the centralized buying of food in world markets; and controls on the labour force adapted from wartime regulations.[73]

Bread, never rationed during the war, became the subject of control between July 1946 and July 1948 to prevent famine in the British zone of occupation in Germany.[74] Altruism in this instance brought much unpopularity. The fuel crisis of January–March 1947, exacerbated by Shinwell's incompetence at the Ministry of Fuel and Power and a prolonged spell of freezing weather, pushed unemployment temporarily up to 3 million and showed just how precariously based the economy was. The second shock – the currency crisis of July and August – in what Dalton described as Labour's 'annus horrendus'[75], spurred the Treasury's contingency planners to produce the most desperate forecasts that have so far turned up at the Public Record Office in postwar files. Clauses attached by the insistent US Treasury to the terms of the American loan obliged a reluctant British Treasury to make sterling freely convertible into dollars one year after the date on which the agreement took effect. As pounds poured across the exchanges in July 1947, eating up the remains of the loan, Whitehall peered into the abyss. A secret group of officials led by the brilliant R. W. B. 'Otto' Clarke of the Treasury drew up for Dalton a 'famine food programme', a scheme for directing labour onto the land, a new sterling bloc and 'a complete and total national mobilisation, as far-reaching as that of 1940'.[76]

The country drew back from the abyss. Convertibility was suspended on 20 August, but the government was shaken to its core. Attlee, with Bevin's help ('I'm sticking to little Clem'[77]), survived an attempt on his leadership from Morrison, Cripps and Dalton (the plan was to make Bevin PM). 'Bright morning', wrote Keith Middlemas, 'never returned after this dismal period.'[78] The first phase of the Attlee administration was over. Innocence was lost. Henceforth reality prevailed. According to Treasury folk memory,[79] the government came of age after August 1947 and gradually acquired the reverential status it still holds among members of the Civil Service, Whitehall's 'permanent governement'.[80]

Certainly Mr Attlee's engine room, his Cabinet machine, achieved a higher order of efficiency once it emerged from the first great currency crisis of the postwar period into the second phase of his administration. Attlee has achieved lasting fame as the supreme Cabinet manager of the twentieth century, keeping bigger talents than his own in check, particularly among the informal inner Cabinet – Bevin, Morrison, Dalton and Cripps, who together with Attlee became known as the 'Big Five'. The image of Attlee that lingers is of the supreme apostle of silence; he used his own as a weapon and crushed those who rambled – with the exception of Bevin, the biggest of the Big Five (in every sense) and the redoubt upon which Attlee could stand when his leadership was threatened. The Attlee style achieved international repute. For example, F. S. L. Lyons, writing, in the standard work on modern Irish history, of W. T. Cosgrave, the interwar Taoiseach, could claim, 'History, perhaps, has not yet done justice to the man who may well ultimately stand to Irish politics in the same relation as Attlee to British politics – an astute, tenacious chairman, excellent in Cabinet but lacking in charisma.'[81] Attlee the silencer is invoked in eighties' Britain. Ferdinand Mount, a former head of Mrs Thatcher's Downing Street Policy Unit, said his old boss 'could, I suppose, keep out of trouble by curbing her tongue and becoming more crisp and taciturn, an Attlee of the Right. Such a style would have saved her from the Westland affair. At an early stage, Mr Heseltine would have been told, in Attlee's words to Harold Laski, that a period of silence from him would be welcome.'[82] Mr Mount was referring to Attlee's most famous put-down in a letter to Professor Harold Laski, the turbulent Chairman of Labour's National Executive Committee during the 1945 general election.[83]

Though, when taken as a whole, Attlee's stewardship of Cabinet justifies his high and enduring reputation, the first two years do not altogether match the image. Though he was effective on issues such as Indian independence, where expert personal background (Attlee had been a member of the Simon Commission to India in the late 1920s) combined with clarity of purpose in his handling of the Cabinet Committee on India and Burma, the Prime Minister's performance in the crucial area of economic affairs could be shaky. This was partly because, in Douglas Jay's words, 'Clem treated economics very much like medicine – a subject on which there were experts and on which it was wise to find a second opinion.'[84] His own grasp of the subject was perfunctory. Another reason for the early inadequacy of performance was Morrison's shortcomings as economic overlord and chairman of the Lord President's Committee, through which the bulk of economic policy-making below the level of Cabinet flowed. Moreover, until the convertibility crisis rubbed their noses in it, Attlee and his ministers tended to discount the impact of external economic factors from overseas (which were handled by a separate Cabinet committee initially) on the domestic economy.[85] Not until his Economic Policy Committee (EPC) was created in September 1947 did Attlee apply his famous grasp to this critical part of the machine.

With Dalton on the backbenches after his Budget leak to a political correspondent, Morrison in partial eclipse and Cripps at the Exchequer after November 1947, the Treasury regained its place as the most powerful Whitehall department for the first time since the early 1940s. From autumn 1947 till ill health afflicted both Bevin and Cripps in 1950, the inner Cabinet rested on a troika of the two of them and Attlee. The period was long remembered as the high-water mark of efficient administration, with disturbance from within the Cabinet confined to arguments about the timing of steel nationalization, very little dissent from the backbenches and not a single by-election lost.[86] 1948 was an excellent year for the government, with Bevin at last entering his kingdom as the architect of postwar Western diplomacy and the economy surpassing the grim expectations of 1947.

Marshall Aid – without which, Otto Clarke feared, there would have been famine in Britain – was approved by the US Congress in March 1948 after herculean efforts by Bevin from the very moment when General Marshall, the US Secretary of State, had floated the idea at Harvard in June 1947. Once Marshall had replaced Byrnes at the State Department, the skies began to clear for Bevin's intuitive genius as a builder of alliances and a reconstructer of shattered West European economies. The European Recovery Programme (ERP), as Marshall Aid was officially known, was crucial to the consolidation of the British welfare state and the maintenance of the standard of living, just as the first phase of Attlee's quiet revolution would have been impossible without the American loan. By December 1950, when Gaitskell, who had replaced Cripps as Chancellor shortly before, announced Britain no longer needed assistance under the ERP, nearly $2700 million of Marshall Aid had been pumped into Britain.[87]

The diplomatic underpinning of British and West European recovery and Bevin's second great monument – sustained resistance to what was then seen as an unmistakable Soviet tendency towards westward expansion – was achieved in stages. In March 1947 at the foreign ministers' conference in Moscow, Bevin laid the foundations of his consistently fruitful relationship with Marshall. Temperament played a part. But the plunging temperature of the Cold War brought to an end any serious American attempts to weaken the economic and political foundations of the British Empire. Shortly before, Bevin had secured the first of the new alliances (if you exempt the special secret UK–USA agreement on gathering and pooling intelligence negotiated in 1946 and signed in 1947[88]) in the shape of the Dunkirk Treaty with France. Sprat caught mackerel (the Brussels Treaty of 1948 extending the embrace of collective defence to Belgium, the Netherlands and Luxembourg) and mackerel caught whale with the signing of the North Atlantic Treaty in 1949 and the creation of the North Atlantic Treaty Organization. Bevin had secured the interlocking circles of British foreign and defence policy: the Commonwealth, North America and Europe – still the basis of the Foreign Office's world view in the 1980's, as Sir Antony Acland, Head of the Diplomatic Service, made plain in a tribute to 'Ernie's legacy' when the last volume of Lord Bullock's biography of Bevin was published in 1983.[89]

The structure of postwar Western foreign and defence policy developed in the late forties, that 'decade of decisions' as Lord Bullock called it,[90] has proved so durable that it now seems to have been inevitable, which it certainly did not at the time. As we have seen, the immediate postwar phase was scarred by suspicion, even hostility, between the United States and Britain. It would have been disastrous, Lord Bullock believes, if Britain had pulled out of world politics in 1945, settling for a kind of Scandinavian existence, as the Americans were markedly reluctant to assume a world role.[91] Events changed that, as they did the Anglo-American relationship. British withdrawal from Greece in March 1947 drew forth the Truman doctrine ('I believe that it must be the policy of the United States to support free peoples who are resisting attempted subjugation by armed minorities or by outside pressures'[92]) and secured an American involvement not just in the Greek Civil War but in the eastern Mediterrean generally. We have examined the crucial economic partnership represented by Marshall Aid. The Communist *coup d'état* in Czechoslovakia in February 1948 confirmed the existence of the Cold War in a brutal fashion and swung opinion in Britain and the United States firmly in the direction of closer trans-atlantic co-operation. One of the fruits of this collaboration, a merger of the British and American zones of occupation in Germany for the purposes of currency and trade, goaded the Russians into blockading the road and rail links from the west to Berlin. The year-long Berlin airlift to supply West Berlin was the first example of shared Anglo-American crisis management since the cease-fires of 1945. Its consequences were profound both in the short term, in the effect on domestic public opinion and the signal sent to the Soviet Union, and for long-term defence arrangements – American bombers, some with an atomic capability, returned to East Anglia and have stayed ever since.[93] There was nothing preordained about the postwar restoration of the Anglo-American special relationship. Doubts sown by the revisionist school of writing on the origins of the Cold War[94] and the passage of time have dimmed the threat that Stalin's Russia seemed to pose at the time. But as Lord Bullock has written,

The most important factor in the criticisms of Bevin between 1945 and 1947 was the reluctance of the British to contemplate the possibility of renewed international conflict now that the war was over. This makes it all the more impressive that the strong lead which Bevin gave in foreign affairs in 1947 steadily gathered support to the point, in 1947–9, when it came as near consensus as any British foreign secretary has been able to count on in time of peace.

This change could never have taken place if British public opinion had not come independently to the same conclusion Bevin had already reached, that there was a real danger of the Soviet Union and other Communists taking advantages of the weakness of Western Europe to extend their power. We know now that this did not follow, but nobody knew it at the time. This was a generation for whom war and occupation were not remote hypotheses but recent and terrible experiences. The fear of another war, the fear of a Russian occupation, haunted Europe in those years and were constantly revived – by the Communist coup in Czechoslovakia, by the Berlin blockade, and the outbreak of war in Korea in 1950 which produced near-panic in France and Germany. It is unhistorical to dismiss these fears as groundless because the war and occupation did not occur.[95]

Yet it would be wrong to see the Attlee government simply as Truman's Cold War British head office placed conveniently close to the European mainland. Bevin was no branch manager; in the crucial early period of the Cold War, he made the running. And he was not averse to resisting American pressure when he thought it misguided, as in 1949, when Britain recognized Communist China, and in 1950, when Britain turned its back on the European Coal and Steel Community, precursor of the EEC.

Bevin liked to remark that given an extra million tons of coal he could give Britain a new foreign policy.[96] Attlee's was a very production-minded administration, the only postwar government to win approval from that relentless chronicler of the nation's relative economic decline, Professor Sidney Pollard. He praises the government for refusing to cut investment even during the convertibility crisis of 1947, as it 'was still sufficiently under the influence of wartime economic logic to insist that the main economic aim must be to "devote all our energies to production and more production." '[97] For Pollard, the postwar economy, 'given a real economic task, a task to produce and create ... performed magnificently'.[98] With Cripps at the Treasury, the priority was production for export. By 1948 exports were 150 per cent above their prewar level in 1938. Output increased at 4 per cent a year in 1948, 1949 and 1950. Cripps in 1948 secured a voluntary wage freeze with the trade unions which held for over two years. Given the harshness of contemporary criticism of the corporate state and its Siamese twin, the mixed economy, it is as well to remember that it, too, had a high tide in peacetime in the Cripps era.

Folk memory tends to concentrate when looking at Labour's postwar economic record on the devaluation of the pound in 1949. Indeed, one of the reasons adduced for Harold Wilson's determination to cling to the 1949 parity of $2.80 in 1964–7 is his fear that Labour would be dubbed for ever the party of devaluation. As Alec Cairncross has shown, no two devaluations are the same, and his explanation of the 1949 adjustment is the most convincing – that it was the sterling bloc and most of the Western economies adjusting sensibly to the primacy of the postwar economic superpower, the United States.[99] But the American economic recession in spring 1949, the pressure it put on sterling and the growing financial speculation of early summer did not see the government and EPC, its economic command post, at its best. There was a refusal to face up to reality and momentary panic when Lord Addison, the Lord Privy Seal, after a meeting of the EPC on 15 June 1949 turned to Dalton and said, '1931 over again'.[100] There was a continued lack of grip by the Prime Minister in July and August, when, in the absence of the ailing Cripps, who was convalescing in Switzerland, Attlee seemed content to delegate the decision on whether to devalue to a team of young, economically literate ministers – Gaitskell, Jay and Wilson.[101]

The devaluation of sterling from $4.03 to $2.80 to the pound threw a shadow over the forthcoming election, as it obliged the government to deflate domestic consumption still further in the hope, successful as it turned out, of freeing more resources for export. Douglas Jay has developed an intriguing theory about the provenance of the thirteen years of Conservative rule between 1951 and 1964 which dates from this period. According to Jay, Cripps, his much-admired chief at the Treasury, would, on issues of probity, speak only to God. He refused outright to contemplate presenting a Budget to Parliament before an election, as it might be construed as a bribe. Attlee, therefore, was forced to go to the country in February 1950 in rotten weather and before the benefits of the September 1949 devaluation had worked through, and scraped home with a majority of five. Had he waited till May, Jay argues, matters would have been different and a workable majority could have been won, allowing Labour to preside well into the fifties over the fruits of its economic efforts of the forties.[102]

Whether we blame the Almighty or Sir Stafford's conscience, the third phase of the Attlee years is one of political and personal decline. Illness and death depleted the government's human capital with the departure of Cripps in autumn 1950 and Bevin in spring 1951. Attlee himself was bed-ridden in St Mary's Hospital, Paddington, when the Cabinet crisis of April 1951 over the cost of rearmament and Health Service charges forced Bevan and Wilson from the Cabinet and re-created that civil war between left and right in the Labour Party which continues, with shifting *dramatis personae*, to this day. The great years of achievement were past (unless zealots for public ownership include the eventual nationalization of iron and steel). From February 1950 to the government's fall in October 1951 it was consolidation at best, damage limitation and crisis management at worst. And crises crowded in in Egypt (a resurgence of nationalism threatening the Canal Zone), Iran (nationalization of the Anglo-Iranian Oil Company by Mossadeq) and, most important of all, Korea.

The invasion of South Korea, when Communist troops from the North poured across the 38th parallel on 25 June 1950, brought the Cold War home to Britain with a vengeance. It was widely assumed to be, in effect, the opening round of World War III. Attlee had no hesitation in committing British troops and recasting the British economy onto a war footing, even to the point where a ruinous trebling and, later, quadrupling of the defence estimates killed off the fledgling export-led boom which has eluded Whitehall's policy-makers ever since. Once more good housekeeping was thrown to the winds. Gaitskell, seen by so many as the last, best hope of British social democracy, has a very patchy record as Chancellor of the Exchequer. His pursuit of rearmament at all costs, included the fracturing of Labour's internal stability and an overstraining of the economy, was later repudiated, ironically enough, by the incoming Conservative government, which scaled down substantially the planned increase in defence spending. Gaitskell has suffered, too, at the hands of the anatomists of decline. Their scalpels have plunged deep into his announcement in the 1951 Budget of the abandonment of Cripps's 'initial allowances' on new plant, machinery and buildings for a paltry saving of £170 million a year.[103]

Kenneth Morgan has captured the flavour of the last eighteen months of the Attlee administration in his phrase 'The retreat from Jerusalem'.[104] The appetite for construction work abroad had gone, too. The Schuman plan for a European Coal and Steel Community was presented to the British Cabinet by the French in such a way and at such speed, as a virtual ultimatum, that its rejection was inevitable in June 1950. Bevin resented being hustled by Acheson at the State Department and Schuman at the Quai d'Orsay. Ministers disliked the idea of a supranational authority above the commanding heights of the British economy. Xenophobia played a part. Britain, a victor in 1945, still at the heart of a worldwide empire, was being jostled by formerly defeated or occupied countries into a technocratic initiative of nil appeal. As Morrison told Kenneth Younger (deputizing at the Foreign Office for the sick Bevin), 'it's no good – the Durham Miners won't wear it.'[105] Retrospectively it appears the first of two golden opportunites for Britain to lead a renascent Europe (the other being the period of the Messina Conference in 1955). It did not appear so at the time to ministers or to the Whitehall machine.[106]

Tired ministers, the absence of new policies, the battering from war and tension abroad and the cracking of the government's economic strategy at home under pressure of surging commodity prices, rising inflation and a renewal of industrial troubles after a decade of relative peace (apart from bouts of trouble from groups such as the London dockers and meatpackers and a rash of strikes in the Yorkshire coalfield in 1947) produced a jaded epitaph for the century's most hyperachieving peacetime administration. Even the timing of the election in October 1951 seemed odd. Attlee, whose relationship with the King had improved markedly from that first meeting in July 1945, when the King emerged to tell his private secretary 'I gather they call the Prime Minister "Clem". "Clam" would be more appropriate!',[107] insisted that the election should be called before George VI's Commonwealth tour (which in the event the ailing King abandoned). It was almost as if Attlee and his ministers had lost the appetite for power. Churchill was returned with a majority of seventeen.

The dismal final phase should not be allowed to tarnish the glow, albeit austere, of the earlier Attlee years. In terms of achievement, the Attlee governments set the standard against which all subsequent administrations have been marked. As Anthony King expressed it, 'The fit between what the Labour Party said it would do in 1945 and what the Labour Government actually achieved between 1945 and 1951 is astonishingly close. Most of *Let us Face the Future* reads like a prospective history of the immediate post-war period.'[108] What impresses eyes glazed by what Derek Rayner has called 'the fatigues and disappointments of the British political and economic systems'[109] is the self-confidence of the governments of 1945–51. They believed they could affect for the better the welfare of the British people, the productiveness of their economy and the condition of international affairs. The price may have been a hubristic overestimate of the country's great-power status. But theirs was a seed-corn not a scorched-earth mentality, a Victorian frame of mind. It was matched by what Paul Addison has called 'the most striking aspect of it all . . . the governability of the British people'.[110] He is right to see Britain as being 'reconstructed in the image of the war effort' as 'the home front ran on without a war to sustain it'.[111] Perhaps the most compelling rebuttal of the Correlli Barnett thesis is Albert Speer's contention that Bevin in Britain was able to do things that he, Speer, in Hitler's Germany, a tyranny, could not.[112] The way in which an open society *voluntarily* transformed itself into first a resistance then a reconstruction machine is the most striking feature of the history of Britain from 1940 to 1950.

The decade from the creation of the siege economy in spring 1940 to the seepage of Attlee's majority in February 1950 has a genuine completeness – with real benchmarks separating it from the historical landscape at either end. This factor has two kinds of historical significance. If you believe, with Professor Martin Wiener, that 'the leading problem of modern British history is the explanation of economic decline',[113] its origins go deep into culture and history, but its onset, in terms of manifestations in the real economy, postdate 1950. According to Sidney Pollard's assessment,

At the end of the war . . . [Britain] was still among the richest nations of the world, ahead by far of the war-shattered economies of Europe. On the Continent, only the neutrals, Sweden and Switzerland, were better off than Britain, and elsewhere only the United States and Canada. Britain was among the technical leaders, especially in the promising high-technology industries of the future: aircraft, electronics, vehicles. The problem that exercised the states-men of the day was whether the rest of Europe, even its industrialised parts, would ever be able to come within reach of, let alone catch up with, Britain. Nor was that lead a temporary fluke, a result of the more destructive effects of the war on the Continent. On the contrary, the British lead in 1950 was fully in line with that of 1938: and even more so with that of earlier decades, when the British position had been firmly in the van of Europe.[114]

Perhaps there is something in the view of scholars sympathetic to the Attlee government, such as Kenneth Morgan, when they contrast the dynamic performance of the British economy, of rising production and an export-led boom, in 1945–51 with subsequent years, when Chan-cellors lacked the 'spartan intensity of Cripps'.[115]

The second reason for taking the austere forties as an entity to be preserved as if in historical aspic is to protect them from excessive, hindsight-laden revisionism. This has come from both Left and Right. Ralph Miliband's *Parliamentary Socialism* has been a classic in the literature for twenty-five years. He portrays the Attlee government as 'the climax of Labourism' yet cautious and unradical in the scope of its nationalization programme, its unwillingness to envisage real industrial democracy, its susceptibility to the views of the Chiefs of Staff, its refusal to map out a third course between the superpowers, its economic and military dependence on the United States, its espousal of consolidation rather than further socialist advance.[116] For those who have lived through subsequent Labour governments, Miliband's grudging attitude towards the Attleean achievement seems misplaced.

More potent, and, therefore, more dangerous, are the twin schools of revisionism fostered by the more polarized politics of the seventies and eighties. Paul Addison is their early historiographer:

When the Marxist Left and the radical Right emerged in the 1970s there was one point on which they were agreed: that many of the seeds of decline were planted in the immediate post-war years. According to the Marxist Left, this was because socialism and the class struggle were betrayed. According to the radical Right, it was because free market forces had been stultified by the Welfare State and the managed economy. Both rejected the social democratic legacy inherited by the Conservatives from Labour in 1951.

I do not believe that either of these theories is plausible as a reading of post-war history or workable as a means of governing Britain. I believe they will and should give way in time to a radically revised version of the spirit of 1945. Yet each theory illuminated a disturbing corner of reality neglected by conventional opinion. The Marxist Left drew attention to the fact that the sources of industrial conflict were just as explosive as ever. The radical Right drew attention to the fact that the public sector sheltered powerful vested interests whose claims for greater resources were theoretically boundless. These were truths and remain so in spite of the fallacious ideological baggage with which they are mixed up. Neither problem reached critical proportions between 1945 and 1951, but with hindsight they cast a shadow over the period.[117]

The best antidote to the poison of ideological distortion distilled from prejudice and hindsight is an abundance of primary evidence and a rich literature based upon it. And here the Attlee governments are well served in the wealth of raw material at the PRO; general studies of the calibre of Morgan's and Pelling's; specialist studies of the intricacy of Cairncross's; and official histories of the quality of Margaret Gowing's two volumes on the atom bomb and Sir Norman Chester's huge study of postwar nationalization.[118] A third official history, of the National Health Service, is in preparation.[119] The period is well served by political biographies: Harris and Burridge on Attlee; Pimlott on Dalton; Donoughue and Jones on Morrison; Bullock on Bevin; Foot on Bevan; Philip Williams on Gaitskell (a biography and an edited diary [120]). Military biographies are plentiful too: Nigel Hamilton on Montgomery;[121] Denis Richards on Portal;[122] Ronald Lewin on Slim.[123]

There are gaps. Cripps is *the* missing biography, which Maurice Shock is going to provide.[124] Harold Wilson still awaits his biographer. There are no biographies yet on such crucial Whitehall figures as Sir Edward Bridges and Sir Norman Brook, though Richard Chapman has begun work on Bridges.[125] John Campbell's life of Bevan, due for publication in spring 1987, should provide the needed antidote to Michael Foot's over-devotional biography. The Civil Service in the Attlee years, which was crucial to its achievement and effectiveness, deserves a study of its own (the government was not seriously interested in Civil Service reform[126]). Alec Cairncross, who maintains that, 'whether one tries to look forward from 1945 or backwards from forty years later, those years appear in retrospect, and rightly so, as years when the government knew where it wanted to go and led the country with an understanding of what was at stake',[127] argues none the less that

The economic problems encountered by the government were not, as a rule, those which it had expected. Equally, the solutions to the problems were rarely of the government's devising. There were exceptions, as when Bevin grasped at what became the Marshall Plan. But more commonly ministers were the reluctant pupils of their officials. On one economic issue after another – the American Loan, the coal crisis, the dollar problem, devaluation, the European Payments Union – they were slow to grasp the true options of policy and had great difficulty in reaching sensible conclusions.[128]

It is on the detailed policy-making of the Attlee government that many a fascinating case study remains to be written after sinking deep shafts into the files.

An intriguing study could be made, too, of what might be called harbingers. For example, on 14 June 1949 the harassed members of Attlee's EPC, grappling with the dollar drain which preceded devaluation, may have failed to notice an item in *The Times* on Manchester University's 'mechanical brain' or 'computing machine'.[129] The computer age, which was to have a dramatic impact on British industry and society, was upon us. Supermarkets, another phenomenon which was to transform the pattern of consumption and alter domestic habits, made their appearance on the high streets in the Attlee years, carefully encouraged by Food Minister, John Strachey, after a visit to Washington.[130]

Hand in hand with steps to develop the colonial empire in Africa went the first moves which were to lead to its unscrambling. At the Colonial Office, Arthur Creech-Jones, aided by the zealous young under secretary Andrew Cohen, 'the King of Africa' as he became known, began the constitutional changes which were to turn the Gold Coast into Ghana and to set a precedent whose hour had come.[131] Ministers became nervous as the Empire began to come home in the shape of colonial immigration. A mild panic ensued in 1948 when the *Empire Windrush* turned up at Tilbury unannounced carrying 400 immigrants from the West Indies. In 1950 Attlee established a Cabinet Committee on Colonial Immigration under Home Secretary James Chuter Ede which in early 1951 came close to recommending controls.[132]

Some hardy perennials began to rear their troublesome heads. Arguments about the scope and efficacy of public ownership began to emerge between what later became the Clause IV left and the 'revisionist' right, with a third group around Wilson arguing that the relationship between the state and industry represented 'a vacuum in socialist thought'.[133] Health-service costs were rocketing. Bevan, like everyone else, was surprised by the accumulated, suppressed demand on the NHS and the cascades of medicine, to paraphrase Bevan, that poured down the nation's throat in the first two years of its existence. In 1950 Attlee took the chair at the newly constituted Cabinet committee on NHS costs. Overall control of public expenditure was rudimentary and by 1950 was causing serious concern at the senior level in Whitehall.[134] Like several Prime Ministers after him, Attlee was plagued by spy scandals and took the first steps to purge Communists and fascists and their sympathizers from the Civil Service in 1948. As Labour left office, the Cabinet, bowing reluctantly to American pressure after the conviction of Klaus Fuchs and the defection of Guy Burgess and Donald Maclean, was about to introduce positive vetting for the public service and the armed forces.[135] Quite apart from keeping the KGB out of Whitehall, Attlee was a firm believer in closed government. Virtually the first Cabinet paper he circulated in August 1945 asserted 'the underlying principle . . . that the method adopted by Ministers for discussion among themselves of questions of policy is essentially a domestic matter, and is no concern of Parliament or the public'.[136] And he did not bat an eyelid when the Home Secretary authorized the tapping of journalists' phones after leaks on Palestine and public-ownership policy.[137] In his passion for secrecy he set a pattern, too. Finally, a little noticed harbinger: on 28 February 1949 Miss Margaret Roberts was adopted as prospective parliamentary candidate by the Dartford Conservative and Unionist Association.[138]

To finish where we began. We do not need a third biography (a fourth if you include Roy Jenkins's interim study of 1948[139]) on the little man in Downing Street. As a Cabinet colleague told the first biographer of Sir Alec Douglas-Home, 'don't search for an answer to an enigma – there isn't an enigma'.[140] From 1945 to 1951 Britain was run by a real-life Captain Mainwaring – and it was run very well indeed.

Chronology

1945

5 July   General election. 3-week delay while forces' votes counted. Result declared (26 July): Labour, 393 seats; Conservatives, 213; Liberals, 12; others, 22. Formation of first Labour government with a majority (146 seats). Bevin surprise appointment at Foreign Office; Dalton to the Treasury. Attlee survives plot against his leadership.

6 August   Truman announces dropping of atom bomb on Hiroshima.

15 August   Japan surrenders. Second World War ends. Parliament opened by George VI. King's Speech announces nationalization of the mines and repeal of the Trade Disputes Act.

21 August   Truman stops Lend–Lease. Attlee appoints Advisory Council on Atomic Energy under Sir John Anderson.

13 October   Dalton's first Budget: income tax and purchase taxes reduced; profits tax introduced; surtax raised.
6 December   US loan agreement signed.

1946

1 March   Bank of England nationalized.
9 April   Dalton's second Budget: purchase tax reduced; income tax allowances increased.
22 May   Trade Disputes Act repealed.
28 June   Minister of Food announces bread-rationing.
22 July   King David Hotel blown up in Jerusalem.
12 November   King's Speech announces nationalization of long-distance road transport and inland waterways.

1947

1 January   Cable and Wireless nationalized. Coal nationalized.
8 January   Cabinet committee authorizes manufacture of a British atom bomb.
5 February   Coal crisis exacerbated by freezing weather.
14 February   Palestine problem referred to UN.
20 February   Attlee announces transfer of power in India not later than June 1948. Mountbatten appointed Viceroy.
12 March   Truman announces US aid to Greece and Turkey.
3 April   National Service reduced to one year.
15 April   Dalton's third Budget: death duties, profits tax, purchase tax, stamp duty and tobacco duties raised.
5 June   General Marshall's Harvard speech on aid to Europe.
12 July   Marshall conference opens in Paris, attended by 16 nations (Eastern bloc boycotts it).
15 July   Sterling made convertible into dollars on the foreign exchanges.
18 August   Financial discussions open in Washington as sterling convertibility puts pound under pressure.
20 August   Convertibility suspended.
26 September   UK government announces relinquishment of Palestine mandate.
29 September   Cripps appointed Minister of Economic Affairs. New Cabinet committee on economic policy created. Attlee survives second plot against his leadership.
1 October   Abolition of foreign-travel allowance. Petrol ration suspended.
21 October   King's Speech. Gas to be nationalized.
12 November   Emergency Budget: profits tax, purchase tax and drink duties raised. (Dalton resigns following day after leaking Budget proposals to a journalist.)
13 November   Cripps appointed Chancellor; Harold Wilson made President of the Board of Trade.
19 December   US Congress passes interim foreign-aid bill.

1948

1 January   Railways nationalized.
7 January   Truman urges Congress to authorize $6800 million in Marshall Aid.

9 February   Cripps' wages freeze launched in White Paper on prices, costs and incomes.

14 March   US Senate passes Economic Co-operation Act. European Recovery Programme (Marshall Aid) begins. US loan exhausted.

17 March   Brussels Treaty signed.

1 April   Electricity supply nationalized.

6 April   Cripps's first Budget: capital levy, tobacco and drink duties up; pools betting tax introduced; income-tax relief given.

12 May   A. V. Alexander announces UK to manufacture atom bomb.

14–15 May   British mandate ends in Palestine.

11 May   Transport nationalized.

16 June   Berlin crisis begins when Russians walk out of joint Allied command.

21 June   Independence for India and Pakistan.

28 June   State of emergency declared to handle dock strikes.

30 June   Dockers return to work.

5 July   National Health Service inaugurated.

25 July   Bread-rationing ends.

2 November   Truman re-elected President in USA.

5 November   Wilson announces 'bonfire of controls'.

1949

4 April   NATO treaty signed.

6 April   Cripps's second Budget: income-tax relief, beer and wine duties reduced; betting tax and death duties raised; food subsidies cut.

11 April   London dock strike begins.

18 April   Eire becomes a republic and leaves the Commonwealth.

12 May   Berlin crisis ends. Transport links restored between Soviet and Western zones.

June   Troops used in London, Avonmouth and Liverpool docks.

1 July   Sterling under pressure; Cabinet Economic Policy Committee in all-day emergency meetings.

7 July   Troops move food in London docks.

14 July   £100 million cuts in dollar imports.

25 July   Dock strike ends.

29 August   Cabinet approves devaluation of sterling.

18 September   Sterling devalued from $4.03 to $2.80 to the pound.

21 September   Mao proclaims People's Republic of China.

23 September   Truman announces Soviets have exploded an atom bomb.

24 October   Attlee announces cuts of £140 million in capital spending and £120 million in current expenditure; bank-loan restrictions; building controls.

19 November   New agreement with trade unions on wages standstill.

24 November   Iron and Steel Bill passed, but nationalization delayed till after general election.

1950

23 February   General election: Labour, 315 seats; Convervatives, 298; Liberals, 9; others 3. Labour majority of 5.

18 April Cripps's last Budget: income tax reduced; fuel tax and purchase tax raised.

25 June North Korean troops invade South Korea. Cabinet rejects Schuman plan for European Coal and Steel Community.

27 June UN resolution calling on members to repel attacks in Korea. Truman announces support for South Korea.

3 August Defence estimates trebled.

2 September Wage freeze breaks down as TUC votes against incomes policy.

15 September National Service extended to two years.

1 October South Koreans cross 38th parallel.

15 October Chinese enter Korean War.

19 October Cripps resigns; succeeded by Gaitskell.

30 November Truman statement raises fears of atom bomb being used in Korea.

4 December Attlee flies to Washington for summit with Truman on bomb and defence burden-sharing.

1951

15 February Iron and steel nationalized.

16 February Defence estimates for 1951–2 over £1000 million.

9 March Bevin leaves Foreign Office; replaced by Morrison.

15 March Iranian parliament nationalizes Anglo-Iranian Oil Company holdings.

19 March European Coal and Steel Community formed.

10 April Gaitskell's first Budget: income tax, purchase tax and petrol duties increased; 'initial allowances' on new plant scrapped.

21 April Bevan resigns over dental and spectacle charges.

22 April Wilson resigns over defence estimates.

2 May Shah approves nationalization of Iranian oil industry.

28 September UK government takes Iranian oil dispute to UN.

25 October General election. Conservative majority of 17.

Notes

1 The story is told by Sir Douglas Wass, Permanent Secretary to the Treasury 1974–83, interview for Brook Productions' Channel Four television series *All the Prime Minister's Men*, 8 April 1986. Transcripts of this and other interviews undertaken for the programme can be consulted at the British Library of Economic and Political Science at the London School of Economics.

2 Roy Jenkins, *Nine Men of Power* (Hamish Hamilton, 1974), p. 64.

3 Peter Hennessy and Andrew Arends, *Mr. Attlee's Engine Room: Cabinet committee structure and the Labour government, 1945–51*, Strathclyde Papers on Government and Politics, no. 26 (1983), p. 1.

4 Only highly sensitive material from 1945–51 remains classified, mostly in the fields of security, intelligence and atomic weaponry.

5   Kenneth Harris, *Attlee* (Weidenfeld and Nicolson, 1982; paperback edn 1984). Trevor Burridge, *Clement Attlee: a political biography* (Cape, 1985).
6   Attlee died on 8 October 1967.
7   Bernard Donoughue and G. W. Jones, *Herbert Morrison: portrait of a politician* (Weidenfeld and Nicolson, 1973).
8   George Jones, 'Missing the mark', *History Today*, June 1986, pp. 58–60. Trevor Burridge, 'Enigma Variations', *History Today*, November 1986, p. 61.
9   Paul Addison, 'Darling Clem', *London Review of Books*, 3 July 1986, p. 4; Eric Hobsbawm, 'Winning was only half of it', the *Guardian*, 27 September 1986.
10 A vivid account of the atmosphere in Bournemouth where the Labour Party Conference was in session as the coalition was formed can be found in Ben Pimlott, *Hugh Dalton* (Cape, 1985), pp. 267–77.
11 Paul Addison, *The Road to 1945: British politics and the Second World War* (Cape, 1975).
12 Kenneth O. Morgan, *Labour in Power 1945–51* (Oxford University Press), 1984, p. 402.
13 See Alan Bullock, *The Life and Times of Ernest Bevin*, vol. II: *Minister of Labour 1940–1945* (Heinemann, 1967), ch. 1. On 25 May 1940 Bevin said to a delegate conference of 2000 trade union executive members, 'I have to ask you virtually to place yourselves at the disposal of the State. We are socialists and this is the test of our socialism' (ibid., p. 20).
14 Minister of Aircraft Production.
15 Bullock, *Bevin*, vol. II, p. 4.
16 Ibid., p. 23 and ch. 3: 'Critics, welfare and wages', pp. 64–97.
17 Correlli Barnett, *The Audit of War: the illusion and reality of Britain as a great nation* (Macmillan, 1986).
18 Ibid., ch. 12: 'New Jerusalem or economic miracle?', pp. 237–64.
19 Ibid., p. 304.
20 Morgan, *Labour in Power*, p. 503.
21 'Michael Foot and the Darlington election', Granada Television, *World in Action*, 28 March 1983.
22 Transcript of party political broadcast of 20 July 1983 supplied by Conservative Central Office.
23 'A cult of Clem the silent?', the *Economist*, 4 September 1982, p. 26. Though articles in the *Economist* are anonymous, I admit to writing this one.
24 Quoted in Anthony Howard, 'We are the masters now', in Michael Sissons and Philip French (eds), *Age of Austerity 1945–51* (Penguin, 1964), p. 16.
25 John Wheeler-Bennett, *King George VI* (Macmillan, 1958), p. 638.
26 Henry Pelling, *Britain and the Second World War* (Fontana, 1970), p. 233.

27 Sissons and French, *Age of Austerity*, p. 16.
28 The story was told to me by Sir Robin Day on 16 July 1986.
29 Attlee wrote this account for the *Observer* in 1959. It is quoted in Harris, *Attlee*, p. 264.
30 Alan Bullock, *Ernest Bevin, Foreign Secretary* (Heinemann, 1983), pp. 65–6.
31 Introduction to D. N. Chester (ed.), *Lessons of the British War Economy* (Cambridge University Press, 1951), p. 2.
32 *Let us Face the Future* can be found in F. W. S. Craig (ed.), *British General Election Manifestos, 1918–1966* (Political Reference Publications, 1970).
33 The best and most authoritative account of the making of the Beveridge Report is available in José Harris, *William Beveridge: a biography* (Oxford University Press, 1977), ch. 16, pp. 378–418.
34 Morgan, *Labour in Power*, pp. 175–6.
35 Ibid., pp. 32–3.
36 Quoted in A. J. P. Taylor, *English History 1914–1945* (Oxford University Press, 1965), p. 513.
37 Alec Cairncross, *Years of Recovery: British economic policy 1945–51* (Methuen, 1985), p. 7.
38 Ibid., pp. 7–8.
39 Tizard, as quoted in Margaret Gowing; *Independence and Deterrence: Britain and atomic energy, 1945–52*, vol. 1: *Policy-making* (Macmillan, 1974), p. 229.
40 Ibid., p. 230.
41 British Ambassador to the United States.
42 Richard N. Gardner, *Sterling–Dollar Diplomacy*, expanded edn (McGraw-Hill, 1969), p. xvii.
43 W. K. Hancock and M. M. Gowing, *The British War Economy* (His Majesty's Stationery Office, 1949), pp. 546–53.
44 For a detailed treatment of the negotiations and the loan, see Cairncross, *Years of Recovery*, ch. 5.
45 R. F. Harrod, *The Life of John Maynard Keynes* (Pelican, 1972), pp. 757–62.
46 Morgan, *Labour in Power*, p. 145.
47 Hugh Dalton, *High Tide and After: memoirs 1945–60* (Muller, 1962).
48 Pimlott, *Dalton*, p. 457.
49 Kenneth O. Morgan, 'Aneurin Bevan 1897–1960', in Paul Barker (ed.) *Founders of the Welfare State* (Heinemann Educational, 1984), p. 106.
50 James Griffiths, *Pages from Memory* (Dent, 1969), pp. 80–1.
51 Peter Calvocoressi, *The British Experience* (Bodley Head, 1978), pp. 35–6. For an account of Bevan's achievement, see Michael Foot, *Aneurin Bevan 1945–1960* (Davis Poynter, 1973), chs 3 and 4, pp. 102–218.
52 For a lively short account of the battle, see Peter Jenkins, 'Bevin's fight with the BMA', in Sissons and French, *Age of Austerity*, pp. 240–65.
53 Morgan, *Labour in Power*, p. 154.

54 PRO, CAB, CC 128/1, 18 October and 20 December 1945.

55 Morgan, *Labour in Power*, p. 99.

56 For the low esteem into which the Morrisonian corporation had sunk by the 1980s, see Simon Jenkins (political editor of the *Economist* and, at the time, a member of the British Railways Board), 'The battle of Britain's dinosaurs', the *Economist*, 6 March 1982, pp. 19–23. For an excellent account of how the nationalization *Zeitgeist* had succumbed to the zest for privatization, see Michael Prowse, 'Old arguments in new bottles', *Financial Times*, 18 April 1986. For a critical philippic from the left on the feebleness of Labour's nationalizations of the forties, see Ralph Miliband, *Parliamentary Socialism*, 2nd edn (Merlin, 1973), pp. 288–9.

57 Donoughue and Jones, *Morrison*, pp. 184–8.

58 Herbert Morrison, *Socialisation and Transport* (Constable, 1933).

59 Morgan, *Labour in Power*, p. 98.

60 *The Times*, 28 October 1946.

61 For the 1946 economic recovery, see Cairncross, *Years of Recovery*, pp. 21–2. For Cripps's rise as President of the Board of Trade, see Morgan, *Labour in Power*, p. 360.

62 PRO, CAB 130/16, GEN 163, 1st meeting, 8 January 1947, Confidential Annex, minute 1, 'Research in atomic weapons'. The historic minute is reproduced as an illustration in Hennessy and Arends, *Attlee's Engine Room*, appendix IV.

63 Quoted in Peter Hennessy, *Cabinet* (Basil Blackwell, 1986), pp. 126–7. This Cabinet committee meeting was not as crucial as some, including myself, have made out. The bomb could have been built without this plant. It is the decision to build plutonium piles at Windscale, taken by the same committee in December 1945, which represents the crucial procurement.

64 Bevin's protest was made in a letter to Attlee on 1 January 1947. See Peter Hennessy, 'Bevin plea failed to stop India "scuttle"', *The Times*, 6 September 1980.

65 Morgan, *Labour in Power*, p. 226.

66 See David Watt, 'Withdrawal from Greece', in Sissons and French, *Age of Austerity*, pp. 106–31.

67 John Gallagher, *The Decline, Revival and Fall of the British Empire* (Cambridge University Press, 1982), p. 146.

68 Ibid.

69 The phrase is Gallagher's (ibid.).

70 Dalton wrote this in his diary, describing his reaction to Attlee's offer of the Colonial Office (which he rejected) after the 1950 general election (Ben Pimlott (ed.), *The Political Diary of Hugh Dalton 1918–40, 1945–60* (Cape, 1986), p. 472).

71 Alan Wood, *The Groundnut Affair* (Bodley Head, 1950).

72   Brian Lapping, *End of Empire* (Granada, 1985), pp. 244–8.
73   Morgan, *Labour in Power*, p. 368.
74   Henry Pelling, *The Labour Governments 1945–51* (Macmillan, 1984), pp. 68–71.
75   Dalton, *High Tide and After*, ch. 22: 'Annus Horrendus', pp. 187–92.
76   PRO, T 229/136. See also Peter Hennessy, 'Otto's horrors: the nightmare we narrowly esacaped', *The Times*, 27 November 1979.
77   Douglas Jay, *Change and Fortune: a political record* (Hutchinson, 1980). p. 135.
78   Keith Middlemas, *Power, Competition and the State*, vol. I: *Britain in Search of Balance, 1940–61* (Macmillan, 1986), p. 152.
79   Conversation with a senior official, 1983.
80   The phrase 'permanent government' belongs to Anthony Vernier, who coined it in *Through the Looking Glass: British foreign policy in the age of illusions* (Cape 1983), p. 4. He in turn adapted it from General Sir William Butler's nineteenth century concept of the 'permanent Conservative government in countless departments of the State' (ibid., p. 55).
81   F. S. L. Lyons, *Ireland Since the Famine* (Fontana, 1973), pp. 525–6.
82   Ferdinand Mount, 'A severe case of Kaunda's contracture of the forefinger', The *Spectator*, 9 August 1986.
83   Kinglsey Martin, *Harold Laski: a biography* (Cape, 1969), pp. 172–3.
84   Hennessy and Arends, *Mr Attlee's Engine Room*, p. 17.
85   Cairncross, *Years of Recovery*, pp. 51–3. For defects in the Attleean engine room, see Hennessy, *Cabinet* pp. 38–44.
86   For a comprehensive account of the condition of the Labour Party and its relationship with the government see Morgan, *Labour in Power*, ch. 2: 'The framework of politics 1945–1951', pp. 45–93.
87   The most easily digested account of the complications of the ERP and the European Payments Union can be found in Pelling, *The Labour Governments*, ch. 10: 'Britain and Marshall Aid, 1947–50', pp. 187–210.
88   See Christopher Andrew, *Secret Service: the making of the British intelligence community* (Heinemann, 1985), pp. 491–2.
89   Peter Hennessy, 'Whitehall brief: timely reminder of a bulldog presence', *The Times*, 1 November 1983. For details of Bevin's treaty-making and his critical role in European recovery, Lord Bullock's volume *Ernest Bevin, Foreign Secretary* will never be surpassed. For an entertaining and strangely moving account of Bevin the man, see the memoir of his junior private secretary, Nicholas Henderson, *The Private Office* (Weidenfeld and Nicolson, 1984), pp. 24–54.
90   In conversation with the author when volume III of his life of Bevin was published.
91   Hennessy, 'Whitehall brief', *The Times*, 1 November 1983.

92   Quoted in Watt, 'Withdrawal from Greece', in Sissons and French, *Age of Austerity*, pp. 108–9.

93   The best account of the Berlin airlift is Avi Shlaim, *The United States and the Berlin Blockade 1948–1949* (University of California Press, 1983). For the agreement governing the stationing of the B29s in East Anglia, see Gowing, *Independence and Deterrence*, vol. I, pp. 310–12.

94   The revisionist literature on the Cold War is now vast. Its founding father was William Appleman Williams – see his *The Tragedy of American Diplomacy*, 2nd edn (Dell, 1962); its most headline-grabbing treatise is Gar Alperovitz's *Atomic Diplomacy, Hiroshima and Potsdam* (Vintage, 1967); and its best general account is Walter La Feber's *America, Russia and the Cold War, 1945–75*, 3rd edn (Wiley, 1976).

95   Bullock, *Ernest Bevin, Foreign Secretary*, pp. 844–5.

96   See Sir Nicholas Henderson's valedictory despatch from the Paris Embassy, 31 March 1979, printed in the *Economist*, 2 June 1979, pp. 29–40.

97   Sidney Pollard, *The Wasting of the British Economy* (Croom Helm, 1982), p. 33.

98   Ibid., p. 31.

99   Cairncross, *Years of Recovery*, p. 209.

100 Quoted in Pimlott, *The Political Diary of Hugh Dalton*, p. 451.

101 The devaluation is fully covered in Morgan, *Labour in Power*, pp. 379–88. and Cairncross, *Years of Recovery*, ch. 7, pp. 165–211, both of which have been prepared with the benefit of the official archive at the PRO. For a diary of the events and discussions leading to devaluation, see Peter Hennessy, *What the Papers Never Said* (Portcullis, 1985), pp. 33–97.

102 Douglas Jay has outlined this thesis in conversation with the author.

103 Pollard, *Wasting of the British Economy*, p. 37.

104 Morgan, *Labour in Power*, ch. 11, pp. 462–504.

105 Quoted ibid., p. 420.

106 The background to the Schuman plan, showing the value of top-flight BBC radio documentary and of modern oral archive techniques, can be found in Michael Charlton, *The Price of Victory* (BBC, 1983), ch. 4: 'The Schuman plan – losing the initiative', pp. 89–123.

107 The story was told to me by the late Lord Helsby, who had heard it from Leslie Rowan, his predecessor as Downing Street principal private secretary. Conversation with Lord Helsby, 2 December 1976.

108 Anthony King, 'Overload: problems of governing in the 1970s', *Political Studies*, XXII, no. 203 (June–September 1975), p. 164.

109 Lord Rayner, 'The Unfinished Agenda', the Stamp Memorial Lecture, University of London, 6 November 1984.

110 Addison, *When the War is Over*, p. 28.

111 Ibid., p. 2.

112 Phillip Whitehead to the author, 1 September 1986, recalling his interview with Speer for Thames Television's *The World at War*.

113 Martin Wiener, *English Culture and the Decline of the Industrial Spirit 1850–1980* (Cambridge University Press, 1981), p. 3.

114 Pollard, *Wasting of the British Economy*, p. 2.

115 Morgan, *Labour in Power*, pp. 496–7.

116 Miliband, *Parliamentary Socialism*, esp. ch. 9: 'The climax of Labourism', pp. 272–317.

117 Addison, *When the War is Over*, pp. vi–vii.

118 D. N. Chester, *The Nationalisation of British Industry 1945–51* (Her Majesty's Stationery Office, 1975).

119 By Dr Charles Webster.

120 Philip Williams, *Hugh Gaitskell: a political biography* (Cape, 1979); Philip Williams (ed.), *The Diary of Hugh Gaitskell, 1945–1956* (Cape, 1983).

121 Nigel Hamilton, *Monty: the Field Marshal 1944–1976* (Hamish Hamilton, 1986).

122 Denis Richards, *Portal of Hungerford* (Heinemann, 1977).

123 Ronald Lewin, *Slim, the Standardbearer* (Hutchinson, 1977).

124 I have not been able to ascertain a publication date for this.

125 Due for publication in 1988.

126 As I wrote in *Cabinet*, p. 37, 'Attlee and his ministers, despite being a radically intentioned government, did not embark on a reform of the Civil Service because they knew the wartime machine personally and liked what they saw. They had seen the recent administrative past and it had worked.'

127 Cairncross, *Years of Recovery*, p. 509.

128 Ibid., p. 20.

129 See Hennessy, *What the Papers Never Said*, p. 45.

130 Hugh Thomas, *John Strachey* (Eyre Methuen, 1973), p. 240.

131 Lapping, *End of Empire*, pp. 369–73.

132 Hennessy, 'Coloured Immigration, 1945–51', *What the Papers Never Said*, pp. 101–9.

133 Middlemas, *Power, Competition and the State*, vol. I, pp. 181–2.

134 For the Cabinet committee on NHS costs, see Morgan, *Labour in Power*, p. 445. On 21 April 1950 Brook minuted Bridges, 'It is curious that in modern times the Cabinet, though it has always insisted on considering particular proposals for developments of policy and their cost, has never thought it necessary to review the development of expenditure under the Civil Estimates as a whole' (PRO, CAB 21/1626).

135 Peter Hennessy and Gail Brownfeld, 'Britain's Cold War security purge: the origins of positive vetting', *Historical Journal*, 25, no. 4 (1982), pp. 965–973.

136 PRO, CAB 66/67, CP (45) 100, II.

137 See 'Tap, tap: is MI5 still there?', the *Economist*, 6 March 1982, p. 28.
138 Nicholas Wapshott and George Brock, *Thatcher: the major new biography* (Futura, 1983), p. 53.
139 Roy Jenkins, *Mr Attlee: an interim biography* (Heinemann, 1948).
140 John Dickie, *The Uncommon Commoner* (Pall Mall, 1964), p. vii.

3

The Churchill Administration, 1951–1955

Anthony Seldon

'The gravity of the crisis we are facing needs no demonstration', proclaimed the *Spectator* the day after the October 1951 general election.[1] Of all the worries afflicting the government, economic and financial concerns were the most vexing. Sterling had had a good year in 1950, but the position soon deteriorated: by the beginning of July 1951, it had been estimated that there would be a dollar deficit for 1951–2 of $500 million. Only two months later, the figure had risen to an incredible $1200 million. Within hours of becoming Prime Minister, Winston Churchill was presented at his London home in Hyde Park Gate with a report, handed personally to him by the nation's two most senior civil servants, Sir Edward Bridges and Sir Norman Brook, foretelling grave consequences if drastic action was not taken.[2] Indeed, some Treasury officials envisaged a collapse greater than had been foretold in 1931 (a view which, with hindsight, appears too alarmist). *The Times* went as far as to compare the crisis of 1951 to that of 1940.[3]

Nor was the economy the only source of anxiety. In colonial affairs the incoming government was faced by a revolutionary position in Malaya following the assassination of Sir Henry Gurney, the British High Commissioner, earlier in October, and by potentially explosive situations in Kenya and Cyprus. In the Middle East, British interests were being threatened by Mossadeq in Persia, and by nationalist agitation in Egypt. The Korean War was temporarily halted by precarious and tense truce talks, but the government was saddled with a crippling rearmanent programme, which in turn fuelled inflation. The panic atmosphere had played its part in turning the electorate to voting Tory at the polls, despite a fierce campaign depicting the Conservatives as warmongers. All eyes now turned on Churchill, a month short of his seventy-seventh birthday, to see whether he had indeed a policy for 1951 as he had had for 1940.

The Conservative government of 1951–5 is one of the most misunderstood, underrated and under-researched administrations of the century. The research position is, at least, beginning to change as growing numbers of scholars come to study the government, with documentary evidence in the Public Record Office now available for the entire three and a half years of the administration. The record of the government at the time was widely seen as one of notable achievement, explaining in part the Conservatives' success at the polls in the May 1955 general election. But from the 1960s, with increasing anxieties about unemployment and industrial decline, the 1950s came to be seen as a period of wasted opportunites, of failed leadership. The government of the day was perceived as having dragged Britain back due to its entertainment of expensive and out-dated notions of world grandeur, while at the same time failing to maintain Britain's economic position relative to other industrial nations.

The suspicion of a government out of touch with postwar realities was given added force by the publication in 1966 of Lord Moran's diaries, bearing the provocative title *Winston Churchill: The struggle for survival, 1940–65.* It created a sensation. Moran, as Churchill's doctor, painted an intimate portrait of a man unfit, for much of the 1951–5 period, for the highest office in the land. So with a Prime Minister depicted lurching from one medical crisis to another, a view widely accepted following publication, the image of the government became further tarnished. Britain's continued economic slide in the 1970s, its apparently uncontrollable trade union movement, and late entry into the EEC in January 1973, only served in their different ways further to discredit the government of 1951–5. Why, people asked, had resolute action not been taken when there was time to avert these, and other, malaises? Keith Middlemas is in agreement with earlier critics when he castigates the Churchill government for, *inter alia*, its failure 'to confront the problem of wages, productivity, investment and exports [and] failure to provide an authoritative case for participation . . . in the early stages of the EEC'.[4]

During her first few years as party leader from 1975, Margaret Thatcher's speech-writers alighted on the Churchill administration as an ideal model of a liberal anti-state government, resolute in its intentions to 'set the people free' after six and a quarter years of socialist dictatorship. Patrick Cosgrave, for example, wrote, 'historically, the most interesting aspect of the emergence of the new right is that it tends to select for praise the only genuinely successful Tory government since the war ... the last Churchill Government'.[5] When Mrs Thatcher's researchers began to delve a little deeper, however, it became clear to them that here was one of the 'wettest' Conservative administrations of the century. True, it decontrolled and derationed, but that process had been set in train by Labour from 1949 at least – notably by Harold Wilson in his 'bonfire of controls'. Worse still, Mrs Thatcher's speech-writers learnt that the government had dodged some key issues, such as trade union reform, pruning the welfare state and immigration. The lauding of the government's record began discreetly to disappear from the polemics of the dry Right.

To the left and moderate sections of the Conservative Party, however, the Churchill government remains a definite success. Here the Conservatives succeeded in hitting upon a popular formula for government in a way never perhaps quite managed by the party in the interwar years, and in doing so restored Conservatives' faith in themselves after the traumas of the later 1940s. The government, sensibly, decided to avoid dismantling many of the social reforms instituted (if not initiated) by Labour during 1945–51, and denationalization was kept to a bare minimum. Social conflict was avoided, and the trade unions were brought closer to a Conservative government than for many years. In economic policy, a middle-of-the-road course was pursued by R. A. Butler at the Exchequer, and unemployment was kept to a minimum. Abroad, the transition from Empire to Commonwealth was given a moderate boost in certain areas. Defence expenditure was meanwhile reduced, and expensive commitments, such as the Suez base, were abandoned (though Churchill himself was never really reconciled to the evacuation of the Canal Zone).

With that type of middle-of-the-road track record, Labour cannot find much with which to quarrel. At the time its criticism was often ineffective. *The Times* in 1953 decried 'the lack of an efficient opposition',[6] while Robert McKenzie, writing a short time after 1955, was even more damning: 'It is inevitably a matter of national concern', he wrote, 'if the leaders of one of the major political parties become so preoccupied with internecine party conflict that they cease to fulfil their duties of Her Majesty's Opposition, and if they fail to behave collectively like a potential government.'[7] There can be no doubt that this was the condition of the Labour Party during much of the lifetime of the 1951 Parliament. Even Harold Wilson, in his latest bout of memoiritis (1986) found this period the unhappiest in his years in the House of Commons.

Internal conflict between the Bevanite left and the Attlee leadership provided the main reason for Labour's poor showing during 1951–5. But almost as important was its lack of clarity on where it wanted to go next, and which Conservative measures it wanted seriously to oppose. Its policy document *Challenge to Britain*, issued in 1953, offered further doses of nationalization, the chemical, machine-tool and parts of the aircraft industries being specifically mentioned, as well as plans to renationalize iron and steel, and road haulage. In social policy it offered the usual formula of abolition of all health charges, independent schools and other left-wing bogeys. But the fact was that, in many areas, Conservative policy post-1951 was largely continuous with Labour's. Where Labour did object strongly, as to aspects of colonial policy, it was often due as much to inept presentation and execution as to the substance of the policy. Since 1955, Labour has tended to look back not unfavourably on the government (for example, in memoirs of former ministers) in as far as it has given it any thought.[8] The hard Left, of course, is heavily critical, but so is it of the Attlee government, for wasting opportunities to abolish private health provision and education, for initiating Britain's independent nuclear deterrent, for aligning itself so closely with the United States, and for not extending nationalization. The hard Left tends indeed to be more bitter about the record of the Attlee than of the Churchill government.

So the early 1950s are only now becoming the subject of concentrated academic interest. Although revealing memoirs have been available for some years, notably those of Lord Kilmuir (David Maxwell Fyfe) (1964), Harold Macmillan (1969) and R. A. Butler (1971), document-based biographies are just reaching the bookshelves.[9] Some of the principal political figures await definitive judgement. Martin Gilbert has yet to complete his last volume of Churchill biography, but this should be with us in the later eighties. Anthony Eden has been the subject of two very different studies, by David Carlton (1981), who depicts him as a 'lightweight' and errs on the side of being too critical, and by Robert Rhodes James (1986), who perhaps goes too far the other way.[10] Butler has had a number of instant biographies, of which the one by Ralph Harris (1956) is interesting. Anthony Howard's official account (1987), written by an author of political subtlety, is especially perceptive.[11] Macmillan again has had a number of instant portraits, of which the one by Anthony Sampson (1967) is still valuable,[12] but the definitive study is his official biography by Alistair Horne, which, following the death of Macmillan in December 1986, will be published during 1987 or 1988.

Much less has appeared about second-rank ministers, although useful biographies have been written about Monckton, Macleod and Swinton by, respectively, Lord Birkenhead (1969), Nigel Fisher (1973) and John Cross (1982).[13] Important studies have still to be written about Salisbury, Woolton, Simonds, Kilmuir, Lyttelton and Thorneycroft. Military figures have been typically well served, notably by biographies of service chiefs Slim, Harding, Templer and Mountbatten by Ronald Lewin (1976), Michael Carver (1978), John Cloake (1985) and Philip Ziegler (1985) respectively.[14] The period is also well served by three outstanding published diaries, those of Lord Moran (1966), John Colville (1985, regrettably brief on Churchill's last years) and Evelyn Shuckburgh (1986), the frank record kept by Eden's principal private secretary (1951–4), which throws new light on the Foreign Secretary and on his often fraught relationship with Churchill.[15] But the period will be even better served if Macmillan's personal diary is published, which should eclipse the other three in terms of value to the historian. By 1987, over 400 books and academic articles had been written which describe part or the whole of the history of government policy during 1951–5. However, so far only one study that deals exclusively with the period has appeared, my *Churchill's Indian Summer* (1981).[16] My intention here was not to write 'a definitive study of the years 1951–1955' but to 'define the territory a little more clearly for the specialised historian on the eve of the release of the government's records at the Public Record Office'.[17] The book argues that the government was remarkable perhaps above all for its consensus approach in most areas of policy, and for its continuity with policies pursued by the Attlee government. Another, more controversial, argument is that Churchill was 'right to remain in office at least until his major stroke in the summer of 1953, and a good case can be made for his retention of power until the autumn of 1954. Only in his last six months in office was he not fully up to the task.'[18] Had he retired earlier, then Eden would have taken over some months or years before he eventually did. Whether the government would have achieved as much under him as it did under Churchill, and whether his successor would have been so successful at the Foreign Office, especially during 1954, are two of the imponderable questions of contemporary British history.

The job of Prime Minister is many-faceted, and needs to be examined under different headings. Churchill took seriously his role as chief appointer, and the government bore strongly his pronounced preference for moderate over right-wing doctrinaire Conservatives. Appointments and dismissals were very much his own; seldom did he yield to pressure, nor did he reveal to any man, even his heir-apparent Eden, his full thoughts on the subject. His previous experience, especially the formation of the caretaker government of May–July 1945, had warned him off listening to ardent would-be Cabinet-makers. In 1951 he determined to have a 'broadly based government', a theme he referred to several times during the election campaign. Wary of being thought controversial, he deliberately opted for a number of Cabinet ministers not originally from politics (Lords Cherwell, Ismay and Leathers), and for others whose origins were not in the Conservative Party (Lords de la Warr, Simonds and Reading, as well as Gwilym Lloyd-George, John Maclay, Walter Monckton and Arthur Salter).

In line with his desire for a moderate complexion to his government, he appointed Butler rather than Oliver Lyttelton to the Exchequer, and the conciliatory Monckton to the Ministry of Labour rather than the more rigid Maxwell Fyfe, who had unsettled the unions during the period in opposition, especially with ideas to legislate on the financial relationship between unions and the Labour Party. The moderate image of the government would have been even more pronounced had Clement Davies, the leader of the Liberal Party, accepted Churchill's offer of the Ministry of Education, and had three non-politicians not declined to serve in 1951 – Sir John Anderson as a co-ordinator, Lord Asquith as Lord Chancellor, and Lord Portal of Hungerford (the former Chief of Air Staff) as Minister of Defence. In the event, Churchill himself took the defence portfolio for four months before handing over to a soldier with no political background, Lord Alexander of Tunis, plucked rudely from his job as Governor General of Canada. (Portal, it might be noted, would have proved far more effective at Defence than did poor Alexander.) Churchill retained the moderate complexion of the Cabinet throughout his three and a half years at No. 10, which witnessed six minor reshuffles and one major one, in October 1954. Throughout all this, Butler remained at the Treasury, and another moderate, Eden, at the Foreign Office. Right-wingers were either kept on the backbenches (as was Charles Waterhouse) or were not allowed too free a rein (as was Lord Salisbury).

In choosing his ministers, Churchill was, therefore, decisive, and made many successful appointments, notably Butler to the Treasury, Macmillan to Housing, and Peter Thorneycroft to the Board of Trade. Initial criticisms that his government was too old, contained too many peers, and was at fault because it did not 'rate specialist knowledge necessarily high'[19] tended to be forgotten, especially as abler younger men were later given senior ministerial office, notably David Eccles (Education) and Alan Lennox Boyd (Colonial Office). However, Churchill can be criticized for hanging on to colleagues long after their unsuitability for office had been demonstrated: both Alexander (Defence) and Florence Horsbrugh (Education) should have been dropped earlier when it became clear that their performance was below standard.

Churchill's personal mark was felt less strongly in his prime ministerial role as chief executive. The appointment of three 'overlords' co-ordinating different government departments and spheres of interest was his own idea. His objective was to cut down on the need for ministerial and official Cabinet committees, both of which he distrusted, especially when peopled exclusively by civil servants. He foresaw major reorganizations of economic departments, and wanted to appoint further overlords to co-ordinate nationalized industries and production departments. He also hoped to implement a number of measures designed to curb the power of the Treasury, which he considered excessive. But his attempts to reorganize the machinery of government proved largely abortive. Churchill's interest in the structure of government gradually faded away, and he became content to defer on Civil Service affairs and appointments to Brook, the Cabinet Secretary, and to Bridges, the head of the Civil Service. Brook established himself as his most influential adviser on administration and governmental matters. Churchill's daily contacts meant his relationship with Brook was far closer than his relationship with Bridges, a fact that accounted in part for a growing coolness between these two most eminent and powerful public servants. Churchill's preference for Brook over Bridges also had an important role in strengthening the position of the Cabinet Office relative to the Treasury.

As a policy-formulator, Churchill's initiatives can be divided into the quirky, the cautious, the reactionary and the inspired. In the very first Cabinet meeting of the administration, on 30 October 1951, he told his ministers to take a £1000 cut in salary to £4000 in view of the economic crisis. Ministers' dismay was scarcely ameliorated by Churchill's announcement that he himself would draw only £7000 of his £10,000 salary.[20] Such idiosyncratic interventions were commonplace. Caution was another touchstone. Anxious to avoid policies that would stir controversy, he was equally concerned to head off any issue before it caused his government embarrassment. In Cabinet on 25 March 1952, for example, the 10 per cent unemployment figure in the textile and clothing industries was discussed. Churchill was prominent in the decision that armed forces and civil defence services should place orders for clothing with them.[21] In consequence, Cabinet was told on 16 December that unemployment had been reduced in those industries by two-thirds, to 67,000.[22] Churchill on certain issues, especially in the realm of foreign affairs, allowed himself to be affected by attitudes more appropriate to Britain in the interwar or even pre-First World War years. The belligerence and impatience he displayed in his early months towards Egypt and Iran, and his clashes with the more realistic Eden over the reduction of British commitments in the Sudan and Egypt, provide good illustrations. But equally it was in the realm of foreign affairs that he produced one of the most inspiring initiatives of his final administration, his desire for a personal meeting with the new Soviet leadership following the death of Stalin in March 1953. To the Foreign Office and several ministers in Cabinet, as well as to the Eisenhower administration, Churchill's enthusiasm for such a meeting, which came to dominate his last two years in office, was a dangerous pipedream. But to Churchill, inspired by a vision of bringing a greater measure of peace to the world, leading perhaps to winning the Nobel Peace Prize (to put alongside his prize for literature), their caution was irrelevant. Until his retirement he held to the view that, if only he could engage in face-to-face talks, unhampered by agendas and retinues of officials, a much-needed breakthrough in polarized Cold War stances might be reached. (At the same time, he appreciated that Britain must bargain from a position of strength, and for that reason fully supported the decision to develop a British hydrogen bomb, taken in 1954.) Personal diplomacy remained very much his style, as witnessed in his enthusiasm also for top-level meetings with Truman and Eisenhower to 'restore' the special relationship after Attlee. He possessed an almost irrepressible confidence in his own personal skills and charm.

Churchill's main interest then lay in the realm of foreign affairs, followed by defence, although he was not without broad aims on the domestic front. Determined to build a relationship of trust with the trade unions, he gave deliberate instructions to Monckton, Minister of Labour, to avoid conflict in industrial disputes. On several occasions, as during the railway strike in 1954, Churchill intervened personally to help ensure peaceful outcomes. In private, he went out of his way to cultivate personal relationships with individual union leaders, to the consternation of some more traditional Conservatives in his Cabinet. Harry Crookshank, Leader of the House, entered in his diary in October 1952 that there were 'eyebrows raised' when Churchill invited three trade union leaders to a party at No. 10.[23] He also played an important part in pushing through the programme of decontrol and derationing. Restrictions on the individual, such as identity cards, he found offensive in peacetime. His anxiety to press ahead with denationalization of the road-haulage industry helped drive the Minister of Transport, Maclay, into a breakdown. Shortly after the general election, Churchill told John Colville, his joint principal private secretary, that his priorities were 'houses and meat, and not being scuppered'.[24] His desire to see houses built, and especially to heal the scars left by widespread bomb sites, meant that he supported Macmillan, Minister of Housing, in his often acrimonious battles (as Howard, Butler's biographer, highlights) for cash against Butler at the Treasury. In Cabinet in November 1952, he thus backed Macmillan against Butler, who said that building resources should be concentrated on increasing industrial productivity.[25] Churchill simply was not prepared 'to ruin the only achievement at home [house-building] which is comprehended by the public'.[26] 'Meat' (or 'red meat' as he often put it) was a rather sentimental idea that his 'island people' should enjoy the best food. 'Not getting scuppered' spoke of his deep worry that Britain should not succumb due to inadequate defence measures.

But he was seldom a man for the fine print of policy during his last years in office. Detail bored him. As has been written, 'he continued his war-time searchlight technique of focusing his attention on particular policy matters, but the beam was dimmer, and moved at a slower tempo'.[27] To education policy, for example, he contributed little, apart from occasional forthright interventions. The peripheral and personal in education, as in many other areas, attracted his attention, rather than the mainstream. Thus he was outraged by the decision of Horsbrugh, the Minister of Education (and the token woman in Cabinet, whom he never much liked), to cut 10 per cent off the adult education budget. To the unwitting Horsbrugh, he sent the following terse minute:

There is more to be said for making economies by reducing the number of small children at one end, and secondly for letting out some of the boys approaching 15 years of age who are now being kept in school against their inclination. . . . Nothing could be worse than to hamper those who in later life feel a strong urge to improve their education. . . . Was the matter specifically approved in Cabinet and have you got any more like this coming along?[28]

Health and other aspects of social policy did not engage his sustained interest. The same story applied to economics; although he apparently spent hours closeted with Butler, he had little to contribute to economic policy, the details of which he found increasingly puzzling – far more complex than when he was Chancellor (1924–9).[29]

The move from Empire to Commonwealth he found uncongenial, but he refrained from intervening to slow the tempo. Keen to foster relations with Commonwealth partners, he personally dominated the two meetings of Commonwealth prime ministers in London (1953 and 1955), but had little of practical value to offer to Commonwealth affairs. Defence policy did engage his sustained interest, and, after relinquishing the defence portfolio to Alexander in March 1952, he continued to chair the Cabinet's Defence Committee. But he had far less to contribute than during the war. In foreign affairs, his chief interest, the initiatives, aside from summitry, successful or otherwise, were Eden's or the Foreign Office's; for all his enthusiasm, he again had little to offer by way of positive policy direction. His role as a policy-formulator was, therefore, not his strongest hand, and he could be criticized for failing to initiate fundamental reassessments of policy overseas, in such areas as industrial policy and in public expenditure. His oversight of the security services was also lamentable. But would an alternative Conservative PM, notably Eden, have been more dynamic? It is doubtful.

Churchill also played a relatively passive role in his capacity as party chief. The Conservative Party in 1951 had been revolutionized since 1945, but the transformation owed little to his own input. Lord Woolton as party chairman had reinvigorated the party organization and finances, and Maxwell Fyfe's reforms of 1948–9 facilitated the arrival of a new middle-class Conservative MP who made his impact strongly in the 1950 and 1951 parliaments. In reforming Conservative policy in the period of opposition, Butler played the key role as head of the Conservative Research Department, where he advanced a number of brilliant young lieutenants, later to come to the fore in the party, including Iain Macleod, Reginald Maudling and Enoch Powell. The policy documents emanating from the office, such as the Industrial Charter, helped to educate the party in progressive ideas in economic and social policy, and helped it to give its adherence to such policies a credibility with the electorate lacked in 1945.

Churchill remained somewhat aloof from all these party developments, although content to see them take place. Indeed, he remained to an extent aloof from establishment Conservative figures: his closest political friends were seldom true-blue Conservatives. His cavalier attitude towards the Conservative *status quo* can be seen in his intention to sack Woolton as party chairman in spring 1952, a deed which would have provoked uproar in the party.[30] The coolness that senior party figures felt towards Churchill was not improved by his government appointments in 1951, or by his periodic requests for an ending to party bickering, implying that the Conservatives were as much at fault as Labour. His pleas in the House of Commons in November 1953 that party strife be kept out of issues of national importance, and that 'it is really not possible to assume that one of these . . . masses of voters possess all the virtues and all the wisdom and the other lot are dupes and fools', antagonized several of his colleagues.[31] But to Chips Channon, as to many others, 'it was an olympian spectacle. A supreme performance which we shall never see again from him or anyone else. In eighteen years in this honourable House I have never heard anything like it.'[32] Indeed, Churchill appeared to regard himself at times as a benign elder statesman, above party politics. In 1952, he even began canvassing support for the creation of a new coalition government on account of the gravity of the economic crisis.[33] But, reluctant Conservative though he may have been, he made a decisive mark on the party as its leader in the ten years after the war by ensuring that it became a mass party, wedded to the welfare state and to the mixed economy. If the transformation occurred at the hands of those he appointed rather than from him directly, its importance should, none the less, not be underestimated. His 'hands-off' style indeed can be compared to Eisenhower's

Churchill's lukewarm attachment to his party meant that he could fulfil his final prime ministerial role, as national leader, better than many other incumbents of No. 10. His desire, to be seen as a national rather than a sectional leader, continued throughout his final period in office. On the eve of the 1951 general election he promised, 'If the government of Britain is entrusted to us . . . we will do our best for all without fear or favour, without class or party bias, without rancour or spite.'[34] The peroration of his penultimate major speech in the House in 1955 reveals his same concern to address the nation as a whole:

To conclude, mercifully, there is time and hope if we combine patience and courage. . . . The day may dawn when fair play, love for one's fellow men, respect for justice and freedom will enable tormented generations to march forth serene and triumphant from the hideous epoch in which we have to dwell. Meanwhile, never flinch, never weary, never despair.[35]

The distracted ramblings of an old man? Some thought so. But these were not idle words. His genuine concern for the condition of the British people as a whole, regardless of class or party affiliation, frequently exercised him. In this respect, at least, there has been no postwar Prime Minister quite like him.

Only in his last six months did his preferred style of Cabinet government, of allowing ministerial colleagues a largely free hand to get on with their work, begin to break down. In October 1954 he presided over a major and effective reshuffle of his government, but after it was over he lacked the physical and mental energy to give to papers and people the attention they merited, and he no longer adequately performed his central role as co-ordinator. His effective, if idiosyncratic, style of chairing Cabinet deteriorated in these last few months. The will to continue in office had been broken. Those who argue that he should have retired in 1953 or even in 1952[36] on account of unfitness for office have, however, to reckon with judgements such as that expressed in an editorial in *The Times* in November 1953: 'His complete authority over the Commons is one of the most important political factors in the new round of the Parliamentary contest that is now beginning.'[37] In similar vein, Hugh Massingham, arguably the astutest contemporary political journalist of his day, wrote in June 1954, 'Now that he is on his last lap, Sir Winston seems to have acquired an ascendancy over his Cabinet that he certainly did not have during the early days of his administration.'[38] Two weeks later, Massingham was writing that there was 'no reason, at least in theory, why he should not lead his party at another general election'.[39] Even in his dismal last six months, Churchill could still rise to the big occasion. The *Scotsman* recorded in April 1955 how his most recent parliamentary performances were 'as brilliant as those of any stage in his career'.[40] Such remarks put paid to the myth that he was 'gaga' through his last few months in office.

Churchill was a Prime Minister who believed strongly in the sanctity of Cabinet government. He practised collective decision-taking, and was proud to be able to boast to Moran that he had 110 cabinets in the year up to April 1953 as opposed to Attlee's 85 in a comparable period. As he said, 'I am a great believer in bringing things before the cabinet.'[41] Even on minor matters, if a majority of colleagues were against his favoured line, he accepted their verdict – as, for instance, in Cabinet on 29 January 1952, over the timing of a speech to the nation.[42] On 31 December 1953 he was again overruled, on the release to Egypt of £5 million to which it was entitled under a 1951 agreement, and which he wanted to halt.[43] His most bitter disagreements with Cabinet came in July 1954 over his plans for a summit with the Soviet leadership; here again he stood down, albeit most reluctantly, in the face of stiff opposition and threatened resignations. (It should be noted that the debacle arose in part because Churchill uncharacteristically tried to ride roughshod over Cabinet.)[44] Unlike many postwar Prime Ministers, Churchill did not rely on an inner circle or inner Cabinet, although such a clique had existed in his earlier Shadow Cabinet, consisting of himself, Eden, Lyttelton and Oliver Stanley. Back in No. 10, he enjoyed the attentions of a coterie of trusted friends and colleagues, whose company he found congenial. These included Brook, Colville, Christopher Soames (his parliamentary private secretary and son-in-law), Lord Cherwell, and political colleagues including Eden, Salisbury, Swinton, Monckton and also Simonds. But they did not constitute a 'kitchen cabinet'; and none, apart from Brook, and to a lesser extent Colville and Soames, had sustained influence on him.

Little evidence exists of his lobbying trusted colleagues to build coalitions of support before he introduced to Cabinet policies about which he felt strongly.[45] Typically, he began a Cabinet meeting by outlining the subject and asking the appropriate minister to open the discussion, which he had to do briefly or run the risk of being cut short. Churchill would then allow a number of ministers to comment, keeping careful watch on the time if he either wished to force a decision, or to procrastinate to avoid reaching an issue lower down the agenda.[46] He himself would sum up matters he considered of particular importance; others he would leave to the Cabinet secretariat. Unlike Attlee, he would often allow discussions to run on longer than necessary, irritating some of the older members who felt his conduct of Cabinet altogether too slack and indecisive. Crookshank's diary, for example, is littered with criticisms of Churchill's management of Cabinet; he is accused variously at different times of being 'intolerably dilatory', 'too woolly for words', 'hopeless' and finally 'ga-ga'.[47] Woolton, another colleague personally unsympathetic to Churchill, was equally critical, complaining in his (also unpublished) diary of Churchill's lack of decisiveness.[48] Some colleagues also found that Churchill's performance compared unfavourably with Eden's crisp style when he was called on to take the chair in Churchill's absence.[49] Outside the Cabinet Room, others were critical; Churchill aroused animosity in non-Cabinet ministers called to No. 10 to discuss a particular item with him. After a long wait, all too often they would find their particular item would be rushed through or not discussed at all. But one can exaggerate Churchill's faults in running Cabinet. Business *was* conducted and decisions taken, although much of the praise was due to Norman Brook.

In one area, foreign affairs, matters tended to be decided away from Cabinet – Egypt proving the main exception, turning up with monotonous regularity on the Cabinet agenda. When foreign policy issues were discussed, few Cabinet ministers would offer much, in part due to the unrivalled ascendancy here of Eden, who preferred to deal direct with Churchill.[50] Eden was one of a group of three who constituted the most influential voices in Cabinet, the other two being Butler and Salisbury. Churchill warmed to Butler after 1951, and gradually removed the watchdogs he had cautiously placed around him at the Treasury, such as the largely ineffective Sir Arthur Salter. Butler's standing in the government increased accordingly, aided by better performances in the House against his opposite number and predecessor, Hugh Gaitskell, than had been expected. But he still remained a curiously mediocre performer in debates (Colville described one of his critical speeches in July 1953 as 'a dull speech, yet more dully delivered. He is certainly no orator'.[51]) Outside Parliament he remained an aloof, isolated figure, with few close friends in Cabinet. Yet his stature was such that by autumn 1952, with Churchill and Eden away, he was taking the chair in Cabinet. He also gained weight from his chairmanship of the key Cabinet Economic Policy Committee and was from early 1952 being talked about as a possible successor to Churchill, a fact that accounted for a marked coolness between him and Eden. (Shuckburgh, Eden's private secretary, recorded that Butler's first Budget 'started off a series of suggestions in the press that he had taken the lead over AE in the Cabinet and was now a serious rival for the succession', and how this view was 'believed by quite a lot of people'.[52]) Salisbury was a popular and trusted figure in Cabinet, but he undermined his position by frequent threats to resign, as well as by ill health, which produced Churchill's jibe that 'Cecils are always ill or resigning.'[53]

Even though these three stood out above their colleagues on account of their influence, it must be stressed that Churchill seldom if ever tried to take key decisions with them, either in a group or singly. Beneath them in importance came five men, Crookshank, Maxwell Fyfe, James Stuart, Philip Swinton and Woolton, none of whom (except Swinton) was very close personally to Churchill, though all, on account of their personalities and positions, had more weight in Cabinet than their colleagues. Not included in this group is Macmillan, still comparatively junior in 1951, but whose star was rising remarkably fast on account of his successful stewardship at the Ministry of Housing and his gift for personal relations (as well as his calculated courting of Churchill); he was tipped as Foreign Secretary in 1953, and in October 1954 emerged as Defence Secretary. Thorneycroft, President of the Board of Trade and the youngest appointee in 1951, was also increasing in influence due to his steady if unspectacular conduct of business at his department. Excluded too were men such as Lyttelton at the Colonial Office, and Monckton at Labour, who, although influential within their own departments, seldom made contributions in Cabinet outside their ministerial specialities.

Churchill's preference for the conduct of business in Cabinet rather than in its committees helps explain the genesis of the ill-fated 'overlord' experiment. The overlords, being in Cabinet, were designed to permit co-ordination at full Cabinet rather than at subordinate level. Churchill had little time for the efficient system of Cabinet and official committees he had inherited from Attlee, and within months of the election officials in Whitehall were bemoaning the loss of order. The only Cabinet committee Churchill relished was the Defence Committee – and this met relatively infrequently. Ministerial and official committees with parallel terms of reference he found particularly unnecessary, and he slashed their number. But Churchill's hostility mellowed with the passing months, and by 1953 a Cabinet committee structure somewhat akin to Attlee's had quietly re-established itself. The overlords system also disappeared in 1953, more because of the unsuitability of the particular incumbents than any inherent weakness in the system. Brook and other mandarins had merely bided their time.[54]

No evidence exists to suggest that the senior Civil Service as a body had hoped for a Conservative victory after the six and a quarter years of socialist government under Attlee, although some officials were certainly relieved by the result. Indeed, trepidation was felt in certain corners about the Conservatives' plan to reduce waste, roll back the state, and reorganize Whitehall. Woolton summed up Conservative hopes, and intentions, when he wrote, 'In opposition, many of us concluded that the country was suffering under a weight of government which was expensive both of money and effort, and we looked forward to a freer society which relied less on either direction or support from government departments.'[55]

In the event the mandarins need not have worried. Woolton recorded despondently in January 1954 that the Cabinet had never discussed the machinery of government, and how to remodel Whitehall to the needs of the country.[56] Woolton, as a retailer and early-day Sir Derek Rayner, found the oversight particularly irksome. Several factors were responsible. Churchill, who spent some considerable time with Brook early on in his administration looking at machinery questions, lost his enthusiasm for reform. Beaverbrook wrote disconsolately in 1953 that he had 'tried some propaganda on Winston about cutting out some of these ridiculous departments, [but he] doesn't want to change anything in his government'.[57] No minister in the government was committed to reform, as Cripps had been under Attlee. Butler, in a similarly commanding position, was only motivated by a desire to reduce the overall size of government; his undoubted creativity was always geared more to policy than to organizational reform. Bridges had been keen to further reform from within, but was outflanked by Brook, who remained sceptical.

The dominant Whitehall officials of the day, Sir Frank Lee (Board of Trade), Sir Godfrey Ince (Ministry of Labour), Sir Frank Newsam (Home Office) and Sir Archibald Rowlands (Ministry of Supply), were all preoccupied with other matters and took little interest in broader machinery-of-government questions. Nor was there pressure for radical reform from academic or journalistic quarters, for whom the inner workings of the Civil Service, protected by an official secrecy vastly more daunting even than now, remained largely a matter of conjecture. A Royal Commission on the Civil Service was, however, set up in November 1953, under the chairmanship of Sir Raymond Priestley.[58] But its report, published in November 1955, although innovatory in some areas such as equal pay and conditions of work, had little to say about machinery of government questions, unlike Fulton (1968). The Priestley Report was, however, appreciated by the Service itself, and set the pattern of employment for the following years. For that reason it has been seen as the most progressive of the five Civil Service royal commissions this century.[59] Changes that did occur in the structure of Whitehall departments owed, therefore, more to practical concerns and a desire for economy, than to any underlying reforming philosophy. Six departments were merged, Transport with Civil Aviation, Pensions with National Insurance, and Agriculture with Food, the first being a sensible rationalization, the latter two the results of a reduction of functions. The one ministry to disappear altogether, Materials, was a direct response to the end of the Korean War.

The government's drive to eliminate waste proved as damp a squib as its reform of Whitehall. As the Conservatives found in 1970, and again in

1979, reducing fat could prove difficult in the face of official inertia. The government's announcements that official cars had been cut from 722 to 444 by February 1953, and that Civil Service numbers had been reduced by 25,640 up to July 1953, were hardly spectacular. Several Conservatives returned in 1951 with grave suspicions about the Civil Service, notably Churchill, Macmillan and Duncan Sandys. Typically it has been Labour that has felt on coming to office that the Civil Service would be antipathetic to its plans, as voiced in 1929, 1964 and 1974. But in 1951 the feeling was that, after twelve years of heavy state controls since 1939, the Civil Service would be reluctant to adapt to the Conservatives' different approach. Not until 1979 was there to be an incoming Conservative administration with a similarly cool attitude to the Civil Service. In the event, the fears in 1951 proved unjustified, and Whitehall readily fell in with the government's plans.

Only one relationship between minister and permanent secretary could have been described as unsatisfactory, that between Sir James Helmore and Sandys at the Ministry of Supply. But that owed more to personal factors than to differences over policy. Macmillan might have encountered greater difficulties with his permanent secretary at Housing, Sir Thomas Sheepshanks, had he not been able effectively to by-pass him and deal direct with the deputy secretary, Evelyn Sharp. Several ministers were eclipsed by abler or more domineering permanent secretaries, notably Horsbrugh by Sir John Maud at Education, Jim Thomas by Sir John Lang at the Admiralty and possibly Lloyd-George by Newsam at the Home Office. But, again, these cases owed more to vacuum-filling due to ministerial weakness than to power-hungry mandarins. Some permanent secretaries also had prodigious influence even with authoritative ministers, especially Godfrey Ince at Labour and Frank Lee at Trade. The influence of Brook on Churchill, and indeed over the whole administration, merits a study in its own right. Churchill's shortcomings, especially towards the end, would have been far more obvious without Brook by his side.

So much for administration: now we turn to policy. As noted above, it was largely continuous with that of the Attlee government. During the 1951 election campaign, Labour predicted divisive and extreme policies at home if the Conservatives proved victorious, and an aggressive and dangerous foreign policy abroad. In economic policy, Lord Croham (a subsequent Head of the Treasury and of the Civil Service) felt that there was less change in 1951 than between any two governments in the entire postwar period.[60] Not for nothing did the *Economist* dream up 'Mr

Butskell', indicating the similarity as Chancellor of Gaitskell and Butler.[61] Butler himself said 'Butskellism really followed upon the demise of Robot [in September 1952]. After that I reverted to normal Keynesian economics.'[62] But not everyone agrees with the thesis of continuity in economic policy. Keith Middlemas, in his important study *Power, Competition and the State* (1986), argues against continuity, citing, for example, the revival of interest in monetary policy and decline in planning.[63] Had the 'Robot' plan for making sterling convertible not been abandoned in 1952, the discontinuity would have been even more pronounced.

Only two of the industries and services nationalized by Labour were denationalized. One, iron and steel, still retained a large measure of control by a central body, the Iron and Steel Board. The other, road haulage, was only partially dismantled as a result of the problems of selling the nationalized concerns back to private enterprise. Little change was the order of the day in other economic ministries. At Trade, a policy of aid was retained for industries and depressed areas; at Agriculture, the radical support system for farmers introduced by Tom Williams in the 1947 Act was retained (although modified to the world of free markets); at Labour, Monckton's softly-softly policy was stuck to, and plans to legislate on industrial relations, which might have upset the unions, were quietly dropped.[64]

Social policy saw similarly little change. Minor charges were introduced in health in 1952, but plans for wider charging were abandoned.[65] The shift of resources to housing was more an astute (short-term) gamble for political popularity than the result of underlying philosophical differences. At Education the priority remained the nonpartisan ones of school-building, ending all-age schools, and bringing new recruits into the teaching profession. No overriding Conservative social philosophy indeed was discernible. The same pattern repeats itself in other spheres. In defence, Labour's commitment to a British nuclear deterrent was maintained (and indeed extended), but conventional forces were run down after the Korean War. A less militaristic policy than withdrawal in 1954 of British forces from the massive Suez base can scarcely be imagined. In colonial policy, the move to self-government was accelerated in West, if not in Central or East, Africa. At the Foreign Office, Labour's rejection of plans of joining in union with Europe was maintained, as was its commitment to the Atlantic Alliance. Eden established himself as a peace-maker on a world scale; his supreme exhibition of diplomatic skills came perhaps at the Geneva Conference in 1954, which brought peace, if only temporarily, to Indo-China. These are only a few examples of the extensive continuity of policy between the Attlee and Churchill administrations. The Churchill government indeed cemented the postwar consensus, which continued, though under increasing strain, until Margaret Thatcher's victory in May 1979.

No government operates in a vacuum, able to do precisely what it would like; constraints are constantly present, distracting it and preventing some favoured policies from being implemented, and causing others to be introduced. The last Churchill administration did, however, possess a number of advantages which should be mentioned before the constraints. It benefited from a relatively united government: although there were differences between left and right, there was also a broad measure of unity on both domestic and overseas policies. Policy disagreements, as over policy to Egypt and the Sudan, were rare, and the only controversial resignation of the administration, Thomas Dugdale's in July 1954, arose on an issue of ministerial responsibility (Crichel Down) and was not sparked by differences with colleagues. The government, therefore, happy (or compliant) under Churchill as leader and Eden as heir-apparent, suffered none of the damaging disputes that had racked Labour's period in office, especially in its latter months. Nor were there disruptive doctrinal differences in the wider party. Unrest there certainly was, especially early on. The *Observer* recorded that 'Disappointment [among backbenchers] with the performance of the Conservative government in its first Parliamentary year is widespread'.[66] Rumblings of discontent were spasmodically heard until Churchill's and Eden's return to health in autumn 1953, after which they faded. The doubts had largely disappeared by 1954, and never constituted a serious anxiety for the government. The unrest, such as it was, always stemmed more from concern about government performance and *ad hoc* issues than from coherent philosophical divisions.

The government was very fortunate to have come to power at a time, in late 1951, when the mood of the nation was in harmony with its desire to end controls and reduce the reach of the state. A leader in *The Times* in 1950 had noted that 'There is a real and mounting distaste for restrictions, whether needed or not, and a resentment of bureaucratic meddling.'[67] But the biggest boon of all to the government was the improvement in the economy during 1952, partly owing to policies pursued by the government, but much more to do with international factors beyond its control, in particular the ending of the Korean War, and the attendant drop in Cold War tension. Yet, deserving or not, the government received the praise. It was indeed an economic miracle that, as *The Times* recorded in December 1954,

there seems to be no [inflation] worth the name in recent movements of prices and wages. With production and consumption in this country at the highest levels of all time, the population fully employed and the external balance of payments still to all outward appearances satisfactory, the present state of the national economy gives little ground for complaint.[68]

Improved conditions also meant more money for public expenditure programmes such as housing, without having to raise taxes. Managing a nation in boom times is far easier than in economic crisis. No government in the postwar world had benefited from such a dramatic change in its economic fortunes during its life.

Finance had remained a constant constraint for the first three years. Butler's pleas for parsimony on departmental expenditure ran like a leitmotif through the Cabinet discussions of 1951–5. Thorneycroft joined forces with him to try to ease the burden on industry of paying for expenditure. In Cabinet in February 1953, Brook's bromide conclusions record that 'it was abundantly clear that the efficiency of British industry could not be maintained, still less increased, unless means were found of reducing the burden of industrial taxation. It was therefore urgently necessary to secure some substantial reduction in the level of government expenditure.'[69] But little heed was paid. In December 1953 Butler sent a memorandum to Cabinet ministers saying, 'I cannot feel that my colleagues have fully grasped the seriousness of the situation. On all sides – defence, agriculture and food, atomic research and development, housing, education and others – I am faced with the prospect of rising expenditure. ... Nonchalance about expenditure will not do.'[70] A pressing item in the government's first Cabinet had been a discussion of the grave economic crisis, based upon a paper submitted by Bridges.[71] The crisis necessitated making economies in many areas. The Cabinet on 20 December 1951 decided to slash £25 million off both education and health estimates for 1952–3 (indicative of the government's priorities).[72] But it was less these meagre economies than the improvement in the world and domestic economies that came to the rescue of Butler. From mid-1954, financial constraints ceased to be an overriding concern.

The small size of the government majority (17) made it more responsive to views of backbenchers than might have been the case with a more comfortable margin. Cabinet records reveal that backbenchers had a decisive influence, in the 1953–4 session alone, in causing the government to speed up or alter several policies, such as over MPs' pay, teachers' superannuation, judges' remuneration and development councils. In consequence of the exceptionally bumpy 1953–4 session, Crookshank, the Leader of the House, suggested that no measures be introduced into the House in the 1954–5 session which would antagonize government supporters.[73] The most important single instance of backbench influence had in fact come earlier, over the introduction of competition in television. Woolton told Cabinet on 3 April 1952 that the Cabinet committee he was chairing on the issue favoured the introduction of commercial television, largely because 'a large majority' of the government's supporters favoured the ending of the BBC monopoly.[74] A more clear-cut illustration of backbench influence could scarcely be found, especially as Churchill, Eden and Lord de la Warr, the Postmaster General (the minister responsible for broadcasting), were all personally opposed to it.

But the small size of the majority also cut the other way: backbenchers were afraid of risking a defeat for the government, and maybe in consequence forcing a general election. Only once did such a defeat appear likely, over the Suez base withdrawal in 1954, when 27 Conservatives voted against the government. But Labour officially abstained, and the vote was carried 257 to 28. Backbenchers were closely controlled by Derek Walker-Smith, chairman of the 1922 Committee, and by Patrick Buchan-Hepburn, the sound if unspectacular Chief Whip. Having so many young MPs eager for office also helped damp down radical fervour. Most of them were too hungry for preferment to want to sacrifice their chances on the altar of rebellion. Parliamentary time was a constraint more often proclaimed than real. It proved on occasion, however, a limiting factor. Because of the government's meagre majority on standing committees, it preferred to take major legislation, such as the bills denationalizing steel and road haulage, on the floor of the House, where its majority was more assured. Time was therefore squeezed, and this was the reason given why some items mentioned in the manifesto, such as bringing nationalized industries within the purview of the Monopolies Commission, were not enacted.

As cases such as the lobby for commercial television illustrate, pressure groups were often dominating influences. The National Farmers Union, traditionally close to the Conservatives, had, however, more influence than many groups.[75] In spite of Butler's plea in Cabinet in

March 1955 that 'an easy settlement with the farmers would be contrary to the main trend of economic policy . . . which ought to be aimed at checking inflationary tendencies', Cabinet decided that it was too late in the Parliament to risk a confrontation, and the farmers were appeased.[76] The same story repeated itself with trade unions, which Churchill realized required very careful handling – especially from mid-1954, when strikes, or threatened strikes, came increasingly to dominate the Cabinet and political agendas. Hugh Massingham wrote, 'In union circles it is often said that [Monckton] is the best Minister of Labour for years, but that is not what some employers think. They feel that he is so anxious to prove that the Conservatives are the true friends of the workers that he will distribute other people's halfpence without a moment's hesitation.'[77] Partly due to this factor, relations with business and the City were possibly less close than with any other Conservative administration since the war. Neither Churchill, Eden nor Butler cared for nor spent much time with business leaders, some of whom never forgave the government for introducing the Excess Profits Levy during 1951–3. The closest channel of communication remained between a limited number of industrialists such as Harry Pilkington (President of the Federation of British Industries, the forerunner of the CBI) and Thorneycroft.

Cabinet records reveal public opinion being a pressure constantly in the minds of ministers, even in matters of no great political import. The closeness of the election result in 1951 (Labour having gained over 200,000 more votes than the Conservatives) and Labour's strong showing in political polls, go a long way to explain their sensitivity. Cabinet records do, however, give a misleading impression of the importance of public opinion over one issue: they suggest Cabinet reversed its initial decision not to televise Queen Elizabeth's coronation in Westminster Abbey expressly on account of 'public outcry' at the decision. In fact, according to Colville, the decision was reversed due to the direct instrutions of the Queen to Churchill.[78]

The question of election timing was bound up inextricably with Churchill's retirement. Soon after Parliament assembled in November 1951, the government made plain its intention not to make an early appeal to the country. Conservative popularity hit a low in 1952, seen in the local government elections in the spring, and even more in the 7.5 per cent swing against the government in the Dundee East by-election in July 1952. Gallup polls meanwhile for the first ten months of 1952 showed a Labour lead ranging from 3.5 to 10 per cent. There was no question of an early appeal to the electorate to obtain a bigger majority while its fortunes were so low. By March 1953, Gallup put the Conservatives in the lead, if only temporarily, and in May confidence was restored dramatically by a by-election swing to the government of 2.4 per cent which enabled it to capture Sunderland South from Labour. Helped by the coronation in June, and better economic figures, the Conservatives continued to gain in popularity. Churchill, however, had decided against an election before 1955, dealing at length with the matter in his speech on the Address in November 1953.

Woolton meanwhile was disconcerted by a secret Conservative Central Office poll in late 1954, which indicated that a change of Prime Minister and government was essential if the party were not to fare badly at a general election. Churchill, however, to the consternation of many of his Cabinet and party colleagues, obstinately refused to stand down – and there was nothing that they could do to prise him out. At one particularly fraught Cabinet meeting in December 1954 (according to a contemporary diary account) he told his stunned colleagues, 'I know that you are trying to get rid of me ... but I won't [go]. If you feel strongly about it you can force my hand by a sufficiently large number of ministers handing in their resignations, in which case an election will be inevitable; but if this happens I shall not be in favour of it and I shall tell the country so.'[79] Two months later, however, and with his final hopes of a summit with the Soviet Union dashed by the fall of Malenkov, he decided to go in the early spring. The ball was now in Eden's court, and after a period of wavering (which led Woolton to record in his diary, 'Eden can't make up his mind, which isn't a very hopeful sign'), he settled on 26 May as the date of the general election.[80] With a popular new Prime Minister, a united party, a record of solid achievement to present to the electorate, and a divided opposition, the result was almost a foregone conclusion. After a quiet but sensible campaign, the Conservatives won 344 seats to Labour's 277, and an overall majority of 58. The Conservatives' share of the vote had risen from 48 per cent in 1951 to 49.7 per cent, and Labour's had correspondingly fallen from 48.8 to 46.4 per cent. Eden's fears that after a fifteen-year wait he might be Prime Minister for less than two months had proved groundless.

What then can be said of the government's work? All sections of the Conservative Party are critical of omissions in the Churchill administration's record. Moderate and left-wing Conservatives point to the failure to introduce a coherent conservative social policy, based on ideas canvassed, for example, by the moderate reforming Conservative pressure group One Nation. Failure to introduce imaginative legislation to bring workers more into decision-taking was another progressive idea in circulation which the government avoided (urged, ironically, by the right-winger Salisbury, among others). Not to have done more to spread capital and create a 'property-owning democracy', an idea on which Eden was especially keen, was another oversight in the eyes of the Conservative left. The old right sees the failure to legislate on immigration as a major error. A memorandum on immigration restriction prepared by Butler and Maxwell Fyfe was debated in Cabinet on 3 February 1954. Churchill said of the continuing increase in the number of coloured people coming to the UK that 'their pressure sooner or later would come to be resented by large sections of the British people'.[81] General support was expressed in Cabinet on 13 January 1955 for restrictions, but plans to legislate were dropped partly because of substantial opposition among MPs.[82]

In the event, very large numbers of coloured immigrants came to the UK (at an estimated rate of 26,000 a year in the latter 1950s) before the first legislation was enacted in 1962. The new right meanwhile was more troubled by the 'appeasement' policy pursued by Monckton (dubbed the 'oil can') towards the unions, and the missed opportunity to legislate on industrial relations. Failure to do more to stimulate productivity and to provide an economic environment conducive to industrial investment and regeneration was also criticized, as was the too-ready acceptance of the welfare state. The government was warned of the dangers of inaction on this front. Early on in the administration, Cabinet considered a paper put up by Butler which argued the need for fundamental solutions to halt Britain's economic decline. The primary causes of it he listed as the growing costs of the welfare state and defence, loss of capital during the war, and deterioration in the terms of trade. Solutions included control of investment, inflation and imports, encouragement to exports, and limitation of defence and overseas expenditure.[83] Others felt the answers lay in an extension of the principle of charging. More efficient and responsive social services would have resulted, it was argued, had the ideas been implemented of those Conservatives such as Ralph Assheton who argued from the backbenches for the introduction of charges. In the event, 'no change' was the order of the day.

Other accusations of missed opportunites are not especially partisan. Foremost among them must be the government's deliberate decision to stay aloof from joining in plans for closer European co-operation, which bore fruit in the Treaty of Rome in 1957. The economic leadership of Europe was there for the taking, protagonists argue. Instead, by remaining aloof, Britain lost out badly, because when it did join the Community, in 1973, it was at a time far less favourable to the British economy than in the early 1950s. Many ardent pro-Europeans have taken this line – for example, the Conservatives Kilmuir, Boothby and Macmillan. Eden and his Foreign Office civil servants are seen as the principal guilty men. In reality, the stay-out view was supported by a majority in Cabinet, whose views were articulated by Salisbury in a Cabinet meeting on 13 March 1952. 'We are not a continental nation,' he said, 'but an island power with a Colonial Empire and unique relations with the independent members of the Commonwealth. Though we might maintain a close association with the continental nations of Europe, we could never merge our interests wholly with theirs. We must be with, but not in, any combination of European powers.'[84] It should also be noted that in the early 1950s the question of closer European co-operation centred not on economic matters, but on defence, with the so-called European Defence Community plan. Churchill's government did well to turn away from this proposal in favour of the more sensible Western European Union of 1954.

Other missed opportunities also had supporters drawn from all shades of the political spectrum. Plans to develop independent technological colleges, advocated forcefully by Lord Cherwell, and which might have given applied science and technology a decisive boost in Britain, fell largely on deaf ears. Plans radically to reform the means of paying for pensions were also abandoned, for political reasons. Cabinet spent some time considering two items of electoral reform before deciding against: the reintroduction of 'university seats', abolished in 1948, which the Conservatives had (unwisely) pledged themselves to reintroduce;[85] and the introduction of proportional representation. Churchill decided to tell the Liberals, urging its introduction, that 'there might be a case at some later stage for considering the introduction of PR in the larger cities', but that moment had not come.[86] A final non-partisan missed opportunity (many others could be stated) was reform of the House of Lords. Some support for reform was expressed in Cabinet, but plans were dropped principally owing to Labour's disagreement with the reforms proposed. Churchill argued in Cabinet that, with no inter-party agreement, the House of Lords' reputation could only be damaged if the government persisted in keeping the subject on the political agenda.[87]

The government justified few of Labour's dire warnings at the time of the 1951 general election that the Conservatives, if elected, would pursue extreme policies. On the home front, the government fell a long way short of introducing a full-blooded capitalist economy, although many controls were finally dispensed with. The *Observer* noted at the time of the 1955 general election that, after three and a half years of Conservative rule, 'Britain is very prosperous, the prosperity is widely diffused, with full employment and higher wages than ever before.'[88] Butler's stewardship of the Treasury, due to a sublime mixture of personal judgement, luck and sound official advice, was mostly successful, although the election Budget in April 1955 remains a blemish.[89] Thorneycroft achieved some notable successes, especially in moving the Conservative Party away from Imperial Preference in the direction of multilateral free trade, and in strengthening the Monopolies Commission in 1953.

Social services were not cut back: instead the government expanded them, and boasted of its record. Pensions and other welfare benefits were increased to become worth marginally more in real terms than in 1951. Houses were built at a quicker rate than under Labour, although at the costs of diverting resources away from industrial building. Although Macmillan achieved his target of 300,000 houses a year at the end of 1953, too many of the new homes were poorly designed and built. Education was neglected until Eccles replaced Horsbrugh in 1954, after which technical schools were given a decisive boost. The NHS was left untouched, but the Minister of Health was removed from Cabinet in 1952, revealing the government's attitude that his was no longer a front-line department. Not until 1960 did health again become a priority concern. In all social policy departments, consolidation rather than inno-vation was the order of the day.

On defence, the government displayed a refreshing willingness to re-examine policy in the light of changed circumstances. The global-strategy paper of 1952 written by the Chiefs of Staff, and principally by Sir John Slessor, Chief of Air Staff, was a radical rethink of defence priorities. In 1951 the Conservatives had inherited a defence capability that in some areas (such as fighter aircraft) was obsolete and in general was not structured with any clear idea of its functions. The 1952 paper helped to define that role, bearing fruit in Macmillan's 1955 defence White Paper, which stated that in the light of the nuclear deterrent Britain's conventional forces should be reduced. Indeed, the Conserva-tives had anyway been presiding over a progressive reduction in the number of servicemen from a Korean War high in 1952. The services were undoubtedly in a healthier state in 1955 than they had been in 1951. For better or worse, the Churchill government gave Britain a pronounced push in nuclear matters: not only did it preside over the explosion of the atom bomb in October 1952 (making Britain the third nation in the world, after the USA and USSR, to possess such a capability), but it also took the decision in July 1954 to build a hydrogen bomb. Further, it produced the seminal White Paper in February 1955[90] on nuclear energy, and oversaw the construction of Calder Hall, the world's first atomic reactor built for civil purposes to feed into the grid.

Colonial policy revealed a certain ambivalence. West Africa was encouraged along the path to self-government, with the Gold Coast (Ghana) and Nigeria being front runners. But East and Central Africa, which had significant white settler minorities, were not deemed fit candidates, or, at least, not in the short term. Under Lyttelton, order was restored in two colonies: Malaya, which threatened to fall under Communist influence: and Kenya, in the grips of the Kikuyu-led Mau Mau revolt. Federation was the formula selected for the Rhodesias and Nyasaland, and for the West Indies, without success. Cyprus remained a source of trouble, and government insensitivity may even have played a hand in exacerbating tensions. In general, Lennox-Boyd's appointment as Colonial Secretary in July 1954 coincided with a marked boost in preparations for self-government in the colonies.

Foreign policy saw perhaps the government's greatest achievements, under the stewardship of Eden. Britain's position in the world was much securer in 1955 than it had been in 1951. The Iran issue had been resolved by a CIA-led coup in 1953 (with British help), which resulted in the return of the Shah and a new deal for British oil. The Sudan was granted its independence, and the Suez base evacuated (though in the event the promise of peaceful relations with Egypt was unfulfilled). For both events, Eden deserves much of the credit, not least for the way he stood up to Churchill and the Conservative rearguard. So too should he be praised for helping bring about a settlement of the Trieste dispute between Yugoslavia and Italy in 1954. (Rhodes James notes that 'Many a Foreign Secretary would have been satisfied with one such achievement in his term of office.')[91] Far more significant was Eden's major contribution to bringing the Federal Republic of Germany into NATO and into the new Western European Union, which supplanted the abortive European Defence Community and involved undertakings by the United States and Britain to maintain troops in Europe: this agreement has been the cornerstone of European security ever since. A final achievement has been described by Shuckburgh: 'He has a large share of the responsibility for preventing [Britain] becoming involved in war in the Far East in the 1950s.'[92] Shuckburgh's praise refers less to Eden's (not insignificant) role in bringing about a successful conclusion to the Korean War than to his co-chairmanship (with Molotov) of the Geneva Conference in 1954, which brought a temporary halt to the war in Indo-China.

So should 1951–5 be seen overall as a period of wasted opportunities, or as a triumph for Tory pragmatism? The answer is both. The Conservatives returned in 1951 with few ideologically coherent policies; what followed emanated in large part from responses to events as they arose, from a desire not to upset the volatile and still left-inclined public, and from a need to conciliate the various other interests in and out of Parliament on whose continued support the government depended. So praise must be qualified, not least because in many areas civil servants were as important, if not more so, than ministers. One is also left with a teasing question. Had Attlee clung on to power for just a few months longer, then the economic crisis would have passed: Gaitskell plus officials would after all have managed to steer Britain through the storm with similar aplomb to Butler plus officials, if not by exactly the same route. Had the election been held in the spring or summer of 1952, then Labour might well have won it, as it came within a whisker of doing in October 1951. It would then have been Labour (assuming it did not squander its opportunities on fratricidal squabbles) and not the Conservatives which would have reaped the benefits of fifties affluence. It is a tantalizing thought.

Chronology

1951

6 October   Assassination of Sir Henry Gurney, High Commissioner for Malayan Federation.

25 October   General election: Conservatives, 321 seats; Labour, 295; Liberals, 6; others, 3. Conservatives gain a majority over Labour, overturning the defeat of February 1950.

7 November   Butler announces in Parliament economic measures to meet the balance-of-payments crisis. Bank Rate rises from 2 to 2.5 per cent.

7 December   Home Guard Act receives royal assent.

1952

15 January   Templer appointed High Commissioner for Federation of Malaya to restore order. Opening in London of conference of Commonwealth finance ministers.

17 January   Churchill addresses the US Congress.

26 January   Serious rioting in Cairo, leading to the murder of 10 British residents.

6 February   George VI dies.

21 February   Churchill suffers an arterial spasm. British identity cards abolished.

22 February   Meeting in Lisbon of Council of NATO.

29 February   Defeat of 'Robot' plan to make sterling convertible.

1 March   Lord Alexander of Tunis appointed Minister of Defence succeeding Churchill.

11 March   Butler's first Budget. Surprisingly mild: food subsidies cut. It is considered a success and Butler's reputation rises.

7 May   Iain Macleod becomes Minister of Health. Job goes out of Cabinet.

22 May   NHS Act receives royal assent. Minor charging introduced for some drugs and dental treatment.

16 June   Meeting of top Conservatives to discuss how to induce Churchill to retire.

18 June   Publication of British government scheme for Central African Federation (Cmd 8573).

23 June   Bombing of North Korean hydro-electric plants on Yalu River.

17 July   Dundee East by-election: 7.5 per cent swing away from Conservatives.

23 July   General Neguib seizes power in Egypt.

25 July   Entry into force of the treaty establishing the European Steel and Coal Community.

14 August   Eden marries Clarissa Churchill.

3 October   British atom bomb detonated at Monte Bello, Australia.

20 October   State of Emergency in Kenya (Mau Mau rising).

4 November   Polling in US for election of President: Eisenhower elected to succeed Truman.

16 November   Announcement of explosion of American hydrogen bomb at Eniwetok Atoll.

27 November   Opening in London of Commonwealth economic conference.

4 December   Churchill announces decision to curtail defence expenditure.

1953

31 January–1 February   East-coast floods. Serious loss of life and damage to property and farm land.

12 February   Conclusion of agreement on Sudan by British and Egyptian governments (Cmd 8766).

5 March   Stalin dies. Succeeded by triumvirate of Malenkov, Molotov and Beria.

8 April   Jomo Kenyatta sentenced to 7 years' hard labour for managing Mau-Mau.

12 April   Eden undergoes an unsuccessful operation. He is out of action for nearly 6 months.

14 April   Butler's second Budget: sixpence off all rates of income tax, purchase tax reduced and the Excess Profits Levy abolished as promised. This is the first Budget since the war to introduce no new taxes or raise ones already in existence.

6 May   Transport Act receives royal assent. Provides for denationalization of British Road Services.

11 May   Churchill's foreign affairs speech during which he proposes a summit meeting with Soviet Union.

13 May   Sunderland South by-election: Conservatives capture seat from Labour.

14 May   Iron and Steel Act receives royal assent. Denationalizes iron and steel, under supervision of a new Iron and Steel Board.

25 May   Successful test of first atomic shell in Nevada, USA.

2 June   Coronation of Queen Elizabeth II.

3 June   Opening in London of conference of Commonwealth prime ministers.

18 June   Proclamation of Republic of Egypt, with General Neguib as President.

23 June   Churchill suffers a major stroke. Cover-up ensues.

27 June   First (of 16) Cabinet meetings presided over by Butler. (Last is on 18 August). He is at the peak of his power during Churchill's and Eden's absences through ill health.

14 July   Rhodesia and Nyasaland Federation Act establishes the Federation of Northern and Southern Rhodesia and Nyasaland.

27 July   Korean War Armistice signed at Panmunjom.

20 August   Soviet press announces explosion of hydrogen bomb. Arrest of Dr Mossadeq, Prime Minister of Iran.

22 August   Shah returns to Iran.

4 September   'Overlords' system of co-ordinating Cabinet ministers formally ended.

7 September   Sir Godfrey Huggins sworn in as Prime Minister of Federation of Rhodesia and Nyasaland.

1 October   Churchill and Eden return to work after their respective illnesses.

6 October   Announcement of decision to send naval and military forces to British Guiana.

29 October   Monopolies and Restrictive Practices Commission Act receives royal assent.

4 December   Meeting in Bermuda of Eisenhower, Churchill and Laniel of France.

8 December   Eisenhower proposes before UN General Assembly international control of atomic energy.

31 December   Macmillan achieves his target of 300,000 new houses a year during the month.

1954

8 January   Commonwealth finance ministers conference opens in Sydney.

25 January–19 February   Berlin Conference.

13 February   Article in the *Economist* headed 'Mr Butskell's Dilemma': coins the term 'Butskellism'.

6 April   Butler's third Budget. Introduces a new 'investment allowance' scheme. Gaitskell calls it 'a tiny, insignificant Budget'. The dullest of Butler's Budgets.

14 April   Cotton Act receives royal assent. Paves way for reopening of Liverpool Cotton Exchange.

18 April   Nasser assumes office of Prime Minister and Military Governor of Egypt.

26 April   Geneva Conference opens.

1 May   Butter, cheese and margarine derationed – among the last items still to be controlled.

7 May   Fall of French post of Dien Bien Phu in Indo-China.

31 May   Declaration of state of emergency in Buganda.

4 June   Departure of Churchill and Eden to see Eisenhower.

21 July   Armistice agreement signed on Indo-China.

23 July   Cabinet in crisis over Churchill's message to Molotov.

26 July   Government reshuffle: Lyttelton retires as Colonial Secretary.

28 July   Cabinet gives final approval to production of a British hydrogen bomb.

29 July   House of Commons agrees to Suez Canal agreement with Egypt by 257 votes to 26.

30 July   Television Act receives royal assent. Establishes Independent Television.

5 August   Iranian government agreement on resumption of operations by Western oil companies.

29 September   Eden announces British government decision to maintain 4 divisions on mainland Europe.

5 October   Conclusion of agreement on settlement of problems of Trieste.

18 October   Ministry of Food integrated into Ministry of Agriculture and Food: rationing formally ended. Major government reshuffle: Alexander, Horsburgh and Simonds retire: Macmillan appointed Minister of Defence and Eccles Minister of Education.

19 October   Anglo-Egyptian agreement on evacuation of Suez base.

21 October   Shoreditch and Finsbury by-election: 5.6 per cent swing away from Conservatives.

23 October   Signature of agreements on end of occupation of Germany and on Western European Union.

17 November   Nasser replaces Neguib as President of Egypt.

30 November   Churchills' eightieth birthday.

9 December   Butler's first wife, Sydney Courtauld, dies.

15 December   Churchill's retirement mentioned in Cabinet.

22 December   Meeting at No. 10 to discuss possible election dates (and Churchill's retirement).

1955

9 February   Reports in press of fall of Malenkov in Soviet Union: crushes Churchill's hopes of a summit meeting with Soviet leaders and precipitates his decision definitely to retire from premiership.

5 April   Churchill retires.

6 April   Eden succeeds as Prime Minister.

7 April   Eden's government reshuffle. Macmillan becomes Foreign Secretary; Home becomes Commonwealth Secretary.

15 April   Eden announces May general election.

19 April   Butler's fourth Budget: sixpence off income tax; personal allowances raised. Considered an 'electioneering' Budget.

5 May   Ratification of Western European Union and end of occupation of Western Europe.

9 May   Federal Germany admitted to NATO.
10 May Western Powers propose a four-power summit.
14 May Warsaw Pact concluded.
15 May Austrian peace treaty Signed.
23 May Dock strike.
26 May General election: Conservatives win 344 seats to Labour's 277 – an overall majority of 58.

Notes

I should like to thank Sir John Colville and Sir David Pitblado for commenting on an earlier draft of this chapter.

1   The *Spectator*, 26 October 1951.
2   PRO, CAB, CC 1/5, 30 October 1951; *The Times*, 27 October 1951.
3   *The Times*, 7 November 1951.
4   Keith Middlemas, *Power, Competition and the State*, vol. I: *Britain in Search of Balance, 1940–1961* (Macmillan, 1986). This book includes the most scholarly account so far of the Churchill government.
5   Patrick Cosgrave, 'The failure of the Conservative Party 1945–75' in R. Emmett Tyrell, Jr (ed.), *The Future that Doesn't Work* (Doubleday, 1977), pp. 98–9. See also Ian Gilmour, *Inside Right* (Hutchinson, 1977), pp. 11–21.
6   A leader in *The Times*, 13 October 1953, commenting on Labour's performance during the first two years of the government.
7   Robert McKenzie, 'Policy decision in opposition: a rejoinder', *Political Studies*, 5 (1957), pp. 178–9.
8   See, for example, Harold Wilson, *The Making of a Prime Minister* (Weidenfeld and Nicolson, 1986), pp. 147–8.
9   Lord Kilmuir, *Political Adventure: the memoirs of the Earl of Kilmuir* (Weidenfeld and Nicolson, 1964); Harold Macmillan, *Tides of Fortune, 1945–55* (Macmillan, 1969); Lord Butler, *The Art of the Possible: the memoirs of Lord Butler* (Hamish Hamilton, 1971).
10 David Carlton, *Anthony Eden* (Allen Lane, 1981); Robert Rhodes James, *Anthony Eden* (Weidenfeld and Nicolson, 1986).
11 Ralph Harris, *Politics without Prejudice* (Staples Press, 1956); Anthony Howard, *Rab: the life of R. A. Butler* (Cape, 1987).
12 Anthony Sampson, *Macmillan: a study in ambiguity* (Allen Lane, 1967).
13 Lord Birkenhead, *Walter Monckton: the life of Viscount Monckton of Brenchley* (Weidenfeld and Nicolson, 1969); Nigel Fisher, *Iain Macleod* (André Deutsch, 1973); John Cross, *Swinton* (Oxford University Press, 1982).
14 Ronald Lewin, *Slim, the Standardbearer* (Cooper, 1976); Michael Carver, *Harding of Petherton* (Weidenfeld and Nicolson, 1978); John Cloake, *Templer* (Harrap, 1985); Philip Ziegler, *Mountbatten* (Collins, 1985).
15 Lord Moran, *Winston Churchill: struggle for survival, 1940–65* (1966;

paperback edn Sphere, 1968). John Colville, *The Fringes of Power: Downing Street diaries 1939–55* (Hodder and Stoughton, 1985); Evelyn Shuckburgh, *Descent to Suez: diaries 1951–56* (Weidenfeld and Nicolson, 1986).

16 Anthony Seldon, *Churchill's Indian Summer* (Hodder and Stoughton, 1981). Unless otherwise indicated, information in this chapter comes from this source.

17 Ibid., p. 1.

18 Ibid., pp. 1–2.

19 The *Spectator*, 9 November 1951.

20 PRO, CAB, CC 1/6, 30 October 1951.

21 PRO, CAB, CC 33/1, 25 March 1952.

22 PRO, CAB, CC 105/3, 16 December 1952.

23 Diary, 15 October 1952, Crookshank Papers, Bodleian Library, Oxford.

24 Colville, *The Fringes of Power*, p. 644 (22–3 March 1952).

25 PRO, CAB, CC 99/6, 6 November 1952; Howard, *Rab*, pp. 184–5.

26 PRO, PREM 11/654, minute from Churchill to Eden, 9 August 1952.

27 Seldon, *Churchill's Indian Summer*, p. 30.

28 PRO, PREM 11/385, minute from Churchill to Horsbrugh, 9 February 1953.

29 Interview with Lord Butler. Churchill appears to have spent fewer hours closeted than Butler imagined.

30 Colville, *The Fringes of Power* p. 646 (26–7 April 1952).

31 House of Commons Debates, vol. 515, cols 897–8, 3 November 1953.

32 *'Chips': the diaries of Sir Henry Channon*, ed. R. R. James (Weidenfeld and Nicolson, 1967), entry for 3 November 1953.

33 Interview with Sir John Colville.

34 Election address, 16.10.51. Newcastle-upon-Tyne.

35 House of Commons Debates, vol. 537, col. 1905, 1 March 1955.

36 John Grigg wrote a powerful essay, 'Churchill, troubled giant' (*Encounter*, April 1977), in which he argues, *inter alia*, that Churchill should have retired in 1953. Norman Brook argued in contrast that Churchill was fit for office until his last few months: John Wheeler-Bennett (ed.), *Action this Day: working with Churchill* (Macmillan, 1968), pp. 37–46.

37 *The Times*, 4 November 1953.

38 The *Observer* 6 June 1954.

39 Ibid., 20 June 1954.

40 The *Scotsman*, 6 April 1955.

41 Moran, *Churchill: struggle for survival* p. 428 (28 April 1953).

42 PRO, CAB, CC 9/2, 29 January 1952.

43 PRO, CAB, CC 81/1, 31 December 1953.

44 PRO, CAB, CC 52/3, confidential annex, 23 July 1954; and CAB, CC 53/2, confidential annex, 26 July 1954. See also Colville, *The Fringes of Power*, pp. 701–2.

45 Interview with Sir David Pitblado.
46 Interview with Lord Amory.
47 Crookshank Diary, 1 May 1952, 17 March and 5 November 1953, 22 March 1954.
48 Diary, 11 March 1955, Woolton Papers, Bodleian Library, Oxford.
49 Crookshank Diary, 14 January 1953.
50 Interview with Sir George Mallaby, in Seldon, *Churchill's Indian Summer*, p. 536.
51 Colville, *The Fringes of Power*, p. 671 (21 July 1953).
52 Shuckburgh, *Descent to Suez*, p. 38.
53 Interview with Sir John Colville.
54 For a full discussion of Churchill's conduct of Cabinet, see Peter Hennessy, *Cabinet* (Basil Blackwell, 1986), esp. pp. 46–50 and 52–3.
55 Comments dated 25 January 1954, Woolton Papers, Box 3.
56 Ibid.
57 Letter from Beaverbrook to Bracken, 7 January 1953, Beaverbrook Papers, Box C57, House of Lords Library.
58 Cmd 9613.
59 Peter Jones to author.
60 Interview with Lord Croham.
61 The *Economist*, 13 February 1954.
62 Interview with Lord Butler.
63 Middlemas, *Power, Competition and the State*, vol. I, p. 267.
64 PRO, CAB, CC 63/6 (c), 26 June 1952.
65 Crookshank Diary, 7 December 1951 and 10 January 1952.
66 The *Observer*, 3 August 1952.
67 *The Times*, 11 January 1950.
68 Ibid., 13 December 1954.
69 PRO, CAB, CC 6/6, 3 February 1953.
70 PRO, PREM 11/658, memo C 355 from Chancellor of the Exchequer, 16 December 1953.
71 PRO, CAB, CC 1/5, 30 October 1951.
72 PRO, CAB, CC 19/3, 20 December 1951.
73 PRO, CAB, CC 68/5, 20 October 1954.
74 PRO, CAB, CC 36/3, 3 April 1952.
75 NFU power was felt, for example, in Cabinet on 27 October 1953. It was, ministers were told, 'in a difficult mood' (PRO, CAB, CC 61/4, 27 October 1953).
76 PRO, CAB, CC 22/3, 9 March 1955.
77 The *Observer*, 17 January 1954.
78 PRO, CAB, CC 90/6, 28 October 1952; letter from Sir John Colville to the author, 4 February 1987.
79 Woolton and Crookshank Diaries, 22 December 1954.

80   Woolton Diary, 5 April 1955. Rhodes James records, 'Eden was deter-
     mined from the moment he entered Downing Street that there must be an
     early General Election' (*Anthony Eden*, p. 404).
81   PRO, CAB, CC 7/4, 3 February 1954.
82   PRO, CAB, CC 3/6, 13 January 1955.
83   PRO, CAB, CC 55/5, 22 May 1952.
84   PRO, CAB, CC 30/3, 13 March 1952.
85   PRO, CAB, CC 55/7, 6 October 1953. See also Seldon, *Churchill's Indian
     Summer*, p. 59.
86   PRO, CAB, CC 6/2, 3 February 1953.
87   Lord Salisbury had said in Cabinet on 5 November 1951 that he hoped
     Cabinet would introduce House of Lords reform (PRO, CAB, CC 4/1; CC
     63/5, 5 November 1953).
88   The *Observer*, 8 May 1955.
89   Middlemas, *Power, Competition and the State*, vol. I, pp. 269–70.
90   *Programme of Nuclear Power*, Cmd 9389.
91   Rhodes James, *Anthony Eden*, p. 355.
92   Shuckburgh, *Descent to Suez*, p. 19.

4
From Eden to Macmillan, 1955–1959
John Barnes

The Conservative government which was confirmed in office by the results of the general election on 26 May 1955 suffered considerable political vicissitudes before it was able to put its own record before the electorate on 8 October 1959, again with success. It had gone to the country in 1955 after a major tax-cutting Budget, but the balance of payments had soon come under strain and in October the Chancellor of the Exchequer, R. A. Butler, had to come back to Parliament with an emergency counter-inflationary Budget. Inevitably the Opposition attacked him for electioneering earlier in the year, and his transfer to the Leadership of the House when Eden reshuffled his Cabinet in December 1955 did neither his own nor the government's reputation much service. Eden's election triumph was soon forgotten, and by spring 1956 the proportion of the electorate approving of his work had fallen from 70 per cent to 40 per cent. By-elections such as that at Tonbridge in June 1956 revealed considerable middle-class discontent with the government. There were already signs of a Liberal revival, which faltered in 1956 only to revive again in the following year and to reach a climax with the Liberal's first by-election breakthrough since the war: Torrington, gained in March 1958.

The Suez affair proved the ultimate test of Eden's leadership and the exploration of its significance tends to dominate discussion of his government's record. The opening of the relevant archives in January 1987 has accentuated this tendency, but in due course it may also induce a sense of proportion. Suez undoubtedly altered public perceptions about Britain's status as a great power, but it had surprisingly little effect on its ability to act, even in the Middle East, and it seems to have had no impact at all on the long-term political fortunes of the government. It did, however, produce a change of Prime Minister. Eden's health, never good, was broken by the crisis, and the choice of Harold Macmillan rather than Butler to succeed him was thought at the time to be significant. As *The Times* observed, Butler had 'long been the hope and the leader of the young Conservatives'.[1] In retrospect it is evident that Eden's decision to transfer Macmillan from the Foreign Office in December 1955 to take Butler's place at the Exchequer was crucial for both men, and it may well have ensured the Conservative Party's third successive election victory. Macmillan had nerve and panache. He had the good fortune also to find the party so shell-shocked that they were grateful for any lead and unlikely to rock the boat. Even so, it does not seem probable that Butler's more donnish style would ever have won him an image to match that of 'Supermac', designed by the cartoonist Vicky to do Macmillan harm but instead perceived in time as something like the truth.

Macmillan, as Lance Siedentop points out in a very perceptive essay,[2] was a master of the use of style and he employed it to good effect both with his own party and people and in international affairs. A leading opponent, Harold Wilson, spoke with admiration of Macmillan's political genius in holding up the banner of Suez for the party to follow while in practice leading it in the opposite direction,[3] and his ability to salvage and use a nation's pride in itself to ease its transition into a less comfortable world was part of the same mastery of the art of politics, put this time to more significant use. Macmillan, as will be seen, had other, more specific achievements, but this is likely to remain the most important in the eyes of historians as well as the hardest to assess. He brought Britain to terms with its new position in the world, and, rather like de Gaulle, did so without doing damage to the national psyche. No doubt it can and should be asked whether it was ultimately good that national confidence should have been preserved in this way, but that it was preserved is beyond question. Nor did Macmillan simply put his command of style to partisan or national advantage. Rather he used it to woo both the American President, Eisenhower, and his Soviet counterpart, Khrushchev, to agree to the idea of a regular series of summits, and he was able to make use of his established position in Eisenhower's confidence to keep the negotiations for a nuclear test-ban treaty alive at a time when the experts had changed their position on the possibility of detection. His personal embassy to Moscow in spring 1959 was conducted with an acute sense of the theatrical, but that should not obscure its serious purpose nor its relative success in furthering detente at a time when there was acute tension over the future of Berlin. It was hard for the Opposition to give him full credit for his efforts at the time, although Wilson has paid him tribute since. His top-level diplomacy was put to good use in the sphere of domestic politics also, and never more so than in summer 1959, when Eisenhower, on an informal visit to London, appeared with his host on television to discuss the international situation. This was theatre of a very high order.

A Trog cartoon may, however, tell us more about the contemporary verdict on the government which the electors expressed when they returned it to power with 100-seat majority. Seated with a car, television, refrigerator and washing machine, Macmillan is saying, 'Well, gentlemen, I think we all fought a good fight. . . .'[4] Nye Bevan unconsciously reflected Conservative election posters when he explained the result: contentment with Conservative prosperity and apprehension that Labour would destroy it.[5] The government had achieved a unique double in postwar politics, a sharp rise in living standards coupled with eighteen months of stable prices. The decision to go for disinflation before resuming the quest for economic expansion, which Macmillan had defended in his only Budget speech, seemed to have paid off, and it had been accomplished without any attack on the social services. Rather than cut them Macmillan had accepted the resignation in January 1958 of the entire Treasury team, headed by the Chancellor, Peter Thorneycroft. By autumn 1958 the government was ready to reflate the economy, but it would be unfair to attribute this to the imminence of a general election. Macmillan was genuinely concerned at growing regional unemployment, and, if politics played any part in his decision to press for action to deal with it, it was because he shared to the full the feeling common to the party's high command that they could not afford to be seen to be adopting any attitude reminiscent of the interwar period when their party had been in power and unemployment was rife. In his moment of victory Macmillan wrote to the Queen about the strong impression he had formed that her subjects did 'not wish to allow themselves to be divided into warring classes or tribes filled with hereditary animosity against each other'[6] and he made this the theme of a message to the nation, both prescient and, as it turned out, premature, that the class war was obsolete.

This cursory survey of the government's fortunes suggests that it was extremely successful, so much so in fact that it ought not to surprise us that so shrewd an observer of the British political scene as Samuel Beer, Professor of Government at Harvard University, was ready to speculate on the possibility of democratic one-party government in Britain.[7] In their obituary tributes to Macmillan following his death in December 1986 commentators tended to look back on the period as something of a golden age, and there are recent textbook accounts which implicitly endorse this view.[8] Nevertheless they note also the obverse of growing British affluence, the rising power of the trade unions, which was to prove one of the central political problems of the next two decades. While Conservative freedom seemed to work, there was an ominous harbinger of these future problems in Frank Cousins's blunt assertion in 1957 that, if there was to be a free-for-all, his union, the Transport and General Workers, wanted to be part of the all.[9] Despite the way in which Macmillan insisted on outfacing the London bus strike in 1958, there has been a growing tendency to feel that his government should have legislated to reform industrial relations. This is not the only missed opportunity highlighted by contemporary historians, although it is perhaps the only one which would find general acceptance among them. In most recent accounts the prevailing tone has been highly critical,[10] but the standpoints from which the criticism has been delivered have been shaped less by the need to understand the preoccupations of the period than by the contemporary political debate about the way in which to remedy Britain's persistent economic decline.

Britain, it is alleged, was prospering in the 1950s for reasons which had little to do with government action, and ministers paid little attention to the problems which were created by this prosperity, cost-push inflation among them. Instead they devoted their energy to maintaining Britain's increasingly illusory role as a world power and devoted too small a share of the nation's resources to investment. This is a criticism that was rather more skilfully argued at the time by a distinguished journalist, Andrew Shonfield,[11] and he at least did not go on to charge that the government also devoted too little of these selfsame resources to hospitals, prisons, subsidized housing, pensions and youth. There is always a case to be made for more spending in a particular area, but the worry at the time, voiced by Thorneycroft and his colleagues and echoed subsequently by a number of economists and students of government, by no means all of a Thatcherite tendency, was that programmes of social spending were getting out of control, and this is a contention many historians of the period seem reluctant to face. To assert simply that 'Tory economic complacency' prevented the economic growth necessary to fund these programmes, and to allow Britain to compete successfully with the Europeans and the Japanese,[12] is to beg some very important questions. More to the point is the argument that the prospects for successful economic growth were destroyed by the government's 'stop–go' policies and that the dangers involved in any sustained pursuit of economic growth could have been overcome by floating the pound and promoting an incomes policy. This is a case which was again made more convincingly by a contemporary journalist, Samuel Brittan, [13] than it has been by any subsequent historian, although Brittan found considerable support from a more academic study published in the same year (1964) by the economist Christopher Dow.[14] While Brittan republished his account of these years in later editions which continued the story to 1969, the last of these was published in 1971 and it seems astonishing that no historian has since reassessed Brittan's arguments in the light of subsequent events and much more detailed econometric study.

The most probable reason for this somewhat sorry state of affairs is that most accounts of the period are textbook in character.[15] As in other key areas of the government's record, the official historian has yet to publish, and there are as yet no substantial monographs. In foreign affairs and certain aspects of defence policy we are much better served by extended surveys,[16] and it may not be wholly accidental that the judgements made on the record of the government in general, and on the conduct of policy by Macmillan and his Foreign Secretary, Selwyn Lloyd, in particular, are a good deal more balanced and could even be said to be sympathetic. Although this is less true of the Suez crisis, it is noticeable that the best of the studies made prior to the opening of the public records, Hugh Thomas's *The Suez Affair*, while highly critical, makes a sustained effort to understand why Eden acted as he did.[17] But most historians, even though they have some good words to say for Macmillan's record on detente, disarmament, and decolonization, find themselves critical of another missed opportunity – that of joining the EEC at its inception. The exclusion of Britain from Europe has even been compared in importance to the Hapsburg Empire's exclusion from the German *Zollverein*, and that makes it all the more remarkable that so important an episode has been studied only as a prologue to Britain's first attempt at entry. Not even the efforts to create a free-trade area to prevent further division within Europe have received any extensive attention.[18]

Much of the criticism made about this government centres on its leadership. Eden tends to be seen as a man innocent of economic understanding and deficient in his knowledge of the domestic scene. His unrivalled expertise in foreign affairs is recognized, but he is thought of as an old-fashioned figure, unwilling to acknowledge Britain's reduced position in the world, building too much on his hopes that the Commonwealth could be made an effective surrogate for Empire, an Atlanticist when it was necessary to be a European. Macmillan by contrast is acknowledged to have had a far shrewder appreciation of the realities of Britain's position, and the criticism therefore centres on his failure to make those realities sufficiently plain to the electorate. The most perceptive of his biographers tends to accept the charge that he offered 'government by camouflage' when leadership was needed, but does not analyse why he thinks a different approach would have been more successful.[19] There is an impression, largely false, that Macmillan in these years concentrated on rebuilding the position of his party, but a more perceptive criticism, hinted at though rarely made explicit, is directed not at his political opportunism but at the fact that in this initial period he operated within the accepted framework of policy, and was simply not radical enough. While there is a good deal to be said for Henry Fairlie's view that the leader should be the 'least Party Man in his Party',[20] there is a limit to the pace with which he can alter its mind. Younger men in search of the succession can challenge the prevailing consensus with the expectation that it will not hinder, and may well advance, their career, but that is not an option open to a party leader. He has to hold the various forces within his party in balance while keeping it in touch with those trends in society which will keep it in power. It is a task to which Macmillan's skills were supremely well fitted.

It is important to realize that, while a case can be made for the rather jaundiced view hitherto taken of the late fifties, most of the writing on the period still reflects the sea-change which swept across British politics little more than a year after Macmillan's almost unparalleled victory at the polls. Until then there had been general satisfaction with Britain's recovery from the economic havoc wrought by the Second World War. Although the position of the balance of payments remained fragile, the controls which had seen the country through the war and postwar period were a thing of the past, and with them the period of austerity. The outward shape of British life, little altered since the war, began to change with great speed in the second half of the fifties. The onset of working-class affluence coincided with the arrival of commercial television and its rapid spread. There was a quite extraordinary surge in consumer credit between 1957 and 1959, and, while it is true that the only consumer durable, apart from television, that could be found in most working-class homes was the vacuum cleaner, the automation of the kitchen was well under way and a private car seemed to be within reach of most families. The number of private cars on the road doubled in the three years from 1955, and the arrival of the jet age in 1958 together with an increasing number of package holidays literally opened up new horizons for family activity. When Macmillan spoke at Bedford in summer 1957 he could say with confidence, 'Most of our people have never had it so good', and the country not only believed him but was content with its lot. As late as 1959, promises by the Labour Party of greater public expenditure financed out of economic growth cut very little ice with the electorate: it was widely believed that an incoming Gaitskell government would have to resort to higher levels of taxation to finance its programme, and Gaitskell's denials of this were taken to be tokens of his dishonesty.

The mood changed with surprising suddenness. There developed a general sense that Britain was lagging behind her European rivals in terms of economic growth, and the ideas which had earlier been canvassed by Shonfield began to pass into general currency. When he wrote his pamphlet *Can Labour Win?* early in 1960, Anthony Crosland thought that economic stagnation was too abstract an issue on which to campaign and added that in any case it would be challenging the government on its own ground. By the autumn, as his *Encounter* article shows, he was less certain,[21] and it is significant that, from further left in the Labour Party, Peter Shore chose to make economic growth and planning one of the five themes in a little noticed policy document, *Labour in the Sixties*. In the following year a Penguin Special called *The Stagnant Society*[22] sold 60,000 copies, and the publishers followed it with a whole series of critical studies, under the all-embracing title *What's Wrong with . . . ?*, which had a ready sale. By the time Crosland reprinted his Fabian pamphlet in 1962 he could confidently omit his reference to the issue of economic stagnation: it had become Labour's central charge against the government in the light of its lurch back into deflationary policies in 1961. Entry into the European Economic Community, considered unthinkable only the year before, became the fashionable nostrum in Whitehall and the media in the course of 1960, and it was pushed hard by British industry. Coupled with modernization, a move to indicative planning and towards a more formal incomes policy, it was to provide the springboard for a future in which large-scale increases in public expenditure would be paid for out of the fruits of economic growth. Inevitably there was a tendency on all sides to look back on the previous decade as a time when opportunity after opportunity had been missed.

Ten, twelve and ultimately thirteen wasted years was a socialist slogan, but one which found a ready echo in the hearts and minds of a far wider audience than the Labour Party. A quarter of a century on, there is an almost equally widely shared scepticism about many, if not all, of the remedies then adopted for Britain's economic problems, but it is also clear that they have not lost their hold on substantial sections of the British intelligentsia. Perhaps that is why the scepticism has not yet led to any radical reassessment of the record of the 1955–9 government, and why the prevalent tone of such writing as there is about the period is still coloured by the assumptions which shaped that *What's Wrong with . . . ?* literature. Much textbook writing simply draws on and reflects those earlier verdicts, even though the confidence with which they were voiced can scarcely have survived the record of the next two decades.

Even the most cursory survey of the scholarly literature available on this period will suggest the enormous task of elucidation and revision which will have to be undertaken once the archives are fully open in 1990. The first biographies based on private papers are only just beginning to appear[23] and there are only a handful of monographs sufficiently thorough to light the researcher's way.[24] Anthony Seldon and I intend to marry our extensive interview records, and those of others, with the public records in order to chart the way for more detailed and extensive research, but that work is unlikely to be complete before the end of the decade. The student in the meantime will probably find the official lives of Eden, Butler and Macmillan the best interim guide to the government's policies; the last of these is not currently available, but publication may be expected in the course of 1987 or 1988.[25]

Political memoirs form a partial substitute for biographies, but, contrary to popular opinion, not all politicians write them. Of the thirty-one who held Cabinet office in the 1955–9 government, only a dozen have published their recollections.[26] Monckton left unfinished memoirs, and at least one of the five survivors who have not so far ventured into print is believed to be actively preparing. In addition to his memoir, Harold Watkinson, then Minister of Transport, wrote some reflections on industrial policy, based on his experience; and his counterpart at the Ministry of Fuel and Power and subsequently Supply, Aubrey Jones, followed the same plan in his book *Britain's Economy*.[27] John Boyd Carpenter, like Jones a minister outside Cabinet, has written a more orthodox memoir with vivid sketches of the Prime Ministers he served under as well as a useful discussion of departmental business.[28] Anthony Nutting, effectively second in command at the Foreign Office, has published useful if discreet records of Britain's attitude to Europe and to disarmament, as well as a very frank account of the Suez crisis,[29] although it should be noted that both Selwyn Lloyd and Rhodes James have challenged parts of this account.

Characteristically, civil servants have been more reticent, with the notable exception of those with a Foreign Office background. Kirkpatrick, Jebb, Hayter, Gore-Booth and Barclay have all set pen to paper: only Maud and Roll have provided a comparable account of more domestic concerns.[30] One free-wheeling member of the Prime Minister's Private Office, John Wyndham, has provided us with an insight into Macmillan's way of doing business and there is much to be gained also from Harold Evans's invaluable *Downing Street Diary*.[31] There is material to be gleaned from obituaries, particularly those in the *Dictionary of National Biography*. Here, for example, may be found Lord Trend's perceptive account of his predecessor as Cabinet Secretary. However, for the most part it has been left to biographers such as Nigel Fisher and historians such as Keith Middlemas to put on record the recollections of the Whitehall mandarins.[32] While oral testimony is not always widely available after it is given, it can be a valuable source. Both Lord Hailsham and Lord Home, for example, have recorded lengthy interviews for the BBC series *The Twentieth Century Remembered*, and particular mention should be made of the way in which highlights from the interviews conducted for the Thames Television series *The Day before Yesterday* were incorporated into the book accompanying the series.[33]

Even when the official records are available, memoirs remain invaluable as evidence for motivation, atmosphere, perspectives and relationships, and may also be the only source for meetings and conversations that do not find their way on to the written record in any other form. That is why Selwyn Lloyd's account of the Suez crisis is likely to retain its importance. Key meetings of ministers at Chequers and elsewhere, which have an important bearing on the issue of 'collusion', are noted by Lloyd but find no place in the very extensive government records. Such sources apart, the most important memoirs are likely to remain those of the Prime Ministers of the day.[34] Not least, they provide a fair indication of the way in which the two men chose to distribute their interest, time and effort. Although Eden is more frank, even about Suez, than has often been supposed, he has a habit of glossing the documents on which he relies in a way which makes a better case for himself than the originals will sustain, and it is likely therefore that historians will rate Macmillan's account of his prime-ministership, for all its omissions, as the more reliable of the two. His volumes are not at all revealing of personality, despite reviewers' claims to the contrary, but they do provide an excellent picture of the man as he appeared to political contemporaries – urbane, courteous, warm, relaxed, witty, always shrewd and frequently wise, delighting in historical context and analogy. The more private figure, with his doubts and perplexities and his occasional steely ruthlessness, does not appear, and it would be hard to guess that behind the studied irony and occasional cynicism could be found a man of deep spiritual conviction. His humanity and compassion too often spilled over into sentimentality, but they were genuine enough, and the memoirs provide good clues as to their roots. But in general they offer less help than one might have supposed to the biographer as he struggles to pin down on paper the elusive secrets of a highly complex personality.

The sheer bulk and range of the Prime Ministers' files in the Public Record Office suggest the extensive role that the Prime Minister must play in modern government. That necessarily gives him (or her) scope to exercise considerable influence, and potential is transformed into reality when he shows himself eager to know what is going on, takes care to be well informed and accessible, and offers good advice. It might be thought that colleagues would resent this, but in practice they acknowledge that he is the one person in government with a synoptic overview of the whole of its work and the ability not only to make it cohere but to make it conform to some longer-term goal. He is the government's principal, some would say only, political strategist. Macmillan was better fitted than Eden for this task, since his experience in office had been far more diverse – hence Eden's wish, in December 1955, to appoint Butler to a senior non-departmental post on the home front, from which he could lend the government's domestic policies some sense of direction.[35] Macmillan, in general more ready to delegate than his predecessor, clearly thought that this task was pre-eminently the Prime Minister's own, and under his chairmanship the steering committee of senior ministers created to prepare the manifesto for the next general election tended to take on a wider role. Macmillan was said also to be working towards a situation where the Cabinet, meeting twice weekly, would devote one of those sessions to more wide-ranging and forward-looking discussion; it was partly the inevitable failure to unclog the Cabinet's agenda of day-to-day problems that led him to use the steering committee for this.

The relationship between the Prime Minister and his Cabinet colleagues is symbiotic and necessarily so. Just as the other members of

Cabinet defer to the Prime Minister because he performs the vital task of setting and maintaining a political strategy, so too he needs strong and successful ministers to manage the component parts of that strategy. There is a limit to the amount any Prime Minister can do, and he is always subject to the constraints of time. Concentration of his efforts in any one field inevitably means that he can devote less time to other areas, and a wise Prime Minister always holds time and energy in reserve to deal with an unexpected crisis. With the growing trend for the Prime Minister to be involved in high-level diplomacy, a trend which neither Eden nor Macmillan was at all anxious to resist, it became increasingly less likely that he would be able to maintain effective oversight of all the work of government, and it is no accident that Macmillan devotes only four of the seventeen chapters of *Riding the Storm*, which deals with the years 1957–9, to domestic affairs. Even these four chapters concentrate on the course of the economy. To take a specific example, it would be hard to guess from Macmillan's memoirs that education formed any part of the government's responsibilities. While Eden clearly took some interest in the proposals for advancing technological education fostered by the Minister, David Eccles, and fathered by a senior official at the Ministry, Antony Part, and treated them publicly as a major theme, Macmillan was content to leave the department to get on with its job, even to the extent of transferring Lord Hailsham, after only eight months in the role of Minister of Education, to the job of party chairman. Nevertheless, while it is clear that Eden was the more active, harrying his ministers with frequent telephone calls, Macmillan was the better placed to influence ministers, partly indeed because he did not nag them, but more because of his wider range of experience in office. Henry Brooke found Macmillan, as a former Minister of Housing, particularly helpful on that subject and related matters, while Macmillan's experience at the Ministry of Defence led directly to his decision to strengthen it at the expense of the service departments in January 1957, and again in the summer of 1958. It was a combination of that experience with insights gained at the Treasury that led him to give Duncan Sandys his full backing as he reshaped Britain's defence policy in 1957 along predominantly nuclear lines.

The appointment of Sandys in place of Anthony Head as Minister of Defence in January 1957 reminds us that a Prime Minister can often have most influence on the development of policy by appointing a particular person to a particular job. The extent to which Eden was consulted about Churchill's reshuffled Cabinet of October 1954 is not clear, but at least one of his colleagues believes that he inherited his Cabinet and did little to make it his own.[36] His most curious appointment on taking office was of Macmillan as Foreign Secretary. The two men did not much like one another, and it was not long before Eden was talking of transferring him to the Treasury. When the occasion arose, Eden made no attempt to use the switch to achieve any major restructuring of his Cabinet. In the course of two reshuffles in 1955, Patrick Buchan-Hepburn, Lord Home, Selwyn Lloyd, Iain Macleod and Lord Selkirk joined the Cabinet for the first time, and Harry Crookshank, Osbert Peake, Philip Swinton and Lord Woolton left. Selkirk was apparently promoted because Salisbury threatened resignation unless more peers were included,[37] and Macleod's promotion to the Ministry of Labour is the only one where Eden conceivably had a policy end in view. Monckton had wanted his loyal lieutenant, Watkinson, to succeed him in the post.[38]

Macmillan is often said to have been more ruthless, but initially he dropped only four of Eden's Cabinet – one of them, Lord Selkirk, being given the non-Cabinet position of First Lord of the Admiralty. There were six new members, three of whom had run departments before, but outside the Cabinet. Before the 1959 election there were three further additions, one of them the result of Thorneycroft's resignation; he was replaced at the Treasury by Derick Heathcoat Amory. There was one other resignation, that of Salisbury in March 1957. Only in the decision to drop Head, with whom he had been arguing as Chancellor about the size of Britain's armed forces and the need for conscription, was Macmillan trying directly to shape policy, although he may have recognized that Brooke's appointment to the Ministry of Housing would lead to some modification of the Rent Act as far as London was concerned. Indeed it has been said that Macmillan cared little about a man's views when appointing him – hence the choice of Amory to replace Thorneycroft.[39] Few at the Cabinet table owed their place there entirely to Macmillan. But for the resignations of Salisbury and Thorneycroft, in October 1951 there would have been four survivors from Churchill's elderly and somewhat idiosyncratic Cabinet of 1951 and eight from his last Cabinet, Macmillan excluded. The Prime Minister had therefore to deal with a body of ministers which included men of considerable experience, seniority and standing, some of them his former rivals for the leadership and a number of them potential successors. Of the eighteen men sitting around the Cabinet table at the end of his first ministry, half had been Macmillan's colleagues in previous

Cabinets and two only, Brooke and Lord Mills, had not headed a department before Macmillan become Prime Minister.

A Prime Minister's standing and hence his influence with his colleagues depends only in part on his personality; it depends also on whether they perceive his judgement to be good and his policies successful. A Prime Minister who transforms the latent power in the office into the successful exercise of power will grow in stature and that in turn will further reinforce his ability to wield power with his colleagues. His standing with the public is also crucial. Eden early attracted a reputation for indecisiveness, largely but not solely because he did not reshuffle his Cabinet in summer 1955 when both press and politicians expected him to do so. His changes of mind over the early recall of Parliament to deal with the economic measures eventually embodied in Butler's autumn Budget confirmed this impression for many at the centre of government, while the mishandling of a number of decisions unimportant in themselves led to grumbling on the back-benches and a *Daily Telegraph*-inspired press campaign calling for the 'smack of firm government'.[40] Eden's response was an ill-judged denial that he was intending resignation and an intemperate attack on the papers – which did little to help him. The official records lend some, but not a great deal of, support to the picture of a temporizing Prime Minister. There were long-drawn-out Cabinet discussions when Eden was at odds with his Chancellors, but that is not altogether surprising, particularly when the Chancellor was threatening resignation as Macmillan clearly was in February 1956. Macmillan proved tougher in similar circumstances in 1958, but more was at stake, and he was at least as careful as Eden in his efforts to carry his colleagues with him, as the series of Cabinet meetings on 3 and 5 January 1958 show.[41] It is even more unfair to see Eden's decision to refer the vexed question of West Indian immigration to a Cabinet committee in November 1955 as evidence of indecision.[42] The Cabinet was clearly divided, with the Colonial Secretary, Alan Lennox Boyd, vehemently against a ban; Salisbury, who feared for the English race and culture, equally emphatically for; while Home from his vantage point at the Commonwealth Relations Office emphasized the dilemma they were in: they would have to legislate on a non-discriminatory basis and yet no one in Britain would want to keep citizens of the old Commonwealth out. In the circumstances the Cabinet Secretary advised caution and Eden can hardly be blamed for taking that advice. There were evident dangers if immigration continued unrestrained – as Duncan Sandys emphasized for the

Ministry of Housing, social disturbances might result from the pressure on housing in Birmingham and Lambeth; but there were advantages also, in the augmentation of scarce labour resources, and it was clearly right to thrash out the balance of argument in committee. Eden himself wished for a temporary ban, but the committee, when it reported the following June, was in favour of taking no immediate action. Salisbury vigorously dissented, and it was evident that the matter would have to be kept under review.[43] The government however, decided to bide its time, and this was to be a major factor in Salisbury's resignation in March 1957.[44] The riots which Sandys had feared came in summer 1958 at Nottingham and Notting Hill, but the government continued to resist the pressures on it to act. It may well have been encouraged in this by the abysmal failure of Sir Oswald Mosley's efforts to exploit the issue, but as Pat Hornsby-Smith, then a junior minister at the Home Office, subsequently recalled, the fact that Britain was then engaged in the effort to bring the African colonies through to independence was far more significant. Lennox Boyd's own sympathies were deeply engaged, and, in the absence of great party and public pressure, it is not hard to see why in 1955 and 1956 Eden gave no strong lead on the subject.

His style in general was to take the lead wherever possible. He was, colleagues testify, a good chairman of Cabinet, much more businesslike than Churchill, and he would, when clear in his own view, make perfectly plain what it was, often leading the discussion. He was not over-fond of opposition. But there were whole areas of business where he had to be content to act as chairman because he simply did not know enough to take a particular line. One at least of his younger colleagues never thought that he had any real grip, and others felt him to be very unsure of himself. They thought this was the reason for his occasional displays of indecision, and the odd flashes of obstinacy, which could have been taken as a sign of strength, were not so interpreted in Eden's case.[45] Kilmuir observed that 'no one in public life lived more on his nerves' and added that there were 'indications that his health was not as good as we had hoped, and he seemed strained and taut in these months'.[46] By the following July the political world was 'full of Eden's moods at No. 10'.[47] Even those who thought that things had gone well in the first few months of his prime-ministership realized the difficulties that his temperament could cause, and his ministers, almost without exception, recall that he was never off the phone. He would worry them about matters which were not yet ready for submission or which were not of sufficient importance for the minister concerned to think it worth taking the Prime Minister's time, and he would question them about niggling details. They felt that he was trying to interfere even when it was patently clear that he did not know enough to do so. Boyd Carpenter, for instance, recalled that he would insist 'on having submitted to him proposed appointments to the boards of nationalised industries. As he knew nothing of the men or the requirements of the jobs, and anyhow hadn't the time to deal with them, the only effect was that they were then held up in his office for embarrassingly long periods.'[48] Nutting was inclined to blame this behaviour on the loneliness of No. 10 and thought that Eden compensated for this by 'continually intervening in the work of his ministers, especially those at the Foreign Office, even to the point of sometimes countermanding decisions which, although they conformed to established policy, had not been specifically referred to him for approval'.[49]

Those close to Eden did not know which they resented more – the sudden and brutal displays of foul temper or the apologies which followed, often within minutes or at the latest the next morning, which have been well characterized as oleaginous. But they noticed too that, while they were always dealing with a prima donna, he never lost his temper over the big questions. In the run-up to the final decision to go ahead with the Suez operation he was amazingly calm, and he allowed his temperament to get the better of him only once, when it seemed that the Cabinet on 4 November was in danger of fragmenting on the question of whether or not to land troops, since they had heard that the Israelis had agreed to a cease-fire.[50]

Although Eden sought to save his Cabinet some of the stress of business by following Baldwin's habit of frequent private consultation with his principal colleagues, and took a high view of the part a Prime Minister has to play in government, there is little evidence that he bypassed the Cabinet on anything that really mattered. The extent to which it was involved in the Suez decisions has been much questioned, but the official records show that, from the initial decision on 27 July that every effort should be made to restore effective international control over the canal – if necessary by the threat and, in the last resort, the use of force – to the final decision on 6 November to accept a cease-fire, the Cabinet was involved in all the key decisions. It was, for example, the Cabinet that took the decision on 11 September to try out the scheme for a Suez Canal Users' Association rather than follow Nasser's rejection of the Eighteen Power proposals with an immediate reference to the UN Security Council, and, while it is true that the Prime Minister and

Foreign Secretary were responsible for the precise timing of the eventual appeal to the Security Council on 23 September, there can be no question but that they were acting in pursuance of an earlier Cabinet decision. The only important exceptions concern the possibility of collaboration with Israel; and it is clear that even here, although they may not have known the full story of Eden's decision to go along with Franco-Israeli collusion, the rest of the Cabinet were told enough to know that their discussions of a possible Israeli break-out against the Egyptians were far from hypothetical and that the British government had an insight into Israeli intentions which had come directly from the Israelis themselves.[51] Nor was this knowledge confined to ministers. In a significant phrase on 2 November Sir Richard Powell told his fellow permanent secretaries on the Defence (Transitional Arrangements) Committee that the French should be asked in their publicity to avoid any material 'which might be construed as confirming the accusation' of collusion.[52]

What was kept from ministers was the precise nature of the arrangement with the Israelis. When the Cabinet discussed the situation on 24 October, ministers were told that the military operations which had been planned could not be held in readiness for many days longer; that, if such an operation were launched, Israel would undoubtedly mount a full-scale attack on Egypt; and that Britain would 'never have a better pretext for intervention against [Nasser] than we had now as a result of his seizure of the Suez Canal'.[53] At the decisive meeting on the following day, in the light of further talks with the French, ministers were told that the Israelis were advancing their attack, that the French wanted to intervene to limit hostilities, and that they would take military action alone or with the Israelis if Britain declined to do so. Eden then sketched the scenario which was actually set in train on 30 October, and added that they 'must face the risk that we should be accused of collusion with Israel'. His argument was that the accusation was inevitable, since the Israelis would launch a parallel attack in any case, and it was better for Britain that it should be seen to be holding a balance between Israel and Egypt rather than appear to be accepting Israeli co-operation in an attack on Egypt alone.[54] This statement was both disingenuous and over-optimistic, and there were evidently some Cabinet ministers clear-sighted enough to voice their doubts at the time. But no one resigned, and it can scarcely be claimed that ministers had not been given sufficient clues to what was really happening. The decision to intervene, therefore, was quite clearly a decision taken by the full Cabinet, and after very full debate. The actual decision to land troops in face of UN pressure for a cease-fire was also the subject of a full, and at times agonizing, debate in Cabinet on 4 November, and it is difficult to see how the charges that have sometimes been voiced against Eden – in effect, that he took his Cabinet for a ride – can now be sustained.

Although the detailed management of the crisis was in the hands of the Egypt Committee, particularly during the parliamentary recess, to some extent its role has been misconstrued. The major political and diplomatic decisions were not withdrawn into this committee, as the leading student of Cabinet government, Professor John Mackintosh, supposed, but it did provide Eden with the means for considering the military plans in great secrecy. When this was questioned by Duncan Sandys, Eden convincingly argued the need to keep these matters in the hands of a small group.[55] This is in marked contrast to his handling of those ministers who evidently felt that the military planning was carrying the Cabinet towards war without sufficient consideration of the political context, both international and domestic, within which it would have to be waged. Given the Cabinet's initial decision that force might have to be used in the last resort, it is relatively easy to understand why Eden should have underestimated the extent of the doubts and worries felt by those of his colleagues not on the Committee; like Butler, they were by no means against the use of force but were anxious that it should be seen and clearly understood that Britain had gone to the limit in seeking a solution by other means. Home took steps to alert the Prime Minister about Butler's position on 22 August,[56] but it was an angry outburst from Monckton, the Minister of Defence, at the Egypt Committee on the morning of 24 August that brought matters to a head. He had evidently been provoked 'by H[arold] M[acmillan]'s speaking as though we were deciding there and then on the date of the operation', the Secretary of the Cabinet wrote; 'And, as Lord S[alisbury] said later, reference to the Security Council would be seen to be a hollow sham if we had already started. ...' Brook's estimate of the position was characteristically shrewd: while reference to the United Nations would contain most of the doubts, there might still be a few who would want Nasser to be seen to provoke military action; hence the attraction for them of Eden's idea that there should be a concerted plan to deny Egypt the canal dues, which would bring matters to a head. Brook's advice to Eden was that he should not put his colleagues 'at the final fence too soon',[57] but it was evidently Eden's own decision to have a full rehearsal of the broad arguments in Cabinet on 28 August. Skilfully working on the proposal of a reference to the Security Council, possibly leading to a Soviet veto, before military measures were used, he succeeded in rebuilding a broad consensus on the probable need for force, winning over an obviously reluctant Monckton and apparently satisfying Butler.[58]

The Egypt Committee itself did not meet between 17 October and 2 November, but there were meetings of senior ministers at Chequers on 21 October, when it was agreed that the Foreign Secretary should talk with the French and Israeli leaders at Sèvres; and again on 23 October, when Lloyd reported on his talks. Brook was certainly present at the first of these meetings, but no record of either has yet come to light.[59] Those present included Butler, Macmillan and Head, who had replaced Monckton as Minister of Defence. It was the same body of ministers which received from Sir Patrick Dean later on 24 October news of the agreement reached with the Israelis about the Anglo-French response to their assault on Egypt, the scenario which was to give the British government the pretext it needed to act. It is surely significant that these were the only meetings to discuss the actual process of collusion, and there are no others of which we know that have not found their way into the public record. By the time the next crucial decisions had to be taken, the Egypt Committee was again meeting and it could be used by Eden if he wanted to prepare for a Cabinet meeting.

Eden took the chair at most of the Egypt Committee meetings, but it was by no means usual for him to chair Cabinet committees. He took the Defence Committee himself, and he also spearheaded the defence review in summer 1956 which led directly to the seminal Defence White Paper of April 1957.[60] In addition he chaired an *ad hoc* committee on the vexed question of the supply of military aircraft. Cyprus was another issue with which he was directly concerned: one of his first actions as Prime Minister was 'to ask Lord Salisbury, Mr Macmillan and Mr Lennox Boyd to work out with me the most promising means of establishing self-government',[6] and he also chaired the *ad hoc* Cabinet committee on security in Cyprus. A third area which aroused his concern was East–West relations, and he took charge of the committee to prepare the follow-up to the successful summit conference at Geneva in summer 1956. The Economic Policy Committee he left to the Chancellor, and, like his successor, he tended to use Butler and Kilmuir as Cabinet committee chairmen.[62]

Macmillan provided, for the most part, a marked contrast in style. In a much-quoted passage Kilmuir wrote of the new feel to the government after Macmillan's succession: 'Eden's chronic restlessness, which had sensibly affected all his colleagues, was replaced by a central calmness which provided a wonderful contrast with 1955–6.'[63] It is a picture confirmed by all those in and around Downing Street, and it was quite clearly an impression which Macmillan wished to convey. 'At one of his first Cabinets,' Watkinson recalls, 'when the problems loomed perhaps overlarge in all our minds, each member of the Cabinet found in front of him on entering the Cabinet room a small packet of tranquillisers. The point was well made and needed no further emphasis. . . .'[64] Macmillan was far from unflappable, as Selwyn Lloyd recalled when interviewed in July 1970, but he knew how to delegate, genuinely believed that 'Quiet calm deliberation disentangles every knot', and had 'this tremendous power of relaxation'.[65] He did not allow himself to brood over problems. 'What's done is done' is a phrase which catches his attitude perfectly, and, if the outcome was a fresh set of problems, he did not repine, but set himself to pick up the pieces.

Unlike Eden, he was not for ever on the telephone, and, while he was always accessible, he did not often send for a minister, preferring to let his colleagues get on with their jobs. But he took good care to know what was going on, relying on the operation of the private-secretary network and the mechanisms of the Cabinet Office. He was, so a senior civil servant recalled, 'always prepared to come in and back up a minister', and was 'very much in control'. If he wanted an explanation, he might invite the permanent secretary to see him or hold a small meeting, but he seems to have been more interested in the broad sweep of policy than in departmental detail. There is some disagreement about his readiness to interfere, John Wyndham recalling that 'because of his seniority both in years and experience, and because, despite that gentleness of manner, he was capable of being ruthless – as were his small staff – [he] managed to interfere time and time again with Ministries over the heads of various Ministers'.[66] The temptation and the tendency may have grown with the years, but to those in the departments it seemed that he did not attempt to interfere unless there was some special reason.

Experienced members of his private office have identified the difficulties which a Prime Minister faces if he tries radically to affect policy through the operations of his private office. He can float an idea or ask pointed questions, but for the most part this has to be 'touch on the tiller stuff'. There may be departmental suspicion, as there undoubtedly was about some of Macmillan's minutes on economic policy, that a private secretary is prompting the Prime Minister with pet ideas of his own; and at best such a method of working leads to 'considerable argey-bargey' and does not make it easy to carry the departments concerned. On the basis of his interviews with Amory, and with the government's Economic Adviser and other senior Treasury officials, Brittan concluded that the latter 'were never quite sure how seriously to take some of the more unorthodox ideas Macmillan expressed in memoranda or over a drink in the evening. They usually found that he was satisfied with a well reasoned brief . . . explaining why his heresies would not work.'[67] Almost certainly, the Conservative Chancellor who told the political scientist A. H. Brown that 'he received about a suggestion a week from the Prime Minister' was speaking about this period. The Treasury found objections to most of them and accepted perhaps half a dozen in the course of a year.[68] Macmillan records his pressure on Amory in February 1958 to have plans ready for major and minor works in case they were needed to reflate the economy, and his subsequent bombardment of the Treasury with arguments about the inadequate liquidity of the free world. He insisted that new ideas, including the possibility of floating the pound, should be widely discussed within the Treasury and with leading bankers.[69] But it is clear that at the time none of these ideas got very far, and it is not surprising to find that his office thought that the Prime Minister had better vehicles for getting his ideas across: in ascending order of importance there were party mechanisms – usually something of a 'sleeping dog', although we have already noted the importance of the steering committee created to prepare the manifesto for the next election; the House of Commons, where the Prime Minister could pre-empt argument and shift the line; and, above all, the mechanisms of Cabinet government.[70] Those who knew the machine well thought that their chief had to operate through the Cabinet and its committees, and that Macmillan was particularly skilful in the way he did so. From the start of his prime-ministership, as one of those politicians closest to him noted, he made systematic use of the committee system to filter business and to prepare it for speedy decision. He estimated that something like 80–90 per cent of it was handled in this way, and that, while use was made of *ad hoc* committees, Macmillan's stress was on the use of standing committees. This ties in well with Kilmuir's observation that another key feature of his approach was his emphasis that 'all important issues would be dealt with by the Cabinet, to remove the very real possibility that some unconsidered independent action by a junior Minister might damage the Government as a whole'.[71] Study of the memoirs confirms that this was the case. Macmillan chaired few committees himself, Defence being the main exception, although Brook recalled that 'he occasionally took the Economic Policy Committee on important occasions'. He would, however, read what had been said in committee and 'would often ask say Rab or Kilmuir to bring a matter to Cabinet'.[72] Macmillan regarded Butler as the best chairman of a committee that he had ever seen, better than himself, and that was no mean tribute from a man whom his ministers universally regarded as 'very adept at leading them and in all the arts of chairmanship'. His domination of the Cabinet was complete but not obtrusive. 'Harold is a very good Prime Minister as far as taking the Cabinet goes', Sampson was told; 'he takes it slowly, lets everyone have his say. . . .'[73] Quick to take in the essentials of a problem himself, he knew better than to rush his colleagues. In fact he liked to let them talk, so long as their discussion was to the point and not too technical. There were few *ex cathedra* pronouncements, nor did he practice 'any of the arts of repression which skilful chairman are tempted to cultivate'.[74] Nevertheless, thanks to Brook's excellent briefing, he could make a good guess at the distribution of views in the Cabinet, would know whom to call and how to steer the discussion. It is worth noting in passing that he never sought to disguise that fact that he had a brief in front of him. If there was criticism it was because he 'liked to talk, sometimes talked too much, but then', as Hare added, 'his conversation was so much better than anyone else's'. 'He could be maddeningly discursive', Macleod recalled; 'it was nothing to reach a decision on rating via the Greek wars and Parnell'. But he had a wide variety of styles. Just when his colleagues were wondering why he was edging them towards a position which could have been achieved by more direct methods, at least in their eyes, he would become 'quick, decisive and wise'. If he found himself in a minority, he gave in with a good grace, as Hill remembered, but in practice he was very rarely overruled. Edward Boyle could recall an outburst on the Japanese trade treaty, for which he felt no love. In general, however, he did not like to disclose his hand too early, and he could therefore cover his tracks, thus safeguarding his authority, if a contrary view seemed likely to prevail. If he really thought it mattered and the discussion looked like going the wrong way, he could and did adjourn the discussion, and he would make good use of the interval between Cabinets to persuade some of his more senior colleagues to see the issue as he did. There were even occasions when he, normally so lucid, summed up in a peculiarly fuzzy way. 'Government by mumble' was a phrase used by colleagues at such moments, and they knew that they would read in minutes precisely the conclusion that Macmillan had wanted them to reach. There was little resentment, and it is obvious that he excelled at keeping his Cabinet together and happy. His colleagues recollect his delight in ironic teases and his impish wit. There is not one who did not say that he made business fun. And at the end of a discussion he was very skilful at drawing together the points of difference and those on which there was general agreement. This was where Macmillan was at his very best. His summings-up were masterly, and it was the sheer 'superiority of mind and judgement' revealed in them which lay at the heart of his dominance.[75]

If anything, he was even better with small groups, and it was these that he used when he wanted to get a real grip on an issue. The press noted that early in 1957 he had summoned to Chequers a group, which it dubbed the 'inner Cabinet', to discuss the economic situation, defence and the American offer of Thor missiles. Those present were Butler, Sandys, Selwyn Lloyd, Salisbury, Thorneycroft and the Chief Whip, Edward Heath.[76] There were several such sessions, some noted by the press and others which escaped their notice, and in his memoirs Macmillan occasionally notes discussions with senior ministers or with his 'principal colleagues'.[77] When the news of the overthrow of the Iraqi government reached London, Macmillan prefaced the meeting of the full Cabinet with a meeting of ministers. Those attending were the Leaders of the Commons and the Lords (Butler and Home respectively), the Foreign Secretary, the Chancellor, the Defence Minister and the Colonial Secretary.[78] Similar meetings took place on other occasions – for example, when Macmillan was trying to avert a possible rail strike in April–May 1958. There was no one group of ministers to whom he turned automatically whatever the subject, and he had few, if any, intimates within the Cabinet. He liked to find time to talk things over with Lord Mills, and he felt it necessary to clear most things with Butler, whom he also asked to deputize for him when he was away. Butler was drawn into many of the meetings which Macmillan had with other ministers. In February 1958, for example, when Macmillan was concerned about the possibility of an American recession, he set up a meeting with the Chancellor and his advisers at which Butler was also present. He was there again on 14 March when Macmillan had Amory to supper to discuss the state of the economy, and he was one of the three ministers with whom, during the brief dinner break between sessions of Cabinet on the evening of Sunday 5 January 1958, Macmillan discussed the way in which he should react to Thorneycroft's threatened resignation.[79] The others were Macleod and Heath. He was evidently very close to the latter in this period, and there were ministers prepared to say that he was 'probably the most influential man around the Prime Minister today. The PM consults him about practically everything. . . .'[80] Butler, if less close, probably carried more weight, and in Cabinet, where domestic issues were concerned, Macmillan would turn to him last of all for some final words of advice. 'If they were delphic in formation, they were none the less profound', he recalled.[81]

It is much easier at this juncture to assess Eden and Macmillan's methods of working than it is to assess the end result, the contribution which they made as Prime Minister to the government's record. In Eden's case the judgement inevitably has to be made largely in terms of foreign affairs. But it should be recalled that he played an active and emollient part in resolving the industrial disputes which troubled the country in the closing stages of the 1955 general election, and in particular the railway strike, which led him to declare a state of national emergency on 31 May. As a result of these strikes, the Cabinet discussed the possibility of legislation to improve arbitration and impose cooling-off periods, but Eden was in agreement with the Ministry of Labour in opposing such action. The problem was one of unofficial disputes, and Eden felt that it could not be resolved by legislation. Much would be lost in terms of goodwill between the government and the TUC, whose co-operation Eden believed to be essential if the country were to deal successfully with wage inflation. He therefore sought instead, and achieved, an informal understanding that the trade unions themselves would in effect operate cooling-off periods where practicable. Nor would Monckton have anything to do with a rather more attractive suggestion urged on Eden by the industrial magnate Lord Nuffield, that there should be secret ballots before strikes and in union elections.[82] In retrospect that seems a major mistake.

Instead the government embarked upon the drafting and redrafting of a White Paper on the implications of full employment. It finally appeared in March 1956 and can be seen to be an attempt to restate the implicit bargain between the government and both sides of industry which was needed if the pursuit of full employment was to be continued. In one of his last actions as Minister of Labour, Monckton had urged Eden in September 1955 to use his personal authority to bring the two sides of industry together in search of a voluntary policy of restraint,[83] but when this was attempted, in July 1956, the trade unions would have none of it. The employers were nagged into price restraint, but to no avail. In

September 1956 the TUC decisively rejected wage restraint. The government had decided earlier in the year against the inclusion in their monopolies and restrictive practices legislation of any shop-floor practices. There was growing criticism within the Conservative party of the government's approach, and some evidence that a younger generation would be ready to tackle the problem along lines first set out in a pamphlet drafted by a number of Conservative lawyers (Geoffrey Howe being one) in 1958.[84] At the 1956 Conservative Conference, Macleod mounted a vigorous defence of his Ministry, and he continued to foster the idea of a responsible and moderate trade union leadership. The government, he observed, was at war not with the trade unions but with inflation. The change of Prime Minister in January 1957 had made no difference to the government's preference for voluntary co-operation: although it sought a sterner approach to pay bargaining from employers, it would have nothing to do with a wage freeze or any formal incomes policy. Efforts by the Treasury to raise the issue of a guiding light, perhaps proclaimed by some body with independent authority, resulted only in the creation of an instrument for more general moral suasion, the Council for Prices, Productivity and Incomes, in August 1957. Its impact was distinctly limited. Towards the end of his time at the Ministry of Labour, Macleod became increasingly concerned with the problem of obsolete labour practices, but the possibility of a royal commission on the trade unions, which he would have favoured as the way forward, was set on one side until after the 1959 general election, and, when the time came for a decision, Macleod's successor, John Hare, proved no more eager to grasp the nettle.[85]

Eden's concern to keep the unions sweet is revealed quite clearly in his minutes to Butler and Macmillan,[86] and was at the heart of his disputes with both men about the abolition of the bread subsidy. He was able to prevent Butler from acting in October 1955, but, when faced with Macmillan's threat to resign in the following February, he had to give way. Nevertheless, Macmillan did not go his own way entirely. It looks as if Eden's evident unhappiness about Butler's use of purchase tax to soak up consumer demand made its mark, and he may well have been behind the decision, which Macmillan later came to regret, to suspend investment allowances. The two men were in any case of one mind about the desirability of drawing off demand into savings, and the result has become part of the national scene, Premium Bonds, which were introduced in the 1956 Budget. Eden's instincts in this matter were sound, and such a close observer as the then Economic Secretary, Edward

Boyle, thought that this was generally the case, but that Eden was handicapped in pushing his views by his obvious economic illiteracy. In this respect Macmillan was far better placed, and there were civil servants who thought that his understanding of really major economic issues was better than that of most of his Treasury advisers. By temperament he was an expansionist. He preferred always to keep demand high and to control the situation in other ways. He flirted with the idea of floating the pound, and clearly resented the straitjacket which sterling's international role placed on the British economy. At home he would have liked to bring inflation under control by increasing production, while on the international front he was a staunch advocate of the need to find a way of generating greater international liquidity. But he was chary about imposing ideas on his Chancellors that he had not pursued himself while at the Treasury, and his efforts were concentrated on the need to avoid increased unemployment, particularly if he thought it was being used consciously to moderate wage claims. Had Thorneycroft not resigned in January 1958 over the level of public expenditure, he would almost certainly have faced a clash with Macmillan over his new-found emphasis on the money supply. Heathcoat Amory found himself under considerable pressure to reflate in autumn 1958, and was urged to slash income tax in 1959. It would be a mistake, however, to characterize Macmillan as an inflationist in this period. When Chancellor he had accepted the need to deflate the economy, and he gave Thorneycroft his support when strong measures were required to protect sterling in September 1957. The 1959 Budget has been much criticized, although more for its timing than its content, but, if there were mistakes in economic policy formulation in 1959, they are more likely to be found in the increases in public expenditure approved later in the year. The major problem, however, was arguably the tendency to underestimate at this time the self-reinforcing qualities of a boom, more particularly when fed by business euphoria over the Conservatives' third successive election victory. In any case, it should be added that the next government rode out the balance-of-payments problems of 1960, albeit almost by inadvertence, and then took action the following year against a boom which had by then already run its course. Had it not done so, economic commentators might well have written a rather different verdict on the success of Amory's chancellorship.

In foreign affairs the Austrian peace treaty and the apparent success of the Geneva summit gave a golden glow to Eden's first months in office, and Macmillan's trip to Moscow in spring 1959, which eased the tension over Berlin had helped pave the way to a further exercise in summitry, brought the period to an end on a similarly successful note of detente. It had been a bumpy ride none the less. The spirit of Geneva had rapidly evaporated in the aridities of the foreign ministers' conference in October–November 1955, and, if Eden had ever nursed any genuine hopes of achieving his declared goal of coupling special security arrangements for the Soviet Union with the reunification of Germany, they cannot have survived those discussions. More realistic were his plans for the creation of a demilitarized zone in Central Europe, although they were strongly opposed by SHAPE and found no favour with the West German government. They were to be revived in a different form by the Polish Foreign Minister in 1958, proved attractive to the Labour Opposition, and formed part of Macmillan's agenda in Moscow in 1959. Disarmament was another field in which Eden had hoped to make progress, and his long experience in the field is reflected in the proposals for arms limitation and inspection in specified areas on which he could hope to build once trust had been established. By the time that Macmillan took up the task of negotiation, hopes for general disarmament had faded and negotiations centred on the possibility of banning nuclear tests. In terms of domestic politics, with concern growing about the effects of fall-out, he needed to find a positive answer to the challenge posed by the Campaign for Nuclear Disarmament, the more so since the Soviet Union had stolen a propaganda march in spring 1958 by unilaterally suspending all nuclear tests. Initially Britain's approach was handicapped by its need to test its own hydrogen bomb, but its success in 1957 in so doing, when coupled with American nervousness about the launching of the first Soviet sputnik, enabled Macmillan to achieve that close nuclear collaboration with the United States which had been denied Britain since 1945. In its turn the agreement with the United States, to which Congress assented in summer 1958, allowed Macmillan to separate the question of nuclear testing from a more general disarmament agreement, and to pursue it whatever the doubts in Washington. However, J. P. G. Freeman's *Britain's Nuclear Arms Control Policy*[87] tends to emphasize Britain's role in pressing for the test-ban conference in autumn 1958 by misrepresenting the position taken by Eisenhower and US Secretary of State John Foster Dulles, although the author is right to suggest that they were vulnerable to the pressures within the United States against an agreement. Perhaps with good reason, most American experts had come to doubt whether underground tests could be detected. Macmillan sought a compromise, and when he visited Moscow in February 1959 he put forward proposals that later became the basis for a Soviet offer. He had informed the President, but had not consulted him, about this initiative. The British delegate to the test-ban conference, Sir Michael Wright, believed that it was Britain's efforts which kept the allies at the conference table, a view with which David Ormsby Gore, then the minister responsible, concurred; Wright pays particular tribute to Macmillan's efforts in spring 1959.[88] Lloyd claimed some of the credit for the idea of the partial test-ban treaty, and on the evidence available it does appear to be an idea developed by Britain. There is also clear evidence that it was the British government which took the lead in August 1959 in announcing that there would be no resumption of tests while the talks continued. But Macmillan's suggestion that a summit might carry the idea forward did not at first meet with Eisenhower's approval, and eventual agreement on it was not reached until late in Macmillan's second period in office.

Macmillan had first suggested a further summit in spring 1958, less than eighteen months after the Soviet invasion of Hungary, and thereafter he pursued the proposal with a mixture of genuine visionary enthusiasm and a keen sense of its electoral possibilities. When Khrushchev took the offensive in the Cold War by threatening the *status quo* in Berlin, with a six-month deadline attached to his ultimatum, Macmillan revived the idea of a personal mission to Moscow and he persisted in this intention despite the evident doubts of his allies. They feared another exercise in appeasement. It is difficult now to recall the war atmosphere which affected the United States in particular, and the hostility with which the Bonn government regarded any attempt at *Ostpolitik*. While Eisenhower's part in controlling the West's response was important, Macmillan's part in defusing the Berlin crisis should not be underestimated. But he had a more far-reaching aim, the creation of a regular series of summits, almost a standing conference of the great powers. Eisenhower was reluctant to commit himself to any meeting of heads of government unless it was prefaced by a successful meeting of foreign ministers, and he reacted angrily when Macmillan, frustrated by the lack of progress made when the foreign ministers met in May 1959, suggested an 'informal' summit.[89] When Eisenhower visited London at the end of August, the two men were still good-naturedly at odds, voicing their differences about summitry in a quite unique duologue on television. To Macmillan's delight, however, Eisenhower had already agreed to a Soviet proposal that Khrushchev should visit the United States in September, and after the success of that visit Eisenhower seemed to warm to the whole idea of a heads-of-government meeting. Macmillan duly reaped the benefit in the general election that October.

His enthusiasm for detente, while real, was fuelled also perhaps by his realization that, in a world dominated by the balance of terror, nuclear weapons could be used to deter but were not a practicable weapon of war. Britain's own defence had been committed to the deterrent quite explicitly by the Defence White Paper of 1957, and the government had put an end to conscription. Britain still had considerable commitments overseas, and its ability to meet them by the deployment of highly mobile professional forces was the subject of considerable debate. Nor was it easy to see how NATO could live with the imbalance of conventional forces in Europe unless the deterrent was conceived as a first-strike weapon. So far as public opinion was concerned, that might well seem an unacceptably high-risk strategy in a tense international climate, but, if Macmillan could demonstrate that the balance of terror had actually led to the possibility of detente and, better still, that Britain's own possession of the bomb had allowed it to mediate between the super-powers, there would be far less public pressure on the government for a change of strategy. The reduction of tension might lead also to the possibility of disarmament, and could not but reduce the strain on the armed forces.

The extent to which this could inhibit Britain's ability to act fast and effectively had been well demonstrated at the outset of the Suez crisis, when Eden asked the Chiefs of Staff on the evening of 26 July what they would recommend by way of a forceful and immediate response. They told him 'that although Britain could deal with Cyprus or Mau Mau or with atomic war, it could not deal militarily with a little local episode in the eastern Mediterranean', William Clark recalled.[90] Their inability to act immediately almost certainly doomed the whole operation to ultimate failure, but, even if Eden had seen this at the time, it would have been an impossible task to convince the Commons.

The Suez expedition brought Eden's Middle Eastern policy to an unsuccessful end, but it is difficult to see that he had any realistic alternative. He had built his policy around the idea of a Middle Eastern counterpart to NATO and he was more than a little disappointed when Dulles, who had fathered the idea, seemed to lose interest in it. In retrospect, it is obvious that he felt that Eden was using the pact to legitimize the continued British interest in the area, and in Iraq in particular. Dulles thought this a perversion of his original plan. Eden had hoped to draw Egypt into the pact, but the whole idea was too closely associated with

Nasser's great rival, Nuri es-Said, for Nasser to stomach that. Instead he set out to destroy the Hashemite rulers of Jordan and Iraq, intensified the conflict with Israel, assisted the Algerians against the French, and engaged on what can only be seen as an attempt to destabilize the whole area in pursuit of his own pan-Arab ambitions. In autumn 1955 he accepted an offer of arms from the Eastern bloc, ostensibly from Czechoslovakia. Britain and the United States countered with an offer to finance the Aswan High Dam. But a major complication in the whole situation was the presence of Israel. Efforts to resolve the long-standing enmity between the Arab power and Israel came to nothing, nor did Eden's dramatic speech at the Guildhall in November 1955 advance matters.

He had not entirely lost hope that Nasser could be kept out of Soviet hands, and it was therefore an extremely unpleasant shock when Nasserite elements in Jordan were able to frustrate British efforts to subsume their treaty arrangements with Jordan into the Baghdad Pact. By the early summer of 1956 Eden was ready to see an end to Anglo-American help with the Aswan Dam, although he would have preferred some less abrupt way of putting an end to it than that chosen by Dulles. Nasser responded by nationalizing the Suez Canal.

Critics of Eden tend to underplay the undoubted threat that Nasser's ambitions posed not only to British interests, or indeed Western interests, but to the political stability of the Middle East. Few had any doubt of this at the time. Dulles described Nasser as an Hitlerite personality, who might become a Soviet tool, while the Labour leader, Hugh Gaitskell, was the first to compare Nasser's action with those of Hitler and Mussolini. His reading of the dangers to Britain's position was acute.[91] The US Joint Chiefs of Staff and the Democratic leader in the Senate wished Eisenhower to back Eden. Even the President believed that the worst likely scenario in the Middle East was precisely that which Eden anticipated, but, crucially, he preferred the long-drawn-out processes of economic and diplomatic action to any use of force, particularly in election year.[92]

The internationalization of the Suez Canal seemed to all these men a worthwhile goal, but, if it was to be secured without military intervention by the British and French, the fullest possible co-operation from the United States was essential. It was not forthcoming. Britain's action were thought to be tainted with colonialism and therefore likely to meet with disapproval in the United Nations. Paradoxically, Eisenhower's refusal to contemplate anything but a peaceful outcome to the crisis seems to have made an Anglo-French military solution more likely. In diplomatic poker it is never wise to show your hand, yet Eisenhower and Dulles did so over and over again. Inevitably they called in question the effectiveness of the strategy which they had enjoined on Eden, a conference of the maritime powers, whose representatives would then take agreed terms to Nasser. Sir Robert Menzies believed to the end of his life that a public pronouncement from Eisenhower had destroyed what little chance that mission had, and he thought that in any case Dulles and not he should have led it.

Dulles himself destroyed his next diplomatic device, the Suez Canal Users' Association. Not only did he fail to make American shipowners pay their canal dues to the Association, but, when challenged, he denied publicly that there were any teeth in the plan. 'I cannot regard it as an element in statesmanship to relieve one's opponent of anxiety', Menzies wrote.[93] In London the anger was intense. In the judgement of those close to Eden, the deliberate undermining of his own scheme by Dulles was decisive. Eden had been persuaded to delay going to the Security Council while the new scheme was tried. As a direct result he had given to the Labour leaders an easy line of retreat from their more strident words at the end of July. They had always ruled out force without the sanction of the United Nations, but they had never asked themselves what would happen if the measures which they had earlier backed failed to secure a settlement. Since Dulles had prevented Eden from going to the Security Council, they could get away with what amounted to unconscious hypocrisy by demanding that Eden should now take that step, adding that Nasser's intransigence was the result of British provocation. They did not ask themselves what would happen in the face of a Soviet veto any more than Dulles asked himself how he could talk with one voice of the need for a just settlement and with the other rule out even the threat of force. At least Eisenhower realized that his policy gave the smaller powers a chance to blackmail the greater: the Labour Party was never as clear-sighted.

Eden had to face a situation, however, in which any humiliating climb-down would be exploited by his enemies within the Conservative Party, and, adversarial politics and the media being as they are, bound to provoke sharp criticism from the Opposition and the press. That Eden would act in these circumstances seems inevitable. His mistake, as Robert Skidelsky has argued,[94] was to cloak his action in a myth, that of 'separating the combatants', which robbed it of much of its essential morality. France's determination to work with Israel, however, particularly when coupled with the latter's skilful employment of a threat to Jordan as a means of putting pressure on Eden, was such as to make it easy to understand why Eden thought his move the lesser of two evils. Probably he played the game too well: a less straightforward man might have got his armada to sea well in advance of any ultimatum. As it was, a Cabinet that had been, broadly speaking, united in support of the scenario sketched for it on 25 October, found itself divided on the question of whether the troops should land in the teeth of a United Nations demand for a cease-fire. Eden prevailed, but only because the Israelis were persuaded to withdraw their own earlier compliance with the resolution. He had become the prisoner of the myth that had been created to justify British intervention, and that, rather than Macmillan's fears for sterling, proved to be the decisive factor when the Cabinet finally agreed to a cease-fire on 6 November. As a result of Canada's efforts at the United Nations, Britain and France had a substantial face-saving device, a UN force to take the place of their own; neither Eden nor his closest colleagues could believe that Eisenhower would fail to use this opportunity to secure a far-ranging Middle East settlement. They had not taken sufficient account of American fears of the taint of colonialism. In fact Eisenhower allowed his aides to withhold oil, and financial support for the pound, until they had forced Britain and France into an unconditional withdrawal of their forces. The Americans seemed unconcerned about the victory they were handing Nasser. Since the British had not occupied the entire Canal Zone, there was no question of their being able to clear the canal, and the government felt compelled to give way. Although the enunciation of the Eisenhower doctrine in January 1957 came as something of a vindication and partially restored the Western position in the Middle East, it came too late to check the enormous surge in Nasser's prestige. The creation of the United Arab Republic, closely allied to the Soviet Union, and the destruction of the kingdom of Iraq can be attributed to the outcome of the crisis, although the actions of Britain and the United States in summer 1958, when American marines landed in Lebanon and British paratroops secured the integrity of Jordan, did a good deal to prevent the position from deteriorating further. The two powers had come a long way since autumn 1956, and for this the close relationship between Eisenhower and Macmillan must take a good deal of the credit.

Richard Neustadt has provided us with a convincing analysis of the misconceptions which bedevilled Atlantic Alliance politics at the time of Suez and of the underlying reasons for them.[95] Macmillan learnt the lesson well. While in public he defended Britain's action, in private he was quite ruthless about the need to get back on terms with the Americans. Eden might well have proved a casualty of this determination had not ill health driven him from office. Once in No. 10 Macmillan made the rebuilding of the special relationship his first priority. Arguably he did his work so well that there has never been a time when it was in better repair. This was essentially the result of the close personal rapport that Macmillan had with Eisenhower and which he established with his successor. As a result he was able to forge a unique arrangement with the United States which amounted to the making of a nuclear alliance, and this has rightly been characterized as 'enormously important' by the official historian of Britain's nuclear projects, Margaret Gowing.[96] The Declaration of Common Purpose which Macmillan agreed with Eisenhower in October 1957 must rank as one of his greatest achievements, and led directly to the amendment of the McMahon Act in the following summer, thus giving Britain its special place within the nuclear framework of the Atlantic Alliance.

Shortly after his return to power in France, de Gaulle sought a share in this nuclear alliance. On 17 September 1958 he suggested to Eisenhower and to Macmillan that they should create within an extended Atlantic Alliance a three-power directorate. Implicit in the proposal was the notion that France would speak for Europe, in itself something which Macmillan would not have found easy to square with his desire that Britain should play an active part in any European grouping. How far the proposition was a serious one is not easy to assess: de Gaulle may well have wished to provoke a refusal in order to justify a course of action which he had always intended to take. Macmillan was anxious that the proposal should not be turned down out of hand, although, like Eisenhower, he found it quite unacceptable. However, it soon became clear that de Gaulle was determined to treat anything less than a complete acceptance of his ideas as a rejection, and he used the outcome to justify, among other things, his decision to prevent a Europe-wide free-trade area from coming into existence. As with the later decision to veto British entry into the EEC, some historians have been prepared to accept de Gaulle's arguments at face value, and to regard this as a heavy price to pay for Britain's special relationship in the nuclear field. The evidence, however, suggests that Macmillan was right to regard it as a pretext, and that de Gaulle's real view was that 'there was room for only one cock on the European dunghill'.[97]

If the government is to be accused of a mistake over Europe, the mistake was made not in 1958, but three years before, when it did not take with sufficient seriousness the relaunching of the European ideal which took place at the Messina Conference. There were divided views within Whitehall about the outcome: Lord Caccia appears to have told Macmillan that it would come to nothing. Hoyer Millar from his vantage point in Bonn recognized that the Organization for European Economic Co-operation (OEEC) did not provide that element of close co-operation in the political field which Adenauer wanted to establish between Western Germany and her European allies, more especially France. But those within the Foreign Office who had to consider the point were split on the issue. It was by no means clear to them that France would see it Adenauer's way, and, even if it did, there were powerful arguments to suggest that Britain ought nevertheless to favour the wider Atlantic community. If Britain became too closely identified with Europe, then the United States might one day withdraw into its own hemisphere. Europe, in any case, was too narrow a base. The Treasury was thinking in terms of building a world economic community. The minds of the official Economic Steering Committee, which had to consider the matter, were fixed on the world of the General Agreement on Trade and Tariffs (GATT) and the International Monetary Fund, and in this context they were determined to protect the OEEC. They had their own links with Washington and they knew that the economic authorities there agreed that the need to build the world community was of more importance than the relatively narrow question of relations with Europe, whatever the President and State Department might think.[98] The powerful voices urging the continuing importance of the Commonwealth to Britain also had their institutional embodiment inside Whitehall and were perhaps even more strongly represented in Parliament. It would be quite wrong, therefore, to exaggerate the part played in the government's decision by Eden's acknowledged Atlanticism and his feelings for the Commonwealth, although they cannot be ignored. Butler's role may have been as crucial. Certainly, when Macmillan reached the Treasury he was able to induce it to take a more positive approach. But the part which Macmillan played while still at the Foreign Office, when he not only acquiesced in the decision not to join the Common Market and Euratom, but actually sent a warning to the West German government that nothing should be done to provoke a clash between the interests of the Six and the OEEC countries,[99] should remind us how anachronistic it is to attribute blame for the failure to see the EEC as the most plausible route forward for Europe as a whole, let alone the free world. In their differing ways, Eden, Butler and Macmillan were all part of a broad consensus within Whitehall which recognized the growing importance of Europe to Britain but which was not yet ready to narrow its horizons to Europe alone. The proposal for a free-trade area, which was pushed by the Board of Trade under Thorneycroft once the decision not to join had been taken, and which Macmillan took up and pushed from the Treasury, was perhaps as far as any man could have taken Britain at that stage, and was in itself a radical proposal. Macmillan's Cabinet was ready subsequently to consider both a measure of supranationality and some concessions on the inclusion of agriculture in order to further the scheme, and did not give up hope of bringing it to fruition until de Gaulle abruptly terminated the negotiations in November 1958. What the Cabinet did then was less than happy, but comprehensible. Although it acted initially under some pressure from the Federation of British Industries, its attempt to bring pressure to bear on the Six through the creation of a rival association and to invoke American aid against the division of Europe was never likely to be successful; by autumn 1959, Britain was not only further removed from the Six than it had been a year before, but the Council of the OEEC had not met since December 1958.

In many ways the smooth passage of the Six towards the signature of the Treaty of Rome was unexpected, and the concept of a free-trade area to include the EEC was not inevitably doomed before de Gaulle's return to power, but Britain's failure to make the most of its close alignment with France over Suez, and, still more perhaps, its ill-judged reaction to the breakdown of the negotiations, bid fair to be considered the major mistakes of this administration; and there is no doubt in retrospect that Britain did pay dearly for its decision to withdraw from the negotiations which led to the EEC. It is important to recognize, therefore, how little support there would have been for any other course. Macmillan, once he had become Prime Minister, set in train both an effort to draw up a balance sheet for the Empire, seeking to establish the advantages and disadvantages of resisting constitutional change where it was likely to lead to a country leaving the Commonwealth,[100] and a more far-reaching study of Britain's place in the world. The group carrying this out under the chairmanship of Sir Patrick Dean was not to be tied to any departmental guidelines. The Chiefs of Staff and the relevant permanent secretaries were less than enamoured of the prospect, and Macmillan agreed that they should comprise a steering group with Brook in the chair. Inevitably, perhaps, they ended by fudging the central question on which the group divided, the choice between becoming 'good Europeans and cutting our losses world wide' and retaining both the nuclear and world roles in order to maintain influence with the United States.[101] Macmillan himself was not yet ready to make the choice, and he had not yet hit on the concept of the United States and Europe as twin pillars of the Alliance, which allowed him to seek entry into the EEC without severing Anglo-American ties.

The failure to get into the EEC at the start has usually been linked to the other main charge against this government, its perceived failure to establish the conditions for faster growth. The turn-around in policies which took place in the early sixties has been taken, rightly, as a tacit acknowledgment that Labour criticisms of 'stop–go' policies were valid. The secular trend downward in the annual average adjusted growth rate of the economy under the governments which followed does not suggest, however, that they had any better idea of how to run the economy. Indeed, Richard Rose suggests that it has little to do with politicians at all, although there are short-term changes about the trend which suggest that the economy is responsive to politicians in search of an election victory.[102] That may be too cynical a view. Prime Ministers will inevitably do their best to time elections to coincide with an upswing in the economic cycle, but, with the choice of date in their hands, they may not need to do much window-dressing. Indeed, if they expect to win, their actions in the medium term at least could prove counter-productive. In this period the evidence suggests less a political calculation than a direct reaction to one of two stimuli, a fall in the reserves or a sharp rise in unemployment.

Writing in 1964, Dow suggested that, as a result, some at least of the fluctuations in economic growth were government-induced.[103] However good the economic statistics, and in the mid-1950s they were far from adequate, the Chancellor always has great difficulty in forecasting the current position of the economy before he can begin to plot its course from there to his desired goal. Both Dow and Brittan believed that in this period government measures were always taken too late in the day and that they were therefore destabilizing.[104] The evidence is less clear than anyone but the most careful reader of Dow might suppose. In 1955, for example, the stimulus to the economy was offset by hire-purchase restrictions and a fall in the government's real current spending and public investment. To have averted the 'crisis', Dow himself notes, Butler would have needed to moderate the whole pace of expansion since 1953! The effect of government policy in 1956 and 1957 is still less clear-cut, and a good deal depends on Dow's argument that it was the credit squeeze that led to the decline in stocks, and on the question of how far, if at all, private investment was affected by government policy. It is almost impossible to resolve whether Dow is right on the first point, but on the second current research would suggest that measures to restrict credit had little effect. Government real spending and public investment remained almost unchanged in 1956; in 1957 defence spending fell, but public investment rose, only to be checked in 1958. Credit policy and budgetary policy were expansionist, however. The slow growth in exports in 1957 and their decline in 1958 were clearly important to the course of the economy but can hardly be attributed to the government. At best, therefore, Dow's argument for these years remains unproven. He is on far surer ground in the period 1958–60, where it is quite clear that government policy influenced substantially the pace of expansion, but it is less obvious that any action was required to moderate the boom. Indeed it is possible to argue that Lloyd's measures in 1961 were not only late, but unnecessary. That contention, however, lies outside the proper scope of this chapter. What may be noted is that Dow's judgement is made in terms of economic growth, that he assumes that stable growth will be more beneficial than the policies actually pursued, and that he makes no assessment of the relative success of the government in combining full employment with a low rate of inflation and a balance-of-payments surplus. Without exception those were the declared objectives of all Chancellors in this period, Thorneycroft perhaps putting more stress than most on the need for a substantial surplus, and arguing also, with apparently little justification, that it was necessary to counter wage inflation by controlling the money supply.

Even if the effects of policy could be shown to be destablizing, it would be important not to exaggerate the extent of the phenomenon. Bispham and Boltho have suggested that over the postwar years the variations about the trend of output and investment, including the impact of demand management, have not been as great in Britain as in many countries with a faster growth rate,[105] nor has the gap between actual GNP and potential GNP (assuming full factor use) differed much from the average achieved even by those European nations which had the fastest rates of growth. Given the underlying buoyancy of both consumption and employment, it seems possible that there was in fact little room for a more expansionary policy.

Arguments about the autonomous impact of domestic policy seem of little significance, however, when we remember the Atlantic orientation of British policy. The key decisions in this period – the move to *de facto* convertibility in 1955 and to full convertibility three years later, and the decisions taken at the 1958 Commonwealth Economic Conference to attempt to make GATT a more effective instrument for dealing with the problems of agricultural protection – may seem minor when compared with the series of decisions taken between 1944 and 1947 which had tied Britain into a world economy dominated by the United States, but they were logically entailed by those earlier decisions. They brought fairly rapid growth to Britain but tied activity in the British economy to the level in the rest of the world economy. A central feature of the entire system was a regime of fixed exchange rates, principally based on the dollar, but with sterling playing an important subsidiary role. It would not have been easy to do as Macmillan wished and phase out the international role of sterling, nor was it that essential in the late 1950s. The benefits of the sterling area might be a good deal more limited than they had been in the immediate postwar period, but it had not yet become a source of weakness. Still more to the point was the widely held view that, without sterling to take some of the strain, the dollar might prove an insufficient base for international liquidity. Sterling had therefore to be protected when under attack, and this constrained the policy-makers. There is little evidence to suggest that in this period Britain's growth record was adversely affected by the primacy given to the external balance, although it is difficult not to believe that one at least of the measures used to restrict demand, hire-purchase controls, was not damaging to particular sections of British industry. But the mild increase in regional unemployment which attracted much attention in the winter of 1958–9, and which led to a reconsideration of regional policy within the Board of Trade,[106] can now be seen to have structural features which were not readily susceptible to Keynesian measures. In fact the most sustained analysis of Britain's growth record in comparison with that of the faster-growing European economies suggests that, to a very considerable extent, 'conditions beyond the control of the United Kingdom were responsible for higher growth rates in other countries'.[107] If the government had been able to reduce its own expenditures overseas, there would have been less strain on the balance of payments, and to that extent Shonfield's contemporary critique still has force.[108] He argued also that investment in Britain was low by international standards and that the government should do something about it, not least by restricting overseas investment. The government did in fact employ substantial tax incentives to improve the position, and presumably deserves some credit for the improved position in the following decade. Indeed, in so far as the blame lies with governments, it should be attributed to the previous Labour government, which chose not to sacrifice social expenditure to industrial investment. Politically it would have been difficult for its successor, after a decade of austerity, to take a different course, although the Cabinet explored ways of bringing social services expenditure under control later in 1955.[109] Nor was its new defence policy, worked out in 1956–7, unrelated to the need to free resources for the domestic economy. But the government's track record does not suggest that direct action on its part would have benefited the country. The Select Committee on Nationalized Industries was scathing, and rightly so, about many aspects of the railways modernization plan and the ease with which it got by the Ministry of Transport,[110] while most economic historians are critical of Britain's massive investment in nuclear power and her overcommitment to the aircraft industry. The debate about overseas investment continues without resolution, but there is, in any case, little reason to suppose that in the late 1950s investment was limited by a shortage of internal funds. However, the major factor conditioning the size of private investment was, almost certainly, industrialists' expectations about the course of the economy, and that is why there came to be so much interest in the French model of indicative planning right at the very end of the decade.

Central to the investigation of the obstacles to faster growth was the realization, spelt out still more emphatically by the Brookings study later in the decade, that the 'level of residual efficiency' within the British economy was the one factor that government actions might conceivably influence for good. The government must be given credit for what was achieved: the Restrictive Trade Practices Act of 1956, the further development of an efficient agricultural industry in a world of free markets by means of the Agriculture Acts of 1957 and 1958, the creation of the colleges of advanced technology and of university institutes of technology, the development of sandwich courses and new awards for technology, and the five-year development plan for technical education. However, the promising development of technical schools was not greeted with any enthusiasm by a grammar-school oriented party, and little was made of the secondary moderns. The Board of Trade did little to build on the postwar involvement of the trade unions in discussions on productivity, and in retrospect it seems clear that both Thorneycroft and his permanent secretary, Sir Frank Lee, relied too much on competition and trade liberalization to induce a new climate in British industry.

They were, in any case, prevented from going as far as they wanted in strengthening the Monopolies Commission by successful pressure from the Federation of British Industries. The Ministry of Labour's reluctance to tackle the necessary task of reforming restrictive labour practices contributed substantially to the problems of industry. Survey after survey noted the under-utilization of capital, overmanning, the shortage of certain skills, the failure to reform apprenticeship, as well as the more publicized evils of demarcation disputes and wildcat strikes. This is a familiar tale, but the problems posed by an antiquated trade union movement, unwilling or unable to reform itself, were compounded markedly by the degree of amateurism among Britain's managers. Dynasticism, administrative corpulence, a reluctance to recruit graduates, a failure to train managers and an inability to use them properly if and when they were trained – all these were characteristic features of British industry, which the government was slow to recognize and slower still to tackle. It was not until the end of the decade that the Ministry of Education began to co-operate with the British Institute of Management on the question of business education.

The Treasury showed scant interest in any of these problems. Its attention was focused on public expenditure. There seemed to be an obvious danger that it would get out of control. The decision to rely mainly on the nuclear deterrent promised to prolong the process of making savings on defence expenditure, but the effects of the postwar baby boom continued to be felt in education, and the social and environmental programmes already launched had now developed a considerable momentum. Local-government expenditure could perhaps be checked by the move away from percentage grants which was a major feature of the 1958 Local Government Act, but the Treasury was now committed to the charges arising from the development programmes of the nationalized industries. Although the motivation for the change was more complex, limited relief was available from the decision to concentrate housing subsidies on slum clearance. But, from his base on the Home and Overseas Planning Staff, Richard Clarke sought to develop a new approach to expenditure control and to use the Parliamentary Estimates Committee to press it on Whitehall. Instead a further inquiry resulted, the Plowden Committee, but Clarke, nothing daunted, set out to convince the Committee in its turn of the virtues of a long-term approach. There was already evidence to support his case, drawn from the complex field of defence, where another Treasury official, David Serpell, working in co-operation with Sir Richard Powell, the permanent secretary, had established long-term costings and a five-year programme.[111]

The work of government does not conform all that easily to the time limits set by general elections, and much of the useful legislation passed by this government perhaps owes more to departmental pressures than the ministers concerned would care to admit. Nevertheless, the record of social amelioration and legislative achievement is solid if not spectacular,[112] and it is some measure of the desperation felt by the Opposition that, in the last months before the 1959 election, it sought to concentrate the minds of the electorate on the government's apparent reluctance to speed certain of its African colonies to independence. Ghana had set the pace, but what the Colonial Secretary had been ready to concede gracefully where there were no white settlers seemed problematic elsewhere. Lennox Boyd spoke of the need to create an educated African middle class, but neither his critics nor the African peoples were ready to wait. That may have been their misfortune, but to hold them back required measures which had become anathema to large sections of British public opinion. The emergency in Nyasaland in spring 1959 had to be dealt with forcibly; the consequence was a decision by Macmillan to bring forward the promised parliamentary review of the future of the Central African Federation. No doubt it played a part also in his determination to resolve the problems of decolonization as speedily as possible once the election was out of the way. But the hopes of the Labour Party that the issue would do damage to the government proved misplaced. As always in those years, the material prosperity of the British people proved the only real issue at the 1959 election.

In many ways the verdict of the electorate has proved a good deal sounder than that offered by the contemporary historians. Their judgement was delivered too soon and needs revision. In particular, the criticisms of the government's economic performance look severe in the light of what later governments have failed to deliver; and it smacks of a very peculiar form of hindsight to deploy at this date criticisms of the government's failure to cope with inflation. In fact it made a better fist of delivering a combination of economic growth, cuts in taxation, full employment and low inflation than any of its successors. Its failure to tackle the in-built inefficiency of British industry is something which it has in common with succeeding governments, and its Thatcherite reliance on trade liberalization to do the job looks less far-fetched in the light of the later failures of more interventionist policies. Certainly the blame in this field must be shared by management in general, which failed to convince the unions of the need for change, and by a trade union leadership which knew the need for reform but failed to give a lead.

Suez remains a questionable operation, but it affected Britain's international position surprisingly little, even in the Middle East, and its main consequence was to spur on some necessary rethinking, as well as putting in No. 10 the politician best fitted for that task. Macmillan saw the need to adjust his country's position in the world to the realities of the new constellation of power, and he had the political skills to take his party with him and to accomplish much of the task without destroying national self-confidence. One major error was made, however explicably, and that was the decision to set Britain's part in creating the new international economy ahead of participation in the EEC. Had Britain resolved to play an active part in the shaping of Europe, it could no doubt have shaped the Community to its liking. Membership might have changed much in Britain for its good. There were few who made this point at the time, however, despite some retrospective claims. As it was, later governments were left to find their own solutions to Britain's ills, and the poor fist they made of it is perhaps the best tribute they could pay to an administration which they criticized so much.

Chronology

1955

26 May   General election: Conservatives, 344 seats; Labour, 277; Liberals, 6; others 3. Conservative government re-elected with an increased majority.
29 May   Footplatemen in ASLEF (Associated Society of Locomotive Engineers and Firemen) come out on strike.
31 May   Government declares a state of national emergency.
13 June   Soviet acceptance of the summit agreement with the USA on the exchange of civil nuclear information.
29 June   Monopolies Commission report on restrictive trade practices.
1 July   First postwar hospital-building programme initiated.
13 July   Thorneycroft foreshadows restrictive practices court. Ruth Ellis hanged.
18–23 July   Summit conference at Geneva.
25 July   Butler announces restrictive economic measures.
8 August   Conference on the peaceful uses of atomic energy.
25 September   Harding appointed Governor of Cyprus.
26 October   Butler's fifth Budget: purchase tax, profits tax increased; housing subsidies cut.
27 October   Four-power conference of foreign ministers at Geneva.
9 November   At the Lord Mayor's Banquet, Eden makes new proposals for a Middle East settlement.

26 November   State of emergency declared in Cyprus.

13 December   Gaitskell elected leader of the Labour Party. US–UK offer of a loan for the Aswan High Dam.

20 December   Ministerial reshuffle: Macmillan Chancellor; Butler Leader of the House; Lloyd Foreign Secretary.

1956

25 January   Guillebaud Committee report on the Health Service.

1 February   Eden and Eisenhower issue the Declaration of Washington.

16 February   Bank rate raised to $5\frac{1}{2}$ per cent – highest since 1932.

17 February   Macmillan announces cuts in food subsidies and public investment; hire-purchase restrictions.

1 March   Selwyn Lloyd visits Cairo; is promised that Egyptian propaganda will cease.

2 March   John Glubb dismissed from command of the Arab Legion.

9 March   Archbishop Makarios deported from Cyprus.

22 March   White Paper *The Economic Implications of Full Employment* published.

16 April   UN ceasefire agreement between Egypt and Israel comes into force.

17 April   Macmillan's first Budget: income-tax reliefs offset by increased profits tax and tobacco duty. Premium Bonds announced.

18 April   Bulganin and Khrushchev visit Britain.

19 April   Gold Coast outlines its proposals for independence.

16 May   Nuclear test at Monte Bello, Australia.

22 May   Calder Hall, world's first atomic power station, goes into operation.

7 June   Tonbridge by-election: Conservative majority slashed.

10 June   Egypt and Suez Canal Company reach agreement.

13 June   Last British troops leave Suez Canal base.

14 June   USA and UK broaden scope of 1955 atomic co-operation agreement.

10 July   House of Lords rejects abolition of the death penalty.

19 July   Dulles rescinds offer of Aswan Dam loan.

26 July   Suez Canal nationalized.

27 July   Cabinet agrees to force as a 'last resort' if all other measures fail to secure the internationalization of the Suez Canal.

2 August   Tripartite statement issued by USA, UK and France.

16–23 August   First London conference of the maritime powers.

3–10 September   Sir Robert Menzies' mission to Cairo to present 18-Power proposals. Nasser rejects them.

11 September   Cabinet agrees to Dulles' proposal for a Suez Canal User's Association.

26 September   UK and France file complaint at United Nations.

13 October   UN Security Council adopts the Six Principles. Soviet Union vetoes machinery for their implementation.

14 October   Eden receives French proposal put by Challe and Gazier at Chequers.

16 October   Eden and Lloyd discuss the French suggestion with Mollet and Pineau in Paris.

18 October   Cabinet discuss the worsening Middle East situation and the possibility of intervention should Israel strike at Egypt.

22 October   Lloyd meets French and Israelis at Sèvres.

25 October   Cabinet agree to a 'police operation' to preserve the peace of the Middle East.

29 October   Israelis attack Egypt.

30 October   Anglo-French ultimatum to Egypt and Israel.

2 November   Cabinet agrees in principle to a UN force.

4 November   Cabinet agrees by a majority to landings.

6 November   UK, France and Israel accept a ceasefire.

7 November   United Nations adopts terms of reference for UN expeditionary force.

14 November   First contingents of expeditionary force reach Suez.

24 November   United Nations votes for immediate withdrawal of Anglo-French forces.

3 December   British and French governments agree to withdraw unconditionally.

22 December   Anglo-French forces leave Suez.

1957

9 January   Eden resigns as Prime Minister.

10 January   Macmillan appointed Prime Minister.

13 January   New Cabinet: Thorneycroft Chancellor; Butler Home Secretary.

7 February   Bank Rate reduced to 5 per cent. Ghana independence Act.

12 February   Council of the Organization for European Economic Co-operation agrees to start negotiations for a European Free Trade Area.

14 February   UK gives notice of a reduction of troops in West Germany.

6 March   Ghana achieves independence within the Commonwealth.

14 March   EOKA (= National Organization of Cypriot Combatants) offers to suspend terrorism in Cyprus on release of Archbishop Makarios.

19 March   Macmillan instructs Sir Brian Robertson to avoid a railway dispute and asks ship building employers to improve their pay offer.

20 March   UK accepts NATO offer of mediation in Cyprus.

21 March   Macmillan meets Eisenhower in Bermuda.

25 March   Treaty of Rome signed.

28 March   Archbishop Makarios released. Lord Salisbury resigns.

4 April   Defence White Paper outlines the 'new look' nuclear defence policy, the ending of conscription and seeping changes in all three services.

9 April   Thorneycroft's first Budget: purchase tax reduced; company tax concessions; surtax allowances raised.

11 April   Singapore constitutional conference agrees internal self-government for Singapore.

15 May   First British hydrogen bomb exploded at Christmas Island.

6 June   Rent Act passed.

26 June   Commonwealth prime ministers conference.

20 July   Macmillan's 'never had it so good' speech at Bedford.

7 August   Maudling appointed to take charge of the Free Trade Area negotiations.

12 August   Council on Prices, Productivity and Incomes appointed.
17 September   Hailsham appointed Conservative Party chairman.
19 September   Bank Rate raised to 7 per cent. Ceiling on public-sector capital spending and bank advances.
28 September   Commonwealth finance ministers meet in Quebec.
11 October   Windscale nuclear reactor overheats.
16 October   Dulles warns the Soviet Union against an attack on Turkey.
22 October   Hugh Foot appointed Governor of Cyprus.
8 November   UK explodes nuclear weapon at high altitude in the central Pacific.

1958

6 January   Thorneycroft redsigns. Heathcoat Amory Chancellor.
7 January   Macmillan departs on his Commonwealth tour.
12 February   Rochdale by-election: Labour gain; Liberals second.
22 February   Publication of Anglo-US agreement on the stationing of Thor missiles in Britain.
27 February   Parliamentary Labour Party split on unilateral nuclear disarmament.
20 March   Bank Rate reduced to 6 per cent.
27 March   Torrington by-election: Liberal gain.
1 April   Macmillan rejects Soviet call to suspend nuclear tests.
15 April   Amory's first Budget: company tax concessions; purchase-tax reductions. Eccles announces creation of development areas.
30 April   Life Peerages Act receives royal assent.
22 May   Bank Rate reduced to $5\frac{1}{2}$ per cent.
19 June   Bank Rate reduced to 5 per cent. British plan for a Cyprus settlement announced.
2 July   McMahon Act amended in USA to permit sharing of military nuclear information.
14 July   King Feisal of Iraq and Nuri es-Said assassinated in revolutionary coup.
22 July   Macmillan proposes that heads of government should attend the UN Security Council discussion of the Middle East crisis.
14 August   Bank Rate reduced to $4\frac{1}{2}$ per cent.
15 August   Modified version of Cyprus plan accepted by Turks, but rejected by Greeks and EOKA.
23 August   Race disturbances in Nottingham.
31 August   Race riots in Notting Hill and Nottingham.
3 September   Government publicly rejects idea of controlling Commonwealth immigration.
15 September   Commonwealth economic conference at Montreal.
30 September   Britain and USA agree a conditional withdrawal of their troops from Jordan and the Lebanon.
6 October   Rent Act comes into operation.
31 October   Three-power conference at Geneva on discontinuance of nuclear testing.
14 November   France rejects proposals for a Free Trade Area.
22 November   Macmillan warns Khrushchev that the UK will uphold its rights in Berlin.

14 December   West agrees to reject the Soviet proposals on Berlin.

1959

5 January   Three-power conference on discontinuance of nuclear tests reassembles.

2 February   Butler publishes White Paper *Penal Practice in a Changing Society*.

19 February   Prime ministers of UK, Greece and Turkey agree on Cyprus settlement.

20 February   Nyasaland disturbances begin.

21 February   Macmillan and Lloyd fly to Moscow.

26 February   State of emergency in Southern Rhodesia.

28 February   Anglo-Egyptian agreement on Suez Canal compensation.

3 March   State of emergency in Nyasaland; Dr Banda arrested.

15 March   Northern Nigeria attains internal self-government.

18 March   First elections in British Somaliland.

19 March   Macmillan and Lloyd fly to Washington after talks in Paris and Bonn.

7 April   Amory's second Budget: ninepence off income tax.

7 May   Anglo-US agreement on purchase of weapons systems and mutual transfer of nuclear material.

11 May   Four-power foreign ministers conference.

13 May   Internal self-government conferred on Jamaica within the West Indies Federation.

24 May   Anglo-Soviet trade agreement.

3 June   Singapore attains independence.

31 June   Final departure of Royal Air Force from Iraq.

9 July   Transport and General Workers Union endorses unilateral nuclear disarmament.

21 July   Announcement of the Monckton Commission to review the Central African Federation.

23 July   Publication of the Devlin Report on the disturbances in Nyasaland.

3 August   Eisenhower announces exchange of visits with Khrushchev.

19 August   Radcliffe Report on the working of the monetary system presented to Parliament.

27 August   Eisenhower visits Britain. US decision to suspend nuclear tests extended.

7 September   Four-power decision to set up new ten-power disarmament conference.

15 September   Khrushchev visits the USA.

28 September   Gaitskell pledges no increase in income tax if Labour wins the General Election.

8 October   General election: Conservative government re-elected with an increased majority.

Notes

1 *The Times*, editorial, 10 January 1957.
2 L. A. Siedentop, 'Mr Macmillan and the Edwardian style' in Vernon Bogdanor and Robert Skidelsky, *The Age of Affluence 1951–1964* (Macmillan, 1970).
3 Quoted in Paul Foot, *The Politics of Harold Wilson* (Penguin, 1968), p. 127.
4 The cartoon is reprinted in David Butler and Richard Rose, *The British General Election of 1959* (Macmillan, 1960), p. 201.
5 Ibid., p. 196.
6 Harold Macmillan, *Pointing the Way* (Macmillan, 1972), p. 15.
7 Samuel H. Beer, 'Democratic one-party government for Britain', *Political Quarterly*, 32 (1961), pp. 114–23.
8 For example Robert Blake, *The Decline of Power 1915–1964* (Paladin, 1985).
9 For context consult V. L. Allen, *Trades Unions and the Government* (Longman, 1960), p. 160; Leo Panitch, *Social Democracy and Industrial Militancy* (Cambridge University Press, 1976), pp. 45–7.
10 For example Alan Sked and Chris Cook, *Post-War Britain*, 2nd edn (Penguin, 1986).
11 Andrew Shonfield, *British Economic Policy since the War*, 2nd edn (Penguin, 1958).
12 Sked and Cook, *Post-War Britain*, p. 224.
13 Samuel Brittan, *The Treasury under the Tories* (Penguin, 1964); republished in updated form as *Steering the Economy* (Penguin, 1971).
14 J. C. R. Dow, *The Management of the British Economy 1945–60* (Cambridge University Press, 1964).
15 The best brief account is that by C. J. Bartlett, *A History of Postwar Britain 1945–74* (Longman, 1977). The essays in Bogdanor and Skidelsky, *The Age of Affluence*, are worth careful study, and there is good material based on oral testimony in Alan Thompson, *The Day before Yesterday* (Sidgwick and Jackson, 1971).
16 Elizabeth Barker, *Britain in a Divided Europe 1945–70* (Weidenfeld and Nicolson, 1971); C. J. Bartlett, *The Long Retreat: a short history of British defence policy 1945–70* (Macmillan, 1972); John Baylis, *Anglo-American Defence Relations 1939–84*, 2nd edn (Macmillan, 1985); Philip Darby, *British Defence Policy East of Suez 1947–68* (Oxford University Press, 1973); Joseph Frankel, *British Foreign Policy 1945–73* (Oxford University Press, 1975); Stewart Menaul, *Countdown* (Hale, 1980); Andrew J. Pierre, *Nuclear Politics: the British experiment with an independent strategic force 1939–1970* (Oxford University Press, 1972); Avi Shlaim, Peter Jones and Keith Sainsbury, *British Foreign Secretaries since 1945* (David and Charles, 1977); John Simpson, *The Independent Nuclear State*, 2nd edn (Macmillan, 1986).

17 Hugh Thomas, *The Suez Affair* (Penguin, 1970). There is also a good recent survey by Geoffrey Warner, '"Collusion" and the Suez Crisis of 1956', *International Affairs*, LV (1979), and he has written with M. Evans a brief account of what is to be found (perhaps more precisely, not found) in the public records. See *The Times*, 1, 2 and 3 January 1987.

18 The most recent account is that by Michael Charlton, *The Price of Victory* (BBC, 1983), but it does not supersede Miriam Camps, *Britain and the European Community* (Oxford University Press, 1964). R. J. Lieber, *British Politics and European Unity* (University of California Press, 1970), should also be consulted.

19 Anthony Sampson, *Macmillan: a Study in ambiguity* (Allen Lane, 1967), p. 258.

20 Henry Fairlie, *The Life of Politics* (Methuen, 1968), p. 68ff.

21 Anthony Crosland's Fabian Society pamphlet *Can Labour Win?* and his subsequent *Encounter* article, dated October 1960, are reprinted with significant alterations in Crosland, *The Conservative Enemy* (Cape, 1962).

22 Michael Shanks, *The Stagnant Society* (Penguin, 1961).

23 The authorized biographies of Monckton and Macleod were the first to appear (in the 1970s), although the biography of Macleod had to depend to a considerable extent on oral testimony in the absence of many papers. Nor did Young have access to more than a few private papers; he drew to a large extent on taped recollections for his biography of Home. Carlton had access to some archival material for his study of Eden, and the authorized life by Rhodes James is, of course, solidly founded on Eden's diaries and his extensive collection of papers. Surprisingly, Rhodes James did not use Sir Evelyn Shuckburgh's diary, which Carlton had put to good use, and which has now been published as *Descent to Suez: diaries 1951–56* (Weidenfeld and Nicolson, 1986). Recent biographies of Mountbatten and Templer are also based on private papers. Neither Sampson nor Fisher could draw on Macmillan's archive, since this was reserved for his official biographer, Alistair Horne.

The following lives repay study: Lord Birkenhead, *Walter Monckton: the life of Viscount Monckton of Brenchley* (Weidenfeld and Nicolson, 1969); David Carlton, *Anthony Eden* (Allen Lane, 1981); Michael Carver, *Harding of Petherton* (Weidenfeld and Nicolson, 1978); John Cloake, *Templer* (Harrap, 1985); Patrick Cosgrave, *R. A. Butler* (Quartet, 1981); Nigel Fisher, *Iain Macleod* (André Deutsch, 1973) and *Harold Macmillan* (Weidenfeld and Nicolson, 1982); Geoffrey Goodman, *The Awkward Warrior: Frank Cousins* (Davis-Poynter, 1979); Robert Rhodes James, *Anthony Eden* (Weidenfeld and Nicolson, 1986); Anthony Sampson, *Macmillan: a study of ambiguity* (Allen Lane, 1967); Kenneth Young, *Sir Alec Douglas-Home* (Dent, 1970); Philip Ziegler, *Mountbatten: the official biography* (Collins, 1985).

In addition, the following may be useful for those interested in the process of decolonization: Darrell Bates, *A Gust of Plumes: a biography of Lord Twining* (Hodder and Stoughton, 1972); Charles Douglas Home, *Evelyn Baring: the last proconsul* (Collins, 1978); David Goldsworthy, *Tom Mboya* (Heinemann, 1982); Jeremy Murray Brown, *Kenyatta* (Allen and Unwin, 1972); David Rooney, *Sir Charles Arden-Clarke* (Rex Collings, 1982).

24 In addition to the studies mentioned in n. 16, a brief list would include: J. M. Barnett, *The Politics of Legislation* (Weidenfeld and Nicolson, 1969); Nancy Crawshaw, *The Cyprus Revolt* (Allen and Unwin, 1978); G. A. Dorfman, *Wage Politics in Britain 1945–67* (Charles Knight, 1973); D. Goldsworthy, *Colonial Issues in British Politics 1945–61* (Oxford University Press, 1971); R. F. Holland, *European Decolonisation 1918–1981: an introductory survey* (Macmillan, 1985); Keith Middlemas, *Power, Competition and the State*, vol. I: *Britain in Search of Balance, 1940–61* (Macmillan, 1986); D. J. Morgan, *Guidance towards Self-Government in British Colonies 1941–71* (Macmillan, 1980); Roger Williams, *The Nuclear Power Decisions* (Croom Helm, 1980).

25 Robert Rhodes James, *Anthony Eden* (Weidenfeld and Nicolson, 1986); Anthony Howard, *Rab: the life of R. A. Butler* (Cape 1987). Macmillan's official biographer, Alistair Horne, agreed not to publish during his subject's lifetime, but had all but completed his work at the time of Macmillan's death. An article, 'Supermac', appeared in the *Sunday Times*, 4 January 1987.

26 Apart from the prime-ministerial memoirs listed below in n. 34, there are the following: Lord Butler, *The Art of the Possible: the memoirs of Lord Butler* (Hamish Hamilton, 1971); Lord Hailsham, *The Door Wherein I Went* (Collins, 1975); Lord Hill, *Both Sides of the Hill* (Heinemann, 1964); Lord Home, *The Way the Wind Blows: an autobiography* (Collins, 1976); Lord Kilmuir, *Political Adventure: the memoirs of the Earl of Kilmuir* (Weidenfeld and Nicolson, 1964); Selwyn Lloyd, *Suez 1956* (Cape, 1978); Reginald Maudling, *Memoirs* (Sidgwick and Jackson, 1978); Lord Stuart, *Within the Fringe: an autobiography* (Bodley Head, 1967); Lord Watkinson, *Turning Points* (Michael Russell, 1986). Lord Woolton, *Memoirs* (Cassell, 1959).

27 Aubrey Jones, *Britain's Economy* (Cambridge University Press, 1986); Lord Watkinson, *Blueprint for Industrial Survival* (Allen and Unwin, 1976).

28 John Boyd Carpenter, *Way of Life* (Sidgwick and Jackson, 1980).

29 Anthony Nutting, *Disarmament* (Oxford University Press, 1959), *Europe will not Wait* (Hollis and Carter, 1960) and *No End of a Lesson* (Constable, 1967).

30 Sir Roderick Barclay, *Ernest Bevin and the Foreign Office 1932–69* (published by the author, 1975); Lord Gladwyn, *The Memoirs of Lord Gladwyn* (Weidenfeld and Nicolson, 1972); Paul Gore-Booth, *With Great*

Truth and Respect (Constable, 1974); Sir Wiliam Hayter *A Double Life* (Hamish Hamilton, 1974); Sir Ivonne Kirkpatrick, *The Inner Circle* (Macmillan, 1959); Lord Redcliffe-Maud, *Experiences of an Optimist* (Macmillan, 1981). Sir Eric Roll, *Crowded Hours* (Faber and Faber, 1985).

31   Lord Egremont (John Wyndham), *Wyndham and Children First* (Macmillan, 1968); Sir Harold Evans, *Downing Street Diary: the Macmillan Years 1957–1963* (Hodder and Stoughton, 1981). William Clark's memoir *From Three Worlds* (Sidgwick and Jackson, 1986) allows us to make an instructive comparison with No. 10 under Eden.

32   Fisher's biography of Macmillan draws on the testimony of Lord Armstrong, Sir Frederick Bishop, Lord Caccia, Sir Alec Cairncross, Neil Cairncross, Sir Philip de Zulueta, Lord Roberthall, Lord Sherfield, Lord Trend and Philip Woodfield. The first volume of Keith Middlemas's *Power, Competition and the State* draws on 137 interviews, but it is not clear what proportion are with civil servants.

33   See above, n. 15.

34   The Earl of Avon, *Full Circle* (Cassell, 1960); Harold Macmillan, *Riding the Storm, 1955–59* and *Pointing the Way, 1959–61* (Macmillan, 1971 and 1972), the fourth and fifth volumes of his memoirs.

35   Interviews. Cf. Clark, *From Three Worlds*, p. 151.

36   Interviews.

37   Clark, *From Three Worlds*, p. 153.

38   Interviews. Cf. Birkenhead, *Walter Monckton*, p. 301.

39   Brittan, *The Treasury Under the Tories*, p. 197.

40   A phrase used by the deputy editor, Donald MacLachlan, in an article in the *Daily Telegraph*, 3 January 1956. Cf. the account in Thompson, *The Day before Yesterday*, p. 122.

41   It would be impossible to guess from the official biography that Eden was in dispute with Butler in September 1955 about the early recall of Parliament and the abolition of the bread subsidy and that he was faced with the possibility of Macmillan's resignation on the latter issue in February 1956. Carlton deals with this later crisis more satisfactorily than with the shaping of the autumn Budget. Macmillan's own account of it and of his own later dispute with Thorneycroft will be found in *Riding the Storm*, pp. 11–15 and 362–72. Cf. also Thompson, *The Day before Yesterday*, pp. 165–7.

42   In an unsigned article, 'In Eden's Day', the *Economist*, 4 January 1986, M. R. D. Foot argues that it was.

43   PRO, CAB 128/29 and 128/30.

44   Information from the late Lord Salisbury.

45   Interviews.

46   Kilmuir, *Political Adventure*, p. 257.

47 Lord Moran, *Winston Churchill: struggle for survival, 1940–65* (Sphere, 1968), p. 734.
48 Boyd Carpenter, *Way of Life*, p. 125; and interviews.
49 H. von Thal (ed.), *The Prime Ministers*, vol. II (Allen and Unwin, 1975), p. 339.
50 Interviews; Butler, *The Art of the Possible*, p. 193. Carlton erroneously supposes that Butler's account refers to the Egypt Committee, while the late James Margach in *The Abuse of Power* (W. H. Allen, 1978), pp. 113–14, relates it to the Cabinet of 6 November. Rhodes James (*Anthony Eden*, p. 567) appears to believe that Butler's recollection was faulty, although his own citation from Clarissa Eden's diary suggests that the discussion was rather more tense than the Cabinet Secretary's record. See below, p. 114.
51 PRO, CAB 128/30. The confidential annexe to the minutes of the meeting of 23 October notes that it was 'From secret conversations which had been held in Paris with representatives of the Israeli government' that Eden had concluded that Israel was unlikely to launch a full-scale attack against Egypt. The printed version of the minutes used by Rhodes James omits this reference to secret conversations. In addition to his extract from the minutes of the Cabinet, Rhodes James quotes freely from the Cabinet meeting of 27 July (*Anthony Eden*, pp. 459–62) and from the meetings of 24 and 25 October (pp. 533–7). Significantly, perhaps, the confidential annexe for the meeting of 25 October is not in the PRO.
52 PRO, CAB 134/815, 2 November 1956.
53 PRO, CAB 128/30.
54 Ibid.
55 PRO, PREM 11/1152; Rhodes James, *Anthony Eden*, p. 499.
56 PREM 11/1152, Home to Eden, 22 August 1956.
57 Ibid., Brook to Eden, 24 August 1956.
58 PRO, CAB 128/30.
59 The records of the Egypt Committee are in CAB 134/1216. The only available account of these meetings of senior ministers is provided by Selwyn Lloyd (*Suez 1956*, pp. 180, 185 and 188).
60 Avon, *Full Circle*, pp. 371–5.
61 Ibid., p. 397.
62 The fullest account of the Cabinet committee structure under Eden will be found in Peter Hennessy, *Cabinet* (Basil Blackwell, 1986), pp. 53–7.
63 Kilmuir, *Political Adventure*, p. 308.
64 Watkinson, *Turning Points*, p. 73.
65 Interview with Lord Egremont. In this and subsequent paragraphs interview material has been used extensively. Full details will be given in John Barnes and Anthony Seldon, *Adjusting to Reality*, a forthcoming study of the government of 1955–9.

66   Egremont, *Wyndham and Children First*, p. 167.
67   Brittan, *The Treasury under the Tories*, p. 195.
68   A. H. Brown, 'Prime ministerial power', *Public Law*, Spring 1968, p. 109.
69   Macmillan, *Riding the Storm*, pp. 708–10.
70   In order to bring pressure to bear on the Treasury in autumn 1958, Macmillan chaired an *ad hoc* Cabinet committee on reflation. See *Riding the Storm*, pp. 726–8, for some indications of its work.
71   Kilmuir, *Political Adventure*, p. 308.
72   Interview, August 1965.
73   Anthony Sampson, *Anatomy of Britain* (Hodder and Stoughton, 1962), p. 134.
74   Hill, *Both Sides of the Hill*, p. 235.
75   Interviews.
76   *Daily Mail*, 25 February 1957. Cf. Andrew Roth, *Heath and the Heathmen* (Routledge and Kegan Paul, 1972), p. 115; Macmillan, *Riding the Storm*, p. 210.
77   Macmillan, *Riding the Storm*, pp. 710, 714. The way in which he used such small meetings to get a grip on the situation and advance policy is well illustrated by the series of meetings which he held in July 1957 to devise a new plan for Cyprus (ibid., p. 660).
78   The *Guardian*, 15 July 1958.
79   Interviews; Macmillan, *Riding the Storm*, pp. 708–9, 368.
80   *Evening Standard* (London), 20 March 1959.
81   Macmillan, *Riding the Storm*, p. 703.
82   Rhodes James, *Anthony Eden*, pp. 415–16.
83   Monckton to Eden, 22 September 1955, Monckton Papers, Bodleian Library, Oxford.
84   *A Giant's Strength* (Conservative Political Centre, 1958).
85   Interviews; Conservative annual conference reports, 1956–8.
86   Avon, *Full Circle*, pp. 314, 321 and 325.
87   J. P. G. Freeman, *Britain's Nuclear Arms Control Policy in the Context of Anglo-American Relations, 1957–68* (Macmillan, 1986).
88   Interviews. Cf. also Freeman, *Britain's Nuclear Arms Control Policy*; and Sir Michael Wright, *Disarm and Verify* (Chatto and Windus, 1964).
89   Stephen E. Ambrose, *Eisenhower: the President* (Allen and Unwin, 1984), p. 526.
90   Clark, *From Three Worlds*, p. 166.
91   The Diary of Hugh Gaitskell, ed. Philip Williams (Cape, 1983), p. 566.
92   The most valuable account of the crisis from the American point of view will be found in Ambrose, *Eisenhower*, but the student should also consult Herman Finer, *Dulles over Suez* (Heinemann, 1964).
93   Sir Robert Menzies, *Afternoon Light* (Cassell, 1967), p. 166.

94 Robert Skidelsky, 'Lessons of Suez', in Bogdanor and Skidelsky, *The Age of Affluence*, p. 186.
95 Richard E. Neustadt, *Alliance Politics* (Columbia University Press, 1970).
96 Personal communication. Cf. Margaret Gowing's essay 'Britain, America and the bomb', in David Dilks (ed.), *Retreat from Power*, vol. II (Macmillan, 1981).
97 As summed up by a member of the British Embassy staff (private information).
98 Interviews; PRO, FO 371/116038–116057.
99 Paul-Henri Spaak, *The Continuing Battle* (Weidenfeld and Nicolson, 1971), p. 233.
100 Morgan, *Guidance towards Self-Government*, p. 96.
101 Private information; Darby, *British Defence Policy East of Suez*, pp. 143–4.
102 Richard Rose, *Do Parties Make a Difference?* (Macmillan, 1980), ch. 7.
103 Dow, *The Management of the British Economy*, ch. 15.
104 Brittan, *The Treasury under the Tories*, pp. 289–92; Dow, *The Management of the British Economy*, ch. 15.
105 J. Bispham and A. Boltho, 'Demand management', in A. Boltho (ed.), *The European Economy: growth and crisis* (Oxford University Press, 1982).
106 D. W. Parsons, *The Political Economy of British Regional Policy* (Croom Helm, 1986), pp. 141–5.
107 R. E. Caves et al., *Britain's Economic Prospects* (Allen and Unwin, 1968), p. 263.
108 Shonfield, *British Economic Policy since the War*, ch. 5.
109 PRO, CAB 128/29. Cf. CP 188 (55) of 3 December 1955.
110 HCP 254 (1959–60), esp. paras 141–221, 386–96.
111 Interviews; also Sir Richard Clarke, *Public Expenditure Management and Control* (Macmillan, 1978), chs 1 and 2.
112 Among the more notable acts passed by this government were the consolidating Food and Drugs Act 1955, the Road Traffic Act 1956, the Clean Air Act 1956, the controversial Homicide Act 1957, the Rent Act 1957, the Life Peerages Act 1958, the Tribunals and Enquiries Act 1958, the Children Act 1958 (dealing with fostering), National Insurance Act 1959 (graduated pensions legislation), the House Purchase and Housing Act 1959, the Mental Health Act 1959, and the Street Offences Act 1959.

5

From Macmillan to Home, 1959–1964

Michael Pinto-Duschinsky

Harold Macmillan's victory in the general election of October 1959 was one of the most notable achievements in British electoral history. The humiliation of Suez was forgotten amid the optimism created by the Tory campaign. The Conservative government was returned to office for a third term. Its 100-seat majority was nearly double that of 1955. Labour's percentage of the vote fell for the fourth election in a row.

The Labour Party plunged into gloom. The growing affluence of British workers seemed bound to weaken their loyalties to the party of the Left. *Must Labour Lose?*,[1] a book published by Mark Abrams, Richard Rose and Rita Hinden after the 1959 defeat, expressed the fear that Labour would be doomed to decline if it failed to adapt to the new prosperity. The American political scientist Samuel Beer anticipated an era of Conservative 'one-party government' for Britain.[2] To make matters worse for Labour, the electoral debacle led to prolonged faction fights between supporters of the leader, Hugh Gaitskell, and of the left wing. Until 1962, there were damaging struggles over Gaitskell's unsuccessful attempt to modernize the party's appeal by abandoning Clause IV of its constitution (which committed the party to a policy of nationalization) and over the issue of unilateral nuclear disarmament. Gaitskell's re-election as leader was challenged by Harold Wilson.

Nevertheless, Macmillan's triumph proved surprisingly short-lived. The government of 1959–64 is remembered mainly for the embarrassments and setbacks it was obliged to endure.

This chapter will outline the problems faced by the Conservative ministry after 1959 and will summarize its apparent successes. It will then discuss its strategy and evaluate its achievements. The discussion will focus unavoidably on Macmillan, the dominant figure of the day.

The government's difficulties started early in the new parliament. In May 1960, Macmillan suffered 'a disappointment amounting to despair'[3] when the East–West summit conference arranged to take place in Paris ended in abrupt failure. Shortly before Macmillan was to meet with the leaders of the two super-powers and with General de Gaulle, the Russians shot down an American U-2 spy plane as it was being flown over Soviet territory. After this, the Russian leader, Nikita Khrushchev, gave the summit short shrift. Thus Macmillan's efforts to lessen tension and to limit the danger of a nuclear conflict between the USA and the USSR met an abrupt halt.

At home, the economic boom, which – conveniently – had been at its height at the time of the 1959 election, was not sustained. Affluence led to a growth of imports and a dangerous trade deficit.[4] In spring 1960, barely six months after the election, the Chancellor of the Exchequer, Derick Heathcoat Amory, demanded a deflationary Budget. Macmillan refused. He felt deflation would be awkward in view of his government's tax cuts and hopeful rhetoric before the 1959 election. As he wrote to Amory,

following the Budget of last year and the Election last autumn, a deflationary Budget would either be very foolish or very dishonest. Unless it is supposed that we would be thought very modern and up-to-date, like those young ladies who oscillate between the stimulant and the tranquilliser. The new Progressive Conservatism will turn out to be a policy of alternation between Benzedrine and Relaxa-tabs. I don't like it at all.[5]

Failure to tackle the trade deficit in 1960 led to a major sterling crisis in 1961. The new Chancellor of the Exchequer, Selwyn Lloyd, was obliged to introduce an emergency Budget in July 1961. This moment of economic difficulty saw the introduction of two important policy innovations, both of which were to end in failure. First, Lloyd introduced a 'pay pause' and, shortly afterwards, created new institutions designed to plan for steady economic growth, the National Economic Development Council ('Neddy') and the National Incomes Commission ('Nicky'). Second, Macmillan announced the government's intention to negotiate British entry into the EEC. The fact that the approach to Europe seemed to be spurred by economic crisis rather than by pro-European convictions weakened Britain's bargaining position.

In the months following the pay pause, the Conservative standing in the opinion polls plummeted. This was not only because of the policy itself but also because the need to introduce emergency measures indicated the hollowness of Conservative promises during the election. The government's efforts to keep wages rises under control led to strikes and protests. The Minister of Education's rejection of a pay award for teachers, which had already been agreed by the Burnham Committee, led to especial resentment.

Disappointment among middle-class Conservatives with the state of the economy was probably the main cause of the spectacular Liberal Party victory in March 1962 in the Orpington by-election. The protest of this middle-class London suburb transformed a rock-solid Conservative majority of 14,760 in the 1959 general election into a handsome Liberal majority of 7855. Macmillan's determination to refurbish the image of his unpopular government and to safeguard his own position led him in July 1962 to dismiss the Chancellor of the Exchequer, Lloyd, and six other Cabinet ministers. The sackings were seen as a sign of panic.

A further crisis faced the Prime Minister in December 1962, when the US Secretary of Defence, Robert MacNamara, announced the cancellation of American plans to develop the Skybolt missile. Britain's Blue Streak missile had been abandoned in 1960. The future credibility of the independent nuclear deterrent – the cornerstone of British defence policy – depended on the American promise to supply Skybolt. Macmillan met President Kennedy for an exhausting meeting at Nassau in the Bahamas. The British mood was set by the Bahamas band which greeted the American delegation with the strains of 'Oh Don't Deceive Me'. With considerable reluctance, Kennedy eventually granted Macmillan's plea to provide Britain with the submarine-launched Polaris missile. Despite this successful outcome, the Skybolt crisis was damaging to the Conservative government. It illustrated British dependence on the United States and the one-sided character of the 'special relationship' between the two nations. It also angered General de Gaulle and was the reason – or the pretext – for his press conference in January 1963 at which he made clear that France would veto Britain's forthcoming application to join the EEC.

By spring 1963, disaster seemed to pile upon disaster. Incidents that would have been insignificant for a strong government now assumed major proportions. An exceptionally cold winter was accompanied by unemployment of nearly 900,000 in February 1963, the highest rate since the bleak winter of 1947. A series of spy cases and revelations brought additional pressures on the Macmillan government.

The 'Portland spies' had been convicted at the Old Bailey in March

1961, for passing secrets about the Navy's Underwater Detection Establishment. In March 1962 George Blake, an MI6 officer in Berlin, had been sentenced to forty-two years' imprisonment. In September 1962 John Vassall, a homosexual cipher clerk at the Admiralty, was arrested, having been blackmailed into spying for the Russians for seven years. Press speculation linked two Admiralty ministers with Vassall. On 8 November the Civil Lord of the Admiralty, Thomas Galbraith, resigned and six days later Macmillan agreed, under pressure, to appoint an independent tribunal of inquiry under Lord Radcliffe. In April 1963, the Radcliffe Tribunal cleared Galbraith of improper links with Vassall and he returned to the government. By this time the affair had already taken its political toll on the Conservatives. Moreover, bad feelings between the government and the press were fostered by the prosecution of two journalists who refused to reveal to the Radcliffe Tribunal the sources of stories about ministerial involvement with the spy.

While the Tribunal was preparing its report, there were further scandals. In January 1963 Kim Philby, formerly head of the Soviet department of MI6, defected to Russia. On 22 March the War Minister, John Profumo, made a personal statement in the House of Commons denying an improper relationship with a call girl, Christine Keeler, whom he had met at Lord Astor's estate at Cliveden. On 4 June, after weeks of mounting speculation, Profumo resigned, admitting that he had lied to Parliament. The affair was a sensation, partly because Keeler had been associating with Captain Ivanov, a military intelligence officer attached to the Soviet Embassy, at the same time as she was having a liaison with the War Minister. Macmillan came under attack for his handling of the matter. When the Profumo affair was debated in the House of Commons on 17 June, twenty-seven Conservative MPs abstained and Macmillan's leadership was challenged by Conservative backbenchers in the 1922 Committee.

The opinion polls continued to show a large Labour lead. By-election results were depressing. Macmillan was becoming weary. On 30 September he told Lord Hailsham that he intended to step down at Christmas, but then changed his mind. In October he told the Cabinet that he intended to lead the party into the next election.

No sooner had Macmillan decided to soldier on than he became acutely ill. Entering hospital for a prostate operation, he resigned as Premier. His illness soon proved curable. In the absence of a formal mechanism to elect a Conservative leader, Macmillan manipulated the 'customary processes of consultation' among Conservative MPs, press and constituency party leaders to ensure that R. A. Butler did not succeed him. In public there was a short struggle between the rival candidates conducted amid a glare of publicity at the annual Conservative conference at Blackpool. In private, Macmillan stage-managed the succession from his hospital bed, finally advising the Queen to ask Lord Home to attempt to form a government.

The struggle for the Tory leadership created bruising divisions within the party. Two ministers, Iain Macleod and Enoch Powell, refused to serve under the new leader. The relatively obscure peer who became Premier seemed an unlikely figure to rescue the party from its difficulties. In October 1964, Home duly lost the general election and, in 1965, resigned as Conservative leader. The Conservatives were to lose four out of five of the general elections held between 1964 and 1974.

Despite its undoubted problems, it can be argued that the Conservative government had major political, economic and foreign policy achievements in the years after 1959. It was in this administration that the most important postwar adjustments in foreign and colonial policy appear to have been made.

Shortly after the 1959 campaign, Macmillan embarked on a long tour of Africa. In February 1960 he spoke at Cape Town to the South African Parliament of the 'wind of change' blowing through the African continent as national consciousness was raised. The Conservative government's response was to speed the granting of self-government to most of the remaining colonial territories. Between 1959 and 1964 the size of the Commonwealth doubled. British Somaliland and Nigeria gained independence in 1960, followed by Cyprus (1961), Sierra Leone (1961), Tanzania (1961), Jamaica (1962), Trinidad and Tobago (1962), Uganda (1962), Kenya (1963), Malawi (1964) and Malta (1964). Several other territories were to become independent soon afterwards as the result of decisions taken in 1959–64. British rule in the Gambia and Singapore ended in 1965, and in Zambia, Guyana, Botswana, Lesotho and Barbados in 1966. The only major unsolved colonial problem was Rhodesia.

As far as the approach to the EEC is concerned, there is a case which supports the view that it was to prove a far-sighted act of statesmanship. Notwithstanding de Gaulle's veto, the negotiations of 1961–3 put Europe firmly on the agenda of British politics and created links between British and European politicians and civil servants which were to be invaluable later on. It was Macmillan's chief negotiator in Brussels in 1961–3, Edward Heath, who was to lead Britain into Europe after the Conservative election victory in 1970.

On the world stage, too, Macmillan could claim success for his attempt to narrow the gap between the United States and the Soviet Union. Britain played an important, positive role in the negotiations that led to the signature of the nuclear test-ban treaty in 1963. Following the failure of the Paris summit in 1960, the erection of the Berlin Wall in 1961 and the Cuban missile crisis of 1962, the treaty was a major event.

In the field of defence policy, the 1959–64 government benefited from the policies of the Defence White Paper of 1957 and from Macmillan's cultivation of Dwight Eisenhower and John F. Kennedy. As decided in 1957, conscription was phased out. The size of the armed forces fell from 702,000 in 1957 and 580,000 in 1959 to 423,000 by April 1964. British nuclear technology was advanced by the exchange of information with the United States, authorized by amendments to the McMahon Act passed by the US Congress in 1958. The Polaris missile provided Britain with a highly sophisticated system for delivering nuclear weapons at a low cost. Polaris cost a total of £350 million and, by 1970, cost a mere £32 million a year to maintain.[6] It was far more effective and less costly in the short term than the French *force de frappe*.[7] At the administrative level, reforms announced in 1963 resulted in the formation of a unified Ministry of Defence and control of inter-service rivalry.[8] The overall effect of these changes was to streamline and modernize the nation's defences.

While the economy failed to fulfil Conservative hopes expressed in the 1959 election campaign, the record of 1959–64 was considerably better than was realized at the time or has generally been granted since. The economy grew by an average of 3.8 per cent a year, an exceptionally high figure by British standards. Unemployment averaged 1.8 per cent and inflation 3 per cent. Investment in manufacturing industry rose by 26 per cent. By 1964, overall investment had reached 20 per cent of the gross national product.

Measures were belatedly introduced to modernize the nation's transport system. In 1963 *The Reshaping of British Railways* (the first Beeching Report) proposed to reduce British Railways' deficit by cutting uneconomic branch lines. Between 1960 and 1964 the country's first 300 miles of motorways were opened. Other plans involved redeployment of manpower from coal-mining to other industries and a programme introduced in November 1963 for long-term regional development and growth in the North East and in Central Scotland.

Among the notable measures introduced in social policy was the growth of higher education, which more than fulfilled the promise in the 1959 Conservative manifesto of a 'massive enlargement of educational opportunity'. The University of Sussex was opened in 1961 and authority was given in 1960 and 1961 for the establishment of the new universities of York, East Anglia, Essex, Kent, Lancaster and Warwick. While this expansion was in progress, the government appointed the Robbins Committee on Higher Education, whose expansionist report of October 1963 was accepted by the Home administration.

The standard of living improved steadily. By 1964, manual workers' wage rates were 19 per cent higher in real terms than in 1959. The proportion of home owners increased from 37 per cent in 1959 to 44 per cent in 1964. 5 million Britons took holidays abroad in 1965 compared with 4 million in 1961 and 1.5 million in 1951. 91 per cent of households possessed a television set by 1964, compared with 82 per cent in 1960 and 4 per cent in 1950. The rise in ownership of washing machines and vacuum cleaners was significant, although a majority of households still lacked a refrigerator.[9] Between 1960 and 1965 the number of private motor vehicles increased from 5.5 million to 8.9 million.[10]

On the political front, too, the government of 1959–64 can claim significant accomplishments. Despite the problems of attempting to win a fourth election running (a feat last achieved in 1868), and despite the malaise of 1961–3, the bad-tempered struggle for the party leadership in 1963 and Home's lacklustre personality and weakness as a television performer, the Conservatives came within a whisker of winning the general election of 1964. Labour gained only 0.2 per cent more votes than the Conservatives and only thirteen more seats. The narrowness of this result was probably due to the skill of the Conservative Party managers and the late date chosen for the election (October rather than June 1964). Heavy expenditure on pre-election advertising (the Conservatives' national campaign of 1964 was the costliest since the Second World War[11]) and the expansion of the economy in the pre-election period may also have helped.

These summaries of the difficulties faced by Macmillan and Home and of their apparent achievements suggest that widely differing evaluations of the record of 1959–64 are possible. Did the government drift from crisis to crisis, or did it have a strategy? Did the Tories cling to outdated visions of national grandeur or did they take positive steps to create a new international role for Britain? Was the task of economic revival properly tackled? Can the Conservative leaders of 1959–64 be blamed for the nation's subsequent economic disasters?

Historians have presented contrasting interpretations of Macmillan. To Ronald Butt, his actions were part of a plan:

When Harold Macmillan took office as Prime Minister in 1957, he had two main objectives in his national policy. The first was to restore the Anglo-American special relationship which had been severely damaged by the Suez affair and to find a new and viable place of influence for Britain within the Western community of nations, having regard to the realities of power. The second was to rebuild the British economy and the status of sterling. . . . Arising from these two general objectives a third practical policy quickly emerged: . . . to switch the emphasis in defence policy from a conventional to a nuclear basis, partly in order to save money. . . . From the same two initial objectives, there also arose, but more gradually, the commitment to a European policy. . . .

Macmillan . . . was a realist who could accept the inevitability of Britain's reduced international status . . . but who had the imagination to understand that national morale depended on finding some positive replacement for what had been lost. He had a sense of history and proportion.[12]

L. A. Siedentop's sensitive essay 'Mr Macmillan and the Edwardian style' gives a similar picture:

Macmillan played the part of an English de Gaulle. . . . Like the General, he believed that change is not only made easier, but is more likely to be for the better if some national virtue or genius is respected. . . . his grand diplomatic manners helped to mitigate, if not conceal, what was probably the most important policy of his administration in its early years – the retreat from Empire.[13]

By contrast, Alan Sked and Chris Cook accuse Macmillan of 'dishonesty' in his approach to Europe:

the motives behind the application had not been those of European federalism and Macmillan had no intention of making Britain a 'European power'. The real reason . . . was the need to find a theatre in which Britain could act the leading role. . . .

Britain's decision to apply for membership of the Common Market . . . should be seen rather as a means of restoring Britain to her old position at the intersection of the three circles – Europe, America and the Commonwealth.[14]

Samuel Brittan too includes the politicians of 1959–64 among the succession of policy-makers who made the mistake of giving 'priority to the maintenance of a world role the country could no longer carry'. This outmoded attitude was

the common factor behind our failure to join the European movement when we could have got in on our own terms ... the long delay in rethinking both the international role of sterling and its exchange parity, the investment of large resources in a series of military and space projects, many of which had to be cancelled before completion, and the growth of overseas defence commitments.[15]

I shall argue that

1 Macmillan did have a vision for the future. Seemingly haphazard actions often fitted into a larger design. Macmillan lacked the analytical genius of a de Gaulle, however.
2 Macmillan was more far-seeing than most of his predecessors and colleagues and more capable of developing a strategy than Labour's premier after 1964, Harold Wilson.
3 His sense of purpose was stronger in foreign than in economic policy.
4 Macmillan's and Home's governments were probably weakened by their narrow social base.

Most postwar British governments can be condemned for failure to make strategic evaluations of the nation's interests. All too often, politicians of both major parties as well as civil servants have been dominated by immediate problems and have omitted consideration of fundamental, long-term reconstruction. Paul Kennedy's study of British foreign policy, *The Realities behind Diplomacy*, argues that governments of the 1950s ignored the realities: 'There were no considered long-term assessments ... of Britain's place in the world, of the processes of decolonization, and of the changing military balance.'[16] Churchill and Eden, argues Kennedy, took for granted that Britain had a continued interest in playing a global role, despite the pressures for withdrawal from colonial commitments.[17]

Macmillan, impressed by the lessons of the Suez humiliation, seems to have thought about the nation's future more consciously. Evidence of his capacity for taking a long view appears in his memorandum entitled 'The Grand Design', composed during Christmas 1960.[18] His use of Cabinet appointments and committees suggests that he was working to a plan. When Heathcoat Amory resigned as Chancellor of the Exchequer in July 1960, no decision had been taken by the Cabinet about a policy towards the European Community. Macmillan saw to it that the three most sensitive Cabinet positions which dealt with Europe went to supporters of the EEC. Edward Heath was appointed Lord Privy Seal and deputy to the new Foreign Secretary, Lord Home, and was given responsibilities for European diplomacy. The two ministries that could be expected to present the greatest opposition to British entry into the EEC, the Ministry of Agriculture and the Commonwealth Relations Office, were allocated two ministers, Christopher Soames and Duncan Sandys, who could be expected to contain their protests. In 1961 Macmillan cleverly neutralized opposition to the European project within the Cabinet. No firm decision to apply for membership was taken (and thus no decision could be directly opposed), since the government merely announced that it would commence negotiations with the Community to explore the possibility of a formal application.[19] By appointing his rival, R. A. Butler, chairman of the Cabinet committee considering the details of the negotiations he deprived Butler of his capacity to campaign against the European project.

As a strategist, Macmillan is pre-eminent among British Premiers between 1951 and 1970. Yet his limitations are apparent when he is compared to General de Gaulle. The precise analysis contained in the French leader's memoirs contrasts with Macmillan's rambling volumes, notable for their evocation of mood, which take a thousand pages to cover his final years of premiership, from 1959 to 1963. In particular, de Gaulle's memoirs display an awareness of the economic foundations of foreign policy that is largely absent from Macmillan's work: 'in short', wrote de Gaulle, 'what a nation is worth in the physical sense of the term and, consequently, the weight it carries in relation to others – these [a nation's resources and labour] are the essential foundations on which its power, its influence and its greatness are based'.[20]

The most durable accomplishments of the British government of 1959–64 were in foreign, particularly colonial, affairs. It is tempting in retrospect to regard the end of Empire as an inevitable and thus unimportant process. The rise of nationalism, the decline of British strength and will, and the dissolution of the colonial empires of France, Holland and Belgium (and eventually Portugal) made it inconceivable that Britain could continue to rule its far-flung possessions.[21]

In the late 1950s, the position was less clear. Precipitate withdrawal could result in local conflicts and massacres (such as had accompanied

Indian independence in 1947), and in some territories, such as Kenya and Rhodesia, might endanger communities of European settlers. As events in 1960–1 showed, following Belgian withdrawal from the Congo, independence could easily be succeeded by chaos, with pro-Communist groups attempting to seize power. Above all, colonial independence risked destabilizing the mother country. Britain was not faced with internal instability on the scale experienced by France during the Algerian conflict, but the movement towards colonial independence did meet strong resistance from some sections of British public opinion and from powerful groups within the Conservative Party. Macmillan's decision, in October 1961, to appoint Iain Macleod Leader of the House of Commons and Conservative Party chairman was partly a response to formidable criticism from Tory diehards of Macleod's willingness as Colonial Secretary to accommodate the forces of nationalism in Africa. Macleod had been attacked in the House of Lords by the Marquis of Salisbury, the head of the Cecil family, for his betrayal of the white communities in Africa. Macleod was 'Too clever by half' and 'unscrupulous', claimed Salisbury.[22] Organized resistance to Macmillan's and Macleod's colonial policies was spearheaded by the 'Katanga Lobby' of Conservative MPs and by the Monday Club, a vociferous Conservative pressure group.

The major unsolved colonial problem was Rhodesia. In 1959, Southern Rhodesia was still part of the Federation of Rhodesia and Nyasaland, which had been formed in 1953. Nyasaland (Malawi) and Northern Rhodesia (Zambia) demanded independence as separate states. Despite resistance from the leader of the European settlers, Sir Roy Welensky, the African demands were eventually met. Within Southern Rhodesia, a self-governing colony ruled by the white community, a new constitution was adopted in 1961 despite African opposition. Africans would receive limited rights; control would remain firmly in white hands. The Conservative government, in attempting to meet both African and white demands, failed to satisfy either. The move towards extremism among the settlers was apparent by 1964 and led in the following year to an illegal 'Unilateral Declaration of Independence' and a further fifteen years of conflict.

Rhodesia apart, the Macmillan era saw the replacement of Empire by Commonwealth. Meetings of Commonwealth leaders were major diplomatic events, especially in May 1960 and in March 1961, when Macmillan unsuccessfully tried to avoid the expulsion of South Africa, and in September 1962, when he consulted the Commonwealth leaders on Britain's proposed entry into the EEC. Yet it was soon clear that the Commonwealth for all its sentimental significance was to be no major instrument of British diplomacy or trade.[23] The loosening of Britain's ties with its old possessions was seen in the Bill introduced in 1961 to restrict the previously uncontrolled influx of immigrants from Commonwealth countries.

Macmillan cannot reasonably be criticized for clinging to an out-moded concept of the Commonwealth as a surrogate for the old Empire. The change in Britain's relations with the white dominions of Canada, Australia, New Zealand and South Africa as well as with the newly independent territories was rapid and clear-cut. Dean Acheson, in his controversial speech of 5 December 1962, stated that 'Great Britain has lost an empire and has not yet found a role.'[24] He based his analysis of British foreign policy partly on the misleading argument that Macmillan was attempting to play a separate power role 'based on being head of a "Commonwealth" which has no political structure, or unity, or strength, and enjoys a fragile and precarious economic relationship by means of the Sterling area'. In fact, Macmillan's policies from 1959 seem to have been based on the premise that Britain's attachments to its former possessions were of declining significance.

Macmillan can be more justifiably criticized for clinging too strongly to the idea that Britain should continue to play the role of a 'great power' on the international stage, and for trying to forge a link with the EEC without relinquishing Britain's 'special relationship' with the United States. By the early 1960s this combination of aims, as Acheson hinted in his speech cited above, was beyond Britain's power to achieve. Macmillan's unwillingness or inability to tackle his problems emerges from the 'Grand Design' memorandum of Christmas 1960, which acknowledges that 'Britain – with all her experience – has neither the economic nor the military power to take the leading role' in the Western struggle against Communism, but none the less envisages a continued world role for Britain. Revealingly, the memorandum was not, as it should have been, an analysis of Britain's specific interests, but rather a vision of how leading Western nations, headed by the United States and Britain, could best confront the Communist challenge. A more logical mind might have reasoned that, if Britain wished to 'lead', then it must first regain that economic and military power whose absence Macmillan remarked upon.

The memorandum also throws light on Macmillan's defensive motives in deciding to direct Britain towards membership of the EEC. Macmillan wrote that he was still uncertain about British relations with 'the new economic, and perhaps political, state which is being created by the Six countries of continental Western Europe'.[25] Britain's main objective was to prevent the split between the six countries of the European Community and the seven countries of the European Free Trade Area (led by Britain) 'from getting worse. This meant reaching an accommodation with de Gaulle. . . . We could woo the French more easily by backing their great power ambitions . . . than by any other means. We might even by able to persuade the Americans to give the French some help in their nuclear plans.'[26]

Britain's pretensions to the status of a great power caused repeated problems after 1959. Macmillan's energy was consumed by discussions over conflicts, such as those about Laos, in which there was no direct British interest. British forces were engaged in far-off lands – Kuwait,[27] Aden, Cyprus and Malaya. Macmillan's concern to act as a broker between the super-powers damaged his relationship with West Germany's aged Chancellor, Konrad Adenauer, and meant that he was unwilling to press de Gaulle to agree to British accession to the European Community. In the late 1950s and early 1960s, West Germany was looking for Western support in the confrontation with the Soviet Union which culminated in 1961 in the erection by the Communists of the wall dividing the Eastern and Western sectors of Berlin. Notwithstanding Soviet provocation, Macmillan remained determined to push America into seeking compromises with the Russian leader, Khrushchev. This offended Adenauer and made him deeply suspicious of Britain's European policy, which he described as 'one long fiddle'.[28] Had Macmillan left the task of assuring world peace to the super-powers, a hurdle facing British entry into the EEC could have been removed.

Britain's position as the world's third nuclear power damaged Macmillan's relationship with de Gaulle. Macmillan made some weak attempts to dangle the carrot of nuclear co-operation before the French President. But de Gaulle realized that Britain had no intention of abandoning its ever-closer technical co-operation on nuclear weapons with the United States. Since the United States would permit Britain to share only a limited range of its nuclear secrets with France, British nuclear co-operation with France could not be complete and would have France in a position of permanent inferiority. This was a central factor in de Gaulle's decision to veto British entry into the EEC.

The unwillingness to come to terms with Britain's status as a second-rank power may also have been the major reason why Macmillan gave priority to the 'special relationship' with the United States and to a long series of meetings with his former wartime colleague, Eisenhower, and, from 1961, with Eisenhower's dashing young successor, Kennedy. The intimate link with the United States brought tangible advantages to Britain, especially in the field of nuclear co-operation. There were close ties between the intelligence agencies of the two nations. Russian military secrets given to the British in 1962 by Colonel Penkowsky and passed to the United States may well have influenced the Kennedy team to accept the cautious line being recommended by Macmillan during the Cuban missile crisis of October 1962. (By showing that Russia's missile capabilities were less than previously thought, Penkowsky's information enabled Kennedy to adopt a more confident, less agressive line.[29])

The ever-increasing imbalance between British and American power was putting the relationship between the two nations under strain, however. Especially after Kennedy's inauguration as President in January 1961, strong forces within the State Department, the Pentagon and the US intelligence community argued that the preservation of a 'special relationship' with Britain was no longer in America's interests.[30] Communism could be more effectively contained by a united Western Europe in which Britain was an ordinary member of a team of nations. Britain should abandon its independent nuclear role and merge its independent nuclear forces into a multilateral NATO force.[31] Macmillan was aware of these pressures and complained about 'the uncertainty of American policies towards us – treated now as just another country, now as an ally in a special and unique category'.[32]

Absorbed as he was in the problems of withdrawal from colonial commitments and in fostering relations with the United States, Macmillan was arguably indecisive, hence slow, in making an approach to the EEC. After the 1959 general election, the Macmillan government was still involved in creating the European Free Trade Area (the 'Outer Seven'), a trading bloc of small countries dominated by Britain. It was hoped that EFTA could negotiate a lowering of tariffs with the EEC. In other words, the tactic was to prevent the EEC from developing into a strong, self-contained unit likely to damage British trading and political interests. Only in 1960, when this approach was an evident failure, did British officials, and Macmillan himself, accept the full reality of the EEC and give serious attention to the question of British entry. Delay in making the initial approach to the Six was followed, after July 1961, by slow, cautious, highly intricate negotiations. Had Macmillan pushed the Cabinet into more rapid concessions over details about trading protections for Commonwealth food producers, had he insisted on a stronger pro-European rhetoric, the negotiations would probably have been completed before the French held a presidential referendum in October 1962 and legislative elections in November, and before the Skybolt missile crisis of December 1962. All these events stiffened de Gaulle's resistance to British entry.[33]

While it would be idle to deny the validity of these criticisms, it would be wrong to exaggerate them or to ignore the constraints upon Macmillan's power to force rapid change. First, the British government's attachment to 'top table' status was not just a matter of vainglory (though this was one element of it). Macmillan's policy objectives were sincere and important. Tension between the Soviet Union and the United States endangered world peace as the debacle at the summit conference of May 1960, Khrushchev's shoe-banging outburst at the United Nations in the same year, the Berlin crisis and the Cuban missile crisis all demonstrated. The atmosphere continued to be polluted by massive above-ground nuclear tests. To Macmillan, who had been schooled in the trenches on the Western Front in the First World War and who continued to suffer the discomforts of his serious wounds, the avoidance of nuclear war and the lessening of tension were overwhelmingly important objectives. Britain's possession of its own nuclear weapons brought it not only prestige but also, probably, some influence in drawing the super-powers together, a policy that bore fruit in the test-ban treaty of 1963.

Second, however keen the desire to end imperial rule, Britain was encumbered by worldwide obligations and ties which could not be severed outright.

Third, Macmillan's cautious approach to the EEC becomes understandable when it is remembered that the Community was not yet developing into a United States of Europe. De Gaulle, no less than Macmillan, was concerned with national prestige and the development of an independent nuclear capability. Moreover, it is open to question whether unreserved British commitment to the idea of a federal European state or the abandonment of the special relationship with the United States would have convinced de Gaulle to accept Britain as a member of the EEC. If undisputed leadership of the Community was de Gaulle's aim, no British concessions were likely to be acceptable to him.[34] Another reason why Macmillan had to be careful in his approach to the Six was the need to preserve British options in case the negotiations ended in failure.

Fourth, Macmillan's foreign policy was hampered by considerable domestic constraints. Public opinion had yet to adjust to the reality of the nation's weakened position. Support for British entry into Europe was to be found in the higher reaches of the Civil Service, within the business community and in the quality press. On the other hand, the Labour leader and most of his party where hostile, as were an active group of Tory MPs, many activists within the Conservative constituency associations, and sections of the Cabinet.[35] Macmillan succeeded in containing these pressures but was obliged to pay a price for doing so. He needed to appease the Cabinet, to avoid offending the Conservative Party conference, and to avoid a damaging party split. This restricted the room for manoeuvre of Edward Heath's team in Brussels which was negotiating terms for British admission to the Community. As argued earlier, it is open to doubt whether more British concessions would have persuaded de Gaulle. But, according to Ronald Butt's study 'The Common Market and Conservative Party politics, 1961–2',

British political attitudes to the negotiations over the 1961–2 period as a whole were a powerful influence on the evolution of the President's [de Gaulle's] own attitude. It was made plain to him at an early stage that Britain's political opinion – and, significantly, Conservative opinion – would not permit the Macmillan government to negotiate terms consonant with de Gaulle's conception of Europe. . . . Surveying the domestic politics of this period, it is difficult to escape the conclusion that Conservative feeling had circumscribed the government's approach to negotiations and in so doing had contributed towards their eventual failure.[36]

It is in the field of domestic policy that the government of 1959–64 is open to stronger criticism, though it should be stressed that the same strictures apply with even more force to other postwar governments, especially the Labour government of 1964–70. Macmillan and Home, like many other Prime Ministers, did not pay enough attention to problems of the economy.

As Chancellor of the Exchequer at the time of Suez, Macmillan had witnessed how economic pressures had made it impossible for the government to carry out its objectives. In the years after the 1959 election, the lesson was repeated again and again. Britain's economic difficulties undermined the credibility of the government's foreign and defence policies. As Adenauer remarked to de Gaulle, 'England is like a rich man, who has lost all his property but does not realise it.'[37]

Macmillan could hardly fail to be aware of the country's economic crises. Yet he failed to make the task of long-term economic reconstruction a top priority. In the last two volumes of his memoirs, which deal with 1959–63, Macmillan devoted only three out of thirty-three chapters to economic questions. The government of 1959–64 could claim credit for a variety of detailed economic reforms but failed to tackle the fundamental problems that were making Britain's economic growth fall ever further behind that of other leading industrialized countries. While British citizens were enjoying holidays abroad and the immediate benefits of owning televisions and cars (the number of cars in Britain increased by about 60 per cent during the 1959–64 Parliament), the future of the economy was being placed in jeopardy. In 1959–64, while the British economy grew (in real terms) by 18 per cent, the equivalent figures for Britain's European rivals were these: Belgium, 29 per cent; the Netherlands, 31 per cent; and France, West Germany and Italy, 32 per cent. Economic growth in Japan was 89 per cent.[38] While the dollar value of British exports grew by 33 per cent, the increase for other countries was far higher: France, 59 per cent; the Netherlands, 61 per cent; West Germany, 62 per cent; Japan, 93 per cent; and Italy, 104 per cent.[39] British exports of manufactured goods continued to decline. In 1950 the British share in the value of world exports of manufactured goods had been a mighty 25.5 per cent. By 1960 it had declined to 16.5 per cent and by 1965 was down to 13.9 per cent. West Germany's share, which had been 7.3 per cent in 1950, had reached 19.3 per cent by 1960 and was at roughly the same level (19.1 per cent) in 1965.[40]

In order to arrest these unfavourable trends, Britain urgently needed, among other things, to invest in the modernization of its industries. Yet, in Britain the proportion of GNP devoted to investment remained exceptionally low by international standards, even though it improved somewhat during the 1959–64 period.[41] The boom in the world economy helped to mask the deterioration in Britain's competitiveness, but the effects of foreign competition were already becoming apparent in such traditional sectors as textiles, steel and shipbuilding.[42] Above all, the failure to maintain Britain's position during the good times of the sixties made the country's economy particularly vulnerable when the world economy declined in the seventies and eighties.

Macmillan's speeches and writings about economic matters lacked the sense of urgency and national purpose shown by de Gaulle. 'Politics and economics', wrote the French leader, 'are as closely linked as action and life.'[43] When de Gaulle came to power in 1958, he launched a 'profound transformation' of the economy, and introduced tough measures, including devaluation and wage restraint. He made no effort to underplay the severity of his economic programme, declaring in a broadcast that, 'without this effort and these sacrifices, we would remain a country in the rearguard, perpetually oscillating between crisis and mediocrity. On the other hand, if we succeed, what a leap forward on the road which leads to the heights!'[44]

Like de Gaulle, Macmillan was a believer in *dirigisme* and aimed to raise living standards. Unlike his French counterpart, he did not face up to the fact that prosperity in the future would entail sacrifices in the present. Whereas de Gaulle in 1958 tackled France's balance-of-payments crisis by devaluation, Macmillan does not seem to have considered this option seriously in 1961 and 1962.

In part, the failure of successive British governments in the fifties and sixties to take tough economic measures was a matter of political expediency. Throughout this period, the Conservative and Labour parties were engaged in a close struggle. The outcomes of general elections were unpredictable and, except in 1959 and 1966, majorities were slim. The rival parties were usually within a few points of each other in the opinion polls. The broad consensus between them on major policy matters meant that the most effective way of attracting electoral support was to provide or to promise tax cuts and consumer benefits. Labour and the Conservatives vied with each other to pledge that they would build more houses, schools or hospitals or would put more money in voters' pockets. Before the 1959 election, Macmillan introduced extravagant tax cuts. In response, Labour promised an even larger pay-out. Economic temptations were again offered by the Conservatives before the 1964 general election and by the Labour government before the 1966 and 1970 campaigns.[45] The resistance to devaluation shown by British governments in the sixties was prompted by the fear that it would be seen by the electors as an indication of failure – an attitude that guaranteed that was exactly how it would be seen.

For Macmillan, short-term consumer benefits were not only a matter of political self-interest. He had a deep-seated, oft-publicized horror of unemployment, dating back to his experience as MP for the Northern constituency of Stockton-on-Tees during the worst years of the Depression. He was a convinced believer in economic expansion and in measures that gave spending power to ordinary people. Though he paid lip service to the problem of inflation, he was far more concerned about the dangers of deflation. His pride in full employment and in improving living standards often blinded him to the need to control consumption and to give priority to projects which would secure the modernization of Britain's industrial base.

By the standards of later years, the immediate economic problems facing the government of 1959–64 were mild. It was not yet clear that there was a fundamental disequilibrium that made devaluation unavoidable. Only in 1960 was there a severe balance-of-payments deficit. The crisis lay in the fact that Britain's rate of economic growth could not continue year after year to lag behind that of other nations without damaging the nation's competitiveness in world markets and without destroying its power and prestige. Macmillan must be criticized for his failure to perceive the crisis and to act with appropriate urgency to increase the pace of investment in industry.

During Selwyn Lloyd's and Reginald Maudling's tenures as Chancellor of the Exchequer (1960–4) a number of significant changes in methods of economic management were introduced. Some of them are listed by Samuel Brittan:

- The setting up of the National Economic Development Council, which introduced indicative planning to Britain.
- Long-term 'forward looks' for the government's spending plans along Plowden lines.
- Acceptance by the government . . . of the *idea* of an incomes policy.
- Setting up of industrial Training Boards.[46]

However, as Brittan comments, 'Some of these changes may have done some indirect harm by encouraging the notion, later to be seized on with such misguided zeal by Labour ministers, that new organizations and procedures could be a substitute for difficult policy choices.'[47] In particular, there was the choice between industrial investment, on the one hand, and consumption or spending on social services, on the other; also, a choice between deflation and devaluation.

Why did Macmillan shrink from presenting electors with a more sobering view of economic reality? Why did he not act more vigorously to channel money into the modernization of the economic infrastructure – roads, rail, telecommunications, ports, factories – rather than into consumer spending, housing or the social services? The answer lies partly in the expansionist economic doctrines of the time and in the same considerations of short-term political expediency that were to influence Harold Wilson even more strongly after 1964. A further explanation is to be found in the character of Macmillan and of his principal colleagues. For all his virtues – his pre-eminent skills as an actor and parliamentary performer, his tactical shrewdness and his vision – Macmillan lacked a compelling sense of national purpose and the determination to convince the public of the need to look to the long term. He enjoyed office too much and was willing to compromise with popular demand. Here again, there is a contrast with de Gaulle, who was unwilling to accept office unless it was offered with the power to implement those policies which he felt would lead to the national revival of France.

Arguably, an additional factor must be taken into account. The Macmillan and Home Cabinets may have been damaged by their narrow social base. Though Macmillan was a canny businessman, active in the family publishing house, and though he always remembered the modest origins of his Scottish ancestors, he was a member of the upper class. His wife, Lady Dorothy, was a duke's daughter. His Foreign Secretary and successor, Home, was a Scottish earl. The backgrounds of other Cabinet members were scarcely less distinguished. After the reshuffle of July 1962, nearly half of the Cabinet consisted of Old Etonians, a proportion which remained unchanged in Home's Cabinet of October 1963.

It would be wrong, of course, to assume that politicians' characters and views are dictated by their social origins, and it must be admitted that not all prominent members of the 1959–64 government came from privileged backgrounds. Heath, for example, came from modest circumstances. Nevertheless, the style and atmosphere of the 1959–64 government was set by the largest group of its members, who came from established families, rooted in the upper reaches of British society.

Since two-thirds of British electors were working-class and half of Conservative voters, the Conservatives could not hope to win elections without appealing for working-class votes. The party did this with considerable success. However, working-class Conservatives played almost no part in party affairs. The measures introduced in 1949 by the Maxwell Fyfe Committee to attract working men and women as Conservative parliamentary candidates had been a complete failure. By prohibiting candidates from contributing more than £25 a year to their Conservative constituency associations, Conservative Central Office had hoped to clear the way for Conservatives of modest means. But, while the financial barrier against working-class candidates had been removed, the social barrier remained.[48] After the 1959 election, there was only one working-class Conservative MP.[49]

The middle classes dominated the middle positions in the party hierarchy. The influence of the upper classes became ever stronger as one approached the top. Of the Conservative MPs elected in 1959, 73 per cent had been educated at a public school, and 16 per cent of the total were Old Etonians. The percentage of Etonians in the Cabinet was three times the percentage of them on the backbenches.

Top Conservative politicians frequently held company directorships when they were not in office, but the party leadership included few whose main careers had been in industry. While Conservative Central Office collected contributions to its national funds from many firms, the business world was surprisingly divorced from the senior counsels of the party.

For politicians who had been brought up amid inherited money, the conservation of wealth rather than its creation was a natural concern. Like the writings of the interwar Conservative leader Stanley Baldwin, Macmillan's are filled with nostalgia for the 'old, quiet, secure' rural world of England before the First World War, the England of his comfortable childhood:

Talleyrand once said that no one who had not known France before the Revolution could understand, in its true sense, 'la douceur de la vie'.

The same is perhaps true of anyone who did not know England before the First World War. . . . It is not easy for the British people, after their long sense of security and their supremacy in many fields – in trade, in industry, in monetary stability, and in undisputed naval power – the country of the Pax Britannica, with ever-growing imperial and colonial responsibilities, to adjust themselves to the new conditions.[50]

It is reasonable to suppose that a Cabinet with more self-made men would have been more determined to construct a modern, vigorous economy rather than to look back to the gentleness of an earlier time. One can speculate that a more middle-class government (such as that of Margaret Thatcher twenty years later) would have been firmer in controlling public expenditure and would have been less prepared to attract working-class votes by offering consumer benefits. A lack of feeling for middle-class interests was also to be seen in the government's education policies. The erosion of the position of selective grammar schools began during the Conservative governments of Macmillan and Home. The personal experience of Tory ministers responsible for the state education system did not equip them to appreciate the concerns of ordinary middle-class Conservatives for the preservation of the grammar schools.

By the early 1960s it had become clear that the rapid growth in affluence, which had seemed assured at the time of the 1959 election, could not be maintained. A mood of disillusionment spread. The social style of Macmillan and his colleagues became a butt of attack. Satirists and young intellectuals mocked or condemned the decadence of the 'Establishment' who ruled Britain. The public schools were criticized for breeding outmoded attitudes, for teaching a traditional classical curriculum that offered no preparation for the task of managing modern industries, for fostering the cult of the amateur, and for training a new generation to rule an empire which had ceased to exist. The 'perpetuation of class-barriers and class-resentment'[51] was condemned in a special issue of *Encounter* as a major cause of Britain's suicide as a leading power. 'It is still true that only exceptionally bright young people of proletarian or lower-middle-class origin are able to cross the barrier, and most of them still carry a traumatizing chip, or cross, through life.'[52]

One reason why the Profumo scandal was so damaging to Macmillan was that it seemed to confirm the image of the Tory government created by publications such as *Private Eye*. Revelations about the government minister and the call girl conjured up a world of naked romps in the swimming pools of aristocratic country houses such as Cliveden. It was not just among outside observers that the issue of class was regarded as a cause for criticism of the Conservative leadership. It was also the theme of Iain Macleod's remarkable article in the *Spectator* on 17 January 1964, which attacked Randolph Churchill's book *The Fight for the Tory Leadership*.[53] In this book, known to have been written in close consultation with Macmillan, Churchill described the informal processes of consultation which had led to the emergence in October 1963 of Lord Home as party leader and Prime Minister. Macleod, who had been Conservative Party chairman at the time (and who refused to serve in Home's Cabinet), condemned the way in which the choice of Home had been manipulated by a 'magic circle' of Old Etonians:

The only interesting part of Churchill's book is the account of the advice Macmillan tendered; of how having first supported Hailsham . . . he switched to Home; of how he organised the collection of opinions by Lord Dilhorne, Lord St Aldwyn, Lord Poole, Mr John Morrison and Mr Martin Redmayne. Eight of the nine men mentioned in the last sentence went to Eton.[54]

It is hard to assess the significance of the discussions about class which were a constant theme in the writings of the early 1960s. Possibly they were merely a symptom of the general mood of self-doubt and discontent which gripped the nation – or, at any rate, the more articulate groups among the young. According to Lord Blake, 'The early 1960s saw one of those mysterious changes in "the climate of opinion" which are as difficult to explain as they are easy to recognize.'[55] Perhaps the change of atmosphere was just a reaction to the fact that the Tories had been in power for too long and were becoming boring. It may also have been a reaction to the loss of Empire and uncertainty about the future. By 1964 the pessimism was pervasive enough to allow the Labour leader, Harold Wilson, to attack the years of Conservative rule since 1951 as 'wasted years'.

The accomplishments of the Conservative governments of 1951–64 made Wilson's epigraph absurd. Peace had been maintained, the Empire had been dissolved without serious mishap and living standards had risen faster than at any time since the First World War. The government of 1959–64 could claim particular credit for these achievements. Wilson was on firmer ground, however, in his implication that opportunities for change had been thrown away. Macmillan had limited Britain's foreign entanglements (though it is open to question whether he could have reduced the nation's commitments more rapidly), yet he had lost a chance to prepare Britain for survival in an increasingly competitive world economy.

Chronology

1959

8 October   General election: Conservatives, 365 seats; Labour, 258; Liberals, 6; other, 1.

14 October   Conservative Cabinet: Prime Minister, Macmillan; Chancellor of the Exchequer, Heathcoat Amory; Foreign Secretary, Selwyn Lloyd; Home Secretary, Leader of the House and party chairman, R. A. Butler.

20 November   European Free Trade Area agreement signed.

19–20 December   Western heads of government meet in Paris (Macmillan, Eisenhower, de Gaulle, Adenauer).

1960

6 January–5 February   Macmillan visits Africa (3 February: 'Winds of change' speech in Cape Town.)

18 January   Conference on constitutional future of Kenya under Colonial Secretary Macleod.

5 March   Macmillan elected Chancellor of Oxford University.

17 March   Conservatives gain Brighouse and Spenborough from Labour in by-election.

21 March   Sharpeville massacre in South Africa.

4 April   Neutral budget (Macmillan rejects deflation).

13 April   Defence Minister Watkinson announces cancellation of Blue Streak missile (£65-100 million had been spent on it).

28 April   Hire-purchase restrictions; credit squeeze.

1 May   American U-2 spy plane shot down over USSR.

3 May   EFTA ratifications complete.

3-13 May   Commonwealth Prime Ministers' conference.

16-17 May   Abortive East-West summit in Paris (de Gaulle, Macmillan, Eisenhower, Khrushchev).

15 June   Nyasaland state of emergency ends.

26 June   British Somaliland independent.

30 June   Belgian Congo independent. (Followed by anarchy and secession of Katanga province.)

1 July   American RB47 shot down over Barents Sea. EFTA tariff cuts begin.

27 July   Cabinet reshuffle following resignation of Heathcoat Amory. Chancellor of the Exchequer, Selwyn Lloyd; Foreign Secretary, Lord Home; Lord Privy Seal, Edward Heath; Commonwealth Secretary, Duncan Sandys; Minister of Agriculture, Christopher Soames.

7 July   Cuba begins expropriating US firms.

16 August   Cyprus independent.

1 September   Khrushchev goes to the United Nations; Nasser, Castro and Macmillan also present.

1 October   Nigeria independent.

1 November   US Polaris submarine base in Scotland announced.

8 November   Kennedy elected US President.

5 December   Abortive conference on Central African Federation.

1961

19 January   Hire-purchase restrictions eased.

10 February   Robbins Committee on Higher Education appointed.

5 March   Deutschmark revalued by 5 per cent.

8-10 March   Commonwealth Prime Ministers' meeting discusses South African membership (South Africa leaves Commonwealth on 31 May).

22 March   Conviction of Portland spy ring.

24 March and 5 April   Macmillan meets Kennedy at Key West and at White House.

17-20 April   Unsuccessful US attempt to overthrow Castro in Cuba.

27 April   Sierra Leone independent.

5 May   Alan Shepard second man in space.

17 May   In parliamentary debate Heath advocates British entry into Common Market. Speech followed by consultations with Commonwealth governments.

4 June   Kennedy visits England.

1 July   British troops sent to Kuwait, which is threatened by Iraq. (Last British troops leave by 10 October.)

25 July   Emergency Budget. Bank rate raised to 7 per cent; government spending checked; credit squeeze; pay pause.

August   Gallup poll gives Labour lead of 4 per cent.

4 August   UK granted IMF credit of £714 million.

8 August   TUC and employers invited to join new National Economic Development Council.

13 August   East Germany closes frontier with West Berlin. (On 17 September the Berlin crisis leads to early recall of House of Commons.)

1 September   Russia tests hydrogen bomb. Russian tests followed by resumption of US (underground) tests.

13 September   UN troops invade Katanga.

9 October   Macleod removed from Colonial Office; becomes Chancellor of the Duchy of Lancaster and Conservative Party chairman.

16 November   Electricity Council breaks pay pause. Butler introduces second reading of Bill to restrict immigration from the Commonwealth.

24 November   De Gaulle visits Birch Grove, Macmillan's home in Sussex.

9 December   Tanganyika independent.

13 December $6000 million IMF 'Group of Ten' set up.

21–2 December   Macmillan meets Kennedy in Bermuda to discuss nuclear testing and Berlin.

21 December   Agreement signed to end secession of Katanga.

1962

1 January   Year opens with government locked in conflict with unions over pay pause. Post Office workers begin work-to-rule.

9 January   Macmillan in talks with Adenauer in Bonn about support costs for British troops in West Germany.

29 January   The Minister of Labour, John Hare, announces pay pause to end 31 March.

2 February   2–2.5 per cent guiding light for incomes announced.

7 February   Sandys arrives in Central African Federation (Federation of Rhodesia and Nyasaland) for talks about Northern Rhodesia.

February–March   Engineering and shipbuilding strikes.

20 March   Defence White Paper, *The Next Five Years*. Defence costs to be kept to 7 per cent of GNP.

3 March   Trial of George Blake for espionage.

14 March   Liberals capture Orpington from Conservatives in by-election (and Labour to maintain Gallup Poll lead throughout the year).

15 March   Butler to take over responsibility for Rhodesian affairs.

5 April   Radcliffe Committee report on security published. Points to Communist activities in Civil Service staff associations.

2 June   Macmillan meets de Gaulle at Château de Champs to discuss EEC.

6 June   Labour wins Middlesborough West in by-election.

13 July   Cabinet reshuffle after Leicester North East by-election. 7 out of 21 Cabinet ministers dismissed, including the Chancellor of the Exchequer, Selwyn

Lloyd. Reginald Maudling becomes Chancellor, Peter Thorneycroft Minister of Defence.

24 July   Heath in Brussels for talks with EEC on crucial question of trade in Commonwealth foodstuffs.

26 July   Government to set up National Incomes Commission.

6 August   Jamaica independent.

10 August   Blue Water missile programme.

16 August   Aden enters Federation of South Arabia.

31 August   Trinidad independent.

10 September   Commonwealth Prime Ministers meet in London. (Communiqué issued on 19 September represents qualified victory for Macmillan on issue of British entry into EEC.)

19 September   Maudling Plan for international expansion opposed by USA at IMF.

9 October   Uganda independent.

20 October   China launches attack on India (Chinese cease-fire and withdrawal on 27 November.)

22 October   Vassall sentenced for espionage. Cuban missile crisis; Kennedy broadcasts conditions.

28 October   Khrushchev agrees to withdraw Soviet missiles from Cuba.

22 November   London Government Bill (Greater London Council to replace London County Council in 1964). Labour captures Dorset South and Glasgow Woodside from Conservatives in by-elections.

11 December   US Defence Secretary MacNamara arrives in London. Announces cancellation of Skybolt missile (which was to have been provided for Britain).

15–16 December   Macmillan visits de Gaulle at Rambouillet.

19 December   Britain accepts Nyasaland's right to secede from Central African Federation.

19–21 December   Kennedy meets Macmillan at Nassau; reluctantly agrees to provide Polaris missiles for Britain.

1963

14 January   De Gaulle's negative press conference about British application to join EEC leads on 29 January to breakdown of negotiations on British entry.

18 January   Hugh Gaitskell dies. Succeeded as Labour leader by Harold Wilson on 14 February.

6 February   NEDC approves 4 per cent growth target.

15 February   Unemployment briefly nears 900,000: 7 per cent in North East.

March   Labour lead in Gallup Poll reaches 15.5 per cent.

22 March   John Profumo makes Commons statement denying improper association with Christine Keeler.

25 March   Meeting in London on Central African Federation. Following walk-out by Kaunda and Nkumbula, Butler allows Northern Rhodesia to secede (29 March).

25 April   Radcliffe Tribunal clears Carrington and Galbraith of involvement in Vassall case.

26 May   Kenyatta elected Kenyan Premier. (Internal self-government granted 1 June.)

30 May   Peerage Bill (on renunciation of titles).

4 June   Profumo resigns as War Minister.

29 June   Kennedy visits Macmillan at Birch Grove.

1 July   Heath names former MI6 Officer Kim Philby as 'third man' involved in defection in 1951 of the Soviet spies Burgess and Maclean.

8 July   Rachman scandal concerning property rental in London.

25 July   Treaties banning nuclear tests in the atmosphere initialled in Moscow by the USSR, USA and Britain.

8 August   The Great Train Robbery.

16 September   Singapore, Sarawak and Sabah gain independence as members of the Malaysian Federation.

8 October   Macmillan taken to hospital on eve of the Conservative Party conference.

10 October   Home delivers Macmillan's resignation statement to conference.

18 October   The Queen visits Macmillan in hospital. He recommends Home as successor.

19 October   Home government formed, with Butler as Foreign Secretary, Heath as Trade Minister, and Lloyd as Leader of the House.

23 October   Home renounces his peerage. Wins Kinross by-election on 8 November.

2 November   Labour gains Luton from Conservatives in by-election.

22 November   Kennedy assassinated.

10 December   Zanzibar independent.

12 December   Kenya independent.

28 December   British troops sent to Cyprus following clashes between Greek and Turkish Cypriots.

31 December   Central African Federation ended.

1964

3 January   Constitution ensuring self-government introduced in Northern Rhodesia.

20–4 January   Mutinies against British officers in Tanganyika, Kenya and Uganda. British troops called in to assist.

22 January   Violence in British Guiana. (Sugar workers' strike January–July; state of emergency declared on 22 May.)

24 January   Comptroller and Auditor General reports Ferranti Ltd made excess profits on Bloodhound missile. Winston Field in London; demands independence for Southern Rhodesia.

12 February   Home sees President Johnson.

4 March   UN Security Council establishes peace-keeping force for Cyprus. (Heavy fighting in Cyprus on 9 March.)

17 March   The government of the South Arabian Federation asks for British help against Radfan tribes of Yemen. (On 28 March RAF planes destroy Yemeni fort in retaliatory raid.)

9 April Statement from No. 10 that general election will not be held before autumn.

14 April Budget. £100 million of increased taxation on drink and tobacco.

23 April Tanganyika and Zanzibar merge after coup in Zanzibar on 12 January.

14 May Labour gains Rutherglen from Conservatives in by-election.

May Labour lead in Gallup Poll 11.5 per cent.

9 June Constitutional conference opens in London on South Arabian Federation. (On 4 July agreement reached on new constitution and independence in 1968.)

6 July Nyasaland (Malawi) independent.

8 July Commonwealth Prime Ministers' conference excludes Southern Rhodesia Premier Ian Smith.

16 July Resale Price Maintenance Act comes into force.

28 July IMF renews $1000 million standby credit to Britain.

17 August Indonesian insurgents attack Johore, Malaysia.

7 September Ian Smith in talks with Home in London.

21 September Malta independent.

15 October General election. Labour gains an overall majority of 4 seats.

Notes

1 Mark Abrams, Richard Rose and Rita Hinden, *Must Labour Lose?* (Penguin, 1960).

2 Samuel H. Beer, 'Democratic one-party government for Britain', *Political Quarterly*, 32 (1961), pp. 114–23.

3 Harold Macmillan, *Pointing the Way, 1959–61* (Macmillan, 1972), p. 185.

4 Samuel Brittan, *Steering the Economy* (Penguin, 1971), p. 228.

5 Macmillan, *Pointing the Way*, p. 221.

6 C. J. Bartlett, *The Long Retreat: a short history of British defence policy 1945–1970* (Macmillan, 1972), pp. 252 and 280.

7 However, there were arguably hidden long-term costs for Britain, since it lost its independent capacity to produce missiles and was to be dependent on purchasing the Trident missile from the United States, at a higher price, when the time came to replace Polaris.

8 Bartlett, *The Long Retreat*, p. 191.

9 See A. H. Halsey, *Trends in British Society since 1900* (Macmillan, 1972), ch. 16.

10 François Bédarida, *A Social History of England* (Methuen, 1979), p. 256.

11 Michael Pinto-Duschinsky, *British Political Finance 1930–1980* (American Enterprise Institute, 1981), p. 143.

12 Ronald Butt, *The Power of Parliament* (Constable, 1969), p. 229.

13 L. A. Siedentop, 'Mr Macmillan and the Edwardian style', in Vernon Bogdanor and Robert Skidelsky (eds), *The Age of Affluence 1951–1964* (Macmillan, 1970), pp. 32 and 36.

14 Alan Sked and Chris Cook, *Post-War Britain: a political history* (Penguin, 1984), p. 169.

15 Brittan, *Steering the Economy*, p. 493.
16 Paul Kennedy, *The Realities behind Diplomacy: background influences on British external policy, 1865–1980* (Fontana, 1981), p. 331.
17 Ibid., p. 372.
18 Macmillan, *Pointing the Way*, pp. 323–6.
19 When Macmillan announced to the House of Commons the decision to open negotiations, 'he emphasized that, although application for membership under article 237 of the Treaty of Rome was a prerequisite of more useful discussion, any decision to join or not to join would not be made until *after* the negotiations had been concluded' – Margaret Laing, *Edward Heath: Prime Minister* (Sidgwick and Jackson), p. 131.
20 Charles de Gaulle, *Memoirs of Hope* (Weidenfeld and Nicolson, 1971), p. 131.
21 As de Gaulle put it, 'the victory [in the Second World War] which the free world owed to the courage of her people had eliminated her from the front rank' (ibid., p. 216).
22 Nigel Fisher, *Iain Macleod* (André Deutsch, 1973), pp. 170–3.
23 See Robert Blake, *The Conservative Party from Peel to Thatcher* (Methuen, 1985), p. 285.
24 Quoted in William P. Snyder, *The Politics of British Defence Policy 1945–1962* (Benn, 1964), pp. 3–4.
25 Macmillan, *Pointing the Way*, p. 324.
26 Ibid., p. 325.
27 See Anthony Verrier, *Through the Looking Glass: British foreign policy in the age of illusions* (Cape, 1983), esp. ch. 5.
28 Quoted in Terence Prittie, *Konrad Adenauer, 1876–1967* (Tom Stacey, 1972), p. 268.
29 See John Ranelagh, *The Agency: the rise and fall of the CIA from Wild Bill Donovan to William Casey* (Simon and Schuster, 1986), pp. 400–2; and Verrier, *Through the Looking Glass*, ch. 6.
30 See the chapters on 'The Special Problem of the United Kingdom' and 'The Disadvantages of the Special Relationship' in George W. Ball, *The Discipline of Power* (Bodley Head, 1968). The Nassau Agreement of December 1962 was an attempt by Kennedy and Macmillan to fudge the issue of whether the 'special relationship' should survive or whether Britain should be pressured into integrating her nuclear weapons into a NATO multilateral force. As Henry A. Kissinger remarked shortly afterwards, the Nassau Agreement was 'a document of extraordinary ambiguity, reflecting an attempt to reconcile the American quest for the integration of all the nuclear forces of the Alliance with the British desire to maintain a measure of independence' – *The Troubled Partnership: a reappraisal of the Atlantic Alliance* (Greenwood, 1982), p. 83.

31 See Andrew J. Pierre, *Nuclear Politics: the British experiment with an independent strategic force 1939–1970* (Oxford University Press, 1972).

32 Macmillan, *Pointing the Way*, p. 324.

33 This view was expressed by Sir Pierson Dixon, the British Ambassador in Paris, who was a member of the British negotiating team. See Piers Dixon, *Double Diploma: the life of Sir Piers Dixon, don and diplomat* (Hutchinson, 1968), p. 288.

34 See Arthur M. Schlesinger, Jr, *A Thousand Days: John F. Kennedy in the White House* (Houghton Mifflin, 1965), pp. 741–2.

35 See Robert J. Lieber, *British Politics and European Unity: parties, elites and pressure groups* (University of California Press, 1970), esp. p. 185ff.

36 Ronald Butt, 'The Common Market and Conservative Party politics, 1961–2' *Government and Opposition*, 1 (1967), pp. 372 and 386.

37 Quoted in Prittie, *Konrad Adenauer*, p. 263.

38 Derived from United Nations, *Statistical Yearbook, 1965*, table 179.

39 Derived from ibid., table 148.

40 G. B. Stafford, *The End of Economic Growth? Growth and decline in the UK since 1945* (Martin Robertson, 1981), p. 91.

41 See Edward F. Denison, 'Economic Growth', in R. E. Caves (ed.), *Britain's Economic Prospects* (Brookings Institution, 1968), p. 271. His research suggested that 'special emphasis' needed to be given to low investment as a cause of slow growth, a view shared by Sidney Pollard in *The Development of the British Economy, 1914–80* (Edward Arnold, 1983), pp. 348–9. For a different view, see J. F. Wright, *Britain in the Age of Economic Management* (Oxford University Press, 1979), p. 46ff.

42 See Pollard, *The Development of the British Economy*, pp. 294–6.

43 De Gaulle, *Memoirs of Hope*, p. 131.

44 Ibid., p. 146.

45 For a development of this argument, see Michael Pinto-Duschinsky, 'Bread and circuses? The Conservatives in office 1961–1964', in Bogdanor and Skidelsky, *The Age of Affluence*.

46 Brittan, *Steering the Economy*, pp. 234 and 290.

47 Ibid., p. 234.

48 See David Butler and Michael Pinto-Duschinsky, 'The Conservative elite 1918–78: does unrepresentativeness matter?', in Zig Layton-Henry (ed.), *Conservative Party Politics* (Macmillan, 1980), pp. 187–90.

49 David Butler and Anthony King, *The British General Election of 1964* (Macmillan, 1965), p. 235.

50 Macmillan, *At the End of the Day, 1961–63* (Macmillan, 1973), pp. 521–3.

51 Arthur Koestler, Introduction to Koestler (ed.), *Suicide of a Nation? An enquiry into the state of Britain today* (Hutchinson, 1963), p. 13.

52 Ibid., p. 14.

53   Randolph S. Churchill, *The Fight for the Tory Leadership: a contemporary chronicle* (Heinemann, 1964).
54   Macleod was not the only prominent Tory to voice such views. Reginald Bevins, Macmillan's Postmaster General, wrote of the Establishment, 'Yes, it has changed a bit, but not all that much. To be landed is no longer a must. Eton is' – *The Greasy Pole: a personal account of the realities of British politics* (Hodder and Stoughton, 1965), ch. 19. Sir Nigel Fisher was later to write of Macmillan, 'he has always been drawn to the background and life-style of the Whig grandees and he admires the best characteristics of the old aristocracy' – *Harold Macmillan: a biography* (Weidenfeld and Nicolson, 1982), p. 365.
55   Robert Blake, *The Decline of Power 1915–1964* (Granada, 1985), p. 406.

Bibliography

Good introductory works for the 1959–64 period are Robert Blake, *The Decline of Power 1915–1964*, Paladin History of England (Granada, 1985); and, for a general background to foreign policy, Paul Kennedy, *The Realities behind Diplomacy: background influences on British external policy, 1865–1980* (Fontana, 1981). Useful collections of essays are David McKie and Chris Cook (eds), *The Decade of Disillusion: British politics in the sixties* (Macmillan, 1972); and Vernon Bogdanor and Robert Skidelsky (eds), *The Age of Affluence 1951–1964* (Macmillan, 1970). Especially relevant chapters are L. A. Siedentop, 'Mr Macmillan and the Edwardian style'; Michael Pinto-Duschinsky, 'Bread and circuses? The Conservatives in office 1951–1964'; William Wallace, 'World status without tears'; and Peter Oppenheimer, 'Muddling through: the economy, 1951–1964'. See also C. J. Bartlett, *A History of Postwar Britain 1945–74* (Longman, 1977); Alan Sked and Chris Cook, *Post-War Britain: a political history* (Penguin, 1984); P. J. Madgwick, D. Steeds and L. J. Williams, *Britain since 1945* (Hutchinson, 1982).

Sources for more detailed investigation are the relevant volumes of Ivison Macadam (ed.), *The Annual Register* (Longman) and *Keesing's Contemporary Archives*. An invaluable, though partisan, source is Conservative Central Office, *The Campaign Guide*, 1964 and 1970. Other reference works are David Butler and Gareth Butler, *British Political Facts 1900–1985* (Macmillan, 1986); B. R. Mitchell and H. G. Jones, *Second Abstract of British Historical Statistics* (Cambridge University Press, 1971); A. H. Halsey (ed.), *Trends in British Society since 1900* (Macmillan, 1972).

Biographical sources on Macmillan are Harold Macmillan, *Pointing the Way, 1959–61* and *At the End of the Day, 1961–63* (Macmillan, 1972 and 1973), the fifth and sixth volumes of his memoirs; Anthony Sampson, *Macmillan: a study in ambiguity* (Allen Lane, 1967); and Nigel Fisher, *Harold Macmillan: a biography* (Weidenfeld and Nicolson, 1982). A full biography by Alistair Horne based on

Macmillan's private papers has been prepared for publication after his death. Reminiscences by members of Macmillan's staff at No. 10 are Lord Egremont (John Wyndham), *Wyndham and Children First* (Macmillan, 1969); and Harold Evans, *Downing Street Diary: the Macmillan years 1957–1963* (Hodder and Stoughton, 1981). For Home, see Lord Home, *The Way the Wind Blows: an auto-biography* (Collins, 1976); Kenneth Young, *Sir Alec Douglas-Home* (Dent, 1970); and John Dickie, *Sir Alec Douglas-Home* (Pall Mall, 1964). There have been a large number of controversial works about Enoch Powell, including Paul Foot, *The Rise of Enoch Powell* (Penguin, 1969); John Wood (ed.), *A Nation Not Afraid: the thinking of Enoch Powell* (Batsford, 1965); Andrew Roth, *Enoch Powell: Tory tribune* (Macdonald, 1970); T. E. Utley, *Enoch Powell: the man and his thinking* (Kimber, 1968); and Roy Lewis, *Enoch Powell: principle in politics* (Cassell, 1979). Biographies of Heath include George Hutchinson, *Edward Heath: a personal and political biography* (Longman, 1970); Margaret Laing, *Edward Heath: Prime Minister* (Sidgwick and Jackson, 1972); and Andrew Roth, *Heath and the Heathmen* (Routledge and Kegan Paul, 1972). Works by or about other members of the 1959–64 government are Lord Butler (R. A. Butler), *The Art of the Possible: the memoirs of Lord Butler* (Hamish Hamilton, 1971) and *The Art of Memory* (Hodder and Stoughton, 1982), which includes chapters on Macleod and Monckton; Lord Birkenhead, *Walter Monckton: the life of Viscount Monckton of Brenchley* (Weidenfeld and Nicolson, 1969); Lord Kilmuir (Sir David Maxwell Fyfe), *Political Adventure: the memoirs of the Earl of Kilmuir* (Weidenfeld and Nicolson, 1964); Reginald Maudling, *Memoirs* (Sidgwick and Jackson, 1978); Lord Hailsham, *The Door Wherein I Went* (Collins, 1975); Lord Hill, *Both Sides of the Hill* (Heinemann, 1964); Nigel Fisher, *Iain Macleod* (André Deutsch, 1973); Lord Stuart (James Stuart), *Within the Fringe: an autobiography* (Bodley Head, 1967); and Reginald Bevins, *The Greasy Pole: a personal account of the realities of British politics* (Hodder and Stoughton, 1965).

Works about public officials include Lord Alport, *The Sudden Assignment: being a record of service in Central Africa during the last controversial years of the Federation of Rhodesia and Nyasaland 1961–1963* (Hodder and Stoughton, 1965); Pierson Dixon, *Double Diploma: the life of Sir Pierson Dixon, don and diplomat* (Hutchinson, 1968); Lord Gladwyn (Sir Gladwyn Jebb), *The Memoirs of Lord Gladwyn* (Weidenfeld and Nicolson, 1972); and Philip Ziegler, *Mountbatten: the official biography* (Fontana, 1985).

Writings on the machinery of government in 1959–64 are H. Daalder, *Cabinet Reform in Britain 1914–1963* (Stanford University Press, 1964); J. P. Mackintosh, *The British Cabinet*, 2nd edn (Methuen, 1968); D. N. Chester and F. Willson, *The Organisation of British Central Government 1912–1964* (Allen and Unwin, 1968); Bryan Keith-Lucas and P. G. Richards, *A History of Local Government in the Twentieth Century* (Allen and Unwin, 1978); Michael Howard, *The Central Organisation of Defence* (Royal United Services Institute, 1970); and D. Vital, *The Making of British Foreign Policy* (Allen and Unwin, 1968).

Surveys of Conservative party politics of the period are included in Robert Blake, *The Conservative Party from Peel to Thatcher* (Methuen, 1985); John Ramsden, 'From Churchill to Heath', in Lord Butler (ed.), *The Conservatives: a history from their origins to 1965* (Allen and Unwin, 1977); Ivor Bulmer-Thomas, *The Growth of the British Party System*, vol. II: *1923–67* (John Baker, 1967); and T. F. Lindsay and Michael Harrington, *The Conservative Party 1918–1979* (Macmillan, 1979). A valuable study based on party documents is John Ramsden, *The Making of Conservative Party Policy: the Conservative research department since 1929* (Longman, 1980). On the leadership struggle of October 1963, see R. T. McKenzie, *British Political Parties: the distribution of power within the Conservative and Labour parties* (Mercury, 1964); Randolph S. Churchill, *The Fight for the Tory Leadership: a contemporary chronicle* (Heinemann, 1964); Macleod's article in the *Spectator*, 17 January 1964, repr. in George Hutchinson, *The Last Edwardian at No. 10* (Quartet, 1980); and Anthony Howard and Richard West, *The Making of the Prime Minister* (Cape, 1965). Studies of aspects of Conservative politics include Ronald Butt, 'The Common Market and Conservative Party politics 1961–62', *Government and Opposition*, 1 (1967); Patrick Seyd, 'Factionalism within the Conservative Party: the Monday Club', *Government and Opposition*, 7 (1972); Hugh Berrington, 'The Conservative Party: revolts and pressures – 1955–1961', *Political Quarterly*, 32 (1961); and Jorgen S. Rasmussen, *The Relations of the Profumo Rebels with their Local Parties* (Institute of Government Research, Tucson, 1966).

On election campaigns and voting behaviour, see David Butler and Richard Rose, *The British General Election of 1959* (Macmillan, 1960); David Butler and Anthony King, *The British General Election of 1964* (Macmillan, 1965); David Butler and Donald Stokes, *Political Change in Britain* (Macmillan, 1969); Eric Nordlinger, *The Working Class Tories* (MacGibbon and Kee, 1967); R. T. McKenzie and A. Silver, *Angels in Marble: working class Conservatives in urban England* (Heinemann, 1968); Ken Young, 'Orpington and the "Liberal Revival"', in Chris Cook and John Ramsden (eds), *By-Elections in British Politics* (Macmillan, 1973); On political advertising, see Richard Rose, *Influencing Voters: a study in campaign rationality* (Faber and Faber, 1967); J. Pearson and G. Turner, *The Persuasion Industry* (Eyre and Spottiswoode, 1966); Lord Windlesham (David Hennessy), *Communication and Political Power* (Cape, 1966); Michael Pinto-Duschinsky, *British Political Finance 1830–1980*, (American Enterprise Institute, 1981). On backbench pressures in the House of Commons, see Ronald Butt, *The Power of Parliament* (Constable, 1969); Robert J. Jackson, *Rebels and Whips: dissension, discipline and cohesion in British political parties since 1945* (Macmillan, 1968); and Philip Norton, *Dissension in the House of Commons: intraparty dissent in the House of Commons division lobbies 1945–1974* (Macmillan, 1975). On the social background of the political leaders, see Anthony Sampson, *Anatomy of Britain Today* (Hodder and Stoughton, 1965); W. L. Guttsman, *The British Political Elite* (MacGibbon and Kee, 1968); Colin Mellors, *The British MP:*

a socio-economic study of the House of Commons (Saxon House, 1978); Samuel H. Beer, *Modern British Politics* (Faber and Faber,1965).

Introductions to the economic background are Sidney Pollard, *The Development of the British Economy 1914–1980* (Edward Arnold, 1983); Derek H. Aldcroft, *The European Economy 1914–1970* (Croom Helm, 1978). An excellent study of economic policy-making is Samuel Brittan, *Steering the Economy* (Penguin, 1971). On incomes policy, see Jacques Leruez, *Economic Planning and Politics in Britain* (Martin Robertson, 1975). Two stimulating studies are Keith Middlemas, *Power, Competition and the State*, vol. I: *Britain in Search of Balance, 1940–61* (Macmillan, 1986); and A. M. Gamble and S. A. Walkland, *The Party System and Economic Policy: studies in adversary politics* (Oxford University Press, 1984). See also G. B. Stafford, *The End of Economic Growth? Growth and decline in the UK since 1945* (Martin Robertson, 1981); R. E. Caves (ed.), *Britain's Economic Prospects* (Brookings Institution, 1968); F. T. Blackaby (ed.), *British Economic Policy 1960–74: demand management* (Cambridge University Press, 1978); Andrew Shonfield, *Modern Capitalism: the changing balance of public and private power* (Oxford University Press, 1965); S. Strange, *Sterling and British Policy* (Oxford University Press, 1971); and J. F. Wright, *Britain in the Age of Economic Management* (Oxford University Press, 1979).

On foreign policy, see F. S. Northedge, *Descent from Power: British foreign policy 1945–1973* (Allen and Unwin, 1974); J. Frankel, *British Foreign Policy 1945–1973* (Oxford University Press, 1975); and Anthony Verrier, *Through the Looking Glass: British foreign policy in the age of illusions* (Cape, 1983). Also Avi Shlaim, Peter Jones and Keith Sainsbury, *British Foreign Secretaries since 1945* (David and Charles, 1977); and Kenneth N. Waltz, *Foreign Policy and Democratic Politics: the American and British experience* (Longman, 1968). On Empire and Commonwealth, useful general works are R. F. Holland, *European Decolonisation 1918–1981: an introductory survey* (Macmillan, 1985); and Brian Lapping, *End of Empire* (Granada, 1985). See also, W. P. Kirkham, *Unscrambling an Empire: a critique of British colonial policy* (Chatto and Windus, 1966); and Colins Cross, *Fall of the British Empire 1918–1968* (Hodder and Stoughton, 1968). As sources, see J. D. B. Miller, *Survey of Commonwealth Affairs: problems of expansion and attrition 1953–1969* (Oxford University Press, 1974); and D. J. Morgan, *The Official History of Colonial Development*, esp. vol. V (Macmillan, 1980). On the political impact of decolonization, see D. J. Goldsworthy, *Colonial Issues in British Politics 1945–1961* (Oxford University Press, 1971); and Miles Kohler, *Decolonization in Britain and France: the domestic consequences of international relations* (Princeton University Press, 1984). Specific studies include P. Gifford and W. R. Louis (eds), *Transfer of Power in Africa: deconolization 1940–60* (Yale University Press, 1982), and a forthcoming volume on the period from 1961; Robert Blake, *A History of Rhodesia* (Methuen, 1977); and Anthony Verrier, *The Road to Zimbabwe 1890–1968* (Cape, 1986). On the issue of immigration into Britain from the New Commonwealth, see E. J. B. Rose et al., *Colour and Citizenship* (Oxford

University Press, 1969); Zig Layton-Henry, *The Politics of Race in Britain* (Allen and Unwin, 1984); and Paul Foot, *Immigration and Race in British Politics* (Penguin, 1965).

A survey of defence policy is included in C. J. Bartlett, *The Long Retreat: a short history of British defence policy 1945-1970* (Macmillan, 1972). Other studies are William P. Snyder, *The Politics of British Defence Policy 1945-1962* (Benn, 1964); Philip Darby, *British Defence Policy East of Suez 1947-1968* (Oxford University Press, 1968); Andrew J. Pierre, *Nuclear Politics: the British experiment with an independent strategic force 1939-1970* (Oxford University Press, 1972); and Lawrence Freedman, *The Evolution of Nuclear Strategy* (Macmillan, 1981), which includes a detailed bibliography. On Anglo-American relations and the Skybolt crisis of December 1962, see Richard E. Neustadt, *Alliance Politics* (Columbia University Press, 1970); Henry Kissinger, *The Troubled partnership; a reappraisal of the Atlantic Alliance* (Greenwood, 1982); and Robert Klieman, *Atlantic Crisis* (Norton, 1964). For a French viewpoint, see A. Grosser, *The Western Alliance* (Macmillan, 1980); Wilfred L. Kohl, *French Nuclear Diplomacy* (Princeton University Press, 1971).

On the application to join the EEC, see Miriam Camps, *Britain and the European Community 1955-63* (Oxford University Press, 1964); Robert J. Lieber, *British Politics and European Unity: parties, elites and pressure groups* (University of California Press, 1970); and E. Barker, *Britain and a Divided Europe 1945-70* (Weidenfeld and Nicolson, 1971).

Material directly relevant to the British government of 1959-64 appears in memoirs and studies of foreign statesmen. See, for example, Arthur M. Schlesinger, Jr, *A Thousand Days: John F. Kennedy in the White House* (Houghton Mifflin, 1965); Ted Sorenson, *Kennedy* (Hodder and Stoughton, 1965); Pierre Salinger, *With Kennedy* (Cape, 1967); David Nunnerley, *President Kennedy and Britain* (Bodley Head, 1972); George W. Ball, *The Discipline of Power* (Bodley Head, 1968); Charles de Gaulle, *Memoirs of Hope* (Weidenfeld and Nicolson, 1971); John Newhouse, *De Gaulle and the Anglo-Saxons* (André Deutsch, 1970); and Terence Prittie, *Konrad Adenauer 1876-1967* (Tom Stacey, 1972).

On the Profumo Affair and spy scandals, see Clive Irving, Ron Hall and Jeremy Wallington, *Scandal '63: a study of the Profumo Affair* (Heinemann, 1963); Wayland Young (Lord Kennet), *The Profumo Affair: aspects of Conservatism* (Penguin, 1963); Bruce Page, David Leitch and Phillip Knightley, *Philby: the spy who betrayed a generation* (Penguin, 1969); and 'Nigel West' (Rupert Allason), *A Matter of Trust: MI5 1945-72* (Weidenfeld and Nicolson, 1982). Contemporary writings on the 'state of Britain' included Arthur Koestler (ed.), *Suicide of a nation? An enquiry into the state of Britain today* (Hutchinson, 1963); Arthur Seldon (ed.), *Rebirth of Britain* (Pan, 1964); Hugh Thomas (ed.), *The Establishment* (Blond, 1959); and Michael Shanks, *The Stagnant Society* (Penguin, 1961).

The large literature on specific areas of domestic policy will not be cited here. There is an admirable bibliography in François Bédarida, *A Social History of England 1851–1975* (Methuen, 1979). See also Arthur Marwick, *British Society since 1945* (Allen Lane, 1982).

6

The First Wilson Governments, 1964–1970

David Walker

It is a matter of when, not whether, Harold Wilson's historical reputation will recover. The publication in 1986 of Wilson's *Memoirs 1918–1964*[1] may have marked the end of a line of self-exculpatory works that have not helped the process. There is, however, material for revisionists. It is time they set to work.

Historiography runs in cycles. The bad cultural odour now issuing from Wilson's decade, the 1960s, will eventually disperse. And there is a demographic reason why Wilson's place in history is likely to be redeemed. It has mostly been in the hands of commentators who, literally or metaphorically, were *young* in 1964, when he first became Prime Minister. They had high hopes. Wilson himself promised a juncture, at least in the nation's economic history. For months indeed the promise was kept: 1965 was Wilson's *annus mirabilis*. And then disappointment. A large cohort passed from 1964 to 1970 through the years of political impressionability; it has carried much literary weight. Writers about those years have, sometimes, been motivated by that most painful of wounds, the death of first, youthful political allegiance. A generation weaned in their grammar-school classrooms on the purple prose of Michael Shanks[2] were bound to apply tests of unusual stringency to the Wilson government. In its maturation lie hopes for a more balanced judgement.

The course of politics since Wilson resigned the premiership in 1976 has extravagantly coloured our preception of his first government. Apologists for Mrs Thatcher for a time set up a fierce antithesis between Wilson and Thatcher, corporatism and free enterprise, statism and liberty. Wilson was an inversion of this woman of principle; his political demeanour the opposite of her steely integrity. On inspection, the contrasts dissolve. By 1987, we can see, Mrs Thatcher's government has travelled far along its 'learning curve'; its U-turns have been accomplished; the revelations of Michael Heseltine serve to paint as lurid a picture of her Cabinet dealings as did Richard Crossman's of Wilson's. The symptoms of the nation's economic and diplomatic decline are as marked in 1987 as ever. Viewed through the prism of 1987's political economy both Harold Wilson and his 1964–70 government deserve at the least a reappraisal and, perhaps, new approbation.

Wilson's leadership of an ideologically fissile party must, first, be reassessed in the light of that stellar event on the left, the formation of the Social Democratic Party. Wilson's skill as a parliamentarian and a tactician have long been recognized; perhaps it is time to add to them an ideologist's contribution to his party.

Wilson's success in 1964 was a work of personnel management. It was not just a question of his succeeding Hugh Gaitskell but of bonding together into a single electoral entity a Shadow Cabinet comprising Wilson's political enemies and rivals, a sluggish and unilateralist party outside Parliament and an aging and cantakerous band of MPs within. Wilson himself spoke of keeping the Labour Party vehicle trundling along so quickly that the occupants were too giddy to have time to look out. His detractors spoke of the party's identity being subsumed into Wilson's style, though they never questioned that the brown sauce and soccer analogies came from the man's instinctive populism rather than from a W1 advertising agent. Either way the inherent tensions within the ideologies of socialism and labourism were forgotten.

Keith Middlemas argued that Wilson's supremacy within the Labour Party 'deep-froze' the incompatibility of socialism – replacing capitalism with a new order – and the practical politics of living in and adjusting to capitalist society; but only between 1963 and 1968.[3] This is faint praise. It underestimates how much, from 1968, Wilson's leadership effected an ideological 'closure' of the Labour Party on the left. His social-democratic stance was offensive to the far left. Equally he maintained the institutional barriers against their penetration of the party, at least until he lost office. To Wilson can be ascribed paternity for extra membership of various far-left groups; honour to the father. What Wilson accomplished was to make Labour a successful electoral force in both 1964 and 1966 (and its acceptability as a governing party was not in question in 1970). This was not done on the basis of socialism but by reconstructing Labour as a popular party of the Left, its ideological baggage as unspecific as possible. In 1987 Neil Kinnock confronts this task and it is instructive to see him copying Wilson's styles and techniques.

Historians will, increasingly, come to see Wilson as a synthesizer of political ideas. By upbringing he was an active *government* Liberal. His personal romance was with Gladstone. His rhetorical triumph was to amalgamate a programme for modernizing Britain with the varied commitments, socialist and otherwise, of the Labour Party. His practice of politics was conservative, even Oakeshottian.

Socialism, Lord Morrison of Lambeth is supposed to have said, is what a Labour government does. The Wilson government realized the maxim. One of the puzzles of Wilson's career is how he continued to be regarded in certain quarters – such as, apparently, sections of the Security Service – as a fanatic. Government by grand strategy or 'principle' was replaced by the civilized and reformist instincts of patricians and experts of the kind recruited for the numerous Royal commissions and committees of inquiry organized during the period. The government's legislative programme relied far more on the agendas of Whitehall departments (including their responses to reformist lobbies) than on paragraphs in the Labour manifestos. The Wilson government was statist; Wilson himself was a believer in active government. But to elide statism and socialism is to make a bad mistake in the history of twentieth-century political ideas. Wilson's foreign policy hinged on the effort – which every postwar administration has perforce had to make – to align Britain's diplomatic and military role with its economic potency. Wilson, like Thatcher after him, swung between the North Atlantic special relationship and joining Europe.

Ideology was replaced, in part, by prime-ministerial whim – issuing, in Wilson's case, from a genuine provincial, a 1940s patriot, an authentic voice of non-metropolitan Britain, perhaps the first to be heard in Downing Street since Lloyd George's. Wilson's credo often boiled down to a weak form of 'social' Christianity, the use of government power to assist identifiable groups of have-nots, notably the old.

Because of the influence on Mrs Thatcher of self-conscious ideologues (advisers, that is, claiming an internally coherent view of the world) 'Thatcherism' has been coined as a ruling doctrine of the 1980s. During the 1960s, and indeed since, it would have been outlandish to ascribe to Harold Wilson any 'ism'. 'Wilsonian', yes, referred to Wilson's demeanour and such tools of the trade as pipe and Gannex raincoat. Yet there was an 'ism', pragmatism, his own favourite. It came to mean Harold Wilson's personal response to events, taking into account state of party, parliamentary votes, the advice of courtiers, bureaucrats, even (as he often said) the weather – in short an empirical response to events serving the immediate end of political equilibrium maintenance. It was this that constantly upset Crossman the diarist. Yet it may be as good a recipe for electorally appealing left-of-centre government as the political circumstances of postwar Britain permit.

The case for revisionism has been aided by the performance of Mrs Thatcher's government. Despite the rhetoric, in seven years it has failed to 'break' with the deep-lying structures of British economic life. Neither economic growth nor the international competitiveness of the British economy can be said to demonstrate success; price inflation has been squeezed out at the expense of employment – secular problems with excess real earnings remain. All of which goes to argue that the relative economic performance of governments should be judged calmly, and empirically. Britain's economic problems (such as high labour costs) appear to be endemic: successive policies should be appraised as if they were coarse experiments rather than final solutions.

Thus the Wilson government patently did not arrest Britain's postwar economic decline as measured by share of world trade or comparative gross national product per head. But its efforts were no less creditable than its successors', given changing economic circumstance. None of the indices as viewed in spring 1987 support a case for excluding the Thatcher government from that continuing failure. Instead, the pointers are to the relative success of the Wilson years. One-to-one comparisons of the tenure of respective Premiers are unsound. Yet it is worth remembering how impressive was the growth of output and trading performance over the period 1964–70; that Wilson's 'supply side' strategy did have some positive effect and there was productivity gain to be registered.

All postwar Prime Ministers stand to be judged on how well they managed the diplomatic and economic decline of the nation. The assumption is easily made both that they could 'manage', and that decline is the right way of describing a geopolitical readjustment. Yet Wilson, like Thatcher, certainly came to office with grand plans for arresting decline. A central question to be asked of his tenure is whether the failure of those plans had some benefit for a nation suffering (as it still does) from delusions of potency. Wilson's handling of Rhodesia's unilateral declaration of independence in 1965 was unheroic; but did it have educational value as a demonstration of military impotence a decade after Suez?

Two decades later the Falklands episode showed how difficult such lessons are to learn. Or perhaps British military involvement with small colonial islands obeys another logic. Wilson himself succumbed to it when in 1969 amidst national ribaldry he ordered the invasion of the Caribbean island of Anguilla by a troop of bobbies. Yet, weighed in the scales, that was a less costly lesson in the decline of British power than the taking of Goose Green.

The grandest context for the Wilson government was 'the sixties'. The decade has come to have a peculiar cultural resonance: the source of moral degradation, sexual promiscuity, libertinism. That ill-defined institution, the 'permissive society', has become a brutal political slogan of the 1980s, and one wielded with zest by Conservatives whose recipe for economic recovery is precisely that of greater permissiveness. The truth is that culture, morality and politics come at each only tangentially. Some writers, notably Christopher Booker,[4] have set themselves to chart great swings in national mood, timetabled with amazing precision by political events. Most are agnostic about the relationship, if any, between – say – the boom in popular music associated with the Beatles and formal politics; perhaps Harold Wilson's good-humouredly opportunistic recommendation of their MBEs said it all.

If we take culture in its broadest sense to include attitudes, then the Wilson government touched and was touched by the decade's movements. This shows most obviously in the government's accommodation of changing attitudes in certain areas of personal conduct. Wilson came to power with no recipe for creating the permissive society; the response was empirical. Brian Lapping is partial but right: 'The Labour government did adapt the laws to changing British moral attitudes at a sufficient rate to encourage some hope that in Britain the law would continue to be respected.'[5] The list of "civilizing" statutes is long: the Abortion Act 1967, introduced by David Steel but passed with the Wilson government's help, the Family Planning Act 1967, the Divorce Act 1968, the Matrimonial Property Act 1970 and the Equal Pay Act 1970.

Such statutes are usually lumped together with, say, the Murder Act 1965, which suspended capital punishment, and a common parentage inferred. This is misleading. Wilson's divorce legislation probably had less effect on the popularization of divorce than changes in the law that came after. Besides, behind it and the other statutes lay a stream of thinking largely independent of Labour policies or personalities. It must be said that the permissive society, which they gave parliamentary space to create, disturbed the Wilson Cabinet little. In personal relationships Wilson and his colleagues were decidedly conventional, even prim. Lord Longford, an acute observer of un-Christian behaviour, counted eleven committed Christians among his Cabinet colleagues *circa* 1965 – including Wilson, Chancellor of the Exchequer James Callaghan and Deputy Prime Minister George Brown.[6] There is indeed a case for identifying the Wilson government as one of the last Christian family Cabinets in modern times – one of the last before the liberalization of the divorce laws showed through in the lives of politicians. It is note-worthy that Anthony Crosland, as Secretary for Education, should have uttered his bloodcurdling threat to kill the grammar schools of England by his wife's bed:[7] iconoclasm about one institution did not necessarily extend to any other. For a Cabinet presiding over the birth of the permissive society, Wilson's availed itself little of the opportunities.

Yet in another way the attitudes of the 1960s were Wilson's. 'What sort of island do we want to be?' Michael Shanks had asked.

A lotus island of easy, tolerant ways, bathed in the golden glow of an imperial sunset, shielded from discontent by a threadbare welfare state and an acceptance of genteel poverty? Or the tough dynamic race we have been in the past, striving always to better ourselves, seeking new worlds to conquer in place of those we have lost, ready to accept growing pains as the price of growth?[8]

That this passage could just as well be used in 1987 (with a caveat about the exclusion of non-white Britons implied in its use of 'race') shows how perennial is the theme; also that the undoubted failure of the Wilson government to realize Shanks's ambition was not singular.

His book was a popular success. It belonged to a genre of institutional and cultural criticism prevalent in the early 1960s, an anti-political strain reflecting in part intergenerational rivalries and in part a search for a grand national idea to replace that of Empire. Suffice it to say that Wilson came to power on a great wave of expectation – mention was widely made of his first hundred days in unembarrassed imitation of the John F. Kennedy myth in the United States. The necessarily large overlap in public policy between the Wilson government and Sir Alec Douglas-Home's was ignored. Wilson was supposed to be the political realization of the lobby for societal change led by Shanks and the host of commentators who, prior to 1964, had excoriated the old and heralded the new.

The honeymoon was surprisingly long-lasting. After the sterling crisis in late spring and early summer 1966 it was realized that Wilsonian macro-economic policy was (inevitably) similar to that pursued by Reginald Maudling in the Douglas-Home government. There were to be no seismic shifts in public policy. It was as if the metropolitan elite which supplies most political commentary had been hyper-ventilating. A spasm of anger and disappointment ran through the salons – if Cecil King's diaries are any guide[9] – and the note then struck has influenced judgements since. In King's case it led, within a year, to that strange episode in which he, Mountbatten and others actually discussed a coup.

Wilson himself cannot be exempted from blame for this pattern of exaggerated expectation and frenzied disappointment. He had written and spoken copiously in the Shanks vein. He had consciously cultivated a central public perception of the 1960s, that the power of government to change men and especially their economic destiny was boundless.

Wilson was a statist, in the archaic sense of someone skilled in the numbers of government. He was, equally, a statist by his belief in the efficacy of government economic interventions, by his biographical experience as an aide to Beveridge, and by necessity. Labour Party doctrine favoured state control of production. Wilson believed in micro-economic intervention to enhance the competitiveness of industry – not because of party dogma, but in the light of his wartime and ministerial experience in the collectivized 1940s, together with a corporatist faith, current at the time, in indicative central planning.

Yet government would have grown big during the sixties regardless of such belief. Each and every government has, regardless of inclination, to accommodate a multitude of past decisions by couples to procreate: the rippling effect of a baby boom through time creates irresistible demands for social and health services. Thus a pre-existing demand for higher education, for education at all levels, had to be catered for. As a matter of fact, many of the buildings within which education is now conducted were put up as a result of Wilsonian public expenditure decisions. These were years, indeed, of large-scale infrastructural investment in the public sector.

The first half of the decade saw the entry into the labour force of the baby boomers, the large birth cohorts of the late 1940s. The proportionate growth of the labour force from 1961 to 1966 was bigger than at any time since 1900.[10] A multitude of new jobs were created. During the Thatcher era it has become a cliché of politics to refer to the 'success' of governments in creating jobs, even outside the public sector; its use has been fulsome even by politicians who otherwise would deny the state can create employment.

In terms of this cliché the Macmillan, Douglas-Home and Wilson governments were eminently successful: the new entrants were absorbed while unemployment stayed low. Since the mid-1960s, however, rates of unemployment have moved upwards, dramatically since the mid-1970s; some might make of 1966 a juncture in the long-term demand for labour in the British economy. 'Since 1966', according to John Ermisch, 'the labour force has been continually diverging from the potential labour supply. A lack of employment opportunities has been discouraging labour force participation, although the extent of the divergence is difficult to estimate.'[11] One aspect of this imbalance is over-pricing of the supply of labour. Until the Thatcher era, this was considered one of those immutable contexts of policy-making – Mrs Thatcher's government has been prepared to consider reform of wages councils and abolition of earnings floors. By not even addressing the issue of imbalance in labour costs, the Wilson government laid the ground for the high and seemingly permanent divergence between employment and labour supply that characterizes the present decade.

The 1960s saw a big increase in the proportion of pensioners in the population – adding to the numbers of those living in a condition where they needed income support from the state.[12] Here was a social fact, and a political opportunity. Providing more generously for the old suited Wilson the social liberal and his party. The only argument was over the degree of generosity. On the eve of the 1964 election Wilson had been in his own constituency of Huyton, now part of the metropolitan district of Knowsley.

His speeches that evening were homely constituency chats about the kind of people and problems he had met during the day. 'Today I asked at the Kirkby Labour club for all the old-age pensioners who had reduced-fare bus passes to put up their hands, and then those who hadn't. It was about 50–50.' This illustrated Wilson's point about the anomalies of the system for giving passes, and his conviction that reduced fares are a matter of real importance. 'In some ways,' he said quietly, 'the loneliness of old-age pensioners is more of a problem than their poverty.'[13]

One of the first Bills introduced by the new government in 1964 empowered local authorities to give the old concessionary fares, thereby delivering an election promise and, in concrete terms, offering a better life to one of the Labour Party's client groups. The use of the state as a mechanism for income redistribution followed almost automatically.

The Wilson government inherited ambitious plans to expand public expenditure. The 1963 survey, conducted by the new Public Expenditure Survey Committee recommended by the Plowden Report,[14] projected real annual average increases of 4.1 per cent to 1967–8. Labour's National Plan projected, to 1969–70, a 4.25 per cent per annum growth rate for spending, exclusive of nationalized industries investment. Both these envisaged spending as rising in line with output growth.[15] In fact spending growth outstripped output, pushing up public expenditure as a share of aggregate national output: the 1960s are a decade of the state in a profound sense. Resources consumed by the public sector, especially manpower, grew apace. During the Wilson years, the public sector took an extra 5 per cent of real national resources. R. W. R. Price points out that a decade which began with the Plowden reforms ended with a spending boom: 'a period which began with concern over the need to contain public expenditure and saw reforms in its management was also one of great expansion.'[16]

If political economy were some exact science, it would be possible to chart the Cabinet discussions which led to this growth. We can certainly get from Crossman little pictures of individual incidents along that curve – a victory in his battle for more housing investment here, a defeat for expenditure on overseas aid there. The big picture is missing. And, we learn from the civil servant responsible for PESC management, it was missing then, too. Sir Richard Clarke, second secretary at the Treasury in charge of public expenditure, makes this admission:

In preparing this chapter ten years later, with the relevant White Papers, and with some familiarity with the business, I cannot satisfy myself about what really happened.

There was a big total increase from 1964–65 to 1965–66, and then a much lower increase from 1965–66 to 1966–67, and then big increases in the following two years until the effect of Mr Jenkins's emergency post-devaluation operation of January 1968, a series of very severe cuts indeed.[17]

It would be easy at that point to throw up one's hands and join the chorus – contemporary as well as subsequent – bemoaning the inadequacy of the public-spending control system; the complaint would not, however, be enlightening about the Wilson years. The stated ambition of a government of very different stripe, Mrs Thatcher's, was to control spending, indeed to cut it as a proportion of national output. By 1986 her government had been convincingly unsuccessful, suggesting some "problem" deeper than the mechanisms of control.

There are, none the less, wider questions about the profligacy of increases in spending in the Wilson years. Anthony Crosland claimed that high spending and high taxation in a climate of moderate output growth gave rise to what by 1970 was 'exceptional resentment of high taxation' with consequent effects on wage bargaining.[18] This line of thinking flourished during the 1970s, predicting various thresholds at which tax revolts would occur because high rates would no longer be tolerable. The fact that the tax burden and associated high marginal rates have persisted into the 1980s without such manifestations and, indeed, with the entire tax issue appearing to have died, suggests some error in the earlier diagnosis.

The obvious error is the failure to link taxation and spending and to emphasize the intervening variable of 'value for money'. This phrase has, again, become fashionable in the 1980s and properly so, for it directs attention to the quality of the public sector and the effectiveness of public services purchased with tax revenue.

Here is a central issue for judging the Wilson years. Did the expansion of public spending 'purchase' acceptable levels of service output? After the collapse of the Ronan Point flats, questions have been posed about the building methods adopted during the expansion of public housing in the 1960s. Little work has yet been done on the bedding-down in schools and, it has to be said, hospitals of practices of work and standards of performance which, upon subsequent examination of outputs, did not provide value for public money. Total local-government expenditure grew faster under Wilson than under any previous government since Disraeli's 1874 administration:[19] the continuous dissatisfaction with local government's product manifest since the mid-1970s is surely evidence that some of that was misdirected. Bacon and Eltis have complained that between 1967 and 1970 total employment in the economy was falling, yet employment in health, education and generic public administration increased markedly, distorting the balance of the economy and requiring the non-government workers to carry an untenable burden.[20]

It seems safe to say that the Wilson government did concern itself with public services in gross. There was a row about postponing the raising of the school-leaving age in 1968, for example: this was a political virility symbol. But, as for discussion about the content and quality of services, there was little, except when service deficiency provoked a political issue. Thus Crossman gets involved in a scandal about a Cardiff mental hospital; but wider issues of management and service delivery are dealt with hermetically within the Department of Health and Social Security.[21]

In a similar way, long threads of public policy-making were carried on with minimal Cabinet supervision. Education is a good example. Wilson's instincts were to cherish the grammar schools of England and Wales as a mechanism for social mobility (the evidence for which contention is ambiguous[22]); but during his government nearly half the existing grammar schools ceased to exist. Neither he nor the social-democratic ministers such as Tony Crosland who were most keen on comprehensive reorganization of secondary schools ever questioned that what they were doing, at best, was tinkering with forms of schooling and with educational organization, leaving its content and children's attainment entirely alone. These were years of astonishing 'hands off' policies in such areas as entry to and organization of initial teacher training and styles of primary education. Wilson's supply-side policies never encompassed the content or the output of the education system; it was considered sufficient to increase inputs.

For a statistician Wilson showed himself little able to connect the costs and benefits of government activity. Sir Richard Clarke recalled

new large subjects coming forward, such as the distribution of population and employment, Buchanan [on urban transport], the Robbins Report [on higher education] the Channel Tunnel, decimalization and so on. These were difficult to grasp, partly because their substance was inchoate and it was difficult to find a way into it that would lead to effective action, and partly because departmental responsibilities were confused.[23]

Perhaps the single greatest disappointment of Wilson's performance was this: that he failed to reconstruct the machinery of central government in such a way that public expenditure decisions could be taken in a conscious, dignified way, with costs and benefits displayed.

No Prime Minister has taken office better equipped to run the machinery of British central government than Harold Wilson. As Oxford don, wartime civil servant and young minister, he had had years to think about and practice upon the bodies of Cabinet and departmental government. The modernization of the Whitehall machine was one of the grand promises before 1964, not least when Wilson sat down with Norman Hunt (later Lord Crowther-Hunt) to record a radio programme full of plans for reform not just of the departments but of the Civil Service itself. By his own account Wilson's desire to 're-skill' the Civil Service went back to conversations during the war. Commissioned in 1966, Lord Fulton, vice-chancellor of the new University of Sussex, produced a report which might have altered recruitment and structures eventually to provide both ministers and Parliament with a better service.[24] Wilson accepted the report. He managed the Cabinet to secure its assent. Implementation ran into the sands because Wilson, ministers and parliamentarians proved to have neither time nor interest enough to track it through the permanent bureaucracy. Wilson, in keeping with a prevalent pattern of thinking, focused on input to public administration, such as the expertise of civil servants, but neglected output, how civil servants actually performed; reorganization was avidly debated instead of function.

Peter Hennessy concluded that Wilson's was 'a hugely disappointing premiership in terms of modernizing the instruments of government'.[25] It is a judgement bolstered by the failure of Wilson and Crossman in their declared intention of giving the House of Lords a better-defined legislative role and the making of Parliament and its select committees a more effective institution. It is mitigated only slightly by such innovations as the Parliamentary Commissioner for Adminstration, the Ombudsman.

The landscape of central government changed piecemeal with the creation of new ministries, for Land and Natural Resources, for Economic Affairs. These were short-lived. Their demise reflected the dropping of the policy initiatives they were supposed to embody. Pollitt described Wilson's Whitehall reforms as manipulating the machine without any consistent principles of strategy or design.[26] The creation of a giant Department of Health and Social Security was in tune with a general preference at the time for administrative grandeur; it also had much to do with finding a suitable job for Richard Crossman given his longstanding interest in the reform of superannuation.

Wilson experimented with decision-taking. At first there was to be a troika with Wilson arbitrating between the Chancellor of the Exchequer, Callaghan, and the First Secretary, George Brown, in charge of the National Plan and the new Department of Economic Affairs. The model degenerated as the supply-side policies of the DEA were subordinated to the Treasury's priorities of demand management. It was replaced, briefly, by a semi-formed inner Cabinet known as the Parliamentary Committee. But Wilson tailored the machinery to the exigencies of policy as he saw them. Callaghan, deemed unsound on trade union policy, was expelled from this inner grouping in 1969 despite his seniority in the government.

The Wilson years saw what we, with twenty years' hindsight, may be tempted to call debate about the effectiveness of the British state, one no nearer a conclusion in 1987. It was a debate begun before Wilson took office. The workings of Parliament had been under attack for their anachronism for some years, and still are; the pertinent question is whether the Wilson years can be called a juncture. Consider local government.

The Macmillan administration had reformed the governance of Greater London according to a recipe of principle (given by the Herbert Committee) and expedience (political pressure within the Conservative Party of the London suburbs and Home Counties). Wilson proposed to do the same for local government at large. One of the consensual ideas of the time – the kind of idea, that is, taken up by royal commissions – was size. Another was participation – to rebuild institutions to secure maximum popular participation. This idea was especially noticeable when applied to town and country planning. A dialectic of such ideas played out over a decade. In *English Local Government Reformed*, Lord Redcliffe-Maud and Bruce Wood described a 'virtually continuous review' of the structure and working of English local government between 1958 and 1974.[27] That should be amended to read the structure and inputs to local government, for the calibre of councillors and their officials was much discussed. The purposes, the outputs of local government received comparatively little attention. Neither, ominously, did its cost. Yet it is difficult to see anything unique about the series of reviews. Since 1974 the rate support grant system has been substantially changed both by Labour and the Conservatives; the abolition of the primary local tax, the rates, has been promised; London government has been altered; and so on.

The greatest test of Wilson's statism was posed by organized labour. Wilson was acutely conscious of the need to keep the trade unions on board: a ministerial job was created for Frank Cousins of the Transport and General Workers Union. The government, on taking office in 1964, bolstered the legal immunities that had been called into question by a sequence of court judgements against the unions in the early 1960s culminating in *Rookes* vs *Barnard*. The 1965 Trade Disputes Act was defined as the sort of legislative assistance a Labour government offered as a matter of course. Wilson's change of emphasis appeared after the seamen's strike of 1966, when he as good as told Parliament that the

Security Service had provided him with evidence of Communist Party involvement; after four years' evidence of wage-push effects; after savouring the political damage caused by the Labour Party's association with unofficial as well as apparently unjustified official strike action. By 1968 redefining the role of the unions within the state had become a test of his own conception of Labour's capacity to govern – indeed its 'naturalness' as Britain's government. On this occasion the royal commission, established under Lord Donovan in 1965, indicated that the spirit of the age still favoured voluntary curtailment of trade union privilege when it reported in 1968. Wilson chose to attempt to balance the unions' power with more state involvement in industrial relations. *In Place of Strife*, the White Paper produced for Wilson by Barbara Castle (an erstwhile left-winger whose association with the project perhaps showed the degree of conviction Wilson's conception of Labour's responsibilities carried), was couched as a positive reinterpretation of union power. It had a 'European' flavour in giving the state an active role in arbitrating industrial disputes. If put into effect it might have had the practical effect of tipping the balance of negotiating power somewhat in employers' favour – with untold consequences for the future cost of labour and, through that, for all-round economic health. Wilson was defeated by Labour parliamentarians, the Trades Union Congress and Cabinet colleagues led by James Callaghan. Callaghan's case, if such a thing can be discerned in amongst personal animus and normal politicking, was that the Wilson proposals would have sundered the Labour Party as the vehicle for the interests of organized labour from its purposes as an instrument of social-democratic government. Perhaps. 'The sequel', as it turned out, 'showed that nothing of value had been gained', according to Keith Middlemas.[28] The solemn and binding agreement made between government and TUC once *In Place of Strife* had been dropped achieved little. 'Unofficial strikes continued, and a crescendo of wage inflation produced conditions in which the British economy almost foundered in the next seven years.' This failure of the Wilson government to demonstrate Labour's transcendence of the interests of organized labour was undoubtedly a sufficient condition, a decade later, of 'Thatcherism'.

In an entry in his voluminous diary for the Wilson years, Richard Crossman noted in 1965, 'What a humdrum Cabinet we are – a gang of competent politicans. Once again Harold Wilson showed himself without a trace of vision.'[29] The historiography of Wilson in power will always be deeply influenced by Crossman's self-conscious judgements, his view of himself as a socialist conscience for the eclectic Wilson, on whom he, Crossman, depended utterly for his political survival.

What are Harold's long-term economic objectives for this country? Does he really want to go in to Europe or doesn't he? I don't think he knows himself. Does he want to devalue? He certainly doesn't want to but is he going to after all? And what about the long-term future of the Labour party? Does he see it as a real socialist party or does he, like the Gaitskellites, aim to turn it into an American Democratic Party or a German SPD? He certainly doesn't confide in me any profound thoughts about the future of the Labour Party and I'm prepared to say as of today that I don't think he has them. . . . His aim is to stay in office. That's the real thing and for that purpose he will use any trick or gimmick.[30]

But there Crossman answered his own question. The 'real thing' for Wilson was to make a Labour government – *his* Labour government – acceptable in British electoral circumstances. That meant, for policy, a social-democratic style and, for the Labour Party at large, subordination to the national figurehead who could appeal beyond the party's core supporters. Wilson put the point pithily in a famous speech to the Parliamentary Labour Party in March 1967, when he warned back-benchers that votes against his government might result in their 'dog licences' not being renewed.

Crossman's diaries, of course, came in two sets (four volumes in all). The lesser known covers the period from the fall of Attlee's government to 1964. The narrative is a repetitive recital of plot-counter-plot but serves usefully to show how much of the Cabinet antagonism of 1964–70 was merely a rerun of personal enmities born in the preceding decade. For what was noteworthy about the Cabinet was how little fundamental disagreement there was about the purposes, indeed the ideology, of government. Crossman postured; but for the most part Wilson's colleagues united in their social-democratic sentiment. Their intense politicking (countered by Wilson's assiduous and justifiably cynical manipulation of the press by means of private briefing) had all to do with position, little with principle.

For Wilson carried no 'socialist' bags. On nationalization he was pragmatic; he was no unilateralist. He received the seal of approval, eventually, from self-appointed custodians of the flame lit to the sainted Hugh Gaitskell. According to John Gyford and Stephen Haseler, the party under Harold Wilson continued to follow a revisionist line. The emphasis in 1964 and 1966 on using varied devices of planning, intervention and public ownership to meet the problems of growth and technology were very much in accord with traditional revisionism. . . . Despite the defeat in 1970, the overall impression of the state of the party at the end of 1970 was that its experience in office had reaffirmed its image of itself as being dedicated, in Max Weber's terminology, to the ethic of responsibility rather than the ethic of ultimate ends; this attitude was nowhere spelled out in any official text, but it was implicit in the experience of the past generation.[31]

Wilson went further than Gaitskell or his acolytes. Social-democratic government was not so much an objective encased in a 'vision' (beyond some elementary tenets of New Testament Christianity) as a *process*. 'From the moment he entered No. 10,' Crossman said, 'he became enraptured by the role of being premier, captivated by the thrilling interplay of today's performance and tomorrow's headlines.'[32] Wilson was constantly seeking to win the immediate game, the argument in Cabinet, the election – Wilson himself says journalist James Margach got it right in attributing such a motive to him as early as November 1964.[33] Wilson was an empiricist and a meliorist. As such he did, and does, annoy utopians and visionaries, left, right and centre.

The Parliamentary Labour Party contained its share of these, and after 1966 his leadership provoked upsets. A special factor was the support the Wilson government, true to the convention of the 'special relationship', offered to President Lyndon Johnson over Vietnam; Vietnam became a left litmus paper.

Yet on the broadest canvas, the performance of the Wilson government as an engine of greater fairness – the essence of social-democratic administration? – rates commendation. Public papers of 1964, 1965 and beyond had resounded with the phrase 'social justice'. The White Paper on prices and income policy of April 1967 said it was necessary 'not only to create the conditions in which essential structural readjustments can be carried out smoothly but also to promote social justice'. 'Given a Labour victory,' Wilson himself wrote in October 1964, 'the test is this: will there be, twelve months from now, a narrowing of the gap between rich and poor, quite apart from any general upward movement there may be as the result of increased national production?'[34]

The figures show that, from an egalitarian standpoint, Labour policy measures 'improved' the distribution of final incomes between 1964 and 1969,[35] so realizing a core ambition of the Wilson government. This did not derive from changes in the share of income going to the lower-paid (though from 1965 to 1969 the earnings of the lowest paid did rise slightly faster than the average, an improvement lost during 1969–70). The main cause of the reduction in inequalities of income under the Labour government was the rapid increase in cash benefits, including pensions, supplementary benefits and family allowances, and of benefits in kind in the form of health and educational expenditures.'[36] Those in receipt of state benefits did better in terms of increases in real disposable income between 1964 and 1969 than the average manual worker or salaried employee. The introduction of rate rebates for low-income rate-payers helped; so did the Wilson government's extensive use of taxes on higher-cost items of consumption.

The 'rediscovery' of poverty at the end of the 1960s has obscured this, substituting utopian dreams of 'abolishing' poverty for real-world increments. That said, the Wilson years saw an increase in funds for income maintenance among the poor without reducing in number households living at the poverty line.[37] The reason was a large increase in the number of pensioner households and an upwards movement in the threshold at which poverty was defined: in other words a real absolute gain (there was in fact also a relative gain for pensioner households in that the long-term supplementary benefit rate rose relative to average earnings).

The Wilson government presided over a sharp fall in the share of profits in national income. This fact is not a testimony to socialism in Downing Street. The economist Michael Stewart says it was 'less an indication of the Labour government's success in improving the distribution of income than of its failure to achieve certain other economic objectives such as faster growth and a slower rate of inflation'.[38] In fact the phenomenon seems something of a freak. Real wages rose, at a rate unjustified by output growth, at the expense of profits; investment was maintained because of an accidental fall in the costs of capital.

In a real sense those pensioners in Kirkby addressed by Harold Wilson on polling day 1964 had benefited from his election, and not just in terms of income transfers. The Wilson years saw a great increase in public expenditure on the social services, broadly defined.

Labour's promise in 1964 was to modernize the British economy. Wilson's remark at the party conference in Scarborough in October 1963 about redefining socialism in terms of the scientific revolution and forging a new Britain in its 'white heat' had quickly entered the lists. The promise was twofold: Labour would make British (private) business more competitive both in terms of international trade and comparative domestic performance; it would also make Britain grow, increased output making the British people better off. As it turned out, the competitiveness of the British economy declined at scarcely a faster rate during the Wilson years than it has, say, during the Thatcher era – notwithstanding her vehement belief in the error of government intervention. According to the National Institute of Economic and Social Research, between 1964 and 1970 the UK's share of world exports of manufactures dropped by 4.5 per cent on average each year; between 1979 and 1985 the equivalent figure, still dropping, was 3.5 per cent per annum. Both Thatcher and Wilson had, one way or another, supply-side strategies. Both overestimated in their different ways the capacity of British industry to respond to politicians' blandishments.

It is easy to underestimate the degree to which the Wilson ambitions of competitiveness and growth were to be realized by using instruments orginated by the Macmillan and Home government. Samuel Brittan listed them:

Industrial Training Boards were set up, more generous grants were provided for training in the high-unemployment areas, 'Little Neddies' were set up for individual industries and new agencies were formed to promote industrial building, all achievements for which the Conservatives were oddly reluctant to claim credit later. Much of the small print of the 1965 National Plan, and Mr Wilson's own 'purposive physical intervention' had already been enacted before Labour came to office.[39]

None the less, the Wilson era provided a conscious test of 'planning', in the shape of the National Plan and the Department of Economic Affairs 'Labour since the war', says Alan Budd, 'has wanted planning to be its distinctive approach to economic policy.'[40] A snap judgement can fairly quickly be made by considering whether planning succeeded in raising output and competitiveness. The National Plan's basic objective was to secure a 25 per cent increase in real gross domestic product between 1964 and 1970 (3.8 per cent per annum). In fact the increase was 14 per cent (2.2 per cent per annum).[41] The Plan failed.

The same round judgement can be made of the new machinery of government set up to make the plan work. The Department of Economic Affairs has attracted much attention because it looked, in 1964, like a means of breaking the Treasury's 'stranglehold' on economic policy-making. Brittan, himself an actor in the politics of the DEA, had influenced public opinion with the publication in a Pelican edition in 1964 of his book *The Treasury under the Tories*. In it he had concluded,

Much in the preceding would point in the same direction as the production or economics ministry favoured by the Labour and Liberal parties. But the snag in most of these plans is that they assume there is something called 'finance' quite apart from economics and production. In fact, of course, the instruments by which production is influenced in this country are the Budget, monetary policy, exchange rate policy. If the Treasury remains responsible for the balance of payments, for taxation, for the Bank Rate, and for the use of devices like the Regulator, it is likely to remain the effective economic ministry.[42]

And in that sentence Brittan encapsulated the failure not just of the DEA but of Wilson's macro-economic policy-making: by giving primacy to the maintenance of a singular external value of the pound, domestic production became a dependent variable.

Of course there was also a 'personal' politics of the DEA. A job had to be found for George Brown, Wilson's rival for the leadership of the Labour Party.[43] Many felt Brown's temperament unsuited to the Foreign Office: creating a new department and putting Brown in charge was a neat solution. Brown subsequently claimed to have thought up the DEA while riding in a taxi with Harold Wilson, a claim rebutted in detail by Wilson.

But defining planning entirely in terms of the National Plan can be misleading. All modern governments plan in the sense that ministers and civil servants make decisions about economic outcomes that anticipate or indeed supplant those of private citizens: the Department of Trade and Industry under the Thatcher government still engages in planning. The Wilson government had policies for industrial investment and for productivity. In 1966 it established an Industrial Reorganization Corporation, which fomented industrial mergers; the government promoted rationalization of shipbuilding through the 1967 Shipbuilding Industry Act; it sought to influence the distribution of employment by means of Nicholas Kaldor's Selective Employment Tax, which came into effect in September 1966.

To what effect? The later part of the 1960s showed impressive gains in productivity. Bacon and Eltis are sanguine:

If productivity is what matters most, things should have gone very much better after 1965 than in the previous decade. Efficiency increased more quickly, which should have meant that all Britain's problems were easier to solve.

Certainly Britain's growth rate of industrial productivity was still low by international standards after 1965, but it was not all that low. West Germany, France and Italy achieved growth at an average rate of 6.0 per cent against Britain's 4.0 per cent, but Britain's growth rate was still exceedingly high by historical standards.

That productivity rose faster is compatible with the view that many of the industrial policies of successive governments were beginning to produce results.

There may have been contributions here from the tougher approach to restrictive practices from the end of the 1950s onwards, which meant that there were fewer price agreements which sheltered the inefficient. There may also have been contributions from the 'little Neddies' set up in the early 1960s which examined the particular productivity problems of a wide range of industries. There was also a great takeover movement in the early 1960s which was often assisted by the government. Successive governments gave substantial tax assistance to investment, and this must have led to the replacement of much obsolete plant.[44]

That quizzical note is necessary. It is so partly because of the difficulty of reading off a particular effect from, for example, the extension of the regime for giving grants for industrial investment contained in the Industrial Expansion Act of 1968. It is so also because of the hydra-headed, sometimes contradictory nature of the Wilson's government's industrial policy.[45] As a young President of the Board of Trade in Attlee's government (1947–51) Harold Wilson had come to favour competition and effected a celebrated 'bonfire of controls' on production. As Prime Minister his policy swung between industrial sponsorship, the promotion of mergers (i.e. the killing of competition) and the active use of a reinvigorated Monopolies Commission (as a result of the 1965 Monopolies and Mergers Act) to promote competition.

There is nothing wrong in principle with such heterogeneity. 'Experience has shown', wrote Thomas Balogh,

that in England at any rate a negative anti-monopoly drive will not result in the much needed rationalization and restructuring of industry.

It was not realised that what was termed a 'restriction' or 'distortion' of competition was, from the point of view of productivity and rapid technical progress, far from being the worst possible industrial structure.[46]

The difficulty, even with hindsight, is assessing the fruits of Wilsonian policy. We now know that rationalization of the old British staples, especially shipbuilding, might have gone much further – the rise of lower-cost production in South Korea and Japan now seems to have had an inevitability about it requiring, sooner or later, massive loss of employment along the Industrial Revolution estuaries. The logic of that is, however, perversely to measure economic 'success' by mounting unemployment; that is a characteristic of the 1980s rather than the 1960s.

The safest measures of performance are the aggregates. Here is the verdict of a Labour sympathizer, Michael Stewart, who played a small walk-on role as an adviser at the DEA:

In 1964 Labour put its economic policy before the electorate ... the policy failed.

Failure was by no means complete. Inheriting a huge balance of payments deficit, Labour transformed it – eventually – into a huge surplus. And under Labour there was an improvement in the distribution of income. Neither achievement compensated for the failure of the central themes of Labour's declared policy – the commitment to maintain full employment, to curb rising prices, and above all to secure a faster rate of economic growth.

Here failure was massive. When Labour took office unemployment was $1\frac{1}{2}$ per cent and falling; when it left it was $2\frac{1}{2}$ per cent and rising.

In the Tories' last year in office, retail prices had risen by $4\frac{1}{2}$ per cent; in Labour's last year they rose by 6 per cent. And under the Tories the rate of economic growth (gdp at constant prices) had averaged 2.7 per cent a year; under Labour it was only 2.2 per cent.[47]

The imperiousness of that judgement does not carry over the years. It was made in 1972. Fifteen years after that, the small increases in inflation and unemployment registered during the Wilson years look considerably better.

If Harold Wilson were a novelist, there would be no doubt that the key to the plot was the deliberate decision, made more than once, to pin macro-economic policy to the 1949 value of sterling. As Brittan has pointed out, such literary criticism is insufficient. What mattered was the government's unwillingness to accept that a particular exchange rate necessarily entailed deflation and to rely on some mysterious 'third way' enabling it to avoid either devaluation or deflation.[48]

The problem of sterling was multiform: was it a problem of the currency's value, or underlying lack of competitiveness showing through in excessive wage costs? It cannot properly be separated from politics, notably the obligation on political leaders to dispel illusion about national power, nor from biography – Harold Wilson's presence at the Cabinet table in 1949 and the impression that devaluation left him with.

It is difficult to disagree with Anthony Crosland's *ex post* judgement that the substitution of short-run payments equilibrium at a hard-to-maintain sterling value for the longer-run objective of economic growth was a 'central failure'. But he goes on, 'It constrained public expenditure. It antagonized the trade unions and alienated large groups of workers. It killed the National Plan and frustrated policies for improving the industrial structure.'[49] At this point, it is clear that the decision not to devalue has become a catch-all excuse, a fig-leaf for utopians.

What is clear is that the external value of the currency had acquired, certainly in Wilson's mind, a supernatural quality that forbade mundane discussion of its political ramifications. Middlemas noted this about the 1949 devaluation: 'Crucial though the political weighting given to sterling was in economic management, this was not something that the Labour Cabinet ever discussed. Yet on that gibbet all subsequent governments were to swing, until the Basle Agreement in 1968 and an end of sterling as a reserve currency.[50]

'Supernatural' is probably the wrong word. The pound was part of the nation's external appearance: the language persists to this day – 'a strong Britain and a strong pound'. In this decade of sliding rates and a $1.03 pound, the defence of $2.80 until 1967 looks like the anachronistic assertion of great power status, a refusal to see that the decline of Britain as a military and diplomatic presence and as an economic competitor might involve decline in the value of the currency. Wilson's political problem was the identification of Labour with incidents in that decline, notably the 1949 devaluation; how was he to resist the equation of socialism and national impotence that would follow from a further devaluation? It was not just Wilson's patriotism, deep and genuine as only a provincial boy scout's could be.[51] It was, in addition, Wilson's great personal project of making Labour a natural party of government and as such capable of managing the currency. Perhaps there is a third element. Roger Opie argued that Whitehall was in the 1960s in thrall to an 'overseas lobby' which propagated a view of economic problems from the point of view of international negotiation and Britain's presence at the 'top table'.[52] It was an 'Establishment' view, and Wilson, Oxford don and former civil servant, was part of the Establishment.

Wilson's conceptual baggage belonged, on relations with the United States, in the 1940s, and, on the Commonwealth, with Labour Party hopes of the 1950s. The two scarcely connected. Wilson's management of decolonization – primarily the withdrawal of military forces from 'east of Suez' – was creditably accomplished. So was his handling of the Rhodesia episode. He revelled in the latter as an issue of constituency management.[53] There was public opinion in Britain, and within that the two parties. The third and fourth constituencies were the Commonwealth and the United Nations. Throughout, it was as much a question how Wilson's actions would be perceived by these as whether they would have any effect. By the publication of the 1968 *Statement on the Defence Estimates*[54] the government had decided on the main lines of military adaptation to a role confined to Europe and the North Atlantic; British defence commitments were, absolutely and relatively, much greater than the nation's economic performance could justify, but significant progress had been made in trimming the cloth. The primacy given to balance-of-payments problems during the Wilson years had the welcome effect of focusing attention on overseas defence expenditure justified only by an anachronistic conception of British power and wealth.

It was in foreign as much as domestic policy that the impression of Wilson as a capable manager of the nation's well-being was formed between 1964 and 1966. And, if that condemns Wilson because his policy choices were expedient, so be it. Expedient they were. On applying for membership of the EEC:

Despite a request from the foreign secretary [Michael Stewart] that a paper advocating this course should be circulated in December 1965, Harold Wilson refused to allow it to go forward for Cabinet discussion.

The reasons are fairly clear. Firstly the effect of changing course so soon after roundly condemning the original application made by the Macmillan government would be tremendous, and, more important, the effect on the Labour Party . . . could easily have disturbed unity.[55]

It is difficult to discern anything as coherent as a Wilsonian foreign policy. Foreign secretaries came and went with speed; none, not least George Brown, was a visionary. The government adapted existing lines of policy: decolonization, retrenchment to a 'European-centred' defence posture, modernization (within cost constraints) of the British deterrent. On one side there were little trips to Moscow; on the other a bid to cultivate a personal relationship with the American President, Richard Nixon, following Johnson. The long lines of continuity in Soviet policy were never likely to be affected by changes of government in London.

The logic of Soviet expansion – aggressive defensiveness – carried the tanks into Prague in 1968 and, Harold Wilson says it clearly in his memoirs, the recall of Parliament was a futile gesture. 'There was little that government or Parliament could do in the face of this assertion of what later came to be known as the "Brezhnev doctrine".'[56]

Foreign policy has not found a great place in this essay. There are two reasons. One is that it is difficult to see a measuring scale against which to stretch the Wilson performance. If an 'ultimate' objective of British foreign policy was the maintenance of international peace, then the peregrinations of Wilson and his Cabinet colleagues in pursuit, for example, of an end to the conflict in Vietnam must be counted vain, but probably not harmful: American policy played itself out unaffected. The second is that the conduct of foreign policy, perhaps even more than domestic, was a matter of governance – response to happening events according to no easily discernible set of principles or logic. Except, first and foremost, keeping government and party going.

Chronology

1964

15 October   General election.

16 October   Labour takes power with 317 seats; Conservatives, 304; Liberals, 9. Creation of Department of Economic Affairs; Ministry of Land and Natural Resources; Ministry of Technology; Ministry of Overseas Development. Title of Welsh Secretary of State created, previously minister, to head new Welsh Office.

26 October   First economic package: import surcharge.

4 November   Curb on London office-building.

11 November   Sterling crisis; Budget raises pensions, abolishes prescription charges.

23 November   Bank Rate raised.

1965

2 February   Appointment of Royal Commission on Reform of Trade Unions and Employers Associations, chaired by Lord Donovan.

4 February   Immigration controls tightened.

11 February   Prices and Incomes Board set up.

17 February   Gambia gains independence.

6 April   Budget: creates corporation tax.

24 May   Metric system announced.

12 July   Circular on comprehensive schools.

2 August   White Paper on immigration control.

5 August   Redundancy Payments Act.

16 September   National Plan published.

8 November   Murder Act (abolished capital punishment). Race Relations Act.
11 November   UDI by Smith regime in Rhodesia.

1966

21 January   Trade embargo against Rhodesia.
25 January   White Paper on Industrial Reorganization Corporation.
17 February   Royal Commission on Tribunals of Inquiry, chairman Sir Cyril
Salmon.
19 February   Christopher Mayhew resigns as Navy Minister over scrapping of
planned aircraft carrier.
22 February   Defence White Paper: east-of-Suez cuts.
25 February   White Paper proposing university of the air.
1 March   Decimal currency announced.
31 March   General election. Labour, 363 seats; Conservatives, 253; Liberals, 12;
Others, 2.
21 April   Parliament meets.
3 May   Budget: Selective Employment Tax introduced.
23 May   State of Emergency declared over seamen's dispute.
24 May   Royal Commission on Local Government in England appointed,
chairman Sir John Maud. Royal Commission on Local Government in Scotland
appointed, chairman Lord Wheatley.
26 May   Guyana independent.
3 July   Resignation of Frank Cousins as Minister of Technology.
14 July   Camarthen by-election: Plaid Cymru victory. Sterling crisis; Implementation of Prices and Incomes legislation.
31 July   Dissolution of Colonial Office.
11 August   Royal Commission on the Examination of Assizes and Quarter Sessions
appointed, chairman Lord Beeching.
3 September   Botswana independent.
4 October   Lesotho independent.
11 November   Barbados independent.
2 December   Wilson–Smith talks, HMS Tiger.

1967

16 January   Wilson and Brown tour Europe talking about EEC entry.
10 February   Herbert Bowden on Far East tour to discuss troop withdrawals
(Defence White Paper 16 February).
22 March   Iron and Steel Act renationalizes steel industry.
1 April   Parliamentary Commissioner (Ombudsman) takes up post.
15 April   Creation of 30 polytechnics announced.
2 May   Britain applies for EEC entry.
27 May   Secession of Biafra from Nigeria.
5 June   Arab–Israeli war.
11 July   Anguilla secedes from St Kitts-Nevis.
25 July   Margaret Herbison resigns as Pensions Minister.
27 July   Defence Statement: timetable for east-of-Suez withdrawal. Criminal

Justice Act: suspended sentences, etc. Sexual Offences Act permits homosexual acts between consenting adults.

26 September   Joint UK–France–West Germany airbus project set.

27 October   Abortion Act: permits abortion in certain circumstances. Leasehold Reform Act.

2 November   Hamilton by-election: Scottish Nationalist victory.

18 November   Sterling crisis: devaluation of the pound.

27 November   Veto of Britain's entry to EEC.

30 November   Aden (People's Republic of South Yemen) independent.

1968

16 January   Public-spending package: postponement of raising of school-leaving age. Earl of Longford resigns.

1 March   Commonwealth Immigrants Act restricts entry of Kenyan Asians.

3 March   Mauritius independent.

15 March   George Brown resigns.

16 March   Special Drawing Rights to support sterling.

20 April   Enoch Powell speaks on race.

26 June   Report of Fulton Committee on Civil Service.

30 June   Ray Gunter resigns as Minister of Employment.

11 July   Defence White Paper: Europe-centred defence.

21 August   Soviet invasion of Czechoslovakia.

6 September   Swaziland independent.

9 October   Wilson–Smith talks on HMS Fearless.

25 October   Transport Act created National Bus Co., National Freight Co., etc.

1 November   White Paper on reform of the House of Lords.

1969

17 January   *In Place of Strife* White Paper on trade unions.

28 January   Earnings-related superannuation scheme proposed.

3 April   Royal Commission on the Constitution appointed, chairman Lord Crowther.

17 April   Representation of the People Act gives 18 year olds the vote.

1 June   Open University chartered.

16 July   Duncan Report on British Representation overseas.

14 August   British troops despatched to Ulster.

24 September   Jeremy Bray resigns from Ministry of Technology.

22 October   Divorce Reform Act. Children and Young Persons Act.

17 November   Strategic Arms Limitation Talks begin.

1 December   Hague summit sets course for renewed British EEC application.

1970

1 January   £50 maximum overseas allowance lifted.

4 February   White Paper on local-government reorganization.

2 March   Rhodesia declares itself a republic.

14 April   Budget: evidence of balance-of-payments equilibrium.

29 May   Chronically Sick and Disabled Persons Act. Equal Pay Act.

4 June   Tonga independent.
18 June   General election. Conservatives win an overall majority.

Notes

1   Harold Wilson *Memoirs 1918–1964: the making of a Prime Minister* (Weiden-feld and Nicolson/Michael Joseph, 1986).
2   Michael Shanks, *The Stagnant Society* (Penguin, 1961).
3   Keith Middlemas, *Politics in Industrial Society* (André Deutsch, 1979), p. 455.
4   Christopher Booker, *The Neophiliacs* (Collins, 1969).
5   Brian Lapping, *The Labour Government 1964–70* (Penguin, 1970), p. 213.
6   Frank Longford, *The Grain of Wheat* (Collins, 1974), p. 57.
7   Susan Crosland, *Tony Crosland* (Cape, 1982), p. 148. To be absolutely accurate, he got her out of bed to deliver the statement 'If it's the last thing I do, I'm going to destroy every fucking grammar school in England and Wales. And Northern Ireland.'
8   Shanks, *The Stagnant Society*, p. 232.
9   Cecil King, *The Cecil King Diary 1965–1970* (Cape, 1972).
10 John Ermisch, *The Political Economy of Demographic Change* (Heinnemann Educational, 1983), p. 127.
11 Ibid., p. 129.
12 Wilfred Beckerman and Stephen Clark, *Poverty and Social Security in Britain since 1961* (Oxford University Press, 1982), p. 3.
13 Anthony Howard and Richard West, *The Making of the Prime Minister* (Quality Book Club, 1965), p. 220.
14 HM Treasury, *The Control of Public Expenditure*, Cmnd 1432 (Her Majesty's Stationery Office, 1961).
15 R. W. R. Price, 'Public expenditure', in F. T. Blackaby (ed.), *British Economic Policy 1960–74: demand management* (Cambridge University Press, 1979), p. 81.
16 Ibid., p. 128.
17 Richard Clarke, *Public Expenditure Management and Control* (Macmillan, 1978), p. 141.
18 Anthony Crosland, *Socialism Now* (Cape, 1975), p. 74.
19 C. D. Foster, R. Jackman and M. Perlman, *Local Government Finance in a Unitary State* (Allen and Unwin, 1980), p. 86.
20 Robert Bacon and Walter Eltis, *Britain's Economic Problem: too few producers* (Macmillan, 1976), p. 55.
21 Richard Crossman, *The Crossman Diaries* (Magnum Books, 1979), pp. 593–4.
22 A. H. Halsey, A. F. Heath and J. F. Ridge, *Origins and Destinations: family, class, and education in modern Britain* (Oxford University Press, 1980), p. 210.

23 Clarke, *Public Expenditure Management*, p. 141.
24 Peter Kellner and Lord Crowther-Hunt, *The Civil Servants* (Macdonald, 1980), esp. chs 2, 3, 4 and 5.
25 Peter Hennessy, *Cabinet* (Basil Blackwell, 1986), p. 70.
26 Christopher Pollitt, *Manipulating the Machine* (Allen and Unwin, 1984), p. 49.
27 Lord Redcliffe-Maud and Bruce Wood, *English Local Government Reformed* (Oxford University Press, 1974), p. 1.
28 Middlemas, *Politics in Industrial Society*, p. 441.
29 Richard Crossman, *Diaries*, p. 141.
30 Quoted in Phillip Whitehead, *The Writing on the Wall* (Michael Joseph, 1985), pp. 10–11.
31 John Gyford and Stephen Haseler, *Social Democracy: beyond revisionism* (Fabian Society, 1971), p. 8.
32 Quoted in James Margach, *The Abuse of Power* (W. H. Allen, 1978), p. 141.
33 Harold Wilson, *The Labour Government 1964–70* (Penguin, 1974), p. 55.
34 Quoted in Michael Stewart, 'The distribution of income', in Wilfred Beckerman (ed.), *The Labour Government's Economic Record 1964–70* (Duckworth, 1972), p. 78.
35 Wilfred Beckerman, 'Objectives and performance', ibid., p. 41.
36 Ibid.
37 Beckerman and Clark, *Poverty and Social Security*, p. 23.
38 Stewart, in Beckerman, *The Labour Government's Economic Record*, p. 78.
39 Samuel Brittan, *Steering the Economy* [the title of later updated editions of *The Treasury under the Tories*] (Penguin, 1971), p. 290.
40 Alan Budd, *The Politics of Economic Planning* (Fontana, 1978), p. 16.
41 Michael Stewart, *Labour and the Economy: a socialist strategy* (Fabian Society, 1972), p. 10.
42 Brittan, *Steering the Economy*, pp. 312–13.
43 Michael Stewart, *The Jekyll and Hyde Years* (Dent, 1977), pp. 36–7.
44 Bacon and Eltis, *Britain's Economic Problem*, p. 9.
45 Andrew Graham, 'Industrial policy', in Beckerman *The Labour Government's Economic Record*.
46 Thomas Balogh, *Labour and Inflation* (Fabian Society, 1970), p. 17.
47 Michael Stewart, *Labour and the Economy*, p. 1.
48 Brittan, *Steering the Economy* pp. 292–3.
49 Crosland, *Socialism Now* p. 18.
50 Keith Middlemas, *Power, Competition and the State*, vol. I: *Britain in Search of Balance, 1940–61* (Macmillan, 1986), p. 155.
51 Leslie Smith, *Harold Wilson* (Fontana, 1964), p. 63.
52 Quoted in Brittan, *Steering the Economy* p. 470.
53 Wilson, *The Labour Government*, p. 235.

54 J. H. B. Tew, 'Policies aimed at improving the balance of payments', in Blackaby, *Britain Economic Policy*, p. 324.
55 Avi Shlaim, Peter Jones and Keith Sainsbury, *British Foreign Secretaries since 1945* (David and Charles, 1977), p. 195.
56 Harold Wilson, *The Labour Government*, p. 698.

Bibliography

Harold Wilson, *The Labour Government 1964–70: A Personal Record* (Penguin, 1974): a blow-by-blow account of the government illustrating Wilson's character and his own assessment of the administration and colleagues.

Brian Lapping, *The Labour Government 1964–70* (Penguin, 1970): a subject-by-subject assessment of the government written by a Labour sympathizer; especially strong on social policy.

F. T. Blackaby (ed.), *British Economic Policy 1960–74: Demand Management* (Cambridge University Press, 1969): a students' edition with sections on budgetary, incomes, and monetary policy.

Wilfred Beckerman (ed.), *The Labour Government's Economic Record* (Duckworth, 1972): a non-technical assessment of the Wilson government's record on economic planning, regional policy, distribution of income, and so on.

Samuel Brittan, *Steering the Economy: the role of the Treasury* (Penguin, 1971): this revised version of Brittan's earlier work, *The Treasury under the Tories*, carries on a decade his analysis of the Treasury's role in policy-making.

Anthony Howard and Richard West, *The Making of the Prime Minister* (Quality Book Club, 1965): a self-conscious, detailed narrative (on the Theodore H. White model) of election year, 1964; gives a full flavour of the time.

Peter Kellner and Christopher Hitchens, *Callaghan: The Road to Number Ten* (Cassell, 1976): until a full biography of Callaghan appears, this journalistic account must serve as an introduction to the man who was omnipresent during the Wilson government.

James Margach, *The Anatomy of Power* (W. H. Allen, 1981): Margach, a political journalist, was close to Wilson and his assessment of the man is acute.

Richard Crossman, *The Crossman Diaries* (Methuen, 1979): one Cabinet minister's view of the inner politics of the government, seasoned with donnish wit and perception.

Michael Shanks, *The Stagnant Society* (Penguin, 1961): a book that set the tone for a decade's debates which gives a clue to the depth of disappointment registered at the Wilson government's 'failure'.

Barbara Castle, *The Castle Diaries 1964–70* (Weidenfeld and Nicolson, 1984): a sympathetic insider's account which fully displays the 'exhaustion factor' in Cabinet life.

Susan Crosland, *Tony Crosland* (Cape, 1982): a partial account which illustrates the lack of trust and mutual confidence at the heart of the Wilson Cabinet.

George Brown, *In My Way* (Penguin, 1972): Brown's apologia does not rehabilitate him, but adds to the sense of pressure on Wilson from colleagues.

Cecil King, *The Cecil King Diary 1965–70* (Cape, 1972): a megalomaniacal story of influence-peddling and intrigue, much of it evidently exaggerated, but as an account of lunches alone a valuable record of the art.

Christopher Booker, *The Neophiliacs* (Collins, 1969): a strange, would-be theoretical account of the sixties, illustrating the self-consciousness of writers and commentators in that decade.

Sir Richard Clarke, *Public Expenditure Management and Control* (Macmillan, 1978): from the 'engine room' of government, the Treasury, Clarke inadvertently shows how little government knows about the outcomes of political decisions.

Michael Stewart, *The Jekyll and Hyde Years* (Dent, 1977): a critique of economic policy during the Wilson years from a 'left' position.

Frank Stacey, *British Government 1966–75* (Oxford University Press, 1975): shows how the reform of institutions such as local government was carried through by successive governments in a 'reform' era.

Peter Kellner and Lord Crowther-Hunt, *The Civil Servants* (Macdonald, 1980): account of a central chapter in the story of the Wilson government – the failure to reform the Civil Service despite Wilson's own determination.

7

The Heath Government, 1970–1974

Dennis Kavanagh

The record of the 1970–4 Conservative government is already overlaid by many controversies and even myths. These concern, *inter alia*, the seriousness of the government's original economic programme, the U-turns in economic policy in 1971 and 1972, the harrowing election defeat in February 1974, the subsequent overthrow of Edward Heath by Margaret Thatcher, and the rival interpretations of the government's record by different wings of the Conservative party. In the bulky *Campaign Guide 1977*, published by the Conservative Research Department, there were just three references to Mr Heath. In *The Campaign Guide 1983* there was only one reference.

In 1970 the programme of the Heath government appeared to mark a clear break with the post-1945 policy consensus. The economic policies in particular were regarded at the time as presenting a major challenge to the postwar collectivist consensus and as a step in the direction of more free-market policies. The policies encompassed trade union reform, reduction of state intervention in the economy, avoidance of a formal prices and incomes policy, cuts in public spending and direct taxes, and greater selectivity in welfare. These measures, it was claimed, would encourage enterprise and initiative; promote economic growth and reverse the country's relative economic decline. Entry into the EEC, combined with reforms of industrial relations and economic policies, would sharpen British industry to face new challenges and grasp new opportunities.

That Edward Heath (and later Margaret Thatcher) came to lead the Tory Party was a sign of a change in the party since 1945. Although frontbench Conservative MPs remained predominantly upper-class products of public schools and Oxbridge, Heath and Thatcher represented a more meritocratic strain. Both came from comparatively modest family backgrounds, won scholarships to grammar schools and Oxford, and were self-made first-generation professional politicians. This was true also of Cabinet ministers such as Anthony Barber, Peter Walker and Robert Carr, all of whom were educated at grammar or minor public schools. The Cabinets of Churchill, Eden and Macmillan had many 'grand' figures who were titled and or who possessed landed estates. In October 1964 the outgoing Conservative Cabinet included eleven Old Etonians, accounting for half its membership. Under Heath in 1970 the figure was down to three. Yet there were important differences between Heath and Thatcher. Although Heath was the first leader chosen by MPs in a contested election, he had long been a member of the party's leadership, ascended the ministerial hierarchy, and might well have 'emerged' under the old system of choosing a leader by a process of informal consultation. He also represented continuity with many of the 'one nation' principles associated with Eden, Macmillan and R. A. Butler. In 1975 Mrs Thatcher, by contrast, was very much an outsider, a product of a backbench rebellion against the leadership, and she had not previously served in any of the major offices of state.

Heath is not an easy man to code as either a *dirigiste* or a free marketeer. He had a managerial view of government; its job was to intervene in industry and social welfare, where there was a proven need. His *dirigiste* tendencies had been shown in his interest in regional policies in 1963–4 when he was Secretary of State for Industry, Trade and Regional Development. Yet the abolition of resale price maintenance in 1964 showed his dedication to increasing competition as well as his determination in the face of opposition in his own party. He was an instrumentalist rather than an ideologue about state intervention in private enterprise, more concerned with making things work better. He was also a great believer in the reasonableness of people. His qualities of patience and doggedness had been illustrated in negotiations for Britain's first application for entry to the European Community in 1961–2 and were again evident in the long search for an incomes policy with the trade unions in 1972.

Mr Heath was not at ease with the party's grass roots or with many of the backbenchers, and dispensed very few political honours to party activists. Lucille Iremonger has said that he was not a 'gut' Conservative and that he was more at home with trade unionists than with people from the City or business.[1] Another Conservative official has described to me Heath's sense of unease with many grass-roots Conservatives.

'Like Macmillan and R. A. Butler, you always had the impression that Ted (and some of his ministers) found some of the activists at Conference distasteful – backward-looking, complacent and reactionary.' On such issues as law and order, tougher sentencing for criminals, education vouchers, repatriation of New Commonwealth immigrants and large-scale denationalization he did not share grass-root views. One of his most memorable remarks was his dismissal of the Lonrho company's proposal to make a Tory MP large tax-free payment for services rendered as 'the unpleasant and unacceptable face of capitalism'.

He had little time for small talk, and the stories of his alleged rudeness and insensitivity to backbenchers are legion. Philip Norton claims that Heath's abrasive personality was an important factor in provoking the record postwar levels of dissent in parliamentary votes among Conservative backbenchers between 1970 and 1974. His Cabinet, having been persuaded of the merits of a change of policy, perhaps too easily assumed that these would be equally obvious to backbenchers. Norton's criticism is that 'Heath was a manager of measures not men'.[2] Heath was perhaps ill served by having spent so long in the whips' office under Churchill, Eden and Macmillan. He had spent only eighteen months as a backbencher before gaining office. He first entered Parliament in February 1950, joined the whips' office when the party gained power in autumn 1951, was promoted to Deputy Chief Whip the following year, and became Chief Whip under Eden in 1955.

Yet there are paradoxes about his record as a party manager. For somebody who was allegedly so stubborn he made some spectacular policy U-turns over incomes and industrial policies. And, for all his remoteness from backbenchers, it is interesting that there were no resignations from the Cabinet over the reversals of policy in 1971 and 1972, and that, for example, among Conservatives only Enoch Powell voted against and only John Biffen and Jock Bruce-Gardyne abstained on the third reading of the Counter-Inflation Bill.

Heath was a dominant leader of the Conservative Party. In opposition this had been seen in his dismissal of Edward du Cann as party chairman (1967) and of Enoch Powell for his speech on immigration in 1968, and in the marked changes in Conservative policy between 1964, when Sir Alec Douglas-Home was still Prime Minister, and 1965, when Heath replaced him as party leader. As Prime Minister, Heath's dominance was reinforced by two events. The first was the unexpected and decisive election victory which the Conservative Party gained in 1970. Although much talk of the presidential trends in British politics is overdone, the concentration of the mass media on the party leaders helps to transform a party's election victory into something of a personal mandate for the party leader. Heath had trailed Harold Wilson in the opinion polls for most of the 1966 Parliament and during the general election. Even supporters and colleagues were worried by his failure to 'break through', and the public appeared to find him cold and boring. But his doggedness and seriousness were vindicated by the election outcome. According to *The Times*,

Achieving so big a victory against the odds puts Mr Heath in a position of great strength. He has no personal obligations to anybody. He has relatively few commitments of policy and those are of his own choosing. . . . He will be a considerably more powerful Prime Minister . . . because he made his victory in such difficult circumstances.

According to the *Economist*, 'Only one man has really won this election and that man is Mr Heath. . . .'

The second event was the death of Iain Macleod on 20 July, thirty-one days after his appointment as Chancellor of the Exchequer. He was the finest orator in the Conservative Party and the only one in a position to challenge Heath. Almost inevitably, his death meant that Heath would exercise a close control over Treasury policy. With the withdrawal from politics of Sir Edward Boyle, the alienation of Enoch Powell, and the resignation of Reginald Maudling from the Home Office in 1972, the 1970 government lacked major personalities.

In line with Heath's belief that opposition was a time of preparation for government, there was much continuity in the frontbench spokesmen (higher than was the case for Labour in 1964 and 1974 and for the Conservatives in 1979); of the seventeen members of the Consultative Committee in the 1969–70 session, fifteen gained Cabinet posts (the other two, Lord Balniel and Joseph Godber, had minister of state appointments outside the Cabinet). Similarly there was a very high degree of continuity in the allocation of departmental duties.

Of the original Cabinet of eighteen, only seven, including Heath, were still in the same post when the government left office in 1974. The other continuous holders of departmental posts were Sir Alec Douglas-Home (Foreign Office), Sir Keith Joseph (Health and Social Security), Lord Hailsham (Lord Chancellor), Margaret Thatcher (Education), Peter Thomas (Wales) and Gordon Campbell (Scotland). There was a recognizable inner Cabinet with which Heath informally discussed policies and personalities. Its regular members were Lord Carrington, Jim Prior, William Whitelaw, Robert Carr, Francis Pym and Peter Walker.

When Heath's colleagues describe him as a civil servant *manqué* they have in mind certain strengths and failings. He believed that an open-minded examination and patient analysis of relevant facts would lead to the emergence of an 'obvious' solution. This should also be apparent to intelligent, 'reasonable' (a favourite Heath word) people. He was not very interested in the art of promoting the policy and deliberately reacted against Harold Wilson's style of media management. Abolition of resale price maintenance in 1963–4, British entry into the EEC, abandonment of an incomes policy and then introduction of statutory incomes policies were all 'obvious'. Peter Hennessy quotes a typical comment of a colleague on Heath's Cabinet style: 'He was rather slow, rather ponderous. … He liked to sit seeing others, including the permanent secretaries, arguing in front of him. He would make up his mind and then he was unshiftable.'[3] Cabinet members became accustomed to long periods of silence from the Prime Minister, particularly when he was tired or uncertain about the course to adopt. He was particularly involved in many of the new policy initiatives – for example, the application for membership of the EEC, the switches to incomes policy and intervention in industry, and the suspension of Stormont and imposition of direct rule in Northern Ireland. He also exercised close control over the Treasury, particularly in the shift to more expansionist policies after 1971, and over industrial policy. He greatly reduced the number of Cabinet committees compared to 1964–70. In a radio conversation in April 1976, with Lord Trend, a former Secretary of the Cabinet, Heath complained that the committees referred too many decisions to the full Cabinet – 'there were too many cases where a Chairman ought to have reached agreement but did not do so'.[4]

In view of Heath's liking for 'rational' solutions, it is not surprising that he came to work very closely with the senior civil servants. He merged the separate Cabinet committees of ministers and officials, a step which weakened the distinction between the 'political' and 'administrative' aspects of government and probably enhanced the political influence of civil servants. According to Stephen Fay and Hugo Young,

The dominant images of Heath's time in Downing Street, which have been carried away by those who served him, rarely include his Cabinets or his inner caucus of Ministers. They are of Heath surrounded by Douglas Allen (Head of

Treasury), Robert Armstrong (his principal private secretary), Burke Trend (Cabinet Secretary), and William Armstrong (Head of the Civil Service). This was the Treasury mandarinate, which nourished Heath's belief in lonely Prime Ministerial power, and was fortified by a leader who seemed to share some of their contempt for the average politician.[5]

Sir William Armstrong, then Head of the Home Civil Service as well as having special responsibilities for prices and incomes and industrial strategy, was so closely identified with the counter-inflation policy, and so often accompanied by Heath at key meetings with the press, the Confederation of British Industries and the Trades Union Congress, that he was called 'deputy Prime Minister' by union leaders. He and Heath had a secret meeting with Joe Gormley, president of the National Union of Mineworkers (NUM), in July 1973, to prepare a Stage III of the incomes policy which would be acceptable to the miners. According to Fay and Young, the Cabinet was kept in ignorance of the meeting. Critics thought that Armstrong's visibility as Heath's personal adviser overrode his position as head of the Civil Service. It is doubtful if he would have been acceptable to the new Labour government, and after a short interval he took early retirement.

Traditionally Conservatives have eschewed detailed policy-making in opposition. They have not been impressed with the idea of the mandate – a concept more often associated with the Labour Party – and have argued that a government derives its authority from election rather than from popular approval of its programme. (Programmes, moreover, imply directed changes and many Conservatives have denied the efficiency and propriety of such social engineering.) Heath differed from previous Conservative leaders in setting up an elaborate policy-making exercise after 1966. By the time he took office in 1970, many commentators and some Conservatives regarded his as the best-prepared government in the postwar era. A number of party professionals, many from the Conservative Research Department, moved into Whitehall either to temporary posts in the Civil Service or to positions as political advisers to ministers. This gave them the opportunity to pursue the plans that they had prepared in opposition. In addition, as early as March 1970, the Research Department had sent Heath a future legislation chart, setting out a full programme covering legislation, ministerial announcements and White Papers.[6] The exercise was probably helpful in assisting the 1970 government to get so much legislation enacted.

Heath argued that 'detail is needed to convince them [the people] that you really intend to carry out your promises'.[7] The 1970 manifesto *A Better Tomorrow*, went well beyond previous Conservative manifestos in specifying so many detailed policy commitments. It made much of Labour's 'broken promises' and pledged that under the Conservative government 'the gap between the politician's promises and government's performance will be closed'. The manifesto was taken seriously and ministers pointed to the many pledges fulfilled, including entry into the EEC, income-tax cuts and reform, industrial relations reform, recasting local housing finance, scrapping compulsory comprehensive education and Labour's Land Commission, selectivity in welfare, and measures of denationalization.

But, for all the impressive correspondence between the many manifesto pledges and government action, opinion polls showed that many people believed that the government had not kept its election promises; according to Gallup in late 1973, the doubters outnumbered the believers by a margin of three to one. This perception probably had more to do with the voters' greater concern about the goals which specific measures failed to promote rather than the measures themselves. For example, one of the aims of the Industrial Relations Act 1971 was to reduce the number of stoppages in industry. But the number of working days lost to strikes increased markedly, and in 1972, the first year of operation of the Act, Britain lost over 23 million man days in stoppages, the largest number since 1926. Again, the government had policies to reduce the rate of inflation. But inflation rose, thanks largely to oil prices and wage settlements. Concern over rising prices grew steadily, and from early 1971 opinion polls showed that the public regard inflation as the major problem facing the government. By the time it left office it was presiding over a postwar record level of inflation.

Much attention focused at the time (and subsequently) upon the manifesto pledges which the government had broken. Critics cited, for example, the abolition of the Stormont Parliament in Northern Ireland in 1973, the growth of government expenditure, and the increase in immigration, due largely to accepting expelled Asian holders of British passports from Uganda. There were also spectacular reversals of original policy in the decision to nationalize Rolls-Royce in 1972, intervene in industrial policy, and introduce a statutory prices and incomes policy in 1972. The manifesto's dismissal of the previous Labour government's statutory incomes policy as a 'failure' which 'we will not repeat' had been absolute.

In retrospect, some Conservatives are prepared to criticize the 1970 manifesto for its bold rhetoric. Item: 'Finally, once a decision is taken, once a policy is established, the Prime Minister and his colleagues should have the courage to stick to it ... courage and intellectual honesty are essential qualities in politics, and in the interest of our country it is high time that we saw them again'. This passage was a clear swipe at the alleged deviousness and supineness of Wilson. The manifesto could also be criticized for rigidity (for example, on industrial relations), for a lack of contingency planning (for example, over a policy to deal with inflation and excessive wage settlements), and for its naïve assumption that industry would readily invest once taxes had been cut.

It is fashionable now to regard the Heath regime as an illustration of the fallibility of policies of demand management and Keynesian economics. The government virtually ignored problems of money supply and the money-supply measure M3 increased rapidly in 1971 and 1972 (by nearly 20 per cent in 1972). The public-spending records of recent governments have been analysed by Richard Rose in his book *Do Parties Make a Difference?*[8] He observes that between 1957 and 1978 there was an increase in constant terms in public spending in eighteen of the twenty-one years; the three years in which there was no increase were all under a Labour government. Over the period public spending has steadily increased as a proportion of the national product, regardless of which party has been in government. On the whole, party incumbency appears to have had little effect on trends in total public spending, which are affected more by shifts in the economy (for example, unemployment) and demographic pressures (which affect, for example, spending on pensions or education). It is interesting to note that on particular programmes the 1970–4 government achieved higher average increases in annual rates of expenditure on education, the National Health Service and housing than the 1964–70 Labour government. Less surprisingly, it also achieved faster rates of annual increases of spending on defence, and law and order.

The Heath government was optimistic about the benefits of structural and institutional change: witness its plans for entry into Europe, trade union reform, and the reorganization of the National Health Service, local government and central government. Changes in government would promote economic growth, enterprise and personal initiative. As David Butler and Michael Pinto-Duschinsky have observed, 'in short, structural reforms would make ideological measures unnecessary'.[9] In opposition Heath had established groups to study ways in which decision-making, policy formulation and the implementation of government programmes might be improved. The government was determined to reduce the number of departments, with a view to producing a smaller Cabinet and to promoting a better sense of strategy and greater co-ordination between policies. The number of major departments had already been reduced from twenty-four to seventeen between 1964 and 1970. Under Heath, these were reduced further to fifteen, with the creation of two giant departments – Environment, and Trade and Industry. The government was smaller than its immediate predecessor: there were eighteen ministers in Cabinet and twenty-five outside, as compared with twenty-one Cabinet and thirty-three non-Cabinet ministers under Wilson in 1964. Heath wanted to avoid overloading ministers with detail and to allow them time to think about strategy. The Central Policy Review Staff, the Think Tank (CPRS), was established to provide periodic reviews of government strategy for the Cabinet and examine subjects which cut across departmental responsibilities, such as Rolls-Royce, energy, race relations and Concorde. The government introduced a scheme of policy audit or 'management by objectives', adapted from the United States, known as Programme Analysis and Review (PAR). It also hived off a number of functions from departments to executive agencies: for example, the government estate management to a Property Services Agency, and weapons supply to the Procurement Executive. Finally it introduced a number of special advisers to Cabinet ministers, extending a process begun by Wilson.

Three major areas of economic policy are worth discussing in some detail. The government's declared intention in 1970 was to stand aside from industrial matters. The travel firm Thomas Cook and the state-owned brewery houses in Scotland and Carlisle were denationalized. In 1970 the regional employment premium was phased out and the Industrial Reorganization Corporation abolished. The giant new Department of Trade and Industry (DTI) was headed by John Davies, who until the election had been Director-General of the CBI. Davies had asserted that the government would not gear its policy to helping the 'lame ducks' – that is, loss-making industries and bankrupt firms. Almost immediately, however, government intervention belied free-market promise. When the Rolls-Royce company fell and attempts to rescue it failed, the government had to nationalize it in February 1971. The company was a prestige maker of aero-engines and it needed support to fulfil a contract to build engines for the Lockeed Tristar. In June 1971 a somewhat similar course of events followed the collapse of Upper Clyde

Shipbuilders (UCS), but in this case ministers were fearful of the increased unemployment which closure would cause. The government was also faced by a 'work-in' of the workforce and was concerned by the Glasgow Chief Constable's warning of an outbreak of violence if the yard was closed. The provision of £35 million saved UCS from liquidation and preserved over 4000 jobs. Despite everything the party manifesto had said about the economy, the Conservative government seemed to be falling prey to events.

In 1972 the change of course was carried further with the Industry Act, which gave the DTI extensive powers to intervene and provided large sums for it to disburse to industry. The run-down of the coal industry was put into reverse, an ambitious investment programme in British Steel was announced and extra funds made available to attract industries to depressed regions. The U-turn was complete, and was made because the original policy did not appear to be working, particularly in stemming the increase in unemployment.

The Industrial Relations Bill was introduced in December 1970. Like the proposals in Labour's White Paper, *In Place of Strife* (1969), the reforms were designed in part to curb unofficial strikes and strengthen official trade union leaders. The Act was dogged by trouble from the start. The trade unions refused to consult with the government when the latter insisted that the basic principles of the Bill were not negotiable. Moreover, the reforms were being introduced at a time when power was seeping from official union leaders to the shop floor. The Bill became law in 1971 and gave trade unions rights of recognition and other favours but at the cost of registration. It created a National Industrial Relations Court and Industrial Relations Commission and provided that agreements between employers and unions would be legally binding unless one of them stated in writing to the contrary. The Act also authorized the government to order a pre-strike ballot and impose a cooling-off period of up to sixty days where a strike would cause serious damage to the community or economy. The last two proposals were invoked by the government to deal with the railway dispute in May 1972, but did not achieve anything. In August 1972 there was a major dock strike over the Industrial Relations Court's decision to fine errant trade unions, and the government backed down. In September the TUC decided to expel any union that registered under the Act – the non-registration policy effectively crippled it. The conflict with the trade unions over this legislation introduced a chill between the government and unions which affected their dealings on other matters. The Act probably added to the number of disputes because of trade union strikes against its provisions, and was effectively placed on ice after May 1972.

Douglas Hurd, who had been head of Heath's political office between 1968 and 1974, claims that disputes over public-sector wages took more of the Cabinet's time than any other issue.[10] The original policy was for government to stand aside from wage negotiations in the private sector and gradually reduce the size of wage settlements in the public sector. But ministers rapidly became concerned at the level of wage settlements. Its policy of achieving N (i.e. the norm) minus 1 per cent in successive wage settlements in the public sector was an *ad hoc* response. In reply to suggestions that they should impose a statutory incomes policy, ministers rehearsed arguments about the inevitable loss of freedom that this would entail, the cumbersome bureaucracy which it would involve and claimed that it would only provide a temporary palliative. At first the policy appeared to be working, but in January and February 1972 occurred the key event which changed ministers' thinking about wages. The miners voted for a full-scale strike in pursuit of a large pay claim. Against a background of ugly picketing and several power cuts, a court of inquiry, under Lord Wilberforce, was hastily convened and recommended a generous wage increase of 21 per cent. The episode dramatically illustrated the power of a determined group of key workers to dislocate society and defy government policy. Inflationary wage demands in the public sector appeared to be just as irresistible as in the private sector. Many ministers felt that they had been humiliated by the miners and there was something of a 'never again' mood in the party. On the day of the Wilberforce award Heath announced, 'We have to find a more sensible way of settling our differences.'

The government then began long and involved talks with the TUC and CBI about the economy, inflation and a prices and incomes policy. Heath was seeking agreement on a voluntary policy of restraint. He failed and in September announced plans for a prices and incomes policy. A compulsory three-month standstill on pay and price increases was declared on 6 November, following the breakdown of the talks. Under Stage II of the policy, which followed in the New Year, a Pay Board and a Prices Commission were established. The government had reluctantly moved to a statutory incomes policy and now defended it as essential for protecting the interests of the community against sectional demands. Many Conservative backbenchers complained in private about the U-turn, but ministers regarded the maintenance of the new line of policy as a test of the government's authority and credibility.

The Heath government for long periods appeared to be under siege and invoked more states of emergency than any other government. (Under the Emergency Powers Act (1920) the government may proclaim a state of emergency if it judges that the essentials of life are threatened. It is empowered to make regulations by Orders in Council which have the force of law. Of the twelve occasions on which the Act has been invoked – usually in connection with strikes – five were under the Heath government.) The country faced power cuts in December 1970, when the power workers began a work-to-rule over pay, in early 1972 and again in early 1974, when the miners went on strike. In 1972 the country was threatened with a national dock strike to protest against the imprisonment of five dockers in 1972 by the National Industrial Relations Court. The government also faced bitter opposition from the Labour Party in the House of Commons, and a number of Conservatives felt that the polarization between the parties was making for a constitutional crisis.

The Conservatives' surprise victory in the 1970 election did not, according to the opinion polls, provide much of a honeymoon with the public. Gallup reported a slim lead for the party over Labour to the end of the year (1 per cent in December), but for the next three years it trailed Labour, until it regained a 2 per cent lead in January 1974. In 1972, when the Conservatives lost the apparently impregnable seat of Sutton and Cheam to the Liberals, it seemed that no Tory seat was safe. In by-elections in July 1973 the party lost two further seats, Ely and Ripon, to the Liberals, who briefly reached 30 per cent in the opinion polls. The Liberal upsurge posed more of a threat to the Conservative Party than to Labour.

The government was also forced to bend its economic policies to cope with pressures of rising unemployment, high wage settlements and then the increase in oil prices. Yet in opposition the party had boasted about its sense of strategy and its determination to stick to well-prepared policies and not resort to ad-hockery. For the first twelve months of office the main battle was against inflation, relying on cuts in income tax and reducing the level of wage settlements in the public sector. Thereafter, particularly when unemployment reached 1 million, the government pursued an expansionist economic policy. In July 1971 a public works programme for the development areas was announced, purchase tax was cut, hire-purchase controls were abolished and the money supply was expanded. These policies were reinforced in late 1972 by the imposition of compulsory controls on wages and prices to stem inflation.

Unfortunately this coincided with, first, a rise in commodity prices and, then, the oil crisis. In December 1973 the government abandoned its dash for growth, reverted to making the fight against inflation its priority, and announced a package of large cuts in public spending. The government was also unlucky in experiencing the failure of Keynesian economic policies. All the devices, such as the CPRS and PAR, designed to avoid overload and short-term decision-making went by the board in face of the oil-price explosion and miner's strike.

The government's major achievement, and one associated with Heath himself, was Britain's entry into the EEC. Ever since 1961, a majority of the party had been pro-European, and Heath had been for longer. But Britain's membership, though central to Heath's vision of Britain's place in world and his hopes for economic revival, never captured the public's imagination. The failure to get Labour Party support was a blow, but one explicable largely in terms of the tensions and rivalries within that party. But, ever since the first application for entry, in 1961, there had been an anti-Market group in the Conservative Party. A small number of opponents (notably Powell) held out to the end, and the government had only a bare majority on the second reading of the accession Bill, a vote which Heath had made an issue of confidence.

The government had inherited a situation in Northern Ireland which was to provide one of its main worries. In August 1970 Reginald Maudling, the Home Secretary, alarmed at sectarian violence, introduced internment. But this alienated Catholics further and was followed by greater violence. Bombings became more frequent all over the province – and there were a few in Britain too. On 30 March 1972, Heath, in what he has decribed as the most difficult decision of his premiership, authorized the suspension of Stormont, the Northern Ireland Parliament, and its constitution and put William Whitelaw in charge of the province. This followed the refusal of Brian Faulkner, the Ulster Premier, to accept London control of law and order. The episode loosened the link between the Conservatives and the Ulster Unionist MPs. It was a constant source of worry to the British government – and it provided a backdrop of domestic violence which added appreciably to the growing sense of national unease.

One has to take account of the sheer pressure of events on the stamina of ministers and officials in these years. During the negotiations with the miners, many ministers and senior civil servants were on the point of physical and nervous exhaustion.[11] In the second week of December 1973, for example, at the height of negotiations, Heath not only entertained visiting heads of states from Italy and Zaire but also had to preside over the Sunningdale Conference on the future of Northern Ireland and attend the European summit in Copenhagen. As Douglas Hurd ruefully observes about these meetings, 'They all involved talks, travel, long meals, extensive briefing beforehand; yet none of them had anything to do with the crisis which was swallowing us up.'[12]

On the eve of the Conservative Party conference at Blackpool in October 1973, none of the party leaders envisaged an early election.[13] The tentative plans of party advisers envisaged a dissolution in late October 1974 or early 1975. Yet by the end of October this leisurely approach had been shot down. The outbreak on 6 October of war in the Middle East resulted in the Arab states' cutting their oil supplies and quadrupling the price, with devastating implications for Britain's energy supplies and balance of payments. The most significant fact for the approach of the election was that the increased oil prices had greatly strengthened the bargaining position of coal-miners and cast a shadow over the government's Stage III incomes policy.

Although this backdrop to the election had never been anticipated, there were several reasons why Conservatives could look forward to an early election. First, there was the continuing disarray of the Labour Party, which had had a disastrous by-election record during the Parliament. A second reason was that on 7 December 1973 an Opinion Research Centre poll put the Conservatives ahead of Labour for only the second time in more than two years and reported a fall for the Liberals, who had recently been riding high in the opinion polls. Third, the unions were not popular and the government's incomes policies enjoyed widespread support. As early as November, a number of Conservative advisers were arguing for an early election, on the grounds that the Middle East war had overturned the government's original 'dash for growth' programme, or that the economic situation was bound to deteriorate and make the government much more unpopular. Ministers had informal discussions about an early election in the light of the worsening industrial situation, although Heath gave no clues to his thinking.

Because the immediate cause of the election was the industrial action by the miners, it is necessary to discuss the circumstances which brought this about. Stage III of the government's prices and incomes policy, published on 8 October, suggested a norm of 8–9 per cent in wage increases but contained special escape clauses which were designed to give the miners more than anyone else. The National Coal Board, to the regret of ministers, immediately offered the maximum amount permissible under Stage III (about 13 per cent), which was dismissed by the miners. It appeared that the escape clause, or bonus provision, was available to other groups of workers which could satisfy the Pay Board – so it was not special enough for the NUM. Many members of the Cabinet believed that a deal had been made in September between Derek Ezra, chairman of the Coal Board, and Joe Gormley, president of the NUM, and felt a sense of betrayal at these developments. But the government's position was weakened by the fact that the package they were defending had been drawn up before the crisis over oil supplies. The situation worsened when the NUM executive voted for an overtime ban to start on 12 November. To save energy, the government declared a state of emergency and eventually authorized a three-day week. Ministers were virtually unanimous in agreeing that it was next to politically impossible to sell to the party any settlement that went much beyond Stage III. They felt that they could not risk another sell-out along the lines of Wilberforce.

In the first two weeks of January 1974, support for holding an early election grew among party officials and backbenchers. However, Heath continued to receive the TUC Economic Committee at Downing Street – on 10 January and again on 14 January, at the height of speculation about a February election. He still hoped for a settlement with the miners or at least a way of avoiding a 'who governs?' election and spurned the chance to call an election on 7 February. He had striven hard to reach some form of long-term agreement with the trade unions, and a bitter general election, even if won by his party, would further damage the prospects of reconciliation. If the Conservative Party won a landslide majority, it was not clear that this would either influence the miners or weaken their bargaining position. Although Mr Heath did not want a 'who governs?' election or one which divided the country, he could not guarantee what would happen once an election was called. A Conservative victory might not make the NUM more conciliatory. On the other hand, Labour might win the election, or the outcome might be indeterminate and he would be blamed. The only case for calling an election was to end the uncertainty. During all the consultations about election timing – and he consulted most of his colleagues in January – he appears not to have shown his hand.

On 4 February it emerged that the NUM had decisively voted for a strike, and a meeting between the TUC and government ministers produced no basis for agreement. An election seemed inevitable. On 7 February, Heath announced that polling day would be 28 February. He called an election simply because he did not know what else to do; he was cornered between the miners' determination to call a strike rather than compromise and his party's resistance to anything that smacked of surrender. There was no little irony in the fact that the government was forced into an election in defence of policies that it had explicitly repudiated when it was elected over three and a half years earlier. The election did not follow a defeat in the House of Commons or occur because Parliament was near the end of its lifespan. It was un-precedented for an outside challenge to government policy to force a dissolution, but the issue was one where ministers genuinely thought it was impossible to change course without a new mandate. There seemed to be no alternative to having an election. According to Hurd, 'The lean years would need new policies and a new vocabulary. There would have to be an end to promises.'[14]

Lord Hailsham has suggested that it is rare for governments in Britain to lose elections; by timing economic booms to coincide with the run-up to an election and taking advantage of the opinion polls for an opportune dissolution, the Prime Minister has a formidable set of advantages.[15] However, since 1945 the party in power has won only six of the subsequent eleven general elections. The Conservatives' private pollsters advised an early dissolution in January 1974 and warned that public opinion was volatile on the issue of the miners' pay claim. Heath's decision to delay the election by three weeks probably cost him the election. He consulted widely, with party officials, Cabinet ministers and private advisers, and went along, reluctantly, with the majority view. He paid a heavy personal and political price for the decision.

The lessons of history are selective and it is unwise to assume that the passage of time will provide its own corrective, as the personalities and events of the past are invariably invoked by rivals to fight contemporary disputes. In the 1980s Conservative 'wets' and Labour critics of the present government point to the 'one nation' policies of the Heath and earlier Tory governments to attack Mrs Thatcher. Thatcherites in turn regard the Heath record as an illustration of the failure of political will and abandonment of political principles; for them the records of the Heath and the succeeding Labour governments confirmed the political bankruptcy of Keynesian and collectivist policies. In many ways Mrs Thatcher has made her reputation by posing as an anti-Heath figure. The contrasts are many. She won her big battle with the miners, made her industrial relations legislation stick, rejected the 'social partners' approach to managing the economy, is more pro-American than pro-European Community, and is deeply suspicious of the ethos of the senior Civil Service. She has wanted to abolish the term 'U-turn' from the political vocabulary ('U-turn if you want to, the lady's not for turning'). The dragons that she claims to have slain, notably over-mighty trade unions and inflation, are largely a legacy of 1974. The spectre of trade union power and fear of inflation were dominant themes in British politics in the mid-1970s and impressions of the Heath government are still dominated by the manner of its downfall. Yet it is worth noting that the succeeding Labour government, in spite of its social contract with the unions, also collapsed on broadly similar rocks to those which proved the undoing of the Heath government.

I have four chief impressions of the 1970–4 government. First, there was Heath's personal dominance in government. As party leader between 1965 and 1970, and as Prime Minister, he got his way on the major issues. The administration and Heath personally suffered many rebuffs, not least from trade unions over incomes policies (though it is worth noting that, until the successful resistance of the NUM, all workers had settled under the guidelines of Stage III) and the Industrial Relations Act. The government's central goal of reversing the country's relative economic decline also failed. By the time it left office, it was presiding over record inflation, a record spending deficit and a record negative balance of payments. Yet, in terms of carrying a united Cabinet and party through spectacular policy U-turns, Heath proved a remark- able leader. The high esteem in which he was held by his Cabinet colleagues was reflected in the large number of them who voted for him on the first ballot in the leadership election in 1975. In spite of the U-turns, there were no resignations from the Cabinet on the grounds of policy disagreement. There were also very few leaks from the Cabinet – probably an indication of high moral and solidarity. The contrast with the well-publicized divisions in the Labour governments of 1964–70 and 1974–9 and the Thatcher government is remarkable.

Yet this very solidarity within the leadership strata of the party may also have been a weakness. The Cabinet was rather like-minded, contained few independent and heavyweight figures and, over time, probably became detached from the mood of many Conservative back- benchers. The discontent was seen in the relatively high levels of dissent in the division lobbies and in the election to important posts by party

MPs of critics of the government. Edward du Cann was elected as chairman of the 1922 Committee, Nicholas Ridley as chairman of the party's Finance Committee and John Biffen as chairman of the Industry Committee. Heath presumed too much on the loyalty and goodwill of backbenchers. The extent of this gulf only became fully apparent when the MPs voted for Margaret Thatcher in preference to him in the subsequent leadership election.

A second impression is of how little remains of the government's legislation. The succeeding Labour government immediately scrapped the industrial relations and housing finance policies and the statutory controls on incomes, and again made it compulsory for councils to introduce comprehensive education. Moreover, the Heath government's major achievements, getting Britain into the EEC, was thrown into the melting pot (by Labour's decision to renegotiate the terms) until the referendum in June 1975. The 1970s were the classic period of 'adversary politics'; indeed, the term came into vogue, thanks to Professor Sammy Finer, in 1974. It referred to the opposition party's determination, for opposition's sake, to reverse most policies of the government of the day. The Labour party after 1970 moved sharply to the left and abandoned many policies which it had pursued in office between 1964 and 1970. Although the 1970 government's policies with regard to industrial relations, incomes policy and membership of EEC resembled those of the previous administration, Labour spokesmen attacked them vigorously in Parliament. The extra-parliamentary wing of the Labour Party, notably some left-wing controlled local authorities, trade unions and the party conference, also became more assertive in the party's decision-making process.

Heath's reform of the machinery of government has also proved short-lived. The Department of Trade and Industry was partly broken up in December 1973, when, in response to the oil crisis, a separate Department of Energy was created. In 1974 the Wilson government further divided the DTI into separate departments for Trade, Industry and Prices, and Consumer Protection. In 1976 the Environment Department was divided by the creation of a separate Transport Department. PAR was formally abandoned in 1979 and the CPRS disbanded in 1983. The Heath government's reorganization of the health service and local government have both been subject to further reorganizations, the most radical occurring under Mrs Thatcher. The machinery set up under the Industrial Relations Act and the Counter-Inflation Act, except for the Prices Commission, was abolished. Apart from membership of the EEC, the Heath government has probably left the fewest policy legacies of any postwar government, apart from the short-lived Home government of 1963–4.

A climate of opinion is a tricky phenomenon to describe, but the government seemed to lack a supportive climate of opinion. It has been argued that many opinion leaders in the mass media and higher education were sympathetic to the egalitarian, welfare and *dirigiste* policies which on balance had prevailed since 1945. A Conservative historian, Lord Blake, claims that the Conservatives won the 1970 election in spite of the intellectual tide of the time; they did not win the election because they had won the 'battle for the mind', but rather because of a general discontent about high prices and general governmental incompetence.[16] According to Douglas Hurd, the Conservatives won the election 'against and not with the tide of intellectual opinion'.[17] Another Conservative critic, Ronald Butt, has condemned the Heath government for its lack of political skills – for instance, in controlling miners' wages at a time of expensive energy, or in making the operation of the Industrial Relations Act contingent upon the voluntary registration of trade unions. According to Butt, 'The Conservative government came to disaster through sheer lack of political instinct about what are and are not workable policies.'[18]

A related failure was that the government suffered a notable lack of ministers who were good communicators. In this the death of Macleod and the absence of Enoch Powell were unfortunate. The government also gained a bad press for imposing museum charges and curtailing free school milk. These two measures produced small financial savings at an enormous political cost and gave the government the image of being hard-hearted. Heath himself was a man who had a vision but who failed to project it, even to many in his party.

A third impression is that the government was overloaded. It undoubtedly attempted to do too much and at times seemed to be fighting battles on several fronts. Survey evidence showed that by 1974 the Conservative Party had lost its traditional reputation for 'competence'. The implementation of so many of the government's policies required the co-operation of other groups. The anti-inflation policy required agreement over wages and prices from domestic producer groups and restraint by commodity producers abroad; the Housing Finance Act depended upon the compliance of the local authorities; and the implementation of the Industrial Relations Act depended upon the co-operation of employers and, above all, of trade unions. This is more than a problem of having public opinion on one's side. Much of the press, notably *The Times* and *Economist*, warmly supported the 1970 programme, and, equally warmly, the shift to the prices and incomes policies. *The Times* on 18 January 1973, for example, praised Stage III of the pay and prices policy: 'Mr Heath has fully discharged [his] special responsibility, and our endorsement is unqualified.'[19] Opinion polls suggested that there was public support for the anti-inflation policy and for the industrial relations reform. But too often the Heath government simply failed to gain the co-operation of the groups necessary for the effective working of a policy. It also faced bitter political opposition from Labour and had to give way to powerful trade unions.

The questions of Britain's membership of the EEC, of bargaining between the major producer interests and government, of the use of an incomes policy as a weapon against inflation, and of reform of industrial relations were inherited from pre-1970 administrations and continued to be problems after 1974. To this extent Heath was part of an era stretching from Macmillan to Callaghan. It is worth noting, however, that the Heath government was the last to use a formal statutory incomes policy. In his determination to preserve the full-employment goals of the 1944 White Paper, Heath was a child of the postwar consensus. Maintaining full employment was not mentioned in the 1970 manifesto because it was taken for granted. Yet 'doing something' about unemployment was important in producing the U-turns. Heath's policies had a desperate air because he had to face the inflationary pressure from the growing problems of trade union bargaining power and the oil-price shock. It was only when the unions overreached themselves in winter 1979 that a new government was able to take action against them. It was not immediately obvious that the consensus was dead by 1974 – the next Labour government had a 'Social Contract' with the unions and an incomes policy. It was the 'winter of discontent' that was important in paving the way for a different approach. Heath's was the last government to make growth the main goal of economic policy.

But the experience of the 1970 government marked an important stage in the evolution of the modern Conservative Party. It saw the emergence of a recognizable New Right group of critics of the government, the most prominent of whom, of course, was Enoch Powell. Philip Norton has found a high degree of overlap in Tory backbench dissent on such issues as entry into the EEC, renewal of Rhodesian sanctions,

changes to the rules for the entry of immigrants (1972) and the imposition of direct rule on Northern Ireland. Opposition to all these policies
came from the party's right wing. Ideology was not central to the leadership election in 1975, though some Thatcherite commentators have
subsequently tried to make it so. The reaction against state control of
incomes and prices, and the more sympathetic hearing for the ideas of
Friedman, Hayek and the Institute of Economic Affairs came after 1975.

A dilemma for the Conservative Party in 1974–5 was, how was it to
come to terms with the legacy of policy trends since 1945? Was it to
accept what Sir Keith Joseph later called the 'ratchet effect of socialism'
and pursue the so-called middle ground, the location of which was partly
defined by what Labour did? Or was it to reverse those policies and
strike out in pursuit of a more market-oriented neo-liberal set of
Conservative policies? Mrs Thatcher and Sir Keith Joseph clearly
favoured the second position. She has made no attempt to deny that her
policies and political values are different from those of her immediate
predecessors as Conservative leader.[20] Heath became increasingly bitter
at what he regarded as the disowning of his government's record by
those who had been members of it, notably Thatcher and Joseph. A
number of his former associates, in particular Sir Ian Gilmour, Jim Prior
and Francis Pym, have stood for a type of Conservatism which is distinct
from that of Thatcher and Joseph.

In one significant sense, however, Mrs Thatcher has operated in the
tradition of Conservative statesmanship. According to James Bulpitt, an
abiding interest of Conservative leaders has been the protection of the
autonomy of central government on matters which they regard as 'high
politics' – for example, defence, foreign affairs and national economic
policy.[21] Other, 'minor' issues could be left to interest groups, local
government or the free market. In economic policy this autonomy of
central government had been seriously compromised by Heath's search
for agreement on incomes policy with the trade unions during 1972–3.
The attraction of monetarism for the new Conservative leadership after
1975 was that it promised a method of controlling inflation without
bargaining with the trade unions and restored some autonomy to the
centre. In this, as in many other features, the Heath government is still
viewed from the vantage point of the personalities and events of the
years since 1979.

Chronology

1970

18 June   General election: Conservatives, 330 seats; Labour, 287; Liberals, 6; others, 7.
30 June   EEC entry negotiations start.
20 July   Iain Macleod dies. Succeeded as Chancellor of the Exchequer by Anthony Barber.
3 December   Electricity work-to-rule with blackouts.

1971

5 February   First British soldier killed in Belfast.
15 February   Decimal currency introduced.
25 February   Rolls-Royce nationalized following bankruptcy.
30 March   First Conservative Budget makes major tax changes and foreshadows value added tax.
27 May   Labour win Bromsgrove by-election.
8 June   Upper Clyde Shipbuilders liquidation followed by work-in.
23 June   EEC negotiations concluded.
5 August   Royal assent to Industrial Relations Act.
20 August   First auction of North Sea oil concessions.
23 August   Pound floated (within limits).
28 October   Commons votes in favour of EEC entry 356–244 (69 Labour MPs vote for).

1972

January   Unemployment exceeds 1 million.
30 January   13 killed in Londonderry ('Bloody Sunday').
18 February   Wilberforce Report to settle 6-week miners' strike.
29 March   First National Industrial Relations Court fines of unions.
30 March   Stormont suspended; William Whitelaw appointed Secretary for Northern Ireland.
7 April   After Cabinet reshuffle Lord Carrington succeeds Peter Thomas as chairman of the Conservative Party.
10 April   Roy Jenkins resigns as Deputy Leader of the Labour Party.
17 April   British Rail work-to-rule (settled on 12 June).
23 June   Pound floated freely.
18 July   Reginald Maudling resigns as Home Secretary.
21 July   Dock strike (till 16 August).
4 August   Expulsion of Asians from Uganda begins.
21 July   Housing Finance Act passed.
4 September   TUC confirms the suspension of unions registering under the Industrial Relations Act.
26 September   Government proposes prices and incomes policy. Abortive tripartite talks follow.

26 October   Liberals win Rochdale (followed by Sutton and Cheam on
7 December).
6 November   90-day wages and prices standstill following failure of tripartite talks
on a voluntary policy (Stage I).

1973

1 January   Britain joins the EEC.
1 March   Dick Taverne re-elected at Lincoln as an independent (having resigned
as sitting Labour MP).
16 March   'Neutral' Budget.
1 April   Stage II of prices and incomes policy.
12 April   First elections to new county authorities under Local Government Act
1972.
May   Unemployment falls to less than the 600,000 inherited from the Labour
Party.
12 May   Lord Lambton and (24 May) Earl Jellicoe resign from government.
26 July   Liberals win Isle of Ely and Ripon by-elections.
4 September   Len Murray succeeds Vic Feather as General Secretary of the TUC.
6–22 October   Middle East war and consequent oil crisis.
31 October   Kilbrandon Report on devolution to Scotland and Wales.
8 November   Scottish Nationalists win Govan by-election; Liberals win Berwick-
upon-Tweed.
12 November   Miners start overtime ban.
6 December   Sunningdale talks on Northern Ireland.
12 December   ASLEF (the Associated Society of Locomotive Engineers and
Fireman) starts work-to-rule.
13 December   3-day week announced, to save electricity.
17 December   Big cuts in public expenditure announced.

1974

10–17 January   Abortive speculation about election on 7 February.
5 February   Miners decide to strike.
7 February   General election announced for 28 February.

Notes

1   Lucille Iremonger, 'Edward Heath', in John Mackintosh (ed.), *British Prime Ministers in the Twentieth Century*, vol. II (Weidenfeld and Nicolson, 1978).
2   Philip Norton, *Conservative Dissidents: dissent within the Conservative Parliamentary Party 1970–74* (Temple-Smith, 1978), p. 229.
3   Peter Hennessy, *Cabinet* (Basil Blackwell, 1986), p. 74.
4   'Edward Heath and Lord Trend on the art of Cabinet government', the *Listener*, 22 April 1976.
5   Stephen Fay and Hugo Young, in *The Sunday Times*, 22 February 1976, p. 33.

6   John Ramsden, *The Making of Conservative Party Policy* (Longman, 1980), pp. 279–83.
7   David Butler and Michael Pinto-Duschinsky, *The British General Election of 1970* (Macmillan, 1971).
8   Richard Rose, *Do Parties Make a Difference?*, 2nd edn (Macmillan, 1985).
9   Butler and Pinto-Duschinksy, *The British General Election of 1970*, p. 19.
10 Douglas Hurd, *An End to Promises* (Collins, 1979).
11 Fay and Young, in *The Sunday Times*, 22 February 1976.
12 Hurd, *An End to Promises*, p. 121.
13 This section draws in part on David Butler and Dennis Kavanagh, *The British General Election of February 1974* (Macmillan, 1974).
14 Hurd, *An End to Promises*, p. 136.
15 Lord Hailsham, *The Dilemma of Democracy* (Collins, 1978).
16 Robert Blake, 'A changed climate', in Robert Blake and John Patten (eds), *The Conservative Opportunity* (Longman, 1976), p. 2.
17 Hurd, *An End to Promises*, p. 149.
18 Ronald Butt, in *The Times*, 7 March 1974.
19 Martin Holmes, *Political Pressure and Economic Policies: British government 1970–74* (Butterworth, 1982).
20 See Dennis Kavanagh, *Thatcherism and British Politics: the end of consensus?* (Oxford University Press, 1987)
21 James Bulpitt, 'The Thatcher statecraft', *Political Studies*, 4 (1986).

Bibliography

To date there have not been many studies of the 1970–4 government or memoirs or 'diaries' from former members. Jim Prior's *A Balance of Power* (Hamish Hamilton, 1986) is not very informative. Edward Heath has promised a substantial book which will deal, in part, with the record of the 1970 government. On Heath himself there have been a number of studies, most of which were written during the early stages of his premiership. Particularly worth reading are George Hutchinson, *Edward Heath* (Longman, 1970); Andrew Roth, *Heath and the Heathmen* (Routledge and Kegan Paul, 1972); and Margaret Laing, *Edward Heath* (Sidgwick and Jackson, 1972). For an unsympathetic commentary, see Lucille Iremonger, 'Edward Heath', in John Mackintosh (ed.), *British Prime Ministers in the Twentieth Century*, vol. II (Weidenfeld and Nicolson, 1978). On the ambitious policy-making exercise when the party was in opposition between 1964 and 1970, see David Butler and Michael Pinto-Duschinsky, *The British General Election of 1970* (Macmillan, 1971); Robert Rhodes-James, *Ambitions and Realities* (Weidenfeld and Nicolson, 1972); and John Ramsden, *The Making of Conservative Party Policy* (Longman, 1980). For 'insider' accounts of the lessons of the government see Jock Bruce-Gardyne, *Whatever Happened to the Quiet Revolution?* (Charles Knight, 1974): Douglas Hurd, *An End to Promises*

(Collins, 1979); Reginald Maudling, *Memoirs* (Sidgwick and Jackson, 1978); and Ian Gilmour, *Inside Right: a study of Conservatism* (Quartet Books, 1978). Also interesting is Sir Keith Joseph's *Reversing the Trend* (Barry Rose, 1975). A good account of the economic record of the government is contained in Martin Holmes, *Political Pressures and Economic Policies: British government 1970–74* (Butterworth, 1982). On specific aspects see Philip Norton, *Conservative Dissidents: dissent within the Conservative Parliamentary Party 1970–74* (Temple-Smith, 1978); Stephen Fay and Hugo Young, *The Fall of Heath* (Sunday Times Publications, 1976); and David Butler and Dennis Kavanagh, *The British General Election of February 1974* (Macmillan, 1974).

8

The Labour Governments, 1974–1979

Phillip Whitehead

What you see is determined by where you stand, in time, and in belief. From 1987, after eight years of a government which has profoundly changed much of British society, the later years of the Wilson–Callaghan generation seem diminished below even their modest pretensions, a muted memory of managed decline. We look at them as Lawrence saw the humming-bird, through the wrong end of the telescope of time. Many on the political left share this view, heightened by that sense of drift and betrayal that sees every Labour leader as a potential shrunken head displayed above the Tory tepee. Within months of the fall of the Callaghan government the Institute for Workers' Control had published *What Went Wrong*. It was a statement, not a question.

What Went Wrong pointed out that after the fall of the Wilson government nine years before it had been excoriated by Reg Prentice for its 'drift to the right',[1] a tendency which he knew well, being now ensconced in Mrs Thatcher's government. Ironically, one of the twelve authors was himself to join the Social Democratic Party less than two years later. The problem with socialism seemed to be that it was more friable than viable. Labour governments are derided for their lack of principle both by those who seek to grasp the wheel and by others who are about to take to the life-rafts. Rapid and explicit publication of diaries and memoirs by those still on board heighten the impression of unseaworthiness. Where Richard Crossman, Barbara Castle and Joel Barnett led, junior office-holders are eager to follow. Few remain to defend the record. Harold Wilson's own memoir of his final term is almost frivolously insubstantial and James Callaghan's account is bland and discreet. There has been far less attention to this period than to the phenomenon of Thatcherism which succeeded it.

There is another reason for the comparative disdain for the 1974-9 Labour governments. Opinion about them was coloured by a press voracious for details of administrative incompetence, always hospitable to apostates. The contemporary impression of any modern Labour government is that it is for ever in a state of terminal decline. So it was with the inquest on the last days of Wilson and Callaghan. Yet the problems of both Prime Ministers were perhaps greater than those faced by any other postwar leader. Against a backdrop of crumbling consensus they had to govern with minority or insubstantial majority support. Their dilemma was that the dominant British preoccupation – inflation, and the fears that it fuelled – made it harder still to carry the socialist policies which their party ardently desired. They sensed public opinion moving to the right, and tried to back and fill accordingly. The party did not find it easy to follow.

Labour leaders sometimes say that their problem has not been winning elections, but winning the right ones. Harold Wilson did not expect to lose in 1970. He did not expect to win in 1974. The party was handed a poisoned chalice in February 1974. It had only 37 per cent of the popular vote, and owed its success to the resurgence of the Liberals, who polled their highest figure for forty years, reducing the Conservatives in turn to their lowest percentage since 1929.[2] The resemblance to 1929 was increased by the severity of the economic crisis. The apparent plateau of 1970 had long vanished in a miasma of uncertainty. The country needed determined and effective leadership. It had to make do with a minority government, starting afresh amid the wreckage of incomes policy, industrial relations law, the interrupted dash for growth, and a fatally weakened power-sharing initiative in Northern Ireland.

Britain had entered the EEC at the worst possible time, on the brink of world recession. Its already efficient agriculture would be cosseted, and the cost passed on to the consumer. But there was to be no stimulus to British industry, with its persistent problems of low productivity, bad labour relations and chronic under-investment. Net company profits as a proportion of fixed assets were to fall throughout the seventies. The quadrupling of world oil prices by the Organization of Petroleum Exporting Countries in 1973-4 had caught Britain unprepared, and accelerating inflation built on already historically high levels. These had been aggravated by the flotation of the pound in 1972 and the credit boom of 1971-3, in which bank advances rose by over 150 per cent in the eagerness of the financial sector to take the waiting out of wanting for every property speculator in town. 'More pounds sterling were created in these three years', wrote one austere observer, 'than in the whole twelve hundred years history of the pound since King Offa.'[3] Flotation of the pound, in itself sensible, prepared a new nightmare: that the pound would float ever downwards, and domestic costs rise inordinately.

The British found their decimalized pound worth only three-quarters of its 1971 value in 1974. By 1978 a pound bought what a shilling had done in 1900. A self-confident trade union movement kept its members' real earnings ahead of inflation, and any thought of restraint was banished by the ostentatious success of the new elite of credit touts and secondary bankers, who boasted that they 'made money, not things'.[4] The unions had defeated Wilson in 1969, Heath in the prolonged war of attrition over his industrial relations law. They were in no mood to be checked. In the last months of the overstretched and exhausted Heath government, the crisis engulfed the country. The Treasury saw the incomes policy, in which it had assisted after Heath's U-turn, purchased at a heavy price in inflationary threshold agreements, fatally damaged. Where the incoming government might usually find policy advice adjusted to its priorities it found a vacuum.

The priorities were there, although they were not Wilson's. 'Promise less and demand more' had been R. H. Tawney's advice in not dissimilar circumstances after 1931.[5] The objective of the party should not be merely to win votes, but to 'wake the sleeping demon' of democratic participation. From 1970 to 1974 the party leadership thought of votes regained, confidence rebuilt. Its activists sought to wake the demon. They distrusted Wilson and his (almost unchanged) frontbench team. They wanted clear commitments against trade union laws and the Treaty of Rome, major extensions of public ownership and investment. There came out to join them Tony Benn, once the youthful technocrat of the first Wilson era, now a born-again socialist radicalized by his experience of workers in struggle. As chairman of the party he had launched 'Participation 72' to rethink party policy. He seemed everywhere 'exciting, inspirational, sometimes dangerous'.[6]

Wilson, who was none of these things, announced that he would veto commitments to a National Enterprise Board which would require a controlling interest in 'twenty-five of our largest manufacturers'[7] and planning agreements with a hundred more. *Labour's Programme 1973* contained an ambitious economic strategy. Its supporters saw it as a socialist continuance of the public investment policies forced on the Heath government, but with the added ingredient of democratic participation. Its opponents thought it as rigid and unworkable as the Russian Gosplan, but did not exert themselves unduly to prevent it passing the party conference.

The Wilson veto led directly to the foundation of the Campaign for Labour Party Democracy. A pressure group which sought to make the leadership more accountable to the rank and file, within seven years it won major constitutional change. The campaigners were not taken seriously at first. Anyone with a duplicating machine and a bedsitter could join, their critics said. But within the shrinking base of active Labour membership they were persuasive and effective – the more so when the left on the National Executive managed to abolish the proscribed list which had previously excluded those with Communist or Trotskyist affiliations. The National Agent's report on the best organised of these, Militant, was conspicuously ignored. There were to be no more witch hunts. It was Wilson, with his view that the conference was there to be inspired or ignored at will, who now lost control of the party machine. From all points of view in the party, his weariness, if understandable, was inexcusable. His latest successor, Neil Kinnock, starting from a much weaker base, has shown what can be done by plain words and close attention; above all by addressing arguments seriously. As it was, a hostile National Executive which represented the spirit of the party in conference, and a government which believed it worked for the interest of Labour voters in the country, were to be in perpetual conflict in the 1970s. The task of the two Labour Prime Ministers was made harder because of it.

On the trade union front Wilson was still bound by the terms of his 1969 surrender. There could be no extension of the law into trade union affairs, and if the trade unions wished to return to unfettered collective bargaining then any counter-inflation policy would have to be so framed. A Labour Party/Trade Union Liaison Committee was to hammer this out. Barbara Castle noted that when, at one of its meetings, 'someone dared to refer to the role of incomes in the management of the economy, Jack Jones jumped in at once: "It would be disastrous if any word went out from this meeting that we had been discussing prices and incomes policy." '[8] Jones held the cards. He recalls that 'I warned them of the danger of a split with the TUC if they persisted, and argued that the priority should be control of prices, plus a comprehensive social policy which would command public support.'[9] Thus began the Social Contract, within which the newly elected minority government would have to operate.

Labour leaders only enjoy one glad confident morning with their party – when it is theirs to command, far enough from power not to take it for granted, and conceding much to a leader who may deliver. Wilson in 1964, like Kinnock in 1987, had his hour. It was not so in 1974. Much of the left of the party distrusted him for his record in government, and his manoeuvres over the EEC in opposition had drawn less understanding from either faction than he deserved. He had no majority, yet a major programme of reform and social ownership to implement. He had to confront the worst inflation of the century with little more than union goodwill. And he knew that the collapse of the Heath government had left some in the country and the security services keen to destabilize him before he began. Yet he seemed curiously serene as he began his last, unexpected tenure of office. Denis Healey had seen him in his days of hubris and hysteria. Now things were different.

When Harold Wilson came back to power in 1974 he stopped interfering with people. I think he'd already made his mind up that he would retire well before his time was up. And he gave everybody a great deal of latitude. He didn't try to stuff the Cabinet with his creatures. But he was still very reluctant to commit himself to difficult decisions.[10]

The decisions awaited. It was a characteristically Wilsonian aphorism that a decision deferred was a decision made. But deferral now was to be disastrous. Wilson's remedy for the British sickness in 1974 would have been managerial social democracy: retain confidence at home and abroad, recognize the limits to what Labour in office can do unilaterally, deal with the special interests upon which the party depended. In such an administration the 1973 programme would not be imposed as a diet, though it might be kept as a flavour. The Labour activists wanted socialism, and the eradication of the legacy of Heath, but the hidden agenda of the Labour Cabinet was not unlike Heath's own: stay in Europe, retain the American alliance and a nuclear defence policy, preserve and make more efficient British industry through the world recession, contain unemployment whilst reducing inflation before it entirely destroyed Britain's competitive position. Instead, Wilson had to win a further election, to which all other considerations were subordinated.

In the period between the two general elections of 1974 economic policy was barely discussed. The Treasury was paralysed. The head of the Downing Street Policy Unit, Dr Bernard Donoughue, noted 'the almost complete absense of economic policy; I think it's true that the Cabinet never really discussed economic policy before the October election.'[11] When he asked a very senior Treasury official why no papers were forthcoming on the inflation crisis he was told, 'Politicians never deal with serious issues until they become *the* crisis. So at the Treasury we're waiting until the crisis really blows up.' The then permanent secretary, Sir Douglas Wass, add this justification:

I think the Treasury was pretty realistic in recognising that these were not conditions under which any big changes of policy could be achieved. . . . I have a feeling in the back of my mind that there was some sort of discussion of economic policy in the summer of '74, but again I'm very sure it was not a full-blooded survey of the whole economy.[12]

The profound consequences of the oil-price rise were ill-digested. Joel Barnett, then chief secretary of the Treasury, describes the policy of the government as 'spending money we did not have'.[13] As Chancellor, Healey took a separate route from the more powerful economies of Japan and the United States, which had deflated in the face of the oil crisis. Britain was to deflate later, and more painfully. For the moment public expenditure was set to rise by 9 per cent in real terms over the 1974 figures, with increases in pensions and food subsidies prominent. The hope was that this combined increase in the social wage and stabilization of basic prices would impress working people and induce moderation in their wage demands. In reality, Donoughue reflected, 'It didn't mean as much to them as it cost us.'[14] By October 1974, when the annual increase in the retail price index was 17 per cent, the figure for wages was 22 per cent, and rising. Matters were worsened by the Treasury's failure to produce an accurate forecast of the public-sector borrowing requirement (PSBR). Its underestimate was a massive £4000 million. Two years later, with the Labour government in the toils of the International Monetary Fund, it was to overestimate by £3000 million.

What was the Prime Minister's principal preoccupation throughout the prolonged crisis? It remained the winning of a fourth election, and then of a referendum on EEC membership. For the former he believed he had to muzzle the minister, Tony Benn, whose characteristic high profile provided both a target for press attacks and, in direct variation, party support. Few Prime Ministers can have devoted so much care to the corralling of a colleague. Benn believed in stumping the country, to awaken the party to its chance to transform society. His colleagues felt that he was appealing over their heads. His White Paper on industrial policy was savaged by Wilson as 'sloppy and half-baked ... polemical, even menacing, in tone, redolent more of an NEC [National Executive Committee] Home Policy Committee document than a Command paper'.[15] Benn might have replied that that was what Labour Command Papers ought to be like.

The policy was rewritten by a Cabinet committee with Wilson in the chair. The money available for the National Enterprise Board was drastically cut back, and planning agreements were to be made voluntary. What Wilson called the 'marauding role' of the NEB was over before it began. The Prime Minister knew the CBI had discussed 'an investment strike [and] a list of things which in themselves would not have been legal'.[16] They had no need for such measures. Wilson himself was orchestrating protests against his Industry Secretary's policies. He later confessed that he had supplied potential protesters against further nationalization with two draft letters, one to himself and his disavowal in reply, which could be published. The letters 'got a reply as quickly as if they had bounced off a satellite, for obvious reasons'.[17]

When the short Parliament of 1974 ended with the October election, all this nimble Wilsonian footwork brought a paltry reward. Labour gained only seventeen seats, and had an overall majority of just three. The election, aptly described as 'an unpopularity contest',[18] left Harold Wilson with a last chance to shape the future course of British politics. In 1975 he did so with considerable skill, but through so many reversals of the policy on which party activists thought they had been elected that he banked the fires of dissent for his successors. Benn's industrial strategy was further dismantled, with the help of the Civil Service. He himself was moved after his position had been weakened by the pro-European vote in the 1975 referendum. That vote, gleaned despite formal opposition from much of the Labour Party organization, effectively ended the argument about British membership for a generation. And, with considerable stealth, Wilson managed to get a substantial modernization of the British nuclear deterrent through the Cabinet without ever submitting a formal paper on the subject. Finally, late in the day, he introduced both cash limits on public expenditure and an incomes policy of rough-and-ready justice. These were no mean feats, achieved with a tiny majority by a Prime Minister who was already determined on retirement. They show both the Wilsonian talent for waiting upon events and an adroit use of the Civil Service. They make the paucity of his achievement when he had a massive parliamentary majority and was at the height of his powers all the harder to comprehend.

It was thought advisable that Tony Benn should remain in the Cabinet, and he was not by nature a resigner. Few senior ministers can have been rebuffed so often. Barbara Castle (always close to Benn and closer still during the referendum campaign by the dissenting ministers), noted in her diary in May 1975,

I suddenly saw why I distrust Wedgie. He is right about certain of his themes, such as the need for a crash programme of positive hope through investment and for the involvement of working people in the decisions of industry. But what is wrong with him is that he never spells out that responsibility involves choice, and that the choices facing this country are by definition grim for everybody. He really cannot eat his seed-corn and sow it. But his whole popularity rests on the belief he is spreading around: that he – and those he hopes to lead – can do just that.[19]

The crash programme meant different things to those concerned. To Benn and his allies in the party it meant taking capitalism out of the intensive-care ward, confronting the crisis by demonstrating that the 'fundamental and irreversible shift' of power towards working people, to which Benn returned like a litany, was actually taking place. The state and the public sector must take up in investment where the City had faltered. Workers' co-operatives would be the alternative to bankruptcy or multinational takeover. This positive lead would swing wavering public opinion before a government which showed something of the resolution of 1945. Wilson saw things differently. He had aged early, and reverted to his natural conservatism. Irritated by Benn's campaign in the country, nervous of a further collapse of public confidence, he looked to Whitehall to muzzle his Secretary of State. Which it did. The relations between Benn and his permanent secretary, Sir Antony Part, were among the worst between minister and mandarin since the war. Something of the acrimony has been preserved in the memoir by Benn's parliamentary private secretary, Brian Sedgemore.[20] Part was unhappy about the Industry Bill. He did not want to give large sums to the worker co-ops at Kirby, Meriden and the *Scottish Daily News*. Stories appeared in the press, leaked from within the Department, that Benn had ignored the warnings of his accounting officer and had been reported to the Prime Minister. The message on the permanent secretaries' network was that he was not to be taken seriously. Donoughue recalls, 'The moment the word got around, as it rapidly did in Whitehall – and the Cabinet Office made sure that it got around – that the Prime Minister was not giving his support to Tony Benn, then the civil servants began to back off from their minister. Although in this case Mr Benn had backed off them from the beginning.'[21]

The Industry Bill was watered down. The National Enterprise Board never became the great institution of national renewal through public ownership which Benn had desired, partly because it became entirely concerned with a series of rescue operations as more and more of British heavy industry came to the brink of collapse. Planning agreements remained a dead letter; the only one signed outside the public sector was with the Chrysler Corporation, in return for a desperate injection of public funds which postponed, though it did not prevent, the departure of Chrysler from Britain. Benn never resigned. He contrived to save the Concorde aircraft, in which he had a vital constituency interest, but became more and more isolated in Cabinet after his removal from the Department of Industry, which Wilson effected after the defeat of the anti-Marketeers in the referendum. Benn was 'castled' with Eric Varley, a Wilson trusty. The Prime Minister remarked smugly to Castle, 'When it is over you will say the old boy has not lost his touch. It is pure poetry.'[22] Under James Callaghan, Wilson's successor, Benn's role became even more ambiguous. He remained in Cabinet, a lonely voice. On the platform and at the annual conference he contrived to be the tribune of the party. His relations with his new permanent secretary, Sir Jack Rampton, were as bad as those with Part. Rampton was a strong supporter of the nuclear industry. Benn, who had had charge of it over two stints for longer than anyone, was increasingly a sceptic. The Department did not keep him fully informed. (He complained bitterly that a radiation leak at Windscale on 10 October 1976 was not reported to him until December, and there were other examples.)

Towards the end of the administration, David Owen, a new member of Callaghan's Cabinet, not usually sympathetic to Benn, noted,

I think the Cabinet was a very happy Cabinet, but the one exception was Tony Benn. He just simply wasn't on the main wavelength of the majority of the Cabinet. . . . You also felt that a lot of his contributions were for his own record of what he had said in Cabinet and not actually for the benefit of the Cabinet. . . . The Civil Service, sensing this disagreement amongst ministers, and the fact that Tony Benn was really an outsider in the Cabinet, did tend to conspire against him, and you would find, in briefing notes for a Cabinet meeting,

'Mr Benn is expected to say the following, and you should argue against it. . . .'
Well, how the hell did they know what he was going to say? Obviously they'd
been told along some sort of mafia.[23]

Owen found himself supporting Benn on issues such as the nuclear
pressurized water reactor, whilst the Civil Service network rallied to the
support of Benn's dissident civil servants.

The problem of Benn, for both Wilson and Callaghan, was therefore
unique to this administration. He spoke with experience. He had been
present at the creation. He spoke in the cadences which the party faithful understood, magnificently unwilling to be part of the sordid
brokerage by which minority governments stay in power. He seemed
almost a leader of the opposition in the very Cabinet Room itself.
Paradoxically, he made fellow ministers huddle closer to the orthodoxies
of the Civil Service. The more they shunned him, and the media
traduced him, the greater was his status in the party and his own sense of
a different destiny, enshrined in the almost verbatim diaries to which he
confided his case, Cabinet by Cabinet.

Witnessed from that vantage point, the last two years of Harold
Wilson could be seen as a gigantic betrayal. Benn has said subsequently 'I
regard the Referendum as the third election, general election, which the
Labour Party lost, but Harold Wilson won.'[24] From the purely tactical
point of view, however, Wilson's conduct of the referendum campaign
was masterly. He secured a double agreement to differ: from the party
(which campaigned lukewarmly for a 'no' vote against the Labour
government), and within the Cabinet, where the seven dissenting
ministers were allowed to campaign against the majority. The heavy use
of an all-party pro-Market team, Heath, Jeremy Thorpe and Roy Jenkins
(almost an all-party coalition in himself), allowed the government's own
heavyweights a certain detachment, like its red, white and blue leaflet,
which went out with the pro- and anti-Market statements to every
household. Sometimes Wilson and Callaghan appeared implausibly
Olympian, as when on one phone-in Mr Callaghan said, 'I am not pro,
nor am I anti. . . . The Prime Minister had taken the same line. It is our
job to advise the British people on what we think would be the right
result.'[25] There was never much doubt that they would get it, and the
referendum must stand as one of the outstanding examples of tactical
skill by a Prime Minister unable to carry his party on a particular course
of action. The issue had destroyed the Norwegian socialist leader,
Bratteli. It had split the Left all over Europe. Now Britain had been

anchored to the main by a Prime Minister with little personal affinity for Europe.

There was a price to pay for these prolonged summer manoeuvres. The Cabinet stagnated as the economic crisis raged. Barbara Castle noted that March, 'No Cabinet. Cabinet government barely exists any more, and is certainly going to be broadly in abeyance until the Referendum is over.'[26] Yet this was only days after the Cabinet had been confronted by the Chancellor with the realities of a 20 per cent inflation and declining world trade. The first cuts in public expenditure programmes followed, over the protests of Benn and the left of the Labour National Executive that the Social Contract with the unions would be destroyed thereby. We now know from published memoirs that an agonized debate was under way behind the scenes, even on the Labour left. Trade union leaders found themselves caught between their sectional role and their national forebodings. Len Murray recalls, 'I remember those conferences passing resolutions calling for wage increases of 30 per cent. I also remember in teas rooms, in bars ... the same delegates who were voting the 30 per cent wage increases saying to me directly, 'Look we've got to do something about this. You've got to do something about this. We can't go on like this.'[27] But the only initiative that mattered had to come from the government, and it was delayed until the referendum was over.

Others then acted. Wilson resisted any return to incomes policy as tenaciously as he had once resisted devaluation. His Policy Unit had first told him that a formal incomes policy would be necessary before Christmas 1974. It had been returned with the comment, 'Analysis fine, except any mention of incomes policy is out.'[28] Then, Downing Street insiders remember, 'We moved from the very idea being taboo, or you can't talk about it, to all of a sudden the acceptance that an incomes policy was going to occur. And the argument became whether or not it would be statutory.'[29] Jack Jones of the Transport and General Workers Union pushed for a flat-rate policy, a voluntary limit of £8–10, later reduced to £6 – rough justice across the board. Now, at last, Wilson turned external pressures to his advantage. Content that Labour had implanted Britain more firmly in Europe, the markets moved against the government's other policies. The pound fell below $2.20. Arab funds poured out of London. Wilson was faced by a midnight ultimatum from the Treasury calling for a statutory policy which appalled his advisers. They saw it as 'a straightforward attempt by the Treasury to make the government put its policies totally in reverse, abandon its manifesto commitments, and commit suicide'[30] – since such a policy could not have passed the Commons, and would have entailed the resignation of the indispensable Michael Foot before it could even be introduced there. The ultimatum was rejected. It had its uses. The deal with the TUC announced a few days later was for a voluntary policy largely drafted in Downing Street, with upper limits for which both Jack Jones and Joe Haines claim authorship.

The new incomes policy succeeded. It was not breached, and it helped to bring down the level of inflation. But it came far too late, and it did not prevent more damaging cuts in public expenditure over the next year. Running on from Heath's U-turn, public expenditure had grown by almost 20 per cent over three years, while output had risen by only 2 per cent. Besides as the deliberate increases in public-sector wages in the National Health Service and elsewhere, there was the upturn in support payments inevitable in any recession. In Harold Wilson's last months in office, while he watched the calendar for a suitable moment to resign, there were heavier public expenditure cuts in forward programmes and the introduction of cash limits. The latter turned into the most effective brake on public expenditure devised in the seventies, with effects which were markedly underestimated by the Treasury. Although Wilson did not mention them in his memoirs (breaking off at the crucial point to describe how he received the freedom of the City of London), they were to be an ineradicable legacy for his successors.

He left other legacies too. For a Prime Minister who had been the leadership candidate of the Labour left in 1963, and whom one hysterical faction in the security services still believed to be a Russian agent, he showed remarkable concern for Britain's nuclear defences. The Prime Minister who had saved Polaris[31] was now presented with a programme, code-named 'Chevaline', for its enhancement. The word was suitably vague. The October 1974 manifesto had pledged that Labour would not move 'towards a new generation of nuclear weapons'. Chevaline involved multiple warheads, but not independently targeted, or, in nuclear jargon, 'MIRVed'. Wilson brought the project once to the Cabinet, as an oral report, not a Cabinet paper. It survives like some ancient settlement seen from the air – bland, puzzling, indistinct – in Barbara Castle's diary for 20 November 1974:

Harold prepared the way carefully by saying that, though we would keep Polaris and carry out certain improvements at a cost of £24 million, there would be no Poseidonisation and no MIRV. The nuclear element represented less than 2% of the defence budget but it gave us a 'unique entrée to U. S. thinking' and it was important for our diplomatic influence for us to remain a nuclear power. . . .

Castle records some half-hearted mumbling by Michael Foot, and a spirited speech by herself, whilst 'Wedgie said nothing.'[32]

'Wedgie' remembers it differently, as an almost casual remark that there was 'a little bit of modernisation going on' followed by a debate in which he was 'the only member of that Cabinet who oppposed it. . . . Wilson left during the middle of that item, to unveil a plaque to Sir Winston Churchill, so he wasn't even present to hear the other ministers speaking.'[33] His unpublished diary bears out this version. The anecdote is revealing for its picture of Wilson's confident, almost audacious handling of a sensitive issue. The 'little bit of modernisation' had cost not £24 million but £595 million before Wilson left office. It did not come back to Cabinet. It was not cash-limited, and the chief secretary to the Treasury, Joel Barnett, never even heard of the project until he was in opposition and chairman of the Public Accounts Committee (by then it had exceeded £1000 million). No other item in the public expenditure programme of the Wilson and Callaghan governments received such cosseted treatment.

Wilson's last days as Prime Minister, some months after he had begun consciously to leave aside matters which could be dealt with by his successor, were overshadowed by the continued weakness of sterling, especially after the markets saw through a botched attempt by the Treasury at a controlled fall in the value of the pound. On Wilson's sixtieth birthday a row between the Chancellor and the Labour left over the new public expenditure White Paper delayed his departure until a vote of confidence had been secured. Thus the actual resignation stunned Cabinet and country alike. His presence, and later his reputation, seemed as evanescent as one of the smoke rings he could produce at will from his oldest stage prop. In his memoir of those last years he presents himself as a consensus man: 'The highest aim of leadership is to secure policies adequate to deal with any situation, including the production of acceptable new solutions and policies, without major confrontations, splits and resignations.'[34] In his terms he had done so.

Historically the reputation of Harold Wilson is low. What can be extricated from the general judgement on the administration of 1974–9, at least as much the creation of his successor, that is peculiar to Wilson? His old weakness for short-term tactics again stood revealed. So did his fondness for delay. It is arguable that he might have saved power-sharing in Northern Ireland had his eyes had not been fixed on the October election date in Britain rather than the tiresome distraction of the Ulster workers' strike. Neither old challenges in Rhodesia nor new ones in Cyprus brought out the best in Wilson and his Foreign Secretary, James Callaghan. On domestic policy he improvised, and his lack of a majority made a necessity of that virtue. If he was less able to articulate the party's vision of an alternative future, a commonwealth of labour, it was because he did not share it. And, just as he did not wish to be educated by his party, so he gave up trying to educate it. On difficult issues such as defence he left no tell-tale tracks. After the failure of *In Place of Strife* in 1969 there were no more cavalry charges at the entrenched positions of the unions. Trade union support, especially in the circumstances of 1974, when the left, enthusiastically, and the right, fearfully, both thought that unions were growing stronger by the day, seemed to him crucial to every move he made.

His achievement was that he retained that support for policies which were anathema to many in his party. The virtual elimination of 'Bennery', the renewed embrace for the EEC, and the abandonment of collective bargaining for a voluntary incomes policy with reserve statutory powers, were all policies unlikely to win fraternal TUC support. All were carried through, not least because the government was able to deliver many of the legislative elements of the Social Contract which it had promised, to improve working conditions and social welfare. This had to be carried through in a more frightening world than in the sixties. There was no large majority to squander. Middle-class panic, as inflation destroyed fixed incomes and organized labour stayed strong through collective bargaining, affected many commentators. There is an irony in the fact that this unfrightening Pooter of politics occupied Downing Street while the press in Britain and abroad saw the collapse of Britain as they claimed they knew it. Terrorism and street violence, exemplified by the 1974 Birmingham bombings, and the riot in Red Lion Square, led to much talk of ungovernability and to Britain as approaching 'proto-communism'. Retired officers schemed and plotted. Right-wing polemicists warned of the nightmare to come. Public opinion quivered in these cross-currents, but it is worth remembering that Labour's standing in the Gallup poll in the month in which Wilson resigned was higher than before his return to office two years before, albeit at a historically low point. This growth of pessimism about future prospects left its mark on the government. Times of contraction do not produce an enthusiasm for radical experiment, but Wilson was happy enough with that. He produced no innovations, apart from his Downing Street Policy Unit, left every stone unturned in the barren fields of constitutional practice. By the time of his retirement there was not a permanent secretary in Whitehall to whom he would have given a moment of unease. The valedictions of the right saw him as Labour's Baldwin, and he was content enough with the epitaph attached to his pipe-smoking likeness in the National Portrait Gallery: 'Achieved a remarkable degree of unity between the different wings of the party'. So he had. Whether the trick cyclist had proved that the bicycle was a safe means of transport, and could retain both wheels, remained to be seen.

If a kind of social Baldwinism now characterized the Labour government, James Callaghan was its most adept practitioner. An elementary schoolboy, he had seen off five Oxford men to capture the Labour leadership. He alone had had some warning of what was afoot, and could prepare his dispositions. Like Harold Macmillan, he became Prime Minister in his mid-sixties. Where Macmillan had been unflappable, Callaghan was avuncular. Both hid their nerves and private doubts, enjoyed their late start at the top, but wearied when the going got rough. Callaghan had already held all the other great offices of state. To the surprise of some who had seen him in these previous incarnations, he proved better as Premier than he had been in any of them. Without exception, his Cabinet ministers found him superior to Wilson in the transaction of business. Denis Healey, who sat in Cabinet from the first to the last day of the 1964–70 and 1974–9 governments, rates Callaghan highly: 'Jim Callaghan was totally different in style. He was a very good prime minister because he always had a clear view about what he wanted to get out of a cabinet discussion, and he guided the discussion in his direction. If it was going off the rails he would intervene and make it quite clear what his own intention was.'[35] Or, as Callaghan himself crisply puts it, 'Try to keep the talkative within bounds, encourage those who are reticent to give you their views. On the whole you try to preserve the theme of the conversation. You have a rigid agenda and you get it finished by lunchtime.'[36]

There was another advantage to Callaghan's long experience in so many departments, while his predecessor had been bunkered in Downing Street. He knew the key permanent secretaries throughout Whitehall, trusted them and was trusted by them. The relationship was entirely free from the mutual suspicion and ignorance with which an incoming Labour Prime Minister and his top mandarins usually regard each other. Callaghan's innate conservatism mattered less in the circumstances in which he found himself. Public attitudes seemed to be moving to the right.[37] A beleaguered minority government, as it speedily became, had to live off the electoral landscape. From the outset Callaghan presented himself as a man who shared the general concern about disorder and falling standards. 'Do you, like me, think that perhaps we've been slipping?' he asked rhetorically in his first broadcast as Prime Minister. In his homilies on public spending (at the 1976 Labour conference), on educational standards (at Ruskin College) and on family values (in his election press conference), he sought to reassure an audience well beyond the Labour Party.

His skills in Cabinet and his gift for reassurance were fused in the first two great tests of his premiership, the International Monetary Fund crisis and the negotiation of the Lib–Lab pact. In each he needed to win time and support for his harrassed government at minimum cost. He bought time in the international markets until the recovery of the pound. He secured votes in Parliament to see the government through until that recovery could be manifest. He was to fail only with the group he knew best, the trade unions.

Callaghan's handling of the application for an IMF loan is a classic of Cabinet government. Within months of assuming office he saw the Bank of England and the Treasury forced into accepting short-term standby credits – one step away from the IMF unless the package of economic cuts introduced in July found favour with the international bankers. The latter are never sensitive to the pain thresholds of the Labour Party. In the words of one of Callaghan's advisers, 'The markets wanted blood and that didn't look like blood. We didn't understand that in No. 10 at the time; we didn't know that what they wanted was a humiliation.'[38] Callaghan knew that despair affected many in the party and the government, well beyond the left. Tony Crosland, then Foreign Secretary, noted in his commonplace book at this time

(a) Demoralisation of decent rank and file: Grimsby L[abour] P[arty]. (b) Strain on T[rade] U[nion] loyalty. (c) Breeding of illiterate and reactionary attitude to public expenditure – horrible. (d) Collapse of strategy which I proposed last year. ... Now no sense of direction and no priorities; only pragmatism, empiricism, safety first, £ supreme. (e) Unemployment, even if politically more wearably = grave loss of welfare, security, choice; very high price to be paid for deflation and negative growth.[39]

Would the Cabinet pay still more? When the pound crashed again during the Labour Party conference that September, Tony Benn delivered his warning from the platform; 'We are also paying a heavy political price for twenty years in which, as a party, we have played down our criticism of capitalism and soft-pedalled our advocacy of socialism.' Callaghan's own speech was brutally candid. In words which 'made the fur fly' borrowed from his monetarist son-in-law, Peter Jay, he told the conference that it could not spend its way out of the recession.[40] 'I tell you in all candour that that option no longer exists, and that, insofar as it ever did exist, it only worked on each occasion by injecting a bigger dose of inflation into the economy, followed by a higher level of unemployment as the next step.' For the faithful this was an invitation to pull on the shirt of Nessus; to the international audience beyond it was intended as a proclamation of prudent housekeeping for the IMF, who were now called in.

Callaghan proceeded circumspectly. The IMF was at first kept waiting while other alternatives were tried, including a trip to Washington by a right-wing sceptic of the need for the IMF, Harold Lever. His attempt to by-pass IMF conditionality got nowhere. Negotiations began in earnest. Callaghan initially stayed aloof, saw the Chancellor's first cuts package turned down. He played matters long, over twenty-six sessions of Cabinet:

Looking back on that period, it seems to me that the strength of the position taken by the Chancellor and myself was that we knew how far we were ready to go, and did not intend to be pushed further. We shared one thing in common with the IMF, namely that both parties were agreed that the total borrowing requirement of £9 billions for 1977–8 which the Cabinet itself had agreed in the previous July must not be exceeded. On the other hand, I had no intention of being pushed seriously below that position.[41]

The cabinet was invited to talk itself out:

I wanted the Cabinet to reach the right conclusion, and to remain united, and the best way of doing that is to have exhaustive discussions. So we did have exhaustive, and exhausting discussion. I knew which way I wanted us to go, but I think that everybody who was in that Cabinet has stated since that they had a fair chance of stating what their views were.[42]

The minister most likely to put up an alternative siege-economy strategy, Tony Benn, was invited to do so, and other ministers were primed to shoot him down. Benn was separated from Foot and other left-wingers once they had placed their reservations on the table. The 'foxy old peasant', as his civil servants described Callaghan, finally showed his hand, telling Crosland and other wavering centrists that he was convinced that there had to be cuts, and simultaneously telling the IMF that the cuts they demanded were too large. Finally Crosland swung over to support the Prime Minister, for political reasons – he continued to think the economic case ludicrous. The Prime Minister had got the most he could for the lowest price in town. Callaghan stored away for future use the memory of Treasury muddle – it had been revealed as substantially overestimating the PSBR – and of those civil servants who had seemed almost eager for the discipline of the IMF and the US Treasury.

The battle was over. It was a real battle, and it could have had a different result. The government was shaky, and might have broken up with less skilful handling. Its standing in the polls and by-election results had never been worse. It was to continue for a further thirty months. This was possible because of the pacts and arrangements which Callaghan showed equal facility in arranging. In March 1977 the government was brought to the brink of defeat by its own rebellious back-benchers. The Opposition pushed its luck with a vote of no confidence, only to be thwarted by a sudden marriage of convenience between the Labour and Liberal parties. The Liberals, overshadowed by the Thorpe affair and wilting in the polls, had no wish for an election. Callaghan knew this, and secured their support on minimum terms. There was no referendum on proportional representation, nor a Speaker's Conference. The system would be unchanged, with the Liberals now buttressing it. Callaghan confided his strategy to the young Liberal leader: 'He says he wants to play the next election as the leader of a left-wing party heading towards the centre while she [Mrs Thatcher] is the leader of a right-wing party heading towards the right.'[43]

The Liberals got less from their published pact than the less congenial Ulster Unionists did from an unspoken arrangement. Whereas Wilson had put his public support behind calls for an ultimately united Ireland, Callaghan relied on tough proconsuls with military backgrounds in Belfast. The Unionists could not get Stormont back, but they got the promise of a conference on parliamentary representation which, in the absence of Stormont, would be bound to offer them extra seats at Westminster. Devolution was not an option for Northern Ireland, but Callaghan kept it firmly in place as a legislative priority for Scotland and Wales, even after the collapse of the first devolution Bill. There was a real possibility that Labour's Celtic base might slip away. The Scottish

National Party had won 30 per cent of the Scottish vote in 1974, and after the defeat of devolution it swept through Labour's heartland in the 1977 local elections.

Callaghan moved swiftly to outflank the SNP. The reintroduction of devolution Bills for Scotland and Wales split the separatists in the SNP and Plaid Cymru from their devolutionist supporters. One SNP strategist who admits to being 'totally outmanoeuvred by the Labour Party' argues that devolution trapped the SNP into disavowing separatism. 'The mistake we made when the separatist charge came up was to try to deny it. And by denying it you made it worse. . . .'[44] A revived Labour Party swept the SNP aside in the by-elections of 1978. The Scottish Development Agency, a Scottish headquarters for the British National Oil Corporation, the rescue of Chrysler and the temporary reprieve of Linwood: all seemed to display a concerned but risk-free Scottish dimension. In Wales devolution seemed to be the device of the Welsh-speaking minority, unlikely to carry the principality whatever the Cardiff MP who was Prime Minister said or did. But in Scotland he defused both economic nationalism ('It's Scotland's oil') and political separatism. The SNP was left formally committed to see devolution through Parliament, and to campaign for a 'Yes' vote in a referendum stacked against devolution by the novel requirement that 40 per cent of those entitled to do vote must do so in the affirmative before the devolved assemblies could be established. Pending these referenda, Callaghan could rest easy. The nationalists would not bring down his government.

In Whitehall he moved effectively to take key areas of decision-making out of the public spotlight altogether, and into those confidential huddles which he found more congenial. The head of his Policy Unit watched this strengthening of prime-ministerial power:

Mr Callaghan had a strong sense of what was secretive and what was sensitive, and it seemed to him that there were two areas where many other ministers did not need to know, and these were the areas of sensitive defence technology . . . he felt that was genuinely secret; and the other was the area of market economics, of money matters and exchange rates and so forth. Those he kept very close.[45]

On defence he continued the Chevaline development without ever bringing it out of a close group of four ministers. The technical, political and military implications of a movement to an entirely new generation of nuclear weapons were entrusted to committees chaired not by ministers, but by civil servants. When he went on his ill-starred expedition to Guadeloupe in 1979, Callaghan was able to ask President Carter if the

United States could and would deliver a version of the Trident system –
if asked. The matter had not come before the Cabinet or the party,
although Callaghan claims to have favoured 'more public discussion of
the issue' before any decision was taken.

Similarly, key market-related issues were discussed in a tight group
called the 'Economic Seminar', to avoid designating it a Cabinet
committee. Ministers whose responsibilities were influenced by the level
of interest rates (housing, for example) knew nothing of all this. For
Callaghan the exercise was intended to give him an early input into what
the Treasury and the Bank intended. He had felt his own ignorance of
the mysteries back in 1964. Ex-Chancellors are best qualified to be
suspicious of the Treasury, and he had not been impressed by its
erroneous estimates of the PSBR during the IMF crisis. The 'Seminar'
allowed him to hear the arguments worked out, with Harold Lever
playing devil's advocate, and to know in advance what the Bank and the
Treasury proposed on interest and exchange rates. The Prime Minister
who had so scrupulously observed the conventions of collective responsibility in the IMF debates was now extending the power of Downing
Street.

Callaghan's natural aversion to what was fashionably called 'open
government' shows up in the significant omissions of his legislative
record. By the beginning of 1979 almost all the major measures
promised in the 1974 manifesto had been completed, although devolution waited upon the Scottish and Welsh referenda. But there had been
no reform of the Official Secrets Act – long promised – despite some
notorious cases under its provisions which besmirched the civil-liberties
record of the Labour government. All moves towards freedom-of
information legislation were blocked, although they would have had the
support of Labour's temporary Liberal allies. Having acted to bring the
direct-grant schools fully into the public sector, the government, with
more discretion than logic, chose to leave the public schools alone. That
other promised leveller, a wealth tax, had been amended to death in a
select committee. These omissions, however, mattered to middle-class
activists. They would therefore be important in how the Wilson and
Callaghan governments were judged by their Labour posterity. They
were less important in forming electoral opinion at the time.

Here all rested on what was seen as Callaghan's trump card: his
special relationship with the unions. The legislation attendant upon the
Social Contract had gone through, as had the remaining nationalization
proposals, though only after ingenious opposition and blue-blooded

dissent in Commons and Lords. The problem was that much of what the government delivered was in the form of packages for the union leaderships – not even for the 'sixty thousand shop stewards' with whom Benn told his Cabinet colleagues they should now deal. The leaders sought a formal share in the power structure, not unlike the position that trade union representatives would have held in their firms had the cumbrous Bullock Report proposals on industrial democracy been implemented. Their members were less happy with a relationship which seemed to be supporting a form of Labour monetarism.

By 1977 the purchasing power of the average worker with two children had fallen by 7 per cent over the two years of pay policy. Stage II (5 per cent increases with an upper limit of £4) had been, as the former permanent secretary at the Department of Employment has written, 'the most severe cut in real wages for twenty years'.[46] A third phase of incomes policy was virtually imposed by the government on the public sector in 1977–8. Later in the day than its competitors, Britain was paying the higher oil price, passed on in reduced living standards for its people. That inflation was now falling, and the economy ready to grow again, was asserted with some truth by the government. Its union allies pleaded with their members to look at other priorities: a shorter working week, more help for the unemployed, in the framework of an 'orderly return to free collective bargaining'. But they were losing control. Skilled workers began to peel away from the Amalgamated Union of Engineering Workers in the car industry. Jack Jones was voted down at his own 1977 conference. And behind these big battalions were the enlarged platoons of local government, education and the National Health Service. They had seen big rises in expenditure, from which they had benefited, before the IMF exercise. Now there were cuts – real cuts Resentment grew, in Labour's own constituency.

Each sectional group confused its own grievance with the generality. Few saw that orgnanized trade unionism was viewed less sympathetically by the general public, and less fairly by the mass media. It suited the latter to exaggerate a strike record which was, in fact, markedly improving, and to present a perception of Britain as 'lawless' or 'ungovernable'. Disputes about union recognition against a maverick employer, notably at Grunwick, were conducted (more out of frustration than conscious design) in ways which showed the unpalatable side of collective action, so that the small group of workers with the grievance became lost to view.

Callaghan, for his part, used the appointments open to him in British industry, where many firms were now within the control of the National Enterprise Board, to usher in a new style of managment. Michael Edwardes, asked to take over at British Leyland under the NEB umbrella, found no one there even knew the price of a Mini, or where the company's profit centres were. The workforce watched a purge of the board and the top management, knowing their turn would come. When Edwardes asked to see Callaghan, and said that it was his aim to bring a profitable BL out of the state sector, the Prime Minister 'just smiled patiently. He was concerned with pragmatic day-to-day matters. The fact that my philosophy was different meant nothing to him. And I think this was the sign of a big man.'[47]

The big man now came fatally unstuck. He had grown up with the trade unions, bone of their bone. His style and tastes were those of one of the classier general secretaries. Within the government he maintained a close and unbreakable alliance with Michael Foot, from 1974 the closest link to Congress House. And now Callaghan and Foot got it wrong. For all the consultation, the coming and going of union barons, they lost everything on the horse they had backed. Due regard, even exaggerated deference, to the principle of consultation did not mean that the consulted were heard. Callaghan reasoned that unemployment had reached its peak at 1.56 million (it was to fall marginally to 1.3 million by December 1978) and that living standards were again rising. Trade unionists would therefore see the virtue of what they had achieved, and agree to more of the same. In the anonymity of the opinion poll they might. In the open debate in branch and factory they did not. Callaghan's facts were right, but his conclusions wrong. When he compounded this error by turning away from an autumn 1978 election, seeing only another hung parliament in prospect, the union leaders were bewildered. Most of them had believed the 5 per cent figure a piece of pre-election window-dressing. Now it had to be taken seriously. With that hindsight of which he always makes copious use, Denis Healey sees the fatal error: 'I'm convinced now that if we had said we want settlements in single figures, we'd probably have come out with something like 12% overall, retained the support of the unions, avoided the Winter of Discontent, and won the election. But hubris tends to affect all governments after a period of success, and by golly it hit us.'[48]

If ever there was a dying fall in politics this was it. The decision to postpone an election is understandable. Callaghan's memory went back to the short, unhappy Parliament of 1950-1; he 'put a ring around

Thursday 5th April 1979'.[49] Elderly Prime Ministers who know they have only one throw tend to prefer the power they have to the gamble that may lose everything. But, from that moment on, Callaghan's luck ran out. The Labour conference rejected incomes policy, egged on by the spokesman of the low-paid workers. A strike at Ford's led to the company settling at 15 per cent, and the government's last desperate attempt to push through sanctions against it was voted down in the House of Commons with the connivance of the Labour left. In the new year, first lorry drivers, then one public-sector group after another, struck. Emotive targets were shut off. Secondary picketing seemed out of control. The press had the ultimate shocking headlines: 'Has everyone gone mad?', 'Target for today – sick children' and 'Now they won't let us bury our dead'. To this they added the apparent insouciance of the Prime Minister, back from the Guadeloupe summit and misquoted as saying, 'Crisis, what crisis?'

It was not that he did not care. In some ways he cared too much, reduced to a near catatonic state by his sudden unpopularity and what he saw as the self-destruction of the unions. Joel Barnett reports him as saying that he 'had never been so depressed in 50 years as a trade unionist'.[50] Some of the radical trade unionists involved in the disputes blamed the government, and blame it still, for public expenditure cuts and rising unemployment which they judged unnecessary. At the start of the winter, at least, they had not taken seriously the possibility that they would bring about more of the same by helping to elect a real conservative government. They thought the government would back off, just as it believed they would. But that is how wars are lost. In the middle of it all the Scottish referendum, which had been built around Callaghan before he became an overnight liability, failed to register a 40 per cent yes vote. The SNP had no reason to support him now; the Liberals had formally cut loose; and last scrambled efforts to secure support from the other minority parties were bound to be as short-lived as they were furtive. The government fell on 28 March, the first to be defeated on a vote of no confidence for fifty years.

Win or lose, had James Callaghan gone to the country in 1978, at his own choosing, his reputation would stand higher. At that time, inflation was in single figures, personal disposable income rising fast, and British industry, for all its problems of overmanning and under-investment, at least preserved in large measure by government intervention to take advantage of the end of the recession. Sterling was strong, oil revenues rising. Callaghan's personal popularity outstripped that of Mrs Thatcher. The Scottish referendum was still to be won, and might have been. There would have been some reflected lustre for Harold Wilson too, for his rebuilding a social-democratic party on the unlikely foundations of the 1973 programme.

Instead the tendency has been to portray them as a pair of shabby pragmatists, waiting for something to turn up, the Estragon and Vladimir of degenerate Labourism. The subsequent split in the Labour Party, and the dominance of a high-profile ideologue of the radical right in the Conservative Party, has accentuated this. Born-again social democrats can decry their reliance on the unions, the immense deference accorded to Michael Foot inside the Cabinet and Jack Jones outside it. The Labour left sees them as premature monetarists, abandoning full employment, alternative economic policies, industrial democracy, the poor and national sovereignty itself, in desperate wheeling and dealing with the forces of international capital. Perhaps James Callaghan is only seen with a certain misty sentiment by those Tories not of Mrs Thatcher's persuasion.

The truth is more complex. Wilson and Callaghan certainly contributed to the later split in the Labour Party – Wilson by his elisions and evasions in the early seventies about what was possible for a socialist party fallen on hard electoral times, Callaghan by losing control of country and party in rapid succession. It was Callaghan and Healey, not Thatcher, who introduced control of money supply, cash limits, and cuts in current rather than future expenditure. Recourse to the IMF won international confidence in inverse ratio to its dissipation within the party. The terms eventually secured from the IMF were not harsh, and the drawings were rapidly paid back as Britain moved into substantial surplus. But the cuts went to the bone of the Labour movement. The confidence lost in late 1976 was translated into the conviction of the Labour left that only through constitutional changes could they take control of the party.

But, as they have subsequently discovered, even leaders chosen by the new methods have to live in the world as it is, though they dream of changing it. Wilson and Callaghan had to cope with the exceptional difficulties of world recession and inherited inflation. Wilson came to power when every expectation of those he led would, in the short run, make matters worse. Yet the short run was all he had, with another election to fight. The climate of the times was one of pessimism and doubt. Inflation stirs atavistic middle-class fears, highlights the power of those with the apparent strength to insulate themselves against it. This meant the trade unions, for whom the 1973–4 miners' strike was a hollow victory. It made them feared, and it made others believe with them that they were stronger than was the case. Their weakness, and inability to change, made them more of a handicap to their Labour allies than their strength. The Labour left were right to discern the need for a new type of trade unionism, based on power and responsibility at the workplace, and unlucky that the co-operative became associated in the public mind with the sit-in at some bankrupt plant, nourished briefly by inadequate public funds.

What was stirring, and what the left failed to read, was a self-assertion that asked for more than the state monolith, the NHS bureaucrat or the local housing manager. It was open to co-operation, but of a different kind. Its collectivities did not always overlap with the hierarchies of trade unionism. The home as leisure centre and personal retreat became a fastness which was impenetrable to some old slogans of fraternity. New notions of freedom as associated with the Right penetrated as easily as the new and strident tabloid press, deeply hostile to the Left. Labour had the opportunity to initiate a genuine pluralism in the press, and failed that test by the traditional means of the royal commission. Limits on proprietorial power would have needed to go hand in hand with home truths for trade unionists in the print. Labour flinched from both.

It is arguable how far the media fed a public mood and how far they created it; probably both. The problem for Labour, for any Labour leader, was that in the 1970s the party had lost ground amongst both those who were habitual personal supporters and those who identified with it from class rather than personal loyalty. Class loyalty was itself weakening through social change, in spite of the threatening climate of the times and the worst unemployment since the war. Yet those whose loyalty to the party was ideological wanted 'real' socialism and not managed capitalism, at odds with apparent majority opinion. Until 1983, at least, they could argue that this had not been put forcefully to the electorate, and that it needed to be tried before it could prove itself and erode the endemic hostility which the political culture provided. There was never any chance that Callaghan would take up this strategy. By 1979 his instinct told him that many Labour voters were closer to Conservative positions on some key policies at issue between the parties. This affected the cherished priorities of both wings of the party, according to the later researches of Ivor Crewe:

It is true that bringing party policy in line with public opinion would oblige the left to abandon some of its major principles (defence cuts, further public ownership, an extension of trade union rights); but it would oblige the right to shed as many of its own (libertarianism, concerted action on behalf of racial minorities, internationalism, foreign aid, constructive membership of the EEC, incomes policy). . . .[51]

Callaghan had the political strength of being identified with many of these reservations and indeed was to fight a good election for the reassurance that he purveyed. But the party he led either stood for the broad coalition of policies about which the electorate were sceptical or ceased advocating a serious socialism. The way to resolve this dilemma was not to be found by the Callaghan generation.

Indeed, what is remarkable about the Wilson and Callaghan years is that they constitute a virtual holiday from institutional reform of any kind. The Heath reforms of the NHS and local government were left for Mrs Thatcher to destroy. The defence of the realm was maintained – Callaghan going to the lengths of taking home a map on which was marked the disposition of the fleet each weekend. From the moment Harold Wilson arrived back from Buckingham Palace in March 1974 to find Sir Robert Armstrong waiting to welcome him on the threshold, the Labour governments remained satisfied with the Civil Service as it was. With the notable exception of Tony Benn in both his posts, and David Owen briefly at the Foreign Office, this was a conformist government. Central Policy Review Staff suggestions for reform of the Foreign Office caused embarrassment (although many of them have since been implemented). Britain remained in the EEC, now the source of a new style of summitry. There were no foreign wars, excepting a brush with Icelandic gunboats, and Harold Wilson was able to participate in a moment of detente at Helsinki. Britain's first and last colonial problems, Northern Ireland and Rhodesia, remained unresolved.

It would be wrong to see these as passive governments, however. On some big subjects the two Prime Ministers were more than mere pragmatists. Wilson's tenacious settlement of the Common Market issue brought him belated recognition from those in the party who had most reviled him. And Callaghan held on to his incomes policy with the tenacity with which Mrs Thatcher was to pursue the Argentines (although his task force sank!). Within the limitations of almost nil growth and low profits there were efforts at redistribution. The emphasis on direct taxation rather than regressive indirect taxes protected the poorest. Pensions and employment subsidies helped other vulnerable groups, though unselectively. Women's pay rose to the unheroic proportion of 75 per cent of men's wages for equivalent work by 1977, before it fell back again, and the new employment protection legislation helped women at work escape from their special vulnerability. For all the disappointments, the Labour governments were sorely missed by the coalition of special interests they served.

Will they be missed, or reappraised, by the population at large and historians in particular? That question depends on the fate of the Thatcher experiment, and the degree to which it permanently changes the political landscape, as the 1906 or 1945 governments did. There are those, some of them Conservatives, who see much merit in the rehabilitation of James Callaghan and his style of government.

Chronology

1974

28 February   General election: Labour 301 seats; Conservatives, 297; Liberals, 14; Ulster Unionists, 11; Scottish National Party, 7; Plaid Cymru, 2; others, 3.

4 March   Heath resigns after failure of negotiations with Liberals. Labour takes office.

6 March   Miners' strike settled.

8 March   Rent freeze announced.

23 March   Scottish Labour Party conference rejects commitment to an elected Scottish assembly.

26 March   First Healey Budget raises income tax and corporation tax.

1 April   EEC renegotiation begins.

2 April   'Slag Heap' affair. Ronald Milhench arrested and charged with forging a letter from Harold Wilson.

15 May   Ulster workers' strike begins

28 May   Brian Faulkner and the Northern Ireland power-sharing executive resign.

15 July   Archbishop Makarios overthrown in Cyprus coup.

22 July   VAT cut to 8 per cent.

August–September   White Papers on industry (15 August), pensions (11 September), land (12 September) devolution (17 September).

18 September   General election announced.

10 October   General election: Labour 319 seats; Conservatives, 277; Liberals, 13; Scottish National Party, 11; Ulster Unionists, 11; Plaid Cymru, 3; others, 1.

21 November   Birmingham pub bombing; 21 people killed. Labour MP John Stonehouse fakes his 'drowning' in Miami; later arrested in Australia.

29 November   Prevention of Terrorism Act passed.

31 December   Retail prices up 19 per cent, wages 29 per cent, in the course of the year.

1975

11 February   Margaret Thatcher elected Conservative leader.

28 February   Second reading of the Industry Bill.

10–11 March   Agreement at EEC Summit on Labour's renegotiated terms to be put in a referendum.

26 April   Special Labour conference calls for a 'no' vote in the referendum.

5 June   EEC referendum: 67.2 per cent vote 'yes'.

10 June   Benn swapped with Eric Varley, and moved from Industry to Energy.

18 June   First landing of North Sea oil, 'turned on' by Energy Secretary Benn.

26 June   Labour loses, Woolwich West by-election, caused by the death of Labour MP Will Hamling.

11 July   Government and TUC announce £6 voluntary pay policy.

14 July   Unemployment passes 1 million.

12 August   Monthly retail price index shows 26.9 per cent increase for the year.

20 November   Announcement that cash limits will be applied to public expenditure in 1976–7.

16 December   Chrysler rescue announced.

1976

18 January   2 Labour MPs defect to set up Scottish Labour Party.

19 February   Public expenditure White Paper shows cuts of £1000 million for 1977–8 and £2400 million for 1978–9. Causes backbench revolt and confidence vote.

2 March   Sterling falls below $2 to the pound.

16 March   Harold Wilson resigns as Labour leader.

5 April   James Callaghan elected Labour leader on third ballot. Takes office as Prime Minister.

6 April   Healey budget announces tax cuts of £1300 million, conditional on a Stage II incomes policy on 4 per cent formula.

10 May   Jeremy Thorpe resigns as Liberal leader.

26 May   Wilson's resignation honours (the 'Lavender notepaper list') published.

2 July   David Steel elected Liberal leader.

22 July   Announcement of further cuts package of £1000 million.

9 September   Unemployment reaches 1,588,000.

10 September   Roy Jenkins resigns as Home Secretary prior to taking up EEC presidency.

28 September   Callaghan's 'borrowed time' speech at the Labour conference.

29 September   Healey calls in the IMF.

27 October   Pound falls to $1.56.

1 November   IMF negotiators fly in.

4 November   Labour loses Workington and Walsall North by-elections.

15 December   After 6 weeks and 26 Cabinet sessions, letter of intent for IMF loan and further cuts package announced.

21 December   Inflation rate now 17 per cent.

1977

19 February   Death of Anthony Crosland. (Succeeded as Foreign Secretary by David Owen.)

22 February   Government defeated on guillotine vote for first devolution Bill.

17 March   Aircraft and Shipbuilding Act passed.

23 March   Lib–Lab pact saves government on confidence vote.

31 March   Labour loses Stechford by-election.

28 April   Labour loses Ashfield by-election (but holds Grimsby).

5 May   Labour loses heavily in local government elections; loses control of Greater London Council (having lost Glasgow on 3 May in substantial losses in Scotland).

9 June   Silver Jubilee of Queen Elizabeth II.

13–24 June   Climax of mass picket at Grunwick.

12 July   High Court rules in favour of the Advisory Conciliation and Arbitration Service (ACAS) against George Ward at Grunwick (ruling overturned by Lord Denning on 29 July).

15 July   Denis Healey outlines Phase III of Labour's Incomes Policy. White Paper on 31 July includes note on sanctions against employers paying over the odds.

9 October   Reg Prentice quits Labour to join the Conservatives.

14 November   Second devolution Bills, for Scotland and Wales, get second reading on successive days.

1978

1 January   Callaghan New Year broadcast trails pay limit target of 5 per cent.

4 January   Pound moves up to $2. UK reserves stand at record £20,600 million.

12 January   Firemans' strike defeated, with the help of auxiliary 'Green Goddess' fire engines and the military.

21 January   Special Liberal Assembly conditionally endorses Lib–Lab pact.

25 January   Amendments setting 40 per cent devolution referendum condition carried against government by rebel backbenchers.

30 January   Mrs Thatcher speaks on television about 'swamping' by immigrants.

17 February   Annual inflation rate falls below 10 per cent for the first time since 1973.

8 March   Labour loses Ilford North by-election.

23 May   Announcement of forthcoming end of the Lib–Lab pact.

31 May   Labour holds Hamilton against SNP by-election challenge.

21 July   White Paper on incomes policy sets out a 5 per cent limit for Stage IV.

4 August   Jeremy Thorpe accused of conspiracy to murder.

5 September   Callaghan's 'waiting at the church' speech teases, but does not amuse, the TUC.

7 September   Callaghan announces that there will be no autumn election.

19 September   Bingham Report on evasions of sanctions against Rhodesia published.

21 September   Ford workers' strike against 5 per cent wage offer begins.

2 October   Labour conference rejects 5 per cent wage limit.

26 October   Labour holds Berwick and East Lothian with positive swing.

13 December House of Commons votes down (by 285 votes to 283) sanctions against employers breaching 5 per cent pay policy.

1979

3 January Lorry drivers' strike begins.

10 January Callaghan returns from Guadeloupe summit to say, 'I don't think other people in the world would share the view that there is mounting chaos', which became 'Crisis, what crisis?' in the press.

22 January Public employees 'day of action', followed by 6 weeks of strikes. Hospitals picketed and code of practice produced, but not immediately implemented.

1 February Callaghan denounces 'free collective vandalism' in the NHS dispute.

14 February Government and TUC announce a concordat on conduct of industrial disputes.

23 February Civil servants begin series of one-day strikes.

1 March Devolution rejected in Welsh referendum by 4–1. Less than 40 per cent of the electorate vote 'yes' in Scotland.

9 March Local-government workers in the National Union of Public Employees accept 9 per cent pay offer.

19 March Hospital workers and ambulance men accept interim offer.

28 March Government defeated 311–310 on vote of no confidence. Election called.

Notes

1 *What Went Wrong* (Spokesman Books, 1979), p. 32.
2 The percentages were (1929) Conservatives 38.2, Labour 37.1, Liberals 23.4; (1974) Conservatives 37.9, Labour 37.1, Liberals 19.3.
3 Douglas Jay, *Sterling, a Plea for Moderation* (Sidgwick and Jackson, 1985), p. 143.
4 Jim Slater, quoted in Anthony Sampson, *The New Anatomy of Britain* (Hodder and Stoughton, 1971), p. 498.
5 R. H. Tawney, *Equality* (Allen and Unwin, 1964), p. 207.
6 Michael Hatfield, *The House the Left Built* (Gollancz, 1975), p. 79.
7 *Labour's Programme 1973*, p. 34.
8 Barbara Castle, *The Castle Diaries 1974–76* (Weidenfeld and Nicolson, 1980), p. 10.
9 Jack Jones, *Union Man* (Collins, 1986). p. 280.
10 Denis Healey, interviewed by Peter Hennessy in *All the Prime Minister's Men*, Channel Four television, 10 July 1986.
11 Quoted in Phillip Whitehead, *The Writing on the Wall* (Michael Joseph, 1985) p. 128.
12 Sir Douglas Wass, interviewed by Peter Hennessy in *All the Prime Minister's Men*.
13 Joel Barnett, *Inside the Treasury* (André Deutsch, 1982), p. 23.

14 Whitehead, *The Writing on the Wall*, p. 126.
15 Harold Wilson, *Final Term: the Labour government 1974–76* (Weidenfeld and Nicolson/Michael Joseph, 1979), p. 33.
16 Whitehead, *The Writing on the Wall*, p. 131.
17 Interview with Terry Coleman in the *Guardian*, repr. in Terry Coleman, *The Scented Brawl* (Elm Tree Books, 1976).
18 David Butler and Dennis Kavanagh, *The British General Election of October 1974* (Macmillan, 1975), p. 272.
19 *The Castle Diaries 1974–76*, p. 393.
20 Brian Sedgemore, *The Secret Constitution* (Hodder and Stoughton, 1980), ch. 5.
21 Whitehead, *The Writing on the Wall*, p. 131.
22 *The Castle Diaries 1974–6*, p. 413.
23 David Owen, interviewed by Phillip Whitehead in *All the Prime Minister's Men*.
24 Whitehead, *The Writing on the Wall*, p. 139.
25 The exchange is quoted in Philip Goodhart, *Full-Hearted Consent* (Davis-Poynter, 1976) p. 173.
26 *The Castle Diaries 1974–76*, p. 357.
27 Whitehead, *The Writing on the Wall*, p. 148.
28 Private information.
29 Private information.
30 Joe Haines, *The Politics of Power* (Cape, 1977), p. 57.
31 See Peter Hennessy, *Cabinet* (Basil Blackwell, 1986), p. 146.
32 *The Castle Diaries 1974–76*, p. 227.
33 Tony Benn, interviewed by Sally-Ann Lomas in *All the Prime Minister's Men*.
34 Wilson, *Final Term*, p. 121.
35 Denis Healey, in *All the Prime Minister's Men*.
36 James Callaghan, interviewed by Phillip Whitehead in *All the Prime Minister's Men*.
37 For a sobering account of the truth of this, see Ivor Crewe, 'The Labour Party and Electorate', in Dennis Kavanagh (ed.), *The Politics of the Labour Party* (Allen and Unwin, 1982).
38 Whitehead, *The Writing on the Wall*, p. 187.
39 Susan Crosland, *Tony Crosland* (Cape, 1982), p. 355. His constituency was Grimsby.
40 James Callaghan, *Time and Chance* (Collins, 1987), p. 425.
41 Ibid., p. 44.
42 James Callaghan, in *All the Prime Minister's Men*.
43 David Steel, *A House Divided* (Weidenfeld and Nicolson, 1980), p. 125.
44 Whitehead, *The Writing on the Wall*, p. 297.
45 Bernard Donoughue, interviewed by Phillip Whitehead in *All the Prime Minister's Men*.

46   Denis Barnes and Eileen Reed, *Government and the Trade Unions* (Heinemann Educational, 1980), p. 212.
47   Whitehead, *The Writing on the Wall*, p. 265.
48   Ibid., p. 279.
49   *Time and Chance*, p. 538.
50   Barnett, *Inside The Treasury*, p. 175.
51   Crewe, in Kavanagh, *The Politics of the Labour Party*, p. 42.

Bibliography

The 1974-9 government has not enjoyed the close attention given to its successor, and there is no comparable literature to that on the Thatcher phenomenon. However, among those books which the author found useful the following deserve mention.

1 Memoirs

The Castle Diaries 1974-6 (Weidenfeld and Nicolson, 1980). Harold Wilson was kind to Barbara. James Callaghan was not. Consequently these diaries end with her removal from office in 1976. Barbara Castle took shorthand and wrote up her entries promptly, so they have a freshness absent from the more analytical Crossman diaries. Barbara rarely conceals her amazement at her triumphs, but there in the frame with her is a vivid fragment of what life seemed like to the battered Wilson cabinet.

Inside the Treasury, Joel Barnett (Andre Deutsch, 1982). This book is like the man, chirpy, candid, disrespectful of persons. The confessions of an 'undoubted pessimist' cover the period when Chancellor Healey was being ground between the upper and nether millstones of the Labour movement and the international monetary system.

Time and Chance, James Callaghan (Collins, 1987). The former Prime Minister's memoirs took much time to produce and leave nothing to chance. A forgiving account of a fortunate life, which adds little to what we know of Callaghan's premiership, slightly more to his time as Harold Wilson's Foreign Secretary.

The Politics of Power, Joe Haines (Cape, 1977). Harold Wilson's Press Secretary from 1969-76 laid bare the cupboard of the 'kitchen cabinet' with a skeletal role for Lady Falkender and some good glimpses of the Civil Service in its manipulative prime.

Downing Street in Perspective, Marcia Falkender (Weidenfeld and Nicolson, 1983). Lady Falkender's second memoir has some insights, but looks forward to the successful gossip columnist she became, rather than back to the powerful political aide she once was.

Tony Crosland, Susan Crosland (Cape, 1982). A beautifully written memoir of a political life cut short, which is also a love story. Its artless glimpses of the rivalries and alliances within the Labour Cabinet catch every politician off guard.

Union Man, Jack Jones (Collins, 1986). Jack Jones's memoir is like himself, doggedly sincere and honest. It illustrates both the strengths and weaknesses of the unions in the 1970s; what you saw was what you got.

Final Term 1974-76, Harold Wilson (Michael Joseph/Weidenfeld and Nicolson,

1979). Though stylish when he is not quoting himself, Wilson's record of his last term is written in the spirit of Safety First. Indeed he ends with the quotation of a Tory epitaph on him as 'Labour's Baldwin'.

The Secret Constitution, Brian Sedgemore (Hodder and Stoughton, 1980). Although clumsily written and not quite the constitutional treatise the author may have intended, this memoir of the tribulations of Tony Benn has some vivid examples of clashes with the Civil Service. A teaser until the Benn diaries are published.

2 Analysis

The David Butler and Dennis Kavanagh studies of the two 1974 elections and that of 1979, together with that by Butler and Uwe Kitzinger of the 1975 Referendum (all Macmillan) retain their usefulness.

For the internal problems of Labour see also: *The House the Left Built*, Michael Hatfield (Gollancz, 1978); *The Forward March of Labour Halted*, Hobsbawm and others (Verso, 1982); *The Politics of the Labour Party*, ed. Dennis Kavanagh (Allen and Unwin, 1982); *What Went Wrong?*, ed. Ken Coates (Spokesman Books, 1979).

For the course of government, 1974–9: *Britain in Decline*, Andrew Gamble (Macmillan, 1981); *Cabinet*, P. Hennessy (Blackwell, 1986); *Labour and Equality*, Nicholas Bosanquet and Peter Townsend (Heinemann, 1980).

For Labour and Scotland: *Labour and Scottish Nationalism*, M. Keating and D. Bleiman (Macmillan, 1979); *The Break-Up of Britain* (2nd edn), Tom Nairn (Verso, 1981); *Mackintosh on Scotland*, John Mackintosh (Longman, 1982); *Breakaway, The Scottish Labour Party*, H. M. Drucker (EUSPB, 1978).

For Labour and Northern Ireland: an indispensable background book is *The Uncivil Wars: Ireland today*, Padraig O'Malley (Blackstaff Press, 1983).

3 Biographies

Most biographies written in the 1970s of active political figures would best be described as interim. Among them are: *Roy Jenkins*, John Campbell (Weidenfeld and Nicolson, 1983); *Michael Foot*, Simon Hoggart and David Leigh (Hodder and Stoughton, 1981); *Callaghan: the road to Number Ten*, Peter Kellner and Christopher Hitchens (Cassell, 1976).

9

The Thatcher Governments, 1979–1987

John Vincent

Margaret Thatcher may be a great historical figure. She may be a very limited woman. She may be both. Such questions will long perplex and divide her biographers. For the historian, however, it is not the essence of her nature that matters, but the context in which she has operated, and the relationship between the Thatcher governments and their times.

Always allow for what would have happened anyway. The collapse of the Victorian economy, and the North–South divide, dated back to the 1920s. Deindustrialization was common to most advanced countries, as industry went the way of agriculture. In society, the collapse of the family in the face of hedonistic individualism, going back to the 1960s, merely continued apace. The cultural revolution of the sixties had come to stay; Mrs Thatcher had an immoral majority, not a moral one, at her back. Even rural Anglicanism had nearly vanished. The downward permeation of intelligentsia and media values made a period of homogenous cultural conservatism, as had occurred in the 1950s, impossible.

Had Mrs Thatcher never existed or her party not held office, the central questions of the 1980s would have been the same. The numbers seeking work were bound to rise alarmingly, for purely demographic reasons. The sharp increase in the very old placed strain on the health and social services, though curiously the decline of the school-age population only made teachers more combative. The social-spending crisis unfolded in slow motion irrespective of politics.

In party politics, the 'degentrification' of the Conservatives was the inevitable result of a middle-class suburban Britain. A party of upper-class public schoolboys changed into a party of middle-class public schoolboys. The non-public-school fringe, if noisy and noticeable, was still a fringe. The decline of the old Labour identity meant the decline of the old, stable predictable system of two class parties, both conservative in outlook, and the decline of strong voter commitment.

So much for what would have happened anyway. To that must be added all those apparently Thatcherite developments of the 1980s which had deep roots in the corporatist 1970s. Consider Mrs Thatcher's inheritance from Labour: the return to financial rectitude in 1976; the explicit rejection of orthodox Keynesianism by James Callaghan; the commitment to 3 per cent per annum growth in defence spending; the demise, beyond all hope of resurrection, of incomes policy in the 'winter of discontent' in 1978–9; and an ominously overpriced pound. To that may be added, on the social side, the ending by Labour of the era of mass council-house building, and the official adoption by Labour of the view that the state of education was a cause for concern. These were legacies. They left no room for manoeuvre. Many of the main decisions that shaped government in the 1980s had already been made under Labour. Even Ian MacGregor and Michael Edwardes were Labour bequests.

Something as contentious today as the 1979 tax cuts, which have since been used to make Mrs Thatcher appear the Robin Hood of the rich, merely embodied what was already in the air. Callaghan had promised a cut in standard-rate income tax from 33 to 30 per cent. The Liberals, exotically, proposed 'income tax starting at 20 per cent with a top rate of 50 per cent', and a major switch to indirect taxation, in their 1979 manifesto. Mrs Thatcher's first Budget cut standard rate to 30 per cent, lowered the top rate to 60 per cent, and involved a major switch to indirect taxation. If she erred, she erred with all the other leading players on the political stage; with the consensus, not against it.

Of course, the financial rectitude of Callaghan and Healey in 1976–9 differed greatly from that of Thatcher. Their policy was enforced, hers voluntary. Theirs relied on state control, hers on the free market, both to an exaggerated extent. But they had a common aim, and, in monetarism of varying sorts, a common method.

Accepting, then, that Mrs Thatcher was faced with a situation where she could no more be the root of all evil than the fount of all good, what cargo of traditions did she carry on board on becoming leader in 1975? The answer is that we do not really know. The two great influences were personal: her father and Denis Thatcher. There are no other mentors in sight. If she lacked the traditional cultural apparatus, it was not because she was a Grantham grocer's daughter, but because she was a scientist. As a politicized schoolgirl and student, daughter of an ex-Liberal Methodist lay preacher with strengths in finance, she absorbed the

Richard Hillary ('my favourite book') emotional patriotism of the 1940s, but not the Beveridge side. Her contempt for, or unawareness of, average opinion started young.

Much less is known about what she read and what she thought between leaving Somerville in 1947 and entering Parliament in 1959. Of those years, lived entirely in the South East, neither public record nor private revelation has anything significant to say. Yet this is perhaps the essential Thatcher, the suburban professional woman of the 1950s, living in a period of naïvely moral anti-totalitarianism, of declining taxes, in a state whose frontiers could, it seemed, be rolled back. Putting aside the symbolism (later to be electorally useful) of Grantham, the fifties were her real formative decade; and what her efforts in the eighties proved was that the fifties could not be brought back.

Long before she entered Parliament in 1959, politics came before family, profession or enjoyments in intensity of commitment. There were no hobbies, no non-political interests. Marriage brought money and approval but did not alter the pattern of her life. Nobody saw her as brilliant; nobody predicted future eminence. Promoted by Macmillan after only two years in Parliament, she has now held responsibility for twenty-five years without a break. Her approach was always strenuous. Her various shadow posts (pensions, housing, energy, transport, education, environment, and economic affairs), if mostly transitory, involved a wide range of subjects. From 1967, she was a member of the Shadow Cabinet. If her experience of office was necessarily limited in 1979, her experience of public business was certainly not.

Between 1959 and 1970, her position is a matter of record. Where did she stand? Perhaps, on balance, on the right; but the evidence is scanty and ambiguous. True, she was a hanger, even perhaps a flogger; true, her 1968 speech at the Conservative Political Centre was pure Thatcherism and effectively destroys any notion that her moral conservatism began in 1974. On the other hand, she allegedly wanted Butler for leader in 1963. She did not attract enough attention for her position to matter; but in retrospect her response to the sixties seems to have been non-existent.

At Education, she attracted all too much attention, becoming a hate figure for the lumpen-intelligentsia and the *Sun* (which called her 'the most unpopular woman in England'). Her policies were made to appear hard even where they were obviously soft. She was the last of the big spenders, with the education budget rising from 4 per cent to over 6 per cent of national income in her time (1970–4). She was supposed to be the hard face of privilege opposing comprehensives; yet while minister she approved all but about 310 of 3420 schemes for comprehensive education submitted to her. Her misfortune was that it mattered little what she did. In a Cabinet of quiet-voiced men, she stood out. In the education world, all that mattered was that she had replaced Sir Edward Boyle, the epitome of centrism, and must therefore be derided as a narrow partisan. It did not help that she was a lawyer who knew her powers under the 1944 Education Act inside out. Without any wish to do so on her part, she was bound to meet the afterglow of the sixties head on.

So loud was the din of battle that it obscured her distinctive position on educational issues. She aimed to reach the parts of the system other ministers had not reached. She favoured primary at the expense of secondary education. She proposed a national system of nursery schools, showing her willingness to enact a great collectivist reform. In this, like Sir Keith Joseph later, she did not share contemporary opinion that educational progress consisted of concentration on the production of an elite. Liberal orthodoxy bit the hand that did not feed it, but perhaps it was orthodoxy that was reactionary.

'Thatcher the milk snatcher' gained in two ways from the attacks on her. She could not be dropped by Edward Heath at the enemy's behest; and, if she had no definite following, at least the backbenchers on the right of the party could hardly not see in her one of their own kind. For all that, when Heath's government fell, nobody, including herself, attached any particular significance to her. She remained an outsider, a non-member of the male club of politics.

The two election defeats of 1974 provoked in the Tories more than the customary wish for a new leader. There was intense awareness that the party faced a historic choice of identity, an awareness enhanced by the highest inflation Britain had known, the apparent supremacy of organized labour, and the Stock Exchange collapse of 1974–5. That is not to say that then or later were most Tories baptized into a new political faith. They were not. But debate went deeper than for a generation; the Butskellite consensus could at last be questioned from within the party mainstream.

Heath's departure was a long-drawn-out, inevitably unpleasant, and deeply personal affair. This only made the tensions within the Conservative Party more interesting than they had been since the war. Mrs Thatcher was not even her own first choice. She supported Sir Keith Joseph. An apparent lack of touch by Sir Keith led to his withdrawal, leaving the field free. She did not rush into the fray. Had she lost, as was highly probable, she would have thrown away a career which was all she had in life. It was a gambler's throw.

Her election to the leadership in February 1975 is best defined by what it was not. It was not a victory for Thatcherism, for a body of doctrine, for no such thing existed. It was not a vote against the postwar consensus on economic and social policy, or for giving the party a new identity. It was a vote for getting rid of Ted Heath, and not much more. And it was a narrow vote, only 130–119 on the first ballot. Tactical voting complicated the issue. There was a majority against Heath, but not for Thatcher; and her campaign managers had used sleight of hand to manipulate the result. Fear of Ted, induced by finesse, had led a significant group of non-Thatcher supporters to vote for her on tactical grounds.

Thus Mrs Thatcher became leader without any real personal following, without any known line on policy, and in a way that the losers found hard to accept as valid. Even her chief backer, Airey Neave, wanted an anti-Heath candidate more than he wanted her. A 'peasants' revolt' on the back benches swept Heath out; but in the Shadow Cabinet all but Sir Keith Joseph appeared to have opposed her. Had she won only to become the prisoner of her Heathite opponents?

As leader, she made up Thatcherism as she went along. Her moral instincts had always been conservative enough. Unlike Sir Keith, once a sixties liberal collectivist, she did not awake in 1974 with the experience of conversion on her lips. But moral outlook had to become economic doctrine before it could become either party policy or national atmosphere. Here she was on her own; the party establishment could only wring its hands among the ruins. Distrusting the official centres of power, the Shadow Cabinet and the Conservative Research Department, she turned elsewhere, above all to Sir Keith Joseph and his Centre for Policy Studies, created in 1974. The resurrection of Peter Thorneycroft as party chairman (1975–81) also meant something, for had he not sat out the Macmillan era as a symbol of principled opposition to its collusion with inflation?

In 1975–9 she saw herself as leader on sufferance. From 1975, Conservative leaders have been subject to annual re-election, and, though no candidate has ever opposed Mrs Thatcher, the presence of this mechanism made it far harder to sail through election defeat as Heath had done in 1966. Before 1979, Mrs Thatcher was right in repeatedly saying, 'I shall have only one chance.' In the 1970s, and probably until 1981, she lacked the normal relationship a leader has with his party. She had to ask, and did ask, whether colleagues were 'one of us'. As the only loyalty she could count on was doctrinal loyalty, doctrine came to the forefront as rarely before in Conservative history.

Neither in 1975 nor in 1979 did she reconstruct the front bench in her own image. In 1975 it was enough to isolate Heath, while in 1979 she seized the Treasury, leaving the Tories to have the rest as they chose. She did not pack the Cabinet; instead she circumvented it. This was not a deliberate constitutional novelty, merely an acknowledgement of the necessities of faction. The rift with Heath remained deep and public. To her great good fortune, Heath's refusal to go through the motions of goodwill sharply reduced his following as 'king over the water' by as early as 1976. Thereafter, he became the opponent any Premier would wish for. Had Heath opted for reconciliation, Mrs Thatcher could hardly have been leader in more than name.

The 'peasants' revolt' was as much a revolt of backbenchers against ministers as an expression of right-wing atavism. In any case, the right meant different things to different people. The Old Right was paternalist, traditionalist, and averse to economic liberalism. The New Right was iconoclastic, radical, committed to modernity and wedded to economic liberalism. Its central political tenet was that the state was over-mighty. Its central financial tenet was that a high-tax economy spelled stagnation and decline. Its central moral tenet was that people should get what they deserved, not what they needed. All these tenets, but especially the last, found an enhanced market in the 1970s, when skilled-worker and middle-class differentials had been eroded by incomes policy. Thatcherism resembles trade unionism in that both are about differentials. The need which Mrs Thatcher intuited in 1975–80 was to give a moral meaning to latent anti-egalitarian feeling among those who had seen their differentials eroded.

The New Right would not have been possible without Enoch Powell's economic teaching. It might have been impracticable without the floating of the pound by Heath (long advocated by Powell). But Powell himself, as an Ulster Unionist, played no part in opposition policy. The creative mornings of desultory chat with Sir Keith Joseph, chairman of the Advisory Committee on Policy, through which everything was channelled, touched on all aspects of an imaginary future. Through Sir Keith she met Alfred Sherman, a Jewish ex-Communist from the East End, who had fought on the Communist side in the Spanish Civil War, and who for several years was important to her. Sir Keith's newly founded

Centre for Policy Studies, with no fewer than sixty committees beavering away, represented an attempt at an alternative Conservatism.

As leader of the Opposition, she moved in two worlds: the world of ideas, whose denizens were often classical Liberals or ex-Labour, and the world of party, which was often unintellectual or anti-intellectual. Since her intellectuals provided reasons for her instincts, and spoke of her leadership in terms of a mission, she found much time for them. By 1979, though not in 1975, rolling back the frontiers of the Macmillan–Wilson–Heath managerial or corporate state had become a set of policies as well as a matter of instinct and slogan. There was nothing forced in this, for, to a professional woman whose formative decade was the 1950s, it was an established fact that taxes could be cut steadily and the frontiers of the state rolled back.

Even before 1979, Mrs Thatcher had stamped a new identity on her party. This was done not through new faces at the top, but by a new departure in policy: the rejection of everything Heath had seemed to embody in 1974. The party leadership, left to itself, might well have rationalized the Heath collapse by taking it as proof that change was impossible. Conservatives might have chosen, as after 1945, to conform to a new and alien consensus. That they did not, owed much to Mrs Thatcher, who interpreted traumatic defeat as meaning that far wider changes were necessary.

The abandonment of incomes policy by nearly all shades of Conservative opinion left only two ways of controlling inflation. Either the power of organized labour could be broken directly, or its effects could be limited by control of the money supply. Since the first option was outside practical politics, monetarism it had to be. Here, with Sir Geoffrey Howe as her new Shadow Chancellor – a kindred spirit from the first – she produced an intellectually consistent policy designed not to treat the symptoms of inflation (high pay rises) but the disease itself.

On trade union policy she faced a principled opponent and possible successor, James Prior, and what emerged bore his stamp of apparent moderation and gradualism. In this area, it was the 'winter of discontent' of 1979 that brought change. The only difference between the 1979 manifesto and the earlier versions of 1976 and 1977 was a promise of tough union policies. The unions had damned themselves so exhaustively in early 1979 in the public eye that the assumption that they could always defy legislation with impunity no longer held good. If anyone broke the mould of the old politics, it was surely the unions by their own actions.

Possibly Mrs Thatcher failed to exploit union unpopularity sufficiently when it was at its height after 1979. But, though the unions had lost the power to carry the public with them, and their membership went into steep decline, they were still believed to have the power to win. Thus caution ruled; in 1981 the Premier insisted on surrender to the demands of the National Union of Mineworkers against the advice of David Howell, her Energy Minister. Here she showed skill. Where Heath had made the soberest Labour men militant, Mrs Thatcher did nothing between 1979 and 1983 to help Labour overcome its disunity. It was only the 1983 election defeat which, within the month, persuaded Labour of the merits of presentability.

Some say that Howe merely continued where Healey left off. The continuity was strong, but the matter is not that simple, for it was partly Howe that made Healey possible. Howe began to define his policy in 1976, the year Healey capitulated to the International Monetary Fund, and by doing so made it easier for Labour to adopt a sternly unpopular line. Had liberal conservatism still held sway, Labour could hardly have lapsed into the conservative immobilism of the late 1970s which its activists found intolerable. The radicalization of Labour at its grass roots, its disintegration as an opposition in 1979–83, and the activation of Labour's betrayal complex, all owed something to the posture of the Thatcher Opposition before 1979. The creation of Foot, of Bennery, and of the Social Democratic Party, and perhaps still more the elimination of Healey, were in part Mrs Thatcher's bequest to Labour.

The 1979 election saw the largest swing between one major party and another since 1945. The Tories' lead in votes was larger than in 1959, their previous postwar high point. The victory was less impressive than it looked. The Conservative share of the vote was low, the lowest of any majority party since 1922. Mrs Thatcher not only consistently trailed behind Callaghan in the polls before and after the election. She was also consistently less popular than her party in 1975–9. Recognition she had achieved, right from the start; but recognition, as a media phenomenon, was very far from popularity. There was no risk of her being an unknown Prime Minister, but she had to work for her votes. Her principal contribution to victory lay in forcing the government to hold an election at a time not of its own choosing, when the public was still in a state of shock from the disruption of the 'winter of discontent'. This forced dissolution in turn hinged on her fight against Scottish and Welsh devolution.

When she became leader, the conventional wisdom, especially among

Scottish Tories, was that appeasement of nationalism was necessary, a line conspicuously endorsed by Heath. By contrast, Mrs Thatcher, in concert with Francis Pym and Tam Dalyell, achieved a triumph of Disraelian manoeuvre within Parliament, and gave Labour no time to regain breath after a disastrous winter. Had Labour had time to recover, the wave of strikes might have receded in the public mind, the electorate could have been bribed, and Callaghan's conservatism would have outshone Thatcher's radicalism. All told, May 1979 must be considered a lucky victory.

By 1979, Mrs Thatcher had achieved a *modus vivendi* with her party. She had let Heath isolate himself, sacked Reginald Maudling, and left Enoch Powell in the wilderness. By 1979, the Conservative leaders of the 1960s were phantoms, not contenders for power. At the top of the party, weakness was unavoidable. The economic Thatcherites were few: Howe, Joseph and Biffen. Lacking a power base in Cabinet, she turned, as Gladstone had, in other directions, to the New Right, to the back-benches, perhaps to the women's vote. Since she could not win supremacy, she defended herself by institutionalizing divisions within the party.

Other Thatchers should not be forgotten. A political leader has many identities. Some survive, some do not. The market, not the politician, decides. To think of the identities that worked as the real her, while forgetting those that failed, would be a mistake. Her anti-EEC identity is a case in point. She judged, correctly, that Heath's Euromania was doing the party no good. While remaining faithful to the letter, she made it clear that she was opposed in spirit. She left the 1975 referendum very much to Heath.

Yet her anti-Europeanism struck no chord. Her financial wrangles upset the liberal press. By 1986, she was isolated on the issue of joining the European Monetary System. The EEC remains an area where she hoped to strike political gold but failed, largely because her ear was so attuned to the anti-Europeanism of the 1970s that it overlooked the anti-Americanism of the 1980s. For her, Americans are wartime allies and Cold War partners – attitudes formed, no doubt, before 1960. The arrival of Reagan in 1980 required a redirection of British chauvinism which she was not equipped to exploit.

There is also the anti-Soviet Thatcher, the Iron Lady. Her difficulty here was that Russia ceased to be feared, just as Reagan's America ceased to be loved. The horse that she backed, the anti-totalitarianism of the 1950s, had long since seen better days. This she came to recognize, becoming a dove of peace soon after Howe began to impart system to foreign affairs in 1983, and entering as enthusiastically as the Foreign Office into the possibilities of an *Ostpolitik* from 1984 onwards. If she could be made to look dated over Europe, by the mid-eighties her Russian policy ably reflected contemporary attitudes.

There is also the Christian Thatcher to consider. Probably she would be happy to present some version of public Christianity. For a time in the late 1970s she seemed to have this in mind. But either she lacked the words, or there were too few Christians for it to matter. This aspect of her also found expression in a later attempt to build a broad, non-economic conservatism around 'the family' – a brief attempt at major moral statement tied to Ferdinand Mount's time as head of the Policy Unit at No. 10, just before the 1983 election.

Mrs Thatcher achieved more in opposition than is generally recognized. Her performance as Prime Minister, however, was at first more muddled than programmatic, causing Sir Keith Joseph to refer to 1979 as 'the lost year'. It was the first instance of the dictum that she is at her worst when things are going well. The momentum of election victory was not maintained. Rash election promises on pay and taxes were rashly honoured. In a crowded year, haste ruled. The theme was not monetarism, but heedless lavishness which added fuel to the inflationary fire.

Inflation there was bound to be. The second oil-price rise and the wages explosion began the trouble. Government action merely made things worse. At times the Clegg Commission on pay, inherited from the Callaghan administration, seemed to have a larger hand in running the economy than the government. Still, the new order was different. Though the situation in 1979 called for an anti-inflationary policy, what it got was a heady dose of economic liberalism. Not having an incomes policy, confiscatory direct taxation, price controls or exchange controls made plain the contrast with all previous postwar governments. Perhaps most important, not only were exchange controls demolished, but the machinery for reintroducing them was dismantled. The spirit of corporatism was dead. Entranced by this pleasant spectacle, it was easy to forget that economic management remained as necessary under economic liberalism as before, and the story of 1980–3 is largely a matter of moving by inches towards the management of a liberal economy afloat on the turbulent waters of world markets. This task was so demanding, even emotionally exhausting, that it left little time for anything else.

Outside this central struggle over the economy, most areas of government went on as before. If the old order persisted, it was partly because it was run by the old faces. The Cabinet, at least until 1981, was non-Thatcherite. Rather, there were two parallel Cabinets, one Thatcherite, running the economic ministries, and one Tory, running everything else. Since the two cancelled out, there was little point in seeking Cabinet views; and accordingly they were not sought.

The Prime Minister made no attempt either to reconstruct the machinery of government, or to radicalize the party leadership. Both in 1975 and 1979 she kept change to a minimum. Her first Cabinet lasted unchanged till January 1981, and without substantial change till September 1981. Mrs Thatcher is not a sacker; her reshuffles have mostly been forced on her by events. There is no reason to suppose that she was unhappy with a Cabinet of broad and diverse views so long as it complied with her on essentials.

Much energy was initially diverted into foreign policy. Rhodesia was interred to the satisfaction of its enemies and of the British public, who asked only that a bothersome problem of Empire should slip into almost decent obscurity. Procedural success – the temporary return of Rhodesia to British rule, a risky business – served to disguise either an element of surrender to 'world opinion', or crude pursuit of British interests, or both. The Establishment – Queen, Prime Minister, Foreign Office, Army – were seen putting on a fine show of competence, and Lord Carrington became the Lord Peter Wimsey of the centrist press, and the only Thatcher minister ever to win a following outside his party.

Later in the year, the Prime Minister made the issue of the EEC budget her own. Her strident nationalism dismayed the sensitive. The sums at stake were less important than the shock given to EEC orthodoxy. Mrs Thatcher had made it clear that Europe as such did not matter and that British interests did. On the whole, she got what she wanted, though controversy rumbled on for years.

Both the Rhodesian and European settlements made sense domestically, for all that one was smooth, the other rough. Both were what people wanted. Both were settlements of sorts. Both implied decisiveness. Both put British interests nakedly first. Both suggested that cutting Gordian knots worked. But they were the right answers to the wrong problems. Public spending and inflation were out of control, and not much was being done about it. The high pound, inherited from Healey, was getting higher, destroying exporters. Economic liberalism might be good in itself, but only in the long term would it change the structure of the economy.

In March 1980, the Southend by-election resulted in a majority down from 10,774 to 430. The honeymoon was over. Public spending remained much as under Labour. The economy was feverishly ill, and had to be saved quickly. Monetarism did not cause crisis, but crisis led to the classical phase of monetarism. By May 1980 inflation was 21.9 per cent. Faced with an emergency, the government gave higher priority to inflation than to unemployment, and it would be surprising if it had not. The Medium Term Financial Strategy (1980), largely Nigel Lawson's work, was a grand scheme for a planned free market, a primer for dealing with the crisis; but, like George Brown's National Plan, it stated what one wanted rather than how to get it.

In 1980 and 1981 Mrs Thatcher's team (but not the Cabinet) wrestled with the question of how to stop inflation. The new ingredient was courage. Other governments had enforced restraint or cut proposed spending increases. What was wholly exceptional was a government willing to persevere with, indeed intensify, deflationary measures while the bottom fell out of the market. Austerity in prosperity is merely prudent; austerity in adversity requires the courage to put all ordinary political considerations in temporary abeyance. It was this courage of 1981, the pivotal year of Thatcherism, not the theoretically radical economic liberalism of 1979, which marked out a new determination by government to govern. The new regime of 1979 had not involved any real test of political will, for economic liberalism was and is as un-contentious as any great reversal of assumptions can be. Few, in 1986, were still sighing for the price, wage, dividend and exchange controls of the 1970s. Changing the economic culture was the easy bit. Reducing inflation by a mixture of fiscal and monetary measures, a problem in financial technology, was a far more desperate business.

Monetarism assumed not just that the money supply should be controlled, but that it could be measured, and that there were people to hand who knew how to do it. Such people either did not exist, or were still learning the job, or were using unreliable yardsticks which altered their dimensions as you looked at them. Whereas fiscal policy involved telling Treasury officials to make changes they had often made before, monetary policy had far more variables. For one thing, it had to operate in a stormy and unprotected international economic environment where huge capital flows mattered more than the normal transactions of trade. Thus in 1980–1 attempts at enforcing a tight money supply by means of high interest rates only drew funds to Britain, augmenting funds in circulation, the exchange rate, and the rate of inflation. Monetarism was very much a curate's egg; but, without earnest attempts at controlling money supply, many strange things might have happened.

But to paint a picture of a government blindly following an impractical dogma would be wrong. As early as autumn 1980, No. 10 diagnosed excessive stringency in monetary policy, and recommended a tougher fiscal policy. This was roughly what ensued. The 1981 Budget, the toughest of all, discreetly hid a relaxation in monetary policy behind far more visible tax increases which produced an 'unthinkably low' public-sector borrowing requirement (PSBR), in an apparent (but not real) inverted Keynesianism. The usual picture can thus be reversed. Instead of credulously trusting in monetarism, Mrs Thatcher's advisers spotted its defects first. Fiscal, not monetary, methods of deflation dominated the agenda. Even the inadequacies of M3, the standard measure of money supply inherited from Labour, were quickly rumbled. Perhaps the Thatcher government should go down as the one which put monetarism in its place. If 1981 was crucial, which it was, it was as a triumph of political will, not of economic doctrine.

Mrs Thatcher's task was to make her measures stick. The least of her problems was fending off Labour, which was busy defeating itself. With Foot replacing Callaghan in autumn 1980, the gods were on her side. Foot started low in public esteem, and sank steadily to the lowest point ever reached by a party leader. With the Opposition in a mess, and the Social Democrats enjoying halcyon days, 1981 was the perfect year for Mrs Thatcher to be unpopular in.

Her main fight was against her own party. She began in January 1981, sacking Norman St John-Stevas and Angus Maude from the Cabinet, and Reg Prentice from his job at minister of state level, and bringing in the eminently biddable, more financially attuned, Leon Brittan and Norman Fowler while replacing Francis Pym at Defence with the economy-minded John Nott. Not a dog barked. Then came the 1981 Budget, cutting the PSBR from £13,500 million to £10,500 million. Cabinet ministers were deeply shocked, but had only hours to decide whether to resign. They were well and truly bounced. The episode taught the Prime Minister that the Cabinet opposition had no guts. By May 1981, enough results were appearing to prevent revolt. Inflation had dropped from 21.9 to 11.7 per cent. Then matters worsened. Riots erupted in cities all over England. Unemployment reached 2.7 million. The Cabinet could not be bounced twice, and they even began to discuss economic policy, leaving the Prime Minister defeated and isolated.

The answer was Mrs Thatcher's most aggressive reshuffle. Doubters were replaced with Thatcherite stalwarts, none from traditional Conservative backgrounds: Nigel Lawson, Cecil Parkinson and Norman Tebbit. The Cabinet was radicalized only when it showed signs of rebellion. After that, it mattered little that the SDP-Liberal Alliance had 45 per cent of the vote by November 1981. With internal and external challenges so inchoate, 1981 could safely be written off.

By March 1982, when Roy Jenkins won a seat in Glasgow, the SDP tide was beginning to ebb. Labour was in the doldrums. The Conservative vote had picked up. Before ever the Argentines set foot in Port Stanley on 2 April, it is argued, Mrs Thatcher again led in the polls, a point that needs the closest investigation. Conceptually speaking, the Falklands War did not exist. Polls after the war showed Mrs Thatcher in much the same position as just before. At parliamentary level, war fever showed a cross democracy putting its emotions before its interests. If Mrs Thatcher saw it as a test of resolve for the West generally, the only terms in which it made sense, she said little to that effect till after the event. She followed opinion, rather than led it, and very wisely too. She did not play the warlord. The divisions of Suez were not repeated. But why she emerged in triumph, still more why she survived the initial blow, remains a little hard to explain.

The ascendancy created in 1982 brought the central episode of Thatcherism to an end. The temporary cessation of inflation in autumn 1982 was astonishing in itself, but it also left Thatcherism without an agenda. Government economic policy had done what it had said it would do, in less time than expected; a rare event, but one which left ministers at a loss what to do next.

The 1983 election merely recorded the inevitable. The Conservative share of the vote was slightly down. To the No. 10 election team, it was a 'soft sell' election, unlike the 'hard sell' used in 1979. The Prime Minister found it advisable to keep away from large centres of population, although she got 50 per cent of the union vote and 55 per cent of the working-class vote. With an almost equally divided opposition, a large and non-Thatcherite Tory majority was inevitable. Backbenchers sitting for normally non-Tory seats and faced, as most were, by Liberal opponents, will on balance behave in a centrist way. Only the miners' strike of 1984–5, fought on the government's terms, prolonged the intensities of the 1970s into the mid-1980s.

Like 1979, 1983 was a lost year, and 1984 a far from productive one. As in 1979, Mrs Thatcher was at her worst when things were going well. The government visibly lacked an agenda. Its attacks on Labour bastions in local government conveyed a preoccupation with battles long ago. After the miners' strike, the Conservatives fell behind in the polls in summer 1985. They recovered in the autumn, only to be more seriously damaged by the Westland episode in 1986 – and this although Britain was enjoying large rises in real wages, a potentially reckless monetary binge, and a reflationary feast of backdoor Keynesianism in the form of the sale of state assets. If Mrs Thatcher had moved the consensus in her direction, she had not moved it very far.

Very soon after the 1983 election, the Opposition began to capitalize on her success. If she stood head and shoulders above her contemporaries, then all faults, all miseries, all shortcomings could be laid at her door. Quite who decided to crucify her is not known, but intelligent minds saw her as the perfect material for psychological warfare. She was stubborn, inflexible, callous, uncaring, divisive, it was said, and not only by the Opposition. Such single-issue propaganda, ably and constantly directed, became the focus of the anti-Thatcher consensus of the mid-1980s, united round personal hostility rather than a doctrine. It was a battle of moral emotions, with the sentimentalism of the centre thirsting for blood. Thus a leader whose creed was individual responsibility found her personal pre-eminence used to fortify the belief that the state was the answer to life's problems.

Mrs Thatcher is an exponent more of presidential than of Cabinet government. These things are relative. She has not sought to build up a White House. Indeed, she rejected plans for a Prime Minister's department and abolished the Think Tank: hardly the actions of a centralizer. Rather, the conduct of business has turned on personality and on faction. By temperament Mrs Thatcher is not a good listener. Her Cabinet technique, it is said, is a brisk exchange of fire with individual ministers on their special topics, not an Asquithian waiting game as discussion unfolds round the table. Moreover, her assertion that her aim is to get things done has to be taken seriously. The Cabinet stopped things getting done. The long list of her defeats in Cabinet is one reason why meetings of the full Cabinet have been kept to the minimum.

The question of where decisions have really been taken is hard to answer. Besides the normal Cabinet committee system, there have also been bilateral negotiations with individual ministers, and delegation to an informal entourage. The entourage has provided few grounds for apprehension. Intellectuals have fluttered around; the turnover has been high. The four economics professors, Walters, Griffiths, Minford and Burns are as professionally reputable as those economists who have anathematized them. Sir John Hoskyns, who was doctrinaire, was succeeded in No. 10 by Ferdinand Mount, who was anti-doctrinaire; neither converted, or was converted by, Mrs Thatcher. Mount had indeed opposed the Falklands War on prudential grounds shortly before becoming the chief speech-writer in the 1983 election. The Prime Minister's appetite for advisers and intellectuals is the same as her appetite for anything else: intense, over-serious, and insatiable. But there has never been any figure in the entourage comparable to Lady Falkender under Harold Wilson. Alan Walters was important in economic matters for a short time, probably more so than the Cabinet; and Bernard Ingham, the press spokesman, attracted notoriety for his colourful personality. For all that, Mrs Thatcher has been both *bien entouré* and independent.

The postwar concordat was based economically on Tory connivance in inflation; and politically on Tory acceptance of the veto power of organized labour. The Labour movement did not and could not rule, but it had an assumed power of veto, similar to that of the pre-1911 House of Lords. Labour's old identity dominated the period up to 1979, because nobody really wished it otherwise. The old identity was based on a morally conservative working class and revolved round the 'holy trinity' of the unions, the welfare state and high taxes. It was statist; it believed in looking after people, but not in radicalizing their lifestyles. Mrs Thatcher's attack on it coincided with a period when it was ripe for the axe; but without her its eclipse would not have happened when it did.

As Labour's old identity waned, with help from Mrs Thatcher, so its new identity waxed strong, also with help from her. It, too, had its 'holy trinity': the media, the educational system and the intelligentsia, and the public-sector payroll vote. It was rooted in the educated class. It, too, was statist, but from a perspective above rather than below the average income. It was not by any means morally conservative.

The Labour veto on change has remained at its most peremptory where the welfare state is concerned. Even under Mrs Thatcher, this is an area where the government has governed only in details and on sufferance. In outline, the Opposition has ruled, the UK working in practice like a multi-party coalition.

The new identity, broadly symbolized by the *Guardian*, was an opponent that Mrs Thatcher was peculiarly unfitted to fight, but well fitted to encourage. Inevitable though the new confederacy was, Mrs Thatcher raised its consciousness by lending it a demonology; and, when the Opposition returns, it will be the new Opposition as shaped by Thatcher.

What stands out is how much Mrs Thatcher has left alone. In four central areas of government, namely defence, social security, health and education, there has been no shake-up. There may have been deterioration, there may have been increased expenditure; perhaps there have been both. But in these four big-spending areas, the landscape would look familiar to Attlee.

In defence and social security, there was a good case in theory for drastic reconstruction. In defence, the conventional wisdom was that Britain was overstretched, and hard decisions would have to be taken. Hard decisions have not been taken; Mrs Thatcher's defeat by the Royal Navy in the Falklands saw to that. At Social Security, Norman Fowler's long reign has been adequate as an exercise in letting sleeping dogs lie, inadequate as a response to the social spending crisis.

In health, Thatcherism has not happened. Nowhere is government so vulnerable and so conscious of its vulnerability. In terms of overall funding, there have been no cuts, but the public believe there have been, which is what matters. For Health Service administrators, there has been an administrative revolution, the first since Bevan. For the patient, death has gone on as before. There is no obvious topic which has attracted prime-ministerial interest, like vouchers in education. The central thrust of policy has been obtaining more value for money from an expenditure which ministers do not believe can be substantially modified.

Education, like health, is an area obsessed with 'cuts', though real expenditure per pupil, class sizes and pupil–teacher ratios reached the best levels ever. Even teachers' pay increased; few teachers believed this. The shock waves from a declining school population did their work. Education had the low morale of a declining industry; and Sir Keith Joseph was made to serve as a hate figure in consequence. Still, when he departed, the school system was visibly as Mrs Shirley Williams had left it in 1979.

The idea that Mrs Thatcher is in rough water because she goes too far is simply inaccurate. As Professor Minford has written, whenever she has 'obeyed her reforming instincts (as over inflation and privatisation) success has followed the predictable turmoil; when she has been persuaded to patch up the old order (as over unemployment, health, education, tax reform) failure and discontent have ensued'. Certainly, since the end of the miners' strike, discontent has centred on health and education; while America has achieved the tax reforms of which Nigel Lawson only dreams.

On the other hand, it is outside the normal system of Whitehall ministries that Mrs Thatcher has done best. Privatization is a success in its own terms, though what those terms are is hard to say. Is it a budgetary wheeze, or a change in economic culture? Certainly, Attlee would have rubbed his eyes to see the state sector nearly halved in size.

With privatization have gone two other trends: a sustained growth in self-employment (which had fallen in the 1970s) and a growth of uncertain dimensions in popular capitalism. There has been a movement towards enrichment, initiative, risk-taking, and a business culture. The jibe, familiar in 1979, that tax cuts would only lead to businessmen spending more time on the golf course, has not been fully borne out. In one respect, economic liberalism has worked wonders. The City has sold British oil at the top and used the proceeds to buy foreign securities at the bottom. Nothing could have worked more neatly. Britain has become per head the largest overseas investor, replenishing the ravages of two wars. British net assets abroad have risen from £2700 million in 1975 to £90,000 million in 1985.

For all her free market credentials, Mrs Thatcher is perhaps happier as a dirigiste. She is the first Premier to instil purpose into, and extract performance, or even profit, from the state industries. She is the best manager the state industries have ever had, the Lord Weinstock of the public sector. Somehow the command economy suits her. The change of economic culture enforced by Thatcherism has reached far outside those industries formally privatized. It applies to those whose privatization was repeatedly postponed, like British Airways, or where it remains a distant prospect, like water. Even agriculture, essentially a state industry working through franchises, has been told to stop being so production-minded. The postwar belief in production for its own sake has been finally laid to rest.

Mrs Thatcher has done more to justify state socialism than any other Prime Minister. She has not only managed existing areas of state power, but has also added to them. By means of the Manpower Services Commission, the thinking man's answer to the educational system, she has virtually nationalized Youth – and done so outside the conventional Whitehall structure. For the first time, the state has accepted full responsibility for the lives of all school-leavers. Quantitatively, this is the largest extension of the welfare state since the 1940s.

On the central economic questions, she has done worse at inflation, better at unemployment, than might appear. To reduce inflation from 21.9 per cent in 1980 to 2.3 per cent in August 1986, the lowest level since 1967, might seem much, especially as for once it was intentional. The defect of this achievement is that it has left untouched a national wage-bargaining system which institutionalizes inflation. Indeed, strong unionism among the skilled employed workforce has kept Mrs Thatcher afloat by raising wages comfortably above inflation.

Where her critics err on unemployment is that they rely on the half-truth that the government accepted high unemployment in 1981–3 without allowing for ministers' belief that this would lead to a fall in unemployment in 1983–6. Had the labour market remained the same size as in 1983, then unemployment would now be down around 2.5 million, and Mrs Thatcher's record might bear inspection. Where things went wrong was in failing to allow for a sharp increase after 1983 in the proportion of adults wishing to work. Those who argue that Mrs Thatcher is indifferent to unemployment can certainly point to the lack of any prime-ministerial initiative in this field, and the absence of any Cabinet committee on unemployment; but then how do they explain Lord Young, the Beveridge of Thatcherism, a social engineer on the grand scale, whose authority derives wholly from the Prime Minister?

Mrs Thatcher rules not two nations but more like five. Scotland, Wales, and Ulster remain ministerial fiefdoms where Thatcherite rules do not fully apply. If parts of the North seem ready to join the Third World, this should not detract from the value of the central Thatcherite achievement: the regional growth of the South in a way that has transcended its weak national base and enabled it (like northern Italy) to share the prosperity of the West European heartland unimpeded. Yet the South, not the North, has exposed the contradictions of Thatcherism. What has made people rich is inheritance and the property market, and, the higher property prices have risen and the more people have inherited, the more unreal have the Thatcherite ideas of 1979 about the relation between work, just deserts and wealth appeared.

Mrs Thatcher fits the rule that there are no bad Prime Ministers. She may lack Heath's architectonic sense, but more than makes up for it in persuasiveness and electioneering flair. She lacks Callaghan's fatalism, most certainly, but not his caution. She has Eden's wish to meddle, but with the energy to support it. If in many ways she is under-read, her appetite for official papers exceeds that of almost all her predecessors. Had she lost the 1987 election, she would have looked like a curious aberration; since she won, she will be seen as marking a change of epochs, whatever her individual qualities. Whatever the future holds, she will go down as one of history's great improbabilities. For the present, it is perhaps safest to assert that she is the only Prime Minister to cook for her private secretaries when they are working late.

She may have slain yesterday's dragon, not today's: her battle was with an archaic union-based socialism, not a pervasive middle-class liberalism. Still, the dragon looked anything but slayable in 1975, and the work had to be done, with but few helpers in her own party. She may outlive the context which made her relevant, but in the process bequeath a broad national governing party. The measure of her achievement is that she has made Thatcherism unnecessary.

Chronology

1979

3 May   General election: Conservatives, 339 seats; Labour, 269; Liberals, 11; others, 16. Conservative majority of 43.

8 May   Sir Derek Rayner of Marks and Spencer appointed to head Whitehall efficiency drive.

10 May   Pay rises for police (20 per cent) and forces (32 per cent). Tony Benn declines to join Shadow Cabinet.

19 May   Heath rejects post of ambassador to the USA.

19 July   Commons decisively rejects death penalty.

1 August   Thatcher at Lusaka conference.

17 September   57 quangos abolished.

November   'Cuts' of £3500 million in the previous Labour government's expenditure plans for 1980–1 announced.

10 November   Mrs Thatcher calls for £1000 million cut in Britain's EEC contribution.

15 November   Blunt named as 'fourth man' in Soviet spy ring.

1 December   Dublin EEC summit ends in deadlock.

21 December   Rhodesian cease-fire signed in London.

1980

2 January   Steel strike begins (called off in April).

17 January   Professor Terry Burns joins Treasury as Chief Economic Adviser.

4 March   Mugabe becomes Zimbabwe Prime Minister.

12 March   Conservatives hold Southend East by 430, down from 10,774.

2 April   Anti-police riot in St Paul's area of Bristol. Inflation at 21.8 per cent.

1 May   Local elections: large gains by Labour.
19 July   Moscow Olympics open.
October   Unemployment 2,062,900.
4 November   Ronald Reagan elected US President on 51 per cent of popular vote.
10 November   Foot defeats Denis Healey 139–129 in second ballot for Labour leadership. Pound reaches $2.45, its highest for 7 years.
December   Unemployment 2,133,000.

1981

5 January   Norman St John-Stevas and Angus Maude dropped, in first Cabinet changes since election. Unemployment 2,236,000.
7 January   Professor Alan Walters appointed as Prime Minister's personal economic adviser.
February   Inflation 13 per cent.
13 February   Pay increases averaging 6 per cent for public sector announced. After local strikes, plans to close 23 pits withdrawn.
1 March   Bobby Sands begins hunger strike (dies 5 May).
4–9 March   British Steel announces loss of £660 million; British Leyland £535 million.
10 March   Budget: road, drink, tobacco and petrol taxes up.
26 March   Social Democratic Party launched.
10–12 April   Brixton riots: 191 arrests.
7 May   Local elections: Ken Livingstone becomes GLC chairman.
10 May   François Mitterand elected French President.
3 July   Toxteth (Liverpool) riots: CS gas used for first time.
16 July   Warrington by-election: Roy Jenkins cuts Labour majority from 10,274 to 1759.
20 July   Michael Heseltine (Environment Secretary) leads task force to Merseyside.
1 August   Tenth hunger striker dies in Northern Ireland.
29 August   Civil Service strike ends after 21 weeks' sporadic action.
14–15 September   Second Cabinet reshuffle: Sir Ian Gilmour, Mark Carlisle and Sir Christopher Soames dropped.
22 October   Liberals win Croydon from Conservatives in by-election.
25 November   Lord Scarman's report on Brixton riots.
26 November   Shirley Williams (SDP) wins Crosby by 5289 (former Conservative majority 19,272) in by-election.
8 December   Arthur Scargill elected President of National Union of Mineworkers. SDP–Liberal Alliance wins 114 local by-elections out of 214 in July–December, a gain of 100 seats.

1982

27 January   Employment Bill published, giving compensation to workers sacked for refusing to join a closed shop.
9 March   Budget: little change. Road, petrol and tobacco taxes up.
19 March   Unauthorized Argentine landing on South Georgia.

25 March   Roy Jenkins gains Hillhead (Glasgow) for SDP in by-election.

2 April   Argentines take Port Stanley.

3 April   First Saturday sitting of Commons since Suez.

5 April   Foreign Office ministers resign: Pym replaces Carrington as Foreign Secretary. Task force sails.

25 April   South Georgia recaptured.

2 May   The *General Belgrano* sunk: Argentine Navy withdraws from war.

20 May   UN peace efforts abandoned.

21 May   UK forces land at San Carlos.

28 May   Goose Green taken.

3 June   Conservatives win Merton from Labour in by-election.

14 June   Cease-fire.

24 June   Labour holds Coatbridge with reduced majority.

2 July   Roy Jenkins elected SDP leader, defeating Owen.

15 July   Rail strike defeated.

18 October   *The Church and the Bomb* published.

2 November   Miners vote 61 per cent against striking.

14 December   National Health Service unions vote to end 33-week dispute.

1983

5 January   Serpell Report on British Rail. Inflation 5.4 per cent, lowest for 13 years.

6 January   Michael Heseltine replaced John Nott at Defence; Tom King becomes Environment Secretary.

8–12 January   Thatcher visits Falklands.

18 January   Franks Committee clears government of negligence on Falklands.

24 February   Bermondsey by-election: Liberals gain safe Labour seat.

10 March   Miners vote against strike on pit closures.

15 March   Budget: drink, petrol, and tobacco up. No income tax cuts.

9 May   Election announced.

12 May   The Speaker, George Thomas, retires.

9 June   General election: Conservatives, 397 seats; Labour, 209; Alliance, 23. Conservatives have slightly reduced share of the vote. Labour has 28 per cent, Alliance 26 per cent.

11–15 June   Reshuffle: Pym replaced by Sir Geoffrey Howe at Foreign Office; Howe succeeded by Nigel Lawson at Exchequer; William Whitelaw created a hereditary peer and replaced by Leon Brittan at Home Office.

16 June   Central Policy Review Staff ('Think Tank') disbanded. Inflation 3.7 per cent, lowest for 15 years.

13 July   Commons rejects death penalty by 145 on free vote.

28 July   Penrith by-election: Conservative majority cut to 552 from 15,421 by Alliance.

September   Unemployment falls for first time since 1979.

2 October   Neil Kinnock and Roy Hattersley elected as Labour leader and deputy.

3 October   Griffiths Report on NHS recommends appointment of 'general managers'.

7 October   Publication of White Paper proposing abolition of Greater London Council and metropolitan councils.

14 October   Cecil Parkinson resigns; John Selwyn Gummer new Conservative chairman.

25 October   US 'liberation' of Grenada condemned by Thatcher.

11 November   First missiles arrive at Greenham Common.

8 December   30,000 women demonstrate at Greenham. According to polls, Tories do better among men than among women, for the first time.

1984

25 January   Staff at GCHQ (intelligence headquarters) Cheltenham deprived of union membership.

2–4 February   Thatcher in Budapest.

5 March   Miners' strike starts.

13 March   Lawson's first Budget: tax reforms well received.

17 April   Libyans open fire in London, killing Policewoman Yvonne Fletcher.

3 May   Local elections: Conservatives lose Birmingham.

14 June   SDP wins Portsmouth South from Conservatives in by-election.

15 June   Scargill detained in hospital after clashes at Orgreave.

18 August   Clive Ponting, a senior official at the Ministry of Defence, charged with leaking *Belgrano* documents.

10 September   Reshuffle: Douglas Hurd to Northern Ireland office; Lord Young Minister without Portfolio; Lord Gowrie replaces Lord Cockfield at Duchy of Lancaster.

28 September   Pit deputies threaten strike.

12 October   IRA bomb at Grand Hotel, Brighton, kills 4, but just misses Prime Minister. Norman Tebbit seriously injured.

24 October   NACODS (pit deputies' union) calls off strike threat.

25 October   NUM assets sequestrated.

3–7 November   Foreign Office minister Macolm Rifkind makes first ministerial visit to Poland since emergency began there in 1981.

6 November   New session of Parliament opens, dominated by local-government issues.

28 November   British Telecom share issue oversubscribed.

3 December   Tory revolt stops Sir Keith Joseph's plan to make rich parents pay more towards student grants.

4 December   Bill to abolish GLC and 6 metropolitan authorities passed.

11 December   Rate-capping of 13 councils announced.

19 December   Sino-British joint declaration on Hong Kong.

15–21 December   Mikhail Gorbachev, Soviet heir-apparent, visits Britain.

1985

30 January   Larry Whitty becomes Labour's new general secretary.

8 February   Howe visits Romania and Bulgaria.

5 March   NUM delegate conference votes 98–91 for return to work. Teachers' strikes begin.

19 March Lawson's second Budget: a disappointment.

2 May County council elections: big swing to Alliance.

3 June Fowler's Green Paper on social-security reform: an exercise in damage limitation.

4 July Liberals win Brecon and Radnor from Conservatives, with a 559 majority over Labour.

16 July Abolition of GLC and metropolitan authorities receives royal assent.

29 July Outcry over high pay rises for senior public servants; Tory MPs revolt.

2–11 September Prime Minister announces 'probably last major reshuffle before the election'. Patrick Jenkin and Peter Rees return to the backbenches. Lord Gowrie resigns to pursue a career outside government. Tebbit becomes party chairman, with the novelist Jeffrey Archer as his assistant; Leon Brittan replaces him at Trade and Industry; Kenneth Baker replaces Jenkin at Environment; Douglas Hurd replaces Brittan at Home Office; Tom King replaces Hurd at Northern Ireland Office; Lord Young and Kenneth Clarke, both in Cabinet, replace King at Employment; John MacGregor replaces Rees as chief secretary to the Treasury.

9–10 September Riots in Handsworth, Birmingham: 400 youths attack police; 2 Asians killed.

28–9 September Riot in Brixton: 220 arrests. Disturbances in Toxteth.

6 October Tottenham riots: policeman murdered. Bernie Grant (Labour leader of Haringey council) achieves prominence.

11 October Peter Walker describes government as appearing 'remote, perhaps uncaring'.

16–22 October Nassau Agreement of Commonwealth leaders on steps to end apartheid described by Thatcher as 'tiny little measures'.

18 October Notts miners vote to set up breakaway union.

15–29 November Anglo-Irish agreement signed at Hillsborough giving Dublin a role in Northern Ireland; Unionist unrest reaches unprecedented levels in next year.

19–20 November Geneva summit between Reagan and Gorbachev.

13 December Westland helicopters controversy erupts; made test of strength by Heseltine (Defence Secretary).

1986

9 January First ministerial changes of year. Heseltine resigns abruptly, George Younger taking his place. Rifkind replaces Younger as Scottish Secretary.

20 January Thatcher and Mitterrand announce decision to build Channel rail tunnel.

24–5 January Second ministerial change: Leon Brittan resigns, being replaced at Trade and Industry by his deputy Paul Channon.

26–7 January Print workers' dispute at News International (Wapping) begins.

February Unemployment 3,407,729.

3 February Government considers, then abandons, sale of Land Rover and BL Trucks to US bidders.

9 February John Biffen says Toryism 'not a raucous political faction'.

18 March   Lawson's 3rd Budget: standard-rate income tax down from 30 to 29 per cent; cigarettes and petrol up, but not drink.

10 April   Fulham by-election; Labour wins traditional Labour seat by 3503 over Conservatives with Alliance doing badly.

14 April   Shops Bill (Sunday trading) defeated despite 3-line whip: seen by many as a 'mercy killing'.

15 April   US bombs Libya, using UK bases.

26 April   Chernobyl nuclear disaster in Ukraine.

4 May   Biffen calls for Tories to fight on 'balanced ticket'.

8 May   Conservatives lose Ryedale (majority 12,000) to Alliance (Liberals) and hold West Derbyshire (majority 15000) by 100.

21 May   Sir Keith Joseph resigns as Education Secretary; replaced by Kenneth Baker. Nicholas Ridley (Transport) replaces Baker at Environment; John Moore joins Cabinet as Transport Minister.

June   Alliance rift on defence; Alliance falls well back in polls.

July   South Africa dominates media, but not public, attention.

17 July   Labour holds Newcastle-under-Lyme by only 799, with Liberals second.

24 July   Commonwealth Games widely boycotted. Thatcher takes strong line against sanctions.

August   Unemployment figures upwards for the eighth consecutive month.

3 August   Thatcher in hospital for hand operation.

September   Minor ministerial reshuffle without cabinet changes.

24 September   Liberal conference rejects David Steel's defence policy.

26 September   Alliance loses credibility and defence issue becomes prominent.

6 October   Conservative conference marked by a restoration of confidence and a sense that the party had put past quarrels behind it.

10 October   Trustee Savings Bank sold to public. Jeffrey Archer, Conservative deputy chairman, resigned following claims by *News of the World*.

29 October   Labour conference a success for Kinnock's designer socialism.

3 November   Cabinet committee on Aids set up under Lord Whitelaw.

5 November   Australian spy case begins; government looks foolish.

6 November   Nigel Lawson announces £5 billion rise in public spending.

12 November   The Queen's Speech announces a light legislative programme.

2 December   British Gas successfully privatised. General signs of economic recovery. Conservatives take the lead for the first time since Westland.

1987

January   Stock market boom. City scandals deepen, continuing through spring.

5 February   End of Wapping dispute.

26 February   Greenwich by-election; SDP easily win seat held by Labour since 1945.

18 March   Budget: income tax down from 29 per cent to 27 per cent.

April   Conservatives consistently lead in the polls. Unemployment figures fall for eighth consecutive month.

1 April   Prime Minister returns from successful Russian trip. Capital punishment rejected on free vote.

7 May   Local elections show Labour weakness, Conservative strength in key regions like West Midlands, and unspectacular Alliance gains.

11 May   Election announced.

14 May   Unemployment figures show drop to almost 3 million.

15 May   Party leaders open campaign with major speeches.

18 May   Dissolution of parliament.

19 May   An unusually short Labour manifesto and an unusually detailed Conservative manifesto published.

28 May   Good trade figures published. Conservatives maintain steady lead in polls, with Alliance vote falling back to a poor third at about 20 per cent. Stock market around record levels.

9 June   Fourth anniversary of 1983 election.

11 June   Polling day.

12 June   A MORI poll showed 80 per cent of Alliance voters and 65 per cent of all voters wanting a merger of the Liberals and SDP under one leader. 52 per cent of voters said that Mrs Thatcher should lead her party into the next election, against 41 per cent who thought that she should resign before then. Among Conservatives, 81 per cent wanted her to fight a fourth election. One in six Labour voters, and nearly half of Alliance voters, said she should remain as Prime Minister for another full term.

General election results: Conservatives 375; Labour 229; Alliance 22 (Liberals 17, SDP 5); others 24 (including Speaker). Majority over all other parties, after allowing for the Speaker, 101, down from 137 at the dissolution: the second largest majority since the war. Votes cast: Conservatives 13,763,134; Labour 10,033,633; Alliance 7,339,912. Share of votes cast: Conservatives 42.30 (from 42.42 in 1983), Labour 30.83 (27.51), Alliance 22.55 (25.36). Average swings: 1.78 per cent Conservative to Labour; 3.13 per cent Alliance to Labour; 1.35 per cent Alliance to Conservative.

Conservatives gain 12 seats against the national trend (6 from Labour, 6 from Alliance), the largest number since the 1920s, but had no MPs in Manchester, Liverpool, Glasgow, Bradford, Leicester, and Newcastle. South of the Humber-Mersey line, Labour won less than a quarter of votes cast, and gained only one seat in the south, one in East Anglia, and none in the South-West. Labour's share of the vote was its second worst since 1931; its MPs were the second lowest since 1935. According to Gallup, Labour took only 3 in 7 votes cast by trade unionists and their families.

In Scotland, Labour won 50 seats (from 41), Conservatives 10 (21). Share of Scottish votes cast: Labour 42.4 (35), Conservatives 24 (28).

Roy Jenkins and Enoch Powell were defeated.

13 June   Cabinet reshuffle. Hailsham, Biffen, Jopling, and Tebbitt leave the cabinet, the last remaining as party chairman. Sir M. Havers became Lord Chancellor; John Wakeham (previously Chief Whip) became Lord Privy Seal; John MacGregor went to Agriculture; Cecil Parkinson to Energy; Paul Channon to Transport; Peter Walker to Wales (from Energy); Lord Young and Kenneth Clarke both move from Employment to Trade and Industry; John Moore to DHSS; John Major to be Chief Secretary to the Treasury (in cabinet); Norman Fowler to Employment.

18 June   For the first time since June 1983, official unemployment figures fall below 3 million. Both the monthly and the 12-monthly falls were the largest since 1948. Vacancies reach their highest level since 1980.

Note: the days of the month have been supplied by David Lawrence.

Bibliography

First, biographies. Russell Lewis, *Margaret Thatcher: a personal and political biography* (Routledge and Kegan Paul, 1975; rev. edn, 1980), is popular in manner but well-informed. George Gardiner's *Margaret Thatcher: from childhood to leadership* (Kimber, 1975) is the work of a leading backbench supporter. Tricia Murray's biography *Margaret Thatcher* (1978) is strong on human interest.

Patrick Cosgrave, a special adviser to the leader in the 1970s, has written three partially overlapping books. *Margaret Thatcher: a Tory and her party* (Hutchinson, 1978) centres on the leadership contest. A somewhat revised version appeared as *Margaret Thatcher: Prime Minister* (Bodley Head, 1979) and a general interpretation in *Thatcher: the first term* (Bodley Head, 1985). Up to about 1981, his inside knowledge is of great value.

Penny Junor's *Margaret Thatcher: wife, mother, politician* (Sidgwick and Jackson, 1983) is perhaps the richest account in terms of human interest. Nicholas Wapshott and George Brock's *Thatcher* (Futura, 1983) is a more political narrative by two *Times* journalists. Not a biography, but of much personal interest, is *The Thatcher Phenomenon* by Hugo Young and Anne Sloman (BBC, 1986).

Secondly, government. *The Thatcher Government* (Basil Blackwell, 1983; rev. edn, 1985) by Peter Riddell, political editor of the *Financial Times*, covers the issues. A collection of essays by many hands, edited by David S. Bell, *The Conservative Government 1979–84: an interim report* (Croom Helm, 1985) also covers the policy spectrum. In a more narrative form, Jock Bruce-Gardyne's *Mrs Thatcher's First Administration* (Macmillan, 1984) is a survey of a single parliament from the standpoint of a Treasury minister. His *Ministers and Mandarins* (Sidgwick and Jackson, 1986) is also relevant.

Ministerial memoirs are confined to James Prior on himself, *A Balance of Power* (Hamish Hamilton, 1986), and Patrick Cosgrave on Lord Carrington, *Carrington: a life and a policy* (Dent, 1985). Hugh Stephenson: *Mrs Thatcher's First Year* (Jill Norman, 1980) and Carol Thatcher's *Diary of an Election* (Sidgwick and Jackson, 1983) can be recommended. Finally, Alan Walters's *Britain's Economic Renaissance: Margaret Thatcher's reforms 1979–84* (Oxford University Press, 1986) tells of the economic history of the Thatcher ministry from the inside.

10
British Politics, 1945–1987
Four Perspectives

Tony Benn

The administrations which have governed Britain in modern times may perhaps best be classified not by reference to the traditional electoral cycle, but by identifying four different periods of consensus, which have followed one after another. The first, the 'pre-war consensus', underpinned the National government and lasted from 1931 to 1940; the second, the 'war-time consensus', ran from 1940 to 1945 when the coalition was in power; the third, the 'welfare capitalist consensus', lasted from 1945 until 1976; and the fourth, the 'monetarist consensus', which began when the Labour Cabinet accepted the IMF terms, has lasted from then until the present day. To lump governments from different parties into the same categories may seem strange, but, looking back on all the various policies that have been followed by successive administrations, it is the similarity between them, quite as much as the differences, which now seem to be so strikingly obvious.

The 'pre-war consensus', marked by unemployment and appeasement, ended with the formation of the coalition in May 1940, brought both Churchill and Attlee together, each of whom had been in direct opposition to the National government throughout the thirties, and the mix of ideas that resulted was a most interesting one. Churchill had been a radical minister in the great reforming 1906 Liberal government and he called back his old colleague Sir William Beveridge, who had worked with him then at the Board of Trade, and they found it relatively easy to operate the 'wartime consensus', designed to plan the economy for victory and provide for the basic needs of the people. All of this fitted in with the moderate Fabian ideas which were brought into government by Attlee, Dalton and Morrison, and with the few Liberal ministers.

Thus, while the Labour landslide of 1945 marked a turning point in British politics, in the sense that it was the first occasion when Labour won an overall majority, it is also true that a great number of the policies it followed had already been agreed in outline during the war years, and this 'welfare capitalist consensus' built around a mild Keynesianism bore more resemblance to Roosevelt's New Deal than to socialism. The boom which followed the war was strong enough to put industry on its feet again, to end unemployment, to pay for the welfare state, and, above all, to strengthen the trade union movement, which could use the bargaining power that full employment confers on labour to wrest concessions from capital. Labour's New Deal found wide support amongst the politicians, and the electorate, in the years that followed, although the breadth of that support was often concealed beneath the sharp personal exchanges between the parties, especially at election times.

But the Civil Service mandarins, brought up in the same wartime tradition, together with the Establishment generally, knew, and accepted, what was going on; the business community felt reasonably safe so long as there was a broad continuity of policy on which they could rely; and the Labour voters recognized the improvements which they enjoyed, as compared to the prewar years.

Labour policy could then, in one sense, be interpreted as a plan to save capitalism, by incorporating the trade union leadership within the governing group, in return for measures that were important to their union members. Having inherited the experience, and mechanisms, of wartime planning made this task a relatively easy one, but it all rested upon the continuation of the postwar boom itself, which provided a market for goods for reconstruction, here and worldwide, at a time when our major industrial competitors – Germany, Japan and Italy – had been virtually destroyed. Thus the huge task of conversion from military to civil production was made possible, and unemployment virtually disappeared, although physical shortages were still experienced.

The postwar Labour government was also realistic enough to concede independence to many of its old imperial territories, thus avoiding the long-drawn-out wars of national liberation that would otherwise have followed, and have been lost, and most intelligent Conservatives knew that there was no alternative to these judicious withdrawals in the face of the inevitable. In the field of foreign and defence policy most of the concessions were made by Labour to the Conservative view of the world. Ernest Bevin, as Foreign Secretary, whose suspicion and dislike of the USSR matched that of Churchill himself, offered one example, and

Attlee another, since he decided, around the time of the Berlin airlift, to build a British atom bomb, and invite the United States to establish bases here, in both cases without telling the full story to his Cabinet, Parliament or the people, thus laying the foundations for a policy that Churchill accepted, welcomed and extended when he returned to power in 1951. Indeed, after 1951, when Labour was defeated, neither Winston Churchill nor Anthony Eden made any serious attempt to return to prewar Tory economic policies, and Harold Macmillan, the veritable 'wet' grandfather of welfare capitalism, lived to become the beneficiary of the very ideas he had advocated as a Tory rebel twenty years earlier in his book '*The Middle Way*', and under which, as he told us, Britain 'had never had it so good'.

With this manifesto Macmillan won a landslide victory against Hugh Gaitskell in 1959 and the Labour leadership then began a long, and highly publicized, revisionist retreat from socialism, in which Harold Wilson, James Callaghan and Michael Foot all played their parts, more discreetly, in their turn. But under these shifts at the top of politics other factors were at work in industry and the economy, which were actually undermining the foundations of our postwar prosperity, and were destined to change British politics more fundamentally. British capitalism, denied its traditional imperial markets, and reluctant to invest in the necessary re-equipment, began to fall behind in the race for markets, and became victim of a series of balance-of-payments crises, which were dealt with, by parties of both colour, by means of 'stop and go', a form of macro-economic masochism that undermined both business confidence and the power of labour. Both Wilson, after ditching the National Plan in 1966, and Heath, after his U-turn in 1972, tried to counter this decline by policies designed to tempt, or bribe, industrialists to invest, coupled with solemn warnings to the trade unions not to use their bargaining strength to raise wages, backed by anti-union legislation.

British membership of the Common Market was then presented as the route to recovery and growth within a wider European framework, in which we were all assured, capitalism could be revived; but, when the OPEC oil crisis occurred in 1973, all the underlying weaknesses of our economic system were exposed.

It became clear that the economic base on which the 'welfare consensus' depended had finally collapsed, actually ending half-way through Labour's term of office, when the IMF demanded, and received, assurances that public expenditure would be cut, supposedly to restore business confidence. At the end of its twenty-one-year life span, it was clear that the 'welfare consensus' had neither revitalized British industry nor had retained public support with the electorate, which successively defeated Wilson, Heath and Callaghan, who had all tried to make it work, thus paving the way for the election of a very different kind of Conservative government.

The 'monetarist consensus' was, however, born three years before Mrs Thatcher came to power, though its seeds had been planted earlier than that, since the Tories, nursing their defeats in 1974, had resolved to elect a leader who would return to the old orthodoxy and settle their own score with the unions. Meanwhile the Labour Party at the grass roots, after its defeat in 1979, resolved to fight more vigorously for its own people, and insist upon more socialist policies and a more account-able leadership. The years from 1979 to 1983 saw the full flowering of these movements back to class politics, and then, in each party, counter-vailing forces began to emerge. The 'wets' in the Tory Party, who did not question the basic tenets of monetarism, but feared for the electoral consequences if it was applied too harshly, came together slowly and hesitantly, partly because of the power of the Prime Minister, and partly because the Falklands War gave a huge boost to the flagging popularity of the government in 1982. For Labour the counter-revolution of the Right was more traumatic when 10 per cent of the Parliamentary Labour Party actually left and formed a new party, the SDP, which, along with the wets and the Labour right, especially after its 1983 defeat, seemed to be agreed that politics should be steered back towards safer arguments about who was best able to administer the economic system that monetarist policies had created.

In the light of this it can be argued that the history of the last forty years has been the story of one long attempt, by all parties, to save British capitalism, by the use of different policies each of which carried at the time a wide measure of public support. Of course the 'monetarist consensus' has been much the harshest, but when it emerged the crisis of British capitalism had become much more serious, and, if it was to survive, such measures were necessary – though it should be noted in passing that at no stage did the Parliamentary Labour Party ever seek to blame the crisis upon the nature of the system, always preferring to focus its attacks upon the record of ministers.

The unions had already been weakened by rising unemployment, by incomes policies, and more recently by crippling legislation, and the Labour leadership itself had long since abandoned any serious socialist critique of the economic system as such, and had fallen back on its claim to be able to run it better. Capital, by contrast, had by 1976 recovered its self-confidence, had developed much stronger international links, and now had a government ready to use the full apparatus of the state to enforce its interests against any group, whether in the unions or Labour local authorities, which tried to resist the policies that were being applied. Though it would be wrong to describe these policies as ever having won a positive and enthusiastic consensus of support, there was, in the absence of any clear socialist alternative, a broad spectrum of opinion that the surgery being applied was inescapable. In that sense the acceptance that for capital to survive it had to recover the ground it has lost to labour in the postwar years became widespread, and an anti-socialist, anti-union and anti-democratic alliance was created, in the formation of which many Labour leaders, some of whom joined the SDP, played a key role, especially in their denunciation of those who engaged in extra-parliamentary struggles or advocated radical policies.

The polarization and confrontations that these class policies produced, were certainly reflected in the thinking of the wider Labour movement, but they were not articulated in the presentation of the case in the House of Commons, where an informal consensus began to develop in which the Tory wets, the SDP–Liberal Alliance and the Labour right were content to limit the argument to the question of which of them was best qualified to administer an unchanged economic system. It is certainly true that many people in the Conservative Party and the Alliance, and some inside the Labour Party, backed by the majority of the Establishment and political commentators, now believe that it may be possible to reconstruct our political system on the old Victorian, or modern American, principle that Whigs and Tories, Democrats and Republicans will for ever play the game of ins-and-outs, within the broad framework of the policies and institutions evolved during the 'monetarist consensus' which any successor will inherit from the Thatcher administration. In that sense, despite all that has been said about the destruction of the consensus by Mrs Thatcher, there still is a wide measure of agreement among parliamentarians as to how the political future might be shaped.

But, despite the renewed evidence of the traditional huddling together at the top, the economic prospects as oil revenues and the privatization windfall profits run down are poor, and the price that has been paid by millions of people in unemployment has created a much stronger resistance to the government of the day than we have seen since the 1930s.

So far the strength of this feeling has been mainly articulated outside Parliament, and if it forces its way upwards then we are heading for a very different sort of politics. Politicians, of all parties, who are now seeking to retain or gain office in a basically unchanged system, may find that the next real radical challenge comes from outside the formal system: there are forces which will seek to be heard and will make demands and back them up with organizational strength. That should neither surprise nor alarm socialists, for looking back over the years since the war it is arguable that our problems today really derive from the failure of consensus and the failure to give the country the chance to face up to the need for the basic reforms that are necessary in its industrial, economic and political structures if social justice is ever to be achieved. Indeed our whole history shows that every period of change has been heralded by some pressure from underneath or outside the House of Commons, Whitehall or the City of London.

Those who believe that the power of labour has been finally eroded by changes in the make-up of the working class may be ignoring the emergence of new and significant social forces, each experiencing oppression of some kind and all with strong demands to make; and the residual feudalism which still hangs like a cloud over British society, together with its modern technocratic counterpart, virtually guarantees that class will remain on the agenda, even though it may take many forms. Those who want Britain to be governed by a consensus, and believe it can be, might also reflect upon the massive apparatus of state repression which has had to be assembled and used to protect the 'monetarist consensus' from the many challenges to it which have emerged.

Looking ahead to the next period in our political history, there are already signs that those challenges will be spearheaded by fresh democratic assaults upon unaccountable power, a reassertion of morality in public affairs, and a new internationalism to replace the present integration of Britain into the American imperial system, and the bureaucratic embrace of ambitious Common Market federalists. If anything like that were to happen then the present 'monetarist consensus' would lose its appeal, and democratic politics would move on to offer a clearer choice about more basic issues, including the issue of socialism, which all the postwar administrations, in their own way, and for their own reasons, have chosen to avoid, and greatly hoped would never surface, as an option which the electors could choose.

For the most important consensus of all in Britain is based upon the principle that parliamentary debates and election choices must never stray far beyond an argument, however fierce, as to which party is best able to administer the economic and political system which we have in this country. Any political leader, or group, on the left who has the effrontery to argue, and mean it, that an election might actually be used to advance socialism or democracy is immediately put beyond the pale, and an Establishment veto is placed upon that person or that group. Those who act as guardians of the outer limits of so-called legitimate debate include the City, the Whitehall mandarins, the Chiefs of Staff, the security agencies and, above all, the mass media, whose co-operation, however limited, is necessary for traditional electioneering. These domestic centres of Establishment power have strong allies in the IMF, the EEC, NATO and the multinationals, all of whom have enormous influence in shaping British policy through direct and indirect means. No Conservative government need ever fear falling foul of these external forces, since it would be unlikely to want to do anything that would anger them. But that is not true of the Labour Party and the Labour movement, which have, consistently, demanded policies which would bring them right up against both the national and international establishments. Successive parliamentary Labour leaders, and Labour ministers have understood precisely how far they would be allowed to go in radical talk without incurring the wrath of those who wield real power.

Of course, some Labour leaders have in the past actually shared the views of the Establishment, and they have justified their policies to the Labour Party by using the all-too-familiar language of 'facing the harsh realities of office', and being ready to 'take responsibility'. So far, every Labour Prime Minister has had to reach an unwritten and unspoken understanding with certain key people in order to have had any prospect of becoming acceptable and being treated as legitimate.

These understandings cover a wide range of subjects, on each of which there have been bipartisan arrangements of one kind or another for many years, and at least since the war. For example, to have any chance of even the minimum of fair media coverage every Labour Prime Minister has had to assure, or reassure, the proprietors that no Labour government would ever touch their personal power over the newspapers that they own and control, and in return they are guaranteed support against the rank and file of their party. Similar assurances have been sought, and from time to time given, to permanent secretaries, military and security chiefs, to the City, and to Brussels and Washington that

Labour would confine itself to the administration of the *status quo*, in return for counter-assurances that there would be no serious attempt at destabilization.

This is the real political consensus that underpins what we call parliamentary democracy in Britain: absolute freedom to put up alternative candidates to run the system, if, but only if, accompanied by secret assurances that the essential nature of that system will not be challenged or altered. This is how the British constitution really works, and understanding the way it works, to maintain a continuing consensus for the *status quo*, may help to explain why democracy and socialism have been successfully kept off the political agenda, under governments of all persuasions, since 1945. Yet, despite all that, the pressure for more democracy and for the ideas of socialism are strongly felt, and widely shared. But, like early trade unionists, the Chartists and the suffragettes, they will only secure their objectives by organized strength and by pressing them onto reluctant parliamentarians and a frightened Establishment, who will only concede when they realize that they can no longer hold the line. It has often happened before.

Michael Fraser

For most of the period under review I have been close to what Iain Macleod used to call 'the centre of the Conservative web'. Without ever serving on their immediate staff, or being a member of the House of Commons, I have done personal work for five Conservative Prime Ministers and leaders of the party, from Churchill to Heath, and for twelve successive Conservative Party chairmen. So, in a sense, I have been a continuity man in Conservative politics for much of the period covered by this book. Though I have never been other than a Conservative and sit on the Conservative benches in the House of Lords, I have held no official position in the Conservative Party for the past eleven years and the opinions I express here are entirely personal.

Political and historical centuries seem rarely to fit the calendar centuries exactly. For me, the eighteenth century lasted in Britain till 1832, the year of the passing of the first Reform Bill, and the nineteenth century continued till 1918, the end of the First World War. That was indeed a watershed both at home and abroad.

The period from 1918 to the present day then divides naturally into two sections, 1918–45 and 1945–87. In the first period the Conservative

Party really had things relatively easy in electoral terms, because the Left was split. The Liberal Party was declining. The Labour Party was taking its place. It is not surprising, therefore, that the Conservative Party was either itself the government or the majority party in coalition or national governments for all but three of those twenty-seven years. It is not surprising either that, in the then-prevailing climate, some members of the Conservative Party began to think of themselves as the 'natural party of government'. To them, and to many others in Britain, the Labour Party's landslide victory in the general election of July 1945 came as a traumatic shock.

In 1945, the spectre of Britain becoming a full-blown socialist state loomed with some reality for the first time. The Labour Party, committed then as it still is in its written constitution to 'the common ownership of the means of production, distribution and exchange', was in power with an overall majority of 147.

In the hubris of the moment, Labour really thought it was in for many years: certainly a decade, perhaps even a generation. For the party it was the culmination of half a century of effort, two minority governments and several severe reverses. Cries of 'We are masters at the moment and not only at the moment but for a very long time to come' and the like, and scenes of unparalleled euphoria, seem strange in retrospect, but did not appear so silly or unrealistic then. Even if the possibility of a full socialist state on the Soviet satellite model was still some way off, there was at least then a distinct possibility that, as happened to a number of conservative parties overseas, the Conservative Party might become a permanent or semi-permanent minority party in Britain.

At the time, indeed, those of us who decided to enter politics and work for the Conservative Party in one way or another on coming out of the armed forces after the war might well have felt, like the Irishman in the story, that if we were aiming at a Conservative Britain along the lines of our own thinking we 'would not start from here'. In fact, of course, though we were not to know it at the time, we were starting in that best of all possible positions, 'coming in at the bottom of the market'. If you lay a ruler across the Gallup poll, ironing out all the ups and downs on the way, you will find a rising Conservative trend from 1945 General Election to the end of 1960 – a long, gradual, upward-swinging fifteen years.

The forty-two years since July 1945 have turned out very different in practice from anything that the triumphant Labour Party of 1945 anticipated. They have been the years when the rising tide of socialism was first contained and then substantially reversed. Not only does Britain have, in 1987, a Conservative government with a large overall majority, but, of the last forty-two years, twenty-five have been with Conservative governments and only seventeen with Labour governments.

While Labour has won five further general elections since its victory in 1945, it has since the 1945–50 Parliament had only one further period – 1966–70 – with an overall majority for the normal duration of a Parliament. The Conservatives, on the other hand, who have won six general elections since the 1945 defeat, have had workable overall majorities for the whole of their twenty-five years in power. Since politics is about power, as without power you can do nothing other than talk, the party has been relatively successful in denying power to Labour to apply its policies, to some of which, notably socialism, Conservatives have always been opposed. The Conservative party has also had more time to give its own policies practical effect.

In a fundamental sense, there must always be a good deal of common ground between the main parties alternating in government in a free society. When in power, after all, they are governing the same country, with the same history, people, problems and elbow-room, or lack of it, within the same world. Because the two main parties coming out of the coalition government in 1945 had already hammered out, not without some hard bargaining and horse-trading, the broad policies for dealing after the war with those social problems that had been identified and prepared for during the war on the basis of the Beveridge Report, the Employment Policy White Paper and the Butler Education Act of 1944, there was for a time an unusual degree of apparent unity of aim. To say, however, that the situation after 1945 amounted to a 'consensus' is a myth of more recent origin. No one thought that at the time. The real position was like that of two trains, starting off from parallel platforms at some great London terminus and running for a time on broadly parallel lines but always heading for very different destinations.

The Attlee government took office on a wave of great popular goodwill. The British people wanted a change after the war. One section looked for a return to what they had previously regarded as normality. A larger section looked for the New Jerusalem. Neither got quite what they expected. The Attlee government had a number of other advantages at the outset, all the more powerful because they were not then fully realized. It had a number of experienced and well-known ministers. Although it inherited severe postwar problems, people were well aware of that and in the early years continued their support and gave the government the benefit of the doubt. More important politically, neither Labour nor its distinctive policy of socialism had been tried in Britain seriously before. Labour had the great advantage of no history in power. Finally, though this turned out to be an elephant trap, it had still at its disposal, to help its socialist and collectivist policies, the whole paraphernalia of wartime centralization, restriction, rationing and control.

The British people gradually began to suspect after a year or two that Labour was quite happy with the prolongation of this situation, which suited its ideological purposes, and that it had no real 'feel for freedom'. The electorate then became increasingly critical as the rest of Europe, friends and former foes alike, began showing more evident signs of recovery, greater individual freedom and rising living standards.

It was this, and the emergence of R. A. Butler from a long ministerial apprenticeship to be the man primarily responsible for initiating and co-ordinating the new postwar Conservative policies, that began the containment of socialism and later its eventual reversal in changed economic and social conditions. It was Butler's persuasion of the postwar Conservative Party to move, at first reluctantly but soon with enthu-siasm, into the centre of postwar political thinking, together with Lord Woolton as party chairman building a modern mass party organization with much-improved internal and external communications, that destroyed the Labour Party's dream of staying in office for many years after its 1945 victory. It was this that got the Conservatives back into office, albeit with a small majority, in the election of 1951. Had the Conservative Party clung to its prewar attitudes, or even adopted then the policies that are now being applied with considerable success in a much changed climate today, Labour would have had at least a full second term and would quite probably have remained in power for even longer than that.

Given the speed with which the Labour government pressed ahead with nationalization in 1945–50 and the degree to which its more moderate ministers were already under pressure from the left by 1951 to accelerate the process, it does not require much imagination to estimate where Britain might have been in socialist terms had Labour continued in office with an overall majority after 1951 for a further full term or longer. Even Gaitskell had many new nationalization proposals in his policy statements between 1955 and 1959. Though he made a brave attempt to get Clause IV dropped from the Labour Party constitution at the party conference in 1960 after the 1959 election defeat, he signally failed to do so and it is still there today, ready to hand to justify further socialist moves should the electoral situation ever make that possible.

Churchill's presence as Prime Minister from 1951 to 1955 gave that government great prestige, both at home and abroad, and remarkable stability considering the small majority, which many thought at first would prove unworkable. Churchill was the great tree under which younger men developed and applied their talents. One example was his appointment of Macleod as Minister of Health straight from the backbenches in 1952. Contrary to a myth that he was unfriendly to Butler, in fact Churchill gave Butler all the greatest opportunities of his career. He appointed him to Education early in the war. He made him chairman of the Conservative Research Department at the end of the war. He made him Chancellor of the Exchequer in 1951.

Though an arguable case can be made from the point of view of the conduct of business and the feelings of some close colleagues in favour of Churchill's retirement after his illness in 1953, in political terms I believe that his continued presence until 1955, the smooth change of leadership then, followed by an early general election, were ideal for electoral success.

The title of the Conservative Party manifesto for the 1955 general election was *United for Peace and Progress*, and every word had its point. 'United' because the Labour Party was already divided. 'Peace' because Eden had had a uniquely successful period of peace-making across the world in the Churchill government. 'Progress' because the country at that time was succeeding in combining full employment, low inflation, rising living standards and a rate of economic growth roughly equivalent to that of similar countries in Europe. Britain also then led the world in the development of nuclear energy for peaceful purposes. Wartime rationing and controls had gone, and the 300,000 new houses a year that had been promised were being built.

Not surprisingly, in these circumstances, the 1955 general election increased the Conservative overall majority from sixteen to fifty-nine. It was also notable electorally because the Conservatives won more seats than Labour in Scotland (36–34), and gained 49.8 per cent of the total vote, both achievements which have not been equalled since in spite of some larger majorities at Westminster.

The whole of the Eden period has, in retrospect, been so overshadowed by Suez as to lead to a considerable underestimation of Eden's achievements in foreign affairs and diplomacy, particularly in the

Churchill government of 1951–5, and his instinctive, almost Baldwinian feel for the genuine aspirations of the British people. It was, after all, Eden who took as his political slogan 'a nationwide property-owning democracy'. The phrase had originated between the wars, but Eden recognized and developed it as the core of his own views for the development of the domestic future in Britain. Though based on wider home ownership, he meant much more than that.

Good things as well as bad emerged from Suez. It swept away some of Britain's nostalgias. It proved that we were not in a position to maintain our 'far-flung Empire', of which we were rightly proud but which would have been a great deal handier, as the modern world regrouped into more convenient economic and political spheres of influence, had we been able originally to 'fling' it a bit nearer.

Macmillan's achievement between 1957 and 1959, with the help of Butler, his defeated rival for the leadership, was amazingly quick and effective damage limitation after Suez. At the same time, Macmillan rapidly succeeded in gaining authority over and winning the respect in turn of his government, Parliament and Whitehall, the Conservative Party in the country and the electorate at large. He also showed an unusual ability to keep his key colleagues thinking politically and to harness separately under his personal control both official and party help in the process of future policy-making, never an easy task in office.

When Macmillan entered his own second term of office and the Conservatives' third with his victory in 1959 and another increased overall majority, there was a strong feeling of optimism in both government and people. The great majority of the British people did indeed feel then, and rightly, that they had 'never had it so good'. Macmillan seemed set to move from the successful containment of socialism to its progressive reversal. He was determined to make progress with detente between East and West and, having taken aboard the lessons of Suez, to reduce Britain's overseas commitments by continuing to turn Empire into Commonwealth. By entry into the EEC, as soon as acceptable terms could be negotiated, he aimed to make Britain less vulnerable both politically and economically, and British industry more efficient and more competitive worldwide.

At this point, however, on both sides of the political divide, events took a powerful hand and, as Bismarck rightly said, they are 'stronger than the plans of men'. The sixties, though no doubt nostalgic for some as the era of the Beatles and other social and artistic phenomena, look in retrospect something of a slow-handclap decade politically when few runs were scored by either side. Britain gradually fell behind other developed countries in adapting its economy to changing world conditions and was beset with inflation, periodic economic crises, increasingly militant trade unions, excessive wage settlements and bad industrial relations, particularly in the nationalized industries.

Meanwhile, Labour reaffirmed Clause IV and its continuing adherence to socialism in 1960. Gaitskell died in January 1963 and was succeeded by Wilson. A clever tactician rather than a strategist, Wilson then spent an undue amount of time and energy in both opposition and government keeping his deeply divided Labour party in one piece, a condition that did not very long outlive his own retirement.

Though the collapse of the Paris Summit was an early setback for Macmillan's plans for detente, he could feel reasonably well satisfied by his support for Kennedy in his handling of the potentially very dangerous Cuban missile crisis and his own success with the test-ban treaty. Seen in perspective, the move from Empire to Commonwealth in this period was also a success, achieved with minimal bloodshed and considerable residual goodwill.

Very little else went right, however, from the summer of 1961. The most serious blows were the de Gaulle veto on Britain's entry to the EEC in 1963, which unbalanced Macmillan's forward policies, both political and economic, and the much-publicized leadership battle at the Conservative Party conference at Blackpool that year. Had that Blackpool episode been avoided, as it could easily have been, the 1964 general election, which was lost by only five seats after thirteen years in office, would, I believe, have been won, with possible political consequences then that have given rise to much interesting speculation ever since and particularly in Robert Blake's book *The Conservative Party from Peel to Thatcher*.

Home had all the appropriate qualities to limit the damage that had been done, and reunited the Conservative Party during 1964 with remarkable success. When the election came in October of that year, however, there had been insufficient time and he had not enough immediate appeal to the uncommitted to prevent a rise in the Liberal vote letting Labour and Wilson in by a whisker.

With the election of Heath as leader of the Conservative Party in July 1965, a new start was made on the reversal of socialism and, despite many differences of style, presentation and method, the Heath–Thatcher period, now covering more than twenty years, needs to be considered as a whole.

Heath, an energetic leader and a strategist, with a clear idea of what he wanted to do and impatient for action in the drift of the mid-sixties, prepared in the opposition years 1965–70 and in much more detail than any of his predecessors a formidable policy for change and modernization. Knowing that he could not hope to win the 1966 election so soon after the narrow Wilson victory – the British electorate would not think that Wilson had had a 'fair chance' – Heath contrived to fight a very successful personal campaign. It impressed the media, made him much better known and enabled him to 'lose in the right posture for next time', by forecasting very accurately the economic chickens that came home to roost with the Wilson government between 1966 and 1970.

Heath's 1970 general election victory, though a severe shock to Wilson and Labour and a surprise to many others, was foreseen with confidence by him and by some others in the Conservative organization. It remains remarkable in our period as the only occasion when a large overall majority for one party has been decisively turned into an overall majority for another in one general election campaign.

One event will be remembered above all in history from the Heath government of 1970–4, when other excitements of the time – incomes policies, 'lame ducks', 'U-turns' and even the quadrupling of the oil price by OPEC – have been forgotten. The entry of Britain 'late but earnestly' into the EEC in January 1973 stands out as the most important development for Britain, both politically and economically, since the formation of NATO after the war. It was a campaign in which Heath had been personally involved for over ten years since the early Macmillan days. It was, moreover, a campaign on two fronts, in the negotiations abroad and in the party battle at home. It was fiercely opposed throughout by most of the Labour Party, who saw entry into a 'rich man's club' as an obstacle to socialism, and by some Liberals and Conservatives on more traditional, though sometimes curious, grounds.

The other development of long-term political and economic significance at this time was the early introduction and passage of Heath's Industrial Relations Bill, which inaugurated the sequence of trade union legislation which has progressed considerably further since. At the time the Labour Party and the trade unions fought both the passage of this legislation and its implementation hard and tenaciously. Heath was unlucky to have to fight his final union battle with the miners when already faced with the quadrupling of oil prices by OPEC in 1973. His defeat in the election of February 1974 was the closest result in recent British political history. Labour won by three seats but with no overall

majority and fewer votes than the Conservatives. Again, as in 1964, a rise
in the Liberal vote let Labour in. As Lord Carrington, who was then
chairman of the Conservative Party, characteristically said to me at that
tantalizing moment, 'What clobbered us, Michael, was the head under
the bedclothes vote.'

The unions then continued to overplay their hand in the 1978 'winter
of discontent' under the Callaghan government. When Callaghan was
forced by a defeat in the House of Commons to go to the country in
1979, Mrs Thatcher won an overall majority of forty-four and her first
opportunity as Prime Minister. Like Heath, she knew clearly what she
wanted to do and had a well-prepared programme for continuing to
stimulate change in the economy and accelerate the reversal of socialism. Unlike him, however, she had caught a changing tide in the world
economy and in attitudes both at home and abroad, and, though, as
always, with many bumps on the way and new problems rising phoenix-
like from the ashes of previous solutions, she has succeeded with great
determination in riding that tide ever since.

Looking back over the whole period 1945–87, the pursuit of socialism
by the Labour Party appears as the great time and opportunity waster
of the postwar years – the great red herring of modern British politics.
Indeed, socialism now appears to be the great red herring of the
developed world as a whole and there are quite marked stirrings even in
the major Communist regimes of the Soviet Union and China. It is
educative to consider where the British economy and standard of living
might have been by now had the Labour Party never been beguiled by
Marxism and tied to Clause IV and nationalization. It is also interesting
to imagine where the Labour Party itself might have been.

Up to date the Conservative Party has remained the most durable
party in Britain, the only party in the 'top two' for the whole period since
the Reform Act of 1832. This is primarily because it has steered clear of
ideology. Its is not some rigid doctrine, some panacea for all problems. It
is rather a general attitude to life as a whole and as such, flexible and
timeless. This has made the party exceptionally adaptable to change but
continually careful not to 'throw out the baby with the bath water' and
permanently lose valuable elements in our society without which Britain
might become unrecognizable and a place where we and our children
might no longer wish to live.

Though our free and lively media keep us all well informed about our
national deficiencies, since good news is by and large no news, that is not
the whole truth nor the way the rest of the world sees us. Though at

present a little way down the league table of material prosperity among the rich and developed nations, Britain still rates highly in the modern world in political influence, in esteem for its institutions and as a desirable place to live. We do not have to build walls to keep our people in. On the contrary, we are a magnet, not only for those from overseas looking for better living standards, but also for many of the rich and successful from other countries who see virtues in our way of life and opportunities in our economy which we have not always fully appreciated ourselves.

Moreover, having been the first country in the world to become fully industrialized, we have, rather like an eldest child, been through all the problems the hard way. As a result, at least psychologically, we are better geared for the fast moving future than most people think. Some other countries, studying our experience, have managed to avoid some of the problems and skip some of the stages but for many, in their own fashion, similar problems lie ahead.

In a way, too, despite all the change and the vastly accelerating rate of change, there is still a great sense of continuity in Britain. We have changed Empire into Commonwealth. We have recently been adjusting very rapidly to major changes in technology and in the world economy. We have absorbed many people of different cultures from abroad. We have joined the European Community. Yet, Britain remains distinct and in many ways as it used to be. Parliament, despite the invention of life peers and select committees, is still much the same as in 1945. The Civil Service remains essentially impartial and non-political. The judiciary, although having to cope with a mass of legislation and a number of new problems, still retains all the characteristics which make Britain a free country.

Christopher Robin can still go down with Alice in this high-tech computerized world to see them changing Guard at Buckingham Palace.

David Marquand

What do they know of England who only England know? What do they know of postwar British history who begin their inquiries in 1945? Three overlapping themes dominate that history: relative economic and absolute political decline; the rise, triumph and subsequent disintegration of the 'Keynesian social-democratic' consensus of the age of Mr Butskell; and a slow loss of self-confidence on the part of the political class whose consensus it was. Each of these themes had its origins in the preceding three-quarters of a century. None can be understood in the foreshortened perspective of the last four decades alone.

Take first the theme of decline. Whatever the rights and wrongs of the debate over the economic record of the Churchill coalition and the post-war Labour government, there is no doubt that the technological and industrial weaknesses to which the 'pessimists' in that debate point were beginning to manifest themselves as far back as the last quarter of the nineteenth century. Britain – the birthplace of the small-scale, atomistic industrial capitalism of the age of steam – was unable to modernize its industrial structure, to transform its state apparatus or to rethink its traditional economic and political doctrines to fit the needs of the organized, scientific, corporate capitalism of the age of electricity. In the old staples of the first industrial revolution, Britain remained ahead of its competitors. Thanks to the surpluses it had earned and reinvested in the days of its industrial and trading supremacy, it enjoyed an enormous investment income. Thanks to Britain's position at the centre of the worldwide financial and trading system which it had brought into existence, it earned substantial surpluses on invisible trade. Thanks to the colonial or semi-colonial relationships which bound large parts of that system to Britain, it was still ahead in exports to what we would now call the Third World. But where it counted – in the new, science-based industries and in exports to the most sophisticated and rapidly-growing markets of the First World – late-nineteenth-century British producers were steadily losing ground to more efficient competitors in the United States and Germany.

Even in the blazing afternoon of late-Victorian grandeur, in other words, Britain's industrial structure was already obsolescent. So were the pattern of its foreign trade, the structure and assumptions of its banking system, the training received by its managers and skilled workers, the structure and attitudes of its labour movement and every level of its skimpy system of public education. The long diminuendo of her post-1945 economic history was the last act of a tragedy of complacency, self-deception and missed opportunities, which began in the days of Britain's glory, and it cannot be understood if it is seen in any other way.

Less obviously, the same applies to the theme of consensus and the disintegration of consensus. There is even more room for debate over this theme than over the first one. Consensus is an imprecise term, denoting an imprecise and usually fluctuating reality; it cannot be caught in the net of number-crunching social science. Besides, what looks in retrospect like consensus often looked at the time like bitter and passionate dissension. The two great political parties of postwar Britain have always differed profoundly, not only about the details of policy, but about the source of political authority and the nature of the good society; these differences went as deep in the age of Mr Butskell as they did in the interwar period or, for that matter, as they do today. Labour-inclined historians can find plenty of evidence to show that the social and economic reforms of the Attlee government went further and cut deeper than those of a single-party Conservative government would have gone if Churchill had won the 1945 election. Those with Conservative inclinations will not find it difficult to show that the Conservative members of the wartime coalition were more conscious of the costs of social welfare than were their Labour colleagues, and correspondingly less prone to burden the resource-starved real economy with welfare services which the nation could not afford.

But this debate, however intriguing, is in the end beside the point. The central, dominating reality of postwar British history is that for thirty-odd years – starting with the commitment of the 1944 Employment White Paper to a 'high and stable level of employment' after the war, and finishing with James Callaghan's speech to the 1976 Labour Party conference, warning that deficit finance breeds inflation – party differences were argued out, and government policies settled, within a framework of common commitments and common assumptions. The three crucial commitments were, of course, to full employment and Keynesian demand management; to the hodge-podge of welfare reforms foreshadowed in the Beveridge Report and enacted by the postwar Labour government; and to what came to be known as the 'mixed economy' – in other words, to the existence of a substantial public sector alongside a still-predominant private sector, and (more vaguely) to the maintenance of a substantial capacity for public intervention in the affairs of that private sector. These three commitments lay at the heart of the 'Keynesian social-democratic' consensus of the postwar period. The inability or unwillingness of more recent governments to honour them have done more than anything else to shape the politics of the late 1970s and early 1980s.

As with economic decline, however, the roots of the postwar consensus go much further back than the 1945 Labour government, or even than the Churchill coalition. The postwar 'Keynesian social democrats' were the heirs of a long tradition of cross-party progressivism. Their intellectual ancestors included such disparate figures as interwar 'planners', among them the young Harold Macmillan, the young Evan Durbin, the authors of the 1928 Liberal Yellow Book and the founders of Political and Economic Planning; the New Liberals of the turn of the century; the early Fabians; and perhaps even the Tory Radicals of the 1830s and 1840s, who fought against the New Poor Law and alongside the emergent working class in the name of an aristocratic ideal of hierarchy, community and the obligations of property to the unpropertied. This long lineage helps to explain both the strengths and the weaknesses of the consensus politicians – their decency, their fair-mindedness, their genuine wish to do their best by their fellow men and their instinctive faith in reason and compromise; and, on the other hand, their complacency, their insularity, their resistance to new ideas and their inability to question their own assumptions. It also helps to explain why, in spite of repeated claims to the contrary, no new consensus has yet replaced the old one: why the radicals of the New Right and the New Left have failed to capture the intellectual commanding heights which 'Keynesian social democracy' has been forced to vacate.

If postwar 'Keynesian social democracy' had been nothing more than a mushroom growth by Beveridge out of Keynes, the product of a lucky marriage between a dated work of economic theory and a tendentious Blue Book, it would have vanished without trace in the storms of the 1970s. On one level, of course, it *has* vanished. No one now thinks that Keynesian demand management can achieve full employment, or that Beveridgean welfare policies can banish poverty. But only on one level. Keynes and Beveridge may be dead, but the attitudes and aspirations which used to be embodied in the consensus for which they provided the intellectual underpinning still live. 'Keynesian social democrats' survive – undeniably bloody but far from bowed – on the 'wet' wing of the Conservative Party and the 'moderate' wing of the Labour Party, as well as in the SDP-Liberal Alliance. They have not yet found an appropriate intellectual or political vehicle for their attitudes and aspira-tions, or winnowed out the strengths in their inheritance from the weaknesses; and it is possible that they never will. If they do not, the tradition to which they belong may eventually evaporate. But it has not evaporated yet, and one of the reasons for its otherwise rather puzzling survival in the harsh climate of the 1980s is simply that it has been part of British political life for a very long time.

This leads on to the third and most complex theme – the theme of dwindling governmental self-confidence. This, it seems to me, is the theme which emerges most powerfully from the earlier essays in this book, and, for that matter, from my own memories of the stories they tell. Of course, I know now that the postwar Labour government did not really consist of the giants I thought I saw as a schoolboy growing up under it. If we are to believe their biographers, the private characters of Dalton and Morrison were both deeply flawed. I still think Attlee was much more than a glorified Captain Mainwaring, but he was plainly no giant and would never have claimed gianthood for himself. Cripps and Bevin were, in different ways, men of genius, towering above their colleagues in force and will. But the government's reputation does not depend on them alone and, in any event, it is not clear that even their abilities were enormously greater than those of the lesser men who held their offices in the 1960s and 1970s. Yet there is no doubt that they and, for that matter, even quite ordinary members of that government had an inner assurance – a moral solidity, a faith in their right and ability to lead – quite absent from the tormented and vacillating Labour governments of twenty and thirty years later. To be sure, the curve of Conservative self-assurance oscillates much more than the Labour one. There was a bleak, inarticulate seriousness of purpose about the Heath government, which redeemed its policy failures and gave it a kind of dignity missing from the later years of the Macmillan government or, for that matter, from the Eden government. Yet even the Conservative curve points down. Dignified though they were, Heath's closing weeks in power could hardly have been less authoritative. There is no way of telling whether he still had private faith in his right and ability to lead: for what it is worth, my own hunch is that he had. The fact remains that he had too few followers.

It is here, not in arcane disputes about the role of the money supply in causing inflation or the capacity of the Keynesian state to master multinational corporations, that we shall find the true origins of the ideological polarization which forced 'Keynesian social democracy' onto the defensive, and among whose consequences we still live. Whatever else governments may be for, they are supposed to govern. A political class which has lost its self-confidence is like a student teacher, unable to hold the attention of a loutish fourth form. Somewhere on the road from the granite self-confidence of 1945 to the strangulated ineptitudes of the three-day week and the tortured uncertainties of the 'winter of discontent', the decent, *bien-pensant*, liberal-minded political class of the postwar period ceased to believe in itself. It was elbowed aside by the counter-revolutionaries of the radical Right, not because it lost the economic argument, but because it had lost its political touch: because it no longer had a moral language in which to speak to its fellow citizens, and allowed social engineering to become a substitute for leadership.

This loss of self-confidence was much more apparent after 1945 than before. Yet here too, I suspect, the origins of postwar failure can be traced back to the previous half-century. The wartime coalition and postwar Labour government were throwbacks: late flowers of an age of moral certainty and tribal unity, whose intellectual foundations had been eroded long before. They spoke a language of national solidarity, common sacrifice and mutual obligation which was still comprehensible to the ordinary public, but which the intelligentsia had been laughing to scorn since the aesthetes of the late-nineteenth century. They appealed – even lifelong anti-militarists in the Labour Party appealed – to the military virtues: to the values of duty, patriotism, self-discipline and self-sacrifice. They did so because, in a nation which was either fighting for its life or had only just finished fighting for its life, even progressive intellectuals could see that the military virtues held the key to survival. They evoked a response because everyone else could see this too.

But these values were already anachronistic before the war; that was one of the reasons why the enlightened, *bien-pensant* sections of the political class had havered so feebly over resisting Hitler. In the 1940s they got a second wind. By the late-1950s, however, they were in full retreat before the relativist hedonistic individualism – by George Moore out of Jeremy Bentham – which had been dominant among the metropolitan literary intelligentsia since the days of the Bloomsbury Group, and which now began to conquer the rest of the educated class as well. By the 1970s, the politicians and publicists of the postwar consensus had forgotten the old language altogether. When Heath and Callaghan tried to talk it, in order to mobilize the general public against the sectional interests which were defying them, they stumbled so grotesquely that no one could understand what they were trying to say. By an extraordinary paradox, the only section of political opinion which still talked the language of duty, patriotism and self-sacrifice with any kind of conviction or persuasive power was the radical New Right, whose economic ideology was suffused with an extreme form of hedonistic individualism. These radicals rushed in to fill the moral vacuum of which 'Keynesian social democracy' was no longer even conscious. They have been filling it ever since.

The postwar consensus, in short, died by its own hand – or, rather, by the hand of its philosophical progenitors. 'Keynesian social democracy' was a philosophy of public intervention, without a clear notion of the public good or the public realm. To succeed, its interventions required public support, but it provided no moral basis on which the interventionists could appeal to the public for support. Its economics were collectivist, but its politics and ethics were individualist. When the going was good, at the height of the long postwar boom, this did not matter. Hard choices could be postponed and predatory interests bought off. But, as the effects of a century of relative economic decline and dwindling competitiveness began to bite, the room for manoeuvre available to the consensus politicians began to narrow. Increasingly, politics became a zero-sum game. More for high-paid workers in the public sector meant less for old-age pensioners; more for consumption, less for investment. But relativist hedonistic individualism provides no consistent basis for choices of this sort. It tells me that it is in my interests for you to sacrifice yourself for the common good. It does not tell me why I should do so. Bereft of a communal ethic, a compelling peacetime substitute for wartime patriotism, 'Keynesian social democracy' became a kind of football for collective greed. The result was the long crisis of governability of the 1970s, a Hobbesian war of all against all, which ended only with Mrs Thatcher's victory in 1979.

But, of course, the story does not end there. The radicals of the New Right did not resolve the crisis: they only suppressed its symptoms. In place of collective greed, they put individual greed; and, in an old and settled society, at any rate, the latter is no more capable of rebuilding a broken-backed economy or healing a fractured polity than the former. Partly because of this, moreover, the radical Right has, in any case, run out of steam. A few economically irrelevant privatizations apart, the counter-revolution has come to a halt – leaving the public sector's share of the gross domestic product slightly larger than it was at the beginning. No matter which political party is in power in the late 1980s and early 1990s, and no matter what kind of rhetoric it engages in, it is clear that the pendulum of action and decision is moving back to the middle ground. The age of Mr Butskell may be over. That of Mr Hurdersley is about to dawn.

The crucial question for the future, then, is whether Mr Hurdersley can recover the moral solidity which Mr Butskell lost: whether a revived 'Keynesian social democracy' can become a philosophy of the public good as well as of public intervention. Plainly, it is too soon to tell. Plainly too, the answers lie in the long and tangled process through which the moral certainties of the Victorian age were slowly undermined in the three-quarters of a century before the postwar consensus came into existence.

David Butler

For the last forty years Britain has been pictured as in decline – some would say for much longer. But decline depends on perspective. Some simple facts conflict with the depressing image. Real income per head, for example, has almost tripled since the beginning of the century and since 1945 it has doubled. The proportion of the population living in owner-occupied houses has grown from 30 per cent at the end of the Second World War to over 60 per cent in 1986. The numbers owning cars and telephones have multiplied sixfold.

The country's much-publicized decline is not absolute; it only represents a failure to match the extraordinary advance of other countries. None the less, although most Britons are far better off than their parents or grandparents, the seeming fall from pre-eminence has done severe damage to national self-confidence. When a quarter of the globe was under the British Crown, it was easy to believe in the virtues of the system under which the country had risen to dominance. Cabinet government and parliamentary democracy, supported by an independent judiciary and a Northcote–Trevelyan Civil Service, with two parties enjoying alternately the exaggerated majorities produced by first-past-the-post voting – all these could be seen as inspired devices for good administration.

But, as the bleak postwar years were followed by the end of Empire, a loss of certainty about national institutions developed. Politicians, as well as journalists and academics, began intermittently to question how well adapted our governmental arrangements were to the needs of the late twentieth century. Yet very little has been done, over the last forty years, to modify things. The position of the monarchy has stayed unaltered. The House of Lords, with the addition of life peers in 1958, has survived with no obvious diminution of influence. The House of Commons, despite some developments on select committees and in the amount of legislation done upstairs in committee, has experienced remarkably little modification to its procedures. Parliament, moreover, has continued with its 600-plus members, just as the Cabinet has continued with its twenty-plus ministers. The full Cabinet, despite the expansion of its committee system, remains in Morley's phrase 'the keystone of the constitutional arch'.[1] The Civil Service has stayed, at least as far as its top ranks are concerned, a civilized Oxbridge elite, free from party entanglement, but exercising vast political power. The traditions of honest, uncorrupt and relatively efficient government have been maintained by politicians and bureaucrats alike.

Every institutional history must focus on the antithesis between continuity and change. Despite the transformation of Britain's position in the world over the last forty years, continuity has been much more evident than change in the ways of her central administration.

The rhetoric of postwar politics has been full of reformist phrases – 'Let us Face the Future',[2] 'Change is our Ally',[3] 'the white heat of the technological revolution',[4] 'Action not Words',[5] 'A New Style of Government'[6] – but these have scarcely been reflected in action. Prime Ministers have essayed limited initiatives – overlords, super-departments, special advisers, a Central Policy Review Staff, a NATO policy unit – but these cannot be said to have had any great consequences. The major efforts of the 1960s and 1970s – Fulton on the Civil Service,[7] Redcliffe-Maud on local government,[8] Kilbrandon on the constitution,[9] the 1977–8 Select Committee on Parliamentary Procedure[10] – have left no large legacy. The electoral system, the Cabinet system, the working of Parliament have altered little in any formal sense.

In policy, too, continuity has been more apparent than change. In the forty years after the war Britain had twenty-three years of Conservative government and seventeen years of Labour government (although for almost half its time in office Labour had a majority that was negligible or non-existent). The Attlee government nationalized major industries and established the country's comprehensive social security and health schemes. If the Conservatives had won in 1945 they would have gone some way along the same road. Certainly when they took office in 1951 they did little to undo what had been achieved. Butskellism was discovered by the *Economist* in 1954; that consensual acceptance of the welfare state and the mixed economy, of decolonization and collective security through NATO, survived to a remarkable degree into the 1980s. Even now the rougher rhetoric of Mrs Thatcher and the brake on welfare-state expenditure (which really goes back to Denis Healey in 1976) has not marked a substantial change in structure. It is true that after 1979 the apparent lurch to the right by the Conservatives and to the left by Labour seemed for a time to mark the end of the consensus.

Certainly it opened up a gap in the centre of which the SDP–Liberal Alliance eagerly took advantage. But in a remarkable number of areas party policies never drifted very far apart: Labour would spend a bit more and tax a bit more – but the percentage of national resources devoted to the various heads of public expenditure would stay surprisingly similar.

This book is a history of administration, but elections provide most of the chapter breaks. Just as the reigns of kings have supplied the milestones for most of the last thousand years, nowadays we make landmarks of these moments of popular choice. Six times since the defeat of Hitler the voters have thrown out the government. Yet it is singular how little most of those dates – 1945, 1951, 1964, 1970, 1974, 1979 – are linked with the decisive happenings discussed in these pages. The financial crises of 1947 and 1949, the Korean War, Suez, the attempts to enter Europe in 1962, 1967 and 1972, the retreat from the Empire and from being a power east of Suez, the oil-price crisis of 1973, the International Monetary Fund cuts in 1976, and the Falklands War were all independent events, hardly echoing any of the themes that dominated the preceding election campaign. Most of them would have occurred whichever party had been voted into power – and most, though not all, would have evoked a broadly similar reaction.

However, although elections may not decide much, the fear of losing them has a powerful influence on politicians. In opposition they prepare manifestos which they hope to be called upon to fulfil; few voters may read these documents, but the promises are very important. Both in Cabinet discussions and in minister–civil servant relations, 'it was in the manifesto' is a very powerful argument. Most governments have taken a pride in meeting their specific manifesto pledges, though they have not satisfied all the hopes implicit in their glittering generalities. The Conservatives boasted in 1964 that they had met ninety-three out of the ninety-four explicit commitments on which the 1959 election had been fought.

But while it is right to stress the continuities in British affairs there are many significant changes which can be missed by individual authors focusing on a four- or five-year period. The style and content of politics have been transformed.

Historiography, for one thing, has certainly changed in the last forty years. In 1945 academics fought shy of instant history. Journalists lacked the space for in-depth examination of political events – and the tradition of investigative journalism was not strong, at least as far as politics was concerned. Until 1958 the total ban of access to Cabinet papers put a ban on the authoritative discussion of major episodes while the participants were still around to comment (and the reductions to a fifty-year ban in 1958 and a thirty-year ban in 1967 have hardly altered the situation). The BBC solved the challenge of neutrality by putting on few political programmes and excluding all election reporting. High politics were far more closed to the interested public than they are today.

Since the late 1950s the scene has changed. Television has become the main source of information about politics. The serious press, unable to trump the immediacy of broadcasting, has turned increasingly to background reporting. 'Insight'-type stories about the Profumo affair, about the repeated attempts to get into Europe, about devaluation and devolution and about Falklands and Westland have transformed (though some would say have distorted) the popular perceptions of what was going on in high places where great issues were being decided. Publishers, too, began to get into the act, sponsoring instant paperbacks on Suez, Profumo, the Falklands War and the miners' strike, as well as more substantial biographies and analyses of major events, suitable for serialization in the Sunday supplements. Academic research has proliferated; doctoral theses have multiplied twentyfold and monographs are now available on the passage of major pieces of legislation and on most aspects of the evolution of administration and policy.

The broadcasters have made their own contribution to popular understanding – and misunderstanding – of how we are governed, with the comic insights of *Yes Minister*, the serious perceptions of *No, Minister*, the Granada 'factitious' reconstruction of crisis management situations, and many other programmes dealing with the handling of past or current issues.

But it is not only the way in which national administration is recorded or perceived that has changed. The substance of government business is different. The percentage of national income spent by central government on non-defence matters rose from 16 per cent in 1936 to 32 per cent in 1984. The amount of time in Parliament and in government devoted to overseas matters has diminished sharply with the end of the Empire.

The style of government has changed. It is arguable how far the full Cabinet was ever the central forum of decision-making. Prime Ministers have always fixed many of the key issues in advance with one or more of their senior colleagues, so that to use the phrase 'rubber stamp' about the Cabinet could at times be almost as fair as to use it about Parliament.

None the less there have been many critical moments round the table at No. 10 when, as this volume shows, argument has changed the course of events. And Prime Ministers, notably Macmillan and Wilson, have testified to the extent that their behaviour was conditioned by considerations of what the Cabinet would stand.

Richard Crossman argued in 1963[11] that the Cabinet had become a dignified, not an efficient, instrument and that Cabinet government had been superseded by prime-ministerial government. Experience of office in 1964–70 led him to retreat slightly from this view, and Patrick Gordon-Walker offered a stoutly revisionist picture of the importance of Cabinet,[12] which found support in many of the accounts of how affairs were managed in the 1970s. But it does seem that a change has taken place since then. Certainly, after her first few years, Mrs Thatcher took to acting more autocratically in No. 10, allowing fewer papers to come to Cabinet and tolerating less discussion. Cabinet committees and unrecorded *ad hoc* meetings of small groups of ministers have become more important. In 1983–6 the number of hours a week spent by full Cabinet was less than at any time since the war.

The style of Parliament has changed, too. To some extent this is a matter of personnel. The percentage of Old Etonians on the Conservative benches fell from 25 in 1945 to 12 in 1983; the percentage of graduates among Labour MPs rose from 32 to 53. Leading industrialists and major union figures had virtually disappeared from the Commons by the 1950s.

More and more politicians became full-timers. They were given offices in or around the Palace of Westminster, with secretaries and research facilities, and the demands on them, often self-generated, grew. So did their salaries.[13] But, while they became more activist and in some ways more independent of the whips, they did not become significantly more influential;[14] Mrs Thatcher has probably worried less about trouble from her backbenches than any of her predecessors.

The style of mass politics has changed even more. Politicians approach the voters in a very different fashion. Contrast the way in which Attlee trundled around the country in the 1950 election, driven from rally to rally by his wife in their old car, accompanied by a single detective, with the 1983 campaigning of Mrs Thatcher: she made fewer speeches than any predecessor but provided more photo opportunities and set the highest priority on the big television encounters with Sir Alastair Burnett, Sir Robin Day and their like.

The electorate, too, has become more educated but less ideological.

Partisan loyalty has declined spectacularly. Surveys show that the proportion feeling 'strongly Conservative' or 'strongly Labour' has halved since the early 1960s. The short-term fluctuations manifest in opinion polls and in by-elections are three or four times as great as thirty years ago. After the disillusioning experience of seeing changes in government that failed to remedy the ills of the nation it became harder to be a true believer in any one party.

But it is probably the sudden arrival of television as the main source of political communication that has done more than anything else to transform the public's perceptions about those who aspire to govern them. Television moved from a negligible audience when the Conservatives came to power in 1951 to near-saturation by the time they left office in 1964. And suddenly, after the coming of commercial television in 1955, politics began to receive full coverage, both in news bulletins and in discussions and magazine programmes.

The partisan balance imposed on the broadcasting authorities led them to project a very different picture of politics from that offered by the popular press. Instead of a simple, very loaded account that a simple Fleet Street paper might offer, the viewer was forced to listen to both sides of the case. Usually two Oxbridge smoothies, first-naming each other, would argue the Conservative and Labour case in a very reasonable way, knowing that the House of Commons stridency would be alienating when they were uninvited guests at the voter's hearthside. The impact was to show that the political world was made up not of angels and devils but of ordinary educated people who actually agreed on a large part of the national agenda.

Volatility increased spectacularly. At one point in 1981–2, within eighteen months, each of the three parties soared to a 50 per cent support in at least one national opinion poll and bottomed at 27 per cent or less. As volatility increased, politicians became more insecure, more anxiously looking at their media image and more eagerly noting the opinion polls, which, though they first forecast an election in 1945, only achieved prominence in the 1960s. Ad-men and campaign consultants came more into evidence.

Plus ça change. . . . The styles of campaigning have been transformed. The personnel of politics is different in its origins and its manners. And, far more important, Britain has moved from the greatest of imperial powers to a second-league position. But, looking at the country's administration, the continuities loom larger than the changes. Mr Speaker Clifton Brown (1943–51) would not be much at a loss sitting in Mr Speaker Weatherill's Chair. Sir Warren Fisher (Permanent Secretary 1919–39) would recognize Sir Peter Middleton's Treasury in 1987. Neville Chamberlain would empathize with much in Margaret Thatcher's operations at No. 10.

Notes

1   John Morley, *Walpole* (Macmillan, 1928), p. 154.
2   Title of Labour manifesto 1945.
3   Title of pamphlet, One Nation group of Conservative MPs, 1950.
4   Harold Wilson's speech at Labour Party conference, 1 October 1963.
5   Title of Conservative manifesto 1966.
6   From Edward Heath's Preface to the Conservative manifesto 1970.
7   Cmnd 368 (1968).
8   Cmnd 4040 (1969).
9   Cmnd 5460 (1973).
10 HC 588 (1977–8).
11 In his preface to a new edition of Walter Bageshot's *The English Constitution* (Fontana, 1963).
12 Patrick Gordon-Walker *The Cabinet*, 2nd edn (Cape, 1972).
13 MPs, with a twenty-eightfold salary increase (from £600 to almost £17,000 leaving out perks) between 1945 and 1985, seem to stand out from ministers in beating inflation: secretaries of state, with a sixfold increase, fell behind. The top Civil Service salary, however, rose twentyfold (from £3500 to £70,000). Prices rose fifteenfold in the same period.
14 See P. Norton, *Backbench Dissent in the House of Commons* (Macmillan, 1975, and Oxford University Press, 1980).

Contributors

Paul Addison is Reader in Modern History at Edinburgh University.

John Barnes is Lecturer in Government at the London School of Economics.

Tony Benn is Member of Parliament for Chesterfield.

David Butler is a Fellow of Nuffield College, Oxford.

Michael Fraser (Lord Fraser of Kilmorack) Life Peer cr. 1974, was Director of the Conservative Research Department from 1951 to 1964, and Deputy Chairman of the Conservative Party Headquarters from 1964 to 1975.

Peter Hennessy is Co-Director of the Institute of Contemporary British History and a Visiting Fellow at the Policy Studies Institute.

Dennis Kavanagh is Professor of Politics at Nottingham University.

David Marquand is Professor of Contemporary History and Politics at Salford University.

Michael Pinto-Duschinsky is Senior Lecturer in Government at Brunel University.

Anthony Seldon is Co-Director of the Institute of Contemporary British History.

John Vincent is Professor of History at Bristol University.

David Walker is Chief Leader-Writer for the *London Daily News*.

Phillip Whitehead is a Visiting Fellow at Goldsmith's College, University of London.

Index